The effects of the
National Health Service
on the
nursing profession
1948–1961

King's Fund Historical Series 3

The effects of the
National Health Service
on the
nursing profession
1948–1961

Rosemary White
SRN SCM OHNC MSc PhD

King Edward's Hospital Fund for London

© Rosemary White 1985
Typeset by J&L Composition Ltd, Filey,
North Yorkshire
Printed in England by Hollen Street Press
Bound by Hunter and Foulis

Distributed for the King's Fund by Oxford University Press

ISBN 0 19 724629 X

King's Fund Publishing Office
126 Albert Street
London NW1 7NF

King's Fund historical series

.

Rosemary White's book forms the third in the King's Fund historical series, following John Pater's *The Making of the National Health Service* and Lindsay Granshaw's *St Mark's Hospital, London: a social history of a specialist hospital*. The purpose behind the series is to document the development of health and social services, particularly (but not exclusively) in the United Kingdom.

I am delighted that this third title deals with nursing history, specifically the effects of the National Health Service on the nursing profession between the inception of the Service and 1961. The story is, in Dr White's opinion, not a very happy one from the viewpoint of the profession. Some of the changes that were taking place, involving some loss of professional cohesion, were independent of the organisational framework of the NHS and of government policy. Nevertheless, it is disturbing that nurses appear, during the period covered by this book, to have had a quite inadequate input to the shaping of health policy.

There are already signs that the nursing profession has begun to absorb this lesson from Dr White's study. We in the King's Fund have been glad to assist, through helping to set up a new unit at the University of Warwick to study nursing policy – an enterprise that Rosemary White herself did much to shape.

In the wake of the Griffiths report and the implementing of general management in the NHS, nurses may find the message of this book only too familiar. That does not for one moment mean that the nursing input to national health policy should be defensive or reactionary. In international terms, British nursing continues to be very highly regarded. And within Britain no professional group demands greater public sympathy, despite its low economic status. As the political sophistication of the nursing profession increases, I hope that the profession's capacity to think first of those it serves will be dominant in its shaping of the future.

Robert Maxwell

The author wishes to acknowledge her debt to the DHSS for permission to publish this book which is based on her doctoral thesis. Research for the thesis was funded by the DHSS and would not have been possible without their support.

The author also wishes to acknowledge the help given to her by the Nurses and Midwives Whitley Council, the General Nursing Council, the Royal College of Nursing and the Queen's Nursing Institute.

Whilst all these bodies allowed her to examine their records and have given permission for their material to be used in this book, the interpretations placed on this information and the views expressed in the text are the responsibility of the author alone.

List of abbreviations used in the text

ANTC   Area Nurse Training Committee

B of G   Board of Governors
BTA   British Tuberculosis Association. Sometimes used as qualifying initials for nurses who had completed the course of training given by the association

CHSC   Central Health Services Council
CMB   Central Midwives Board
COHSE   Confederation of Health Service Employees
CTHV   Council for the Training of Health Visitors. After 1971 became
CETHV   Council for the Education and Training of Health Visitors

DHSS   Department of Health and Social Security
DN   District Nurse

GCE   General Certificate of Education, taken at Ordinary ('O') level and Advanced ('A') level
GMC   General Medical Council
GNC   General Nursing Council
GP   General Practitioner

HMC   Hospital Management Committee
HV   Health Visitor

JCC   Joint Consultative Committee

King's Fund)
KEHF   ) King Edward's Hospital Fund (for London)

LA   Local Authority
LEA   Local Education Authority
LHA   Local Health Authority

M & CW   Maternity and Child Welfare
MDU   Medical Defence Union
MOH   Medical Officer of Health

NALGO	National Association of Local Government Officers
NHS	National Health Service
NPHT	Nuffield Provincial Hospitals Trust
NUPE	National Union of Public Employees
PTS	Preliminary Training School
QIDN	Queen's Institute of District Nursing, later
QIN	Queen's Institute of Nursing
RCN	Royal College of Nursing. In 1963 it became
Rcn	Royal College of Nursing and National Council of Nurses when the logo was changed
RHB	Regional Hospital Board
RMN	Registered Mental Nurse
RMPA	Royal Medico-Psychological Association, sometimes used as qualifying initials for nurses trained under the association's syllabus
RSI	Royal Sanitary Institute. In 1955 it became
RSH	Royal Society for the Promotion of Health
SEAN	State Enrolled Assistant Nurse. In 1961 became
SEN	State Enrolled Nurse
SNAC	Standing Nursing Advisory Committee
SRN	State Registered Nurse
UGC	University Grants Committee
UKCC	United Kingdom Central Council for Nursing, Midwifery and Health Visiting
WHO	World Health Organization
WPHO	Women Public Health Officers' Association

Contents

TABLES

Introduction

This study is the second in a series called *Social Change and the Development of the Nursing Profession*. The first one, *A Study of the Poor Law Nursing Service, 1848–1948,*[1] was originally undertaken in a search for the reasons why nurses have apparently failed to gain professional authority and an appropriate degree of power in health service politics.

The first study was made in 1972–75, effectively before the reorganisation of the NHS in 1974. This one was completed as the second reorganisation took place in 1982. Both studies rested on the assumption that nurses, in fact, do not have the political power that a numerically large occupation might be expected to have in the health service.

There are people who might dispute this assumption. Garrison[2] has discussed the difficulties of measuring influence and also aspects of the cost of influence. We make no pretentions to have measured the degree of power which the nursing profession may have in the health service. Our study demonstrates that whatever gains nursing may have achieved during 1948–61 they were very slow to come and cost the profession quite a lot in terms of schisms between the nurses as well as within their professional representative association, the Royal College of Nursing. It is probably true to say that nurses have slowly gained managerial power in the health service, especially since the implementation of the Salmon report[3] and, later, in the 1974 reorganisation of the health service. Whether or not it continues with this position after the 1982 reorganisation is a matter for conjecture.

There is, however, the matter of professional authority which the profession still lacks. This is observed in the unwillingness of the media to invite nurses to discuss health matters, the image drawn by the television series 'The Angels', the continuing dominance of the medical profession in the health service and of the doctors and lay administrators in the DHSS. Many other examples could be found.

This study finds that the Royal College of Nursing had to fight a hard battle in order to establish itself as the officially recognised representative body for nurses. In its struggle the College was forced to compromise its own official objectives for the sake of what was perceived as the public good. Our own conclusions are, however, that the perceived public good was a short-term goal which generated longer-term problems.

To the best of our knowledge, this is the first study of national nursing policy to have been undertaken and it opens up a new field for historians and social scientists of the future. There have, of course, been a few other studies of nursing policy which were made by social scientists, at least one of whom was also a nurse.[4,5]

There are several important differences between this study and the others. In the first place, this one deliberately avoided any pre-emptive theoretical framework. We considered that that would have directed the search unduly. Instead, it relied on insights gained from the first study and predicated that three separate streams of nurses with disparate ideologies and roots had come together in the new National Health Service and that they would all thereafter be subjected to common national policies (see page xiii). Furthermore, other studies have discussed professionalising or work-control strategies, thus taking for granted nurses' objectives. We have found that nurses' objectives are various and may not be taken for granted.

Indeed, this study concludes that nursing is a pluralist system with several primary groups, each with its own value system. These primary groups are bound together in a common nursing society by a common ideology. If this finding has been satisfactorily demonstrated, it must follow that any discussion of strategies should take into consideration the pluralist nature of the nursing society: to discuss nursing as a unitary system can no longer be productive.

Only a few studies of nursing policy have been made by nurses and those are usually related to units, hospitals or one specialist area. This study has covered most branches of nursing (excluding midwifery) from a national perspective. It has been made by a nurse whose career started in 1947 and therefore spanned the period included in the study. In this respect the study is also unusual and may be described as a form of internal history.

Macro-policy is a strangely neglected area of research in nursing. There have been numerous publications which examined the National Health Service, health care systems, the effects of social policy on health care etc. Some of these included a brief over-view of nursing and some have included nursing as a rather secondary influence in the politics of the health service. None, so far, has examined the influences of macro-policy on the nursing profession nor the effects of nursing policy on the macro-system.

We have earlier referred to three streams of nursing which entered the health service in 1948. These three streams were described in our first study[1] and it may be helpful to discuss them briefly here.

The voluntary hospitals were the charitable hospitals, and their nurses worked within a Lady Bountiful ethos, almost entirely bounded by acute medicine. Within this group were the teaching hospitals, whose nurses were the élite of the profession. Before our first study of the Poor Law nurses, histories of British nurses were invariably based on those of the voluntary hospitals. The image of nursing in the nineteenth and twentieth centuries was therefore largely of them.

The municipal hospitals were founded within the great public health movement of the nineteenth century and their ideology was consequently derived from that of the medical officers of health, the arch proponents of preventive and environmental medicine.

The last of the three streams were the remnants of the Poor Law nurses and those who worked in the public assistance institutions. These institutions were founded on the less-eligibility principle and the ideology of custodial care and constraint.

The hypothesis considered that the nurses of each of these types of hospital would have been socialised in the institutional roots of their respective foundations and that all would be, from 1948, subjected to a common national policy. We proposed to study the changes that the health service wrought on the profession in these new circumstances. The starting date for the study, 1948, was chosen because it was the end of the first study and, of course, because it was when the NHS came into being.

The end of this study was rather arbitrarily set at 1961 because we wished to avoid stepping into the period surrounding the Salmon report.[3] This date was reasonably convenient, but historical continuity has to be respected and 1961 was often passed for the sake of following up or completing a theme.

The primary sources used for this project were official reports and papers from the Public Records Office, the annual reports of the Ministry of Health, *On the State of the Public Health* (the annual reports of the Chief Medical Officer), the minutes of the General Nursing Council, the Royal College of Nursing, the management and staff sides of the Nurses and Midwives Whitley Council, the Queen's Nursing Institute (formerly the Queen's Institute of District Nursing) and the Council for the Education and Training of Health Visitors (formerly the Council for the Training of Health Visitors). Periodic papers published by voluntary organisations or central organisations, such as the Central Health Services Council, and a number of others that have now ceased to exist were examined. A wealth of material was found in the archives of the Royal College of Nursing and in the library of the DHSS.

National newspapers, specifically *The Times*, proved to be disappointing since, when items on nursing were published, they were invariably reports rather than comment. There was very little discussion on nursing and letters to the editor (usually from officials of one of the nursing institutions) provoked no debate.

The nursing journals were obviously helpful. The study concentrates on policy issues and *Nursing Times* was the official outlet for the Royal College of Nursing until 1966. We did observe that *Nursing Times* often failed in its objective of keeping its readers properly informed. It was, for some reason, selective as well as inconsistent in its presentation of reports and memoranda. It gave a great deal of coverage to the Wood report[6] but very little to the Horder reports[7] and hardly mentioned the Bradbeer report[8]. Invariably, cover was characterised by a summary only: there was most often no discussion or debate. Their readers were therefore left to assess these reports on their own and, unless they obtained copies for themselves, this assessment had to rely on the journal's précis.

Unfortunately, but not unexpectedly, Government papers in the Public Records Office were only available to about 1951. What was not expected, since the Ministry showed such obvious contempt for nurses, was the closure of certain early files beyond the 30 years' period. These files related to the appointment of nurses on to committees of the health service. A number of other sources were also found to be helpful. A full bibliography is provided, but one or two that have contributed particularly to this work may be discussed here.

The Acton Society Trust[9] made a comprehensive study of the health service between the years 1955–59. This study was concerned to examine the effects of large scale organisations on the people who worked in them and the people who were served by them. There were six sections, the second of which was undertaken by Cyril Sofer, a member of the Tavistock Institute.

Sofer's study[10] was made, as he explained, whilst changes were still in progress. Since no pre-nationalisation study had been made, he was not able to make a comparative one and, instead, the field research developed into a study of staff relationships as they existed in a changed and changing organisation. He used, as his base, organisation theory, contrasting hospital characteristics with other working organisations, and concluded that whilst the formal rules had been changed there was not a corresponding adjustment in the internal social structure nor in the 'culture' of the hospital. He found, as an outstanding observation, 'the manner in which individuals or groups affected or threatened by changes give them meanings quite foreign to those intended'.

This observation was supported by the findings of our study and also supports the need for further studies such as this. Change is often directed towards the achievement of certain goals or the resolution of certain perceived problems. Too often the inadvertent consequences of change are not perceived. Sometimes these may undermine the unity of the whole or effect change directly contrary to that planned.

The other sections of the Acton Society Trust were helpful although comments on the nursing service (No 3) tended to be rather general. The studies were perceptive of developing trends and many of its observations have been borne out with the passing of time.

The Acton Society's study was particularly interesting as it demonstrated the value of an analytical approach to policy making. With the exception of Sofer's study, it offered no theoretical structure. It did, however, recommend further, similar studies. 'The marked absence of research and study in the organisation and provision of services is a gross lack closely related to the deficiency of training for administration in the field of medical care. Systematic research and experiment in medical care are as much needed as in bacteriology or in surgery.' (No 1)

One of the earlier studies of nurses was made by Isabel Menzies,[11] also at the Tavistock Institute. Whether or not it is wise to generalise her allegedly Freudian theory, derived from one large hospital situated in London, is debatable. Unfortunately, her theory was not tested, and we have already described nursing as a pluralist society. But since, as we have also found, there is a binding common ideology and since there is no better theory to use in those particular circumstances, we have found it very helpful.

Another study of the health care system which included a chapter on nurses was made by MacKenzie.[12] He examined the concepts of power and responsibility as they related to the health service. Although he might have been expected to examine the health service as a macro-economic organism, he did, in fact, deal with issues at the unit level. MacKenzie preferred a model of interaction to the traditional professional models, since he preferred to deal with the occupational groups as parts of the whole system. His approach to nursing was undermined as he used Abel-Smith's[13] work as his framework. Abel-Smith described mostly the London teaching hospital nurses and therefore derived a rather specific and narrow view. Certainly his picture of the matrons is incomplete, as our study demonstrates. MacKenzie's comparison of the Briggs report[14] with the Salmon report[3] was interesting, even if events have failed to support him fully.

Bellaby and Oribabor[4] wrote two papers which were particularly useful. They used a Marxist framework, equating specialised knowledge and delegated authority with the means of production. They polarised professionalism and unionism and considered that three forces had tended to proletarianise nurses. These were loss of control over the labour market; secondly, the development of complex hierarchies and the division of labour; and, thirdly, the fragmentation of the nursing task itself. They then considered the strategies that nurses may have used to control the work situation. Whilst we have agreed with their theory of the proletarianisation of nurses, we have not agreed with all their reasons for this, nor do we concur with their selection of strategies for reasons that we have already given.

Barraclough[15] offered a theory of contemporary history which requires the student to distinguish the different patterns or trends by reversing the usual perspective and working backwards. He suggested that the contemporary historian should identify today's problems and trace their roots in the past.

One of the difficulties of following Barraclough's method very closely is that of recognising or defining our problems. Both Simon and Audley[16] found that assumptions are built into different branches of social sciences and in decision making, which influence both the way in which problems are perceived and in what terms they are identified. Lindblom[16] went further and found that problems have to be formulated or, when new opportunities make new goals possible, they have to be invented. He decided, therefore, that there is room for controversy over what the problem may be and that analysis does not necessarily settle the controversy.

We did not follow Barraclough's method precisely but in the search for trends in the mass of data that was available, our present day concerns and insight (augmented by the understanding given by our earlier study) certainly helped in their identification. Probably because of this 'dialogue' between the present and the past, some of the issues which raised most concern when they first developed, could be safely ignored. They had been dealt with by time or administrative action. Conversely, some of the issues which did not at the time appear to be of great significance, were recognised as being of interest to us today. In this way, a study of contemporary history, as Barraclough said, gives us a clearer perspective and insight into present day problems.

We made much use of the works edited by Castles et al[16] for the discussion in our last chapter. Decision making theory served largely to explain the inconsistencies which appeared in the events described in the text. But decision making theory, whilst useful as a key, did not serve to explain fully the way in which nursing was affected by the NHS after 1948 and we had to turn to Shils[17] for a final synthesis.

Our study is, then, an historical one which uses social science theories as keys to interpretation. The work has covered nursing in most fields of work in England and Wales only.

Although the title includes the term 'profession', we have not offered any definition in this context. Some discussion of themes of professions is included in the text, but in a different context. Nursing went into the National Health Service as a fragmented occupation, and many would say that it remains so. On the other hand, it is possible to demonstrate a broad movement along certain paths by a core of nurses. To try to offer a concrete definition of the term 'nursing profession' would have risked this possibility. It seems more important to try to distil a core movement than to describe events or developments relating to a number of groups.

In writing the text, one specific problem was identified: this relates to the naming of people. We realised that many people, significantly concerned with events and developments during the period, might still be living. It was thought to be of some historical importance that certain names should be identified. On the other hand, we also considered that the use of names, especially if this might be within a context of criticism, would be unfair and perhaps damaging. We therefore took the decision that names only of public people and the authors of published papers would be used. All other names remain unidentified. In the interests of further historical studies, a reference is invariably used which would help students in the future to identify the person if they so wish. It is of passing interest to note that it is already difficult to link names (such as those on the RCN or GNC Councils) with posts and positions: *tempus edax rerum*.

In reading discussions recorded by the institutions and the nursing journals, it has been interesting to realise how much time was spent on items which can now be regarded as trifling, since they were capable of resolution by administrative adjustments. On the other hand, certain facts were glossed over or missed in debate which can be seen today as deserving much greater consideration. Some of them are still with us today; some have not, until now, been recognised as being of significance. A study such as this becomes important if it helps to decipher, unravel and explain them.

The events that took place between 1948 and 1961, the discussions, negotiations and developments, present themselves as a confusion with little continuity. At the same time, certain themes identified themselves and it was possible to distinguish many connecting links and symbiotic relationships. It would have been confusing to use a chronological form and we therefore decided to use the form of case-studies. This treatment sacrifices continuity to some extent (although each case-study is treated chronologically), but it does offer greater depth to the topics, as well as more opportunity for discussion.

Eckstein[18] wrote that 'case-studies never prove anything; their purpose is to illustrate generalisations which are established otherwise, or to direct attention towards generalisations'.

Whilst this may be true of a single case-study, we have found that a collection of case-studies such as is now presented has, in fact, helped to establish something more than a generalisation because it has demonstrated the complexity of nursing together with the complexity of its objectives and the strategies that may have been used towards their fulfilment.

The use of the case-study technique for the analysis of social policy or social change is a developing one. Hall et at[19] used a series of case studies of different issues to demonstrate a particular theory or explanation of social policy changes. Each of the four authors was responsible for at least one of the studies. They described one of the major defects of this technique as being the difficulty of comparing individual studies in one field with a similar study in another field, undertaken by a different researcher.

In order to reduce this problem, Hall and her colleagues described several safeguards: there should be a delimiting context, the collection of cases should share a common framework, there should be a search for regularities and, lastly, the case or cases should be set in the context of what else was or was not happening so that they are related to a relevant history and other concurrent, overlapping and competing events.

There is one important difference between the work of Hall et al and ours. Whereas in their work six different and unrelated studies were made by four people, in our work 12 related studies were made by one person. This has allowed a common approach to all the studies and, we believe, the application of all the safeguards stipulated by Hall et al.

The study has thrown up three major findings which it may be helpful to describe briefly here.

We believe that nursing may not be treated as a single occupation or unitary social system. We believe, now, that to continue to do so is to over-simplify a very complex subject which has for far too long defied explanation and understanding. Nursing is a pluralist system with a series of groups with different objectives and values. Consequently, each of the major groups has a different set of strategies. This finding implies that a common general policy for the whole of nursing is no longer functional. We do, however, seek to demonstrate that all the groups have a core ideology which binds them together and helps to maintain their adherence to the centre. This then implies that a common policy may sometimes be helpful, so long as subsidiary policies allow each of the major groups to develop their own goals.

Secondly, we have identified two major factions in nursing and three separate major interest groups which function within the two factions. The factions include the generalists and the specialists or, as we have often described them, the proletarians and the professionalists. We have preferred to use the second set of descriptive labels as the terms 'generalists' and 'specialists' suffer from considerable ambiguity and misunderstanding between nurses and social scientists. The development of this ambiguity is discussed in the text.

The three major interest groups consist of the clinical nurses, the nurse teachers and the managers. Each of these groups has evolved its own prior set of values but also, within each of the groups, there are nurses who tend more towards either the proletarians or the professionalists. Whereas, therefore, the objectives of those in any one of the interest groups are shared by the members of that group, there may be some difference in the choice of strategies by which the members seek to achieve them.

The third and last major finding is the demonstration of how the first and second points affected the way in which decisions were taken and, conversely, how decisions affected the groups.

Throughout the period studied, we found that the Royal College of Nursing was a central factor in decision making. With hindsight, we have found how little was the influence of the General Nursing Council in the development of the profession. This is probably due to two factors: the GNC was concerned only with establishing a minimum standard of qualification for nurses and nurse tutors. Its potential influence over the profession was aborted by the omissions of the Nurses Act 1949. Secondly, the GNC was not a free agent and was very much under the control of the Ministry of Health which, in its turn, was considerably responsive to the established power groups, the doctors and the administrators, including the employing authorities.

This study, then, represents the struggles of the nursing profession to find its own identity in the new circumstances presented by the National Health Service. Until it succeeded in that struggle it was in no position to gain entry to the power bloc which determined the policies of the health service.

Chapter 1/Nursing before 1948

The new National Health Service in 1948 was not so much a social revolution as a reorganisation of the health services already existing in the country. That medical provision formed the nucleus of the NHS which, then, slowly re-formed and re-defined those services into a national system. The process has been a slow one and the evolution goes on: changes continue to be made. However, whereas today changes can be made within the national system, the coming of the NHS involved establishing new, comprehensive machinery to nationalise a number of local systems which varied widely in both the quality and quantity of provision.

Before 1948, hospitals were principally administered by the voluntary agencies, the local authority public health committees and the Poor Law or public assistance committees. Whilst it is doubtful whether the voluntary hospitals were subject to any specific statutory framework, each of the other types of hospitals was based on the enactments of a different law. Their derivations were therefore fundamentally different and the central values and beliefs which governed their conduct were different.

The voluntary hospitals were derived from a pre-Victorian and Victorian philanthropy, and they were funded by charitable donations from mainly upper class benefactors. The municipal hospitals derived from the Public Health movement to protect the community from health hazards and were therefore protective (or preventive) in origin. The public assistance hospitals were the remnants of the Poor Law infirmaries which had not been 'municipalised' under the 1929 Local Government Act. They were institutions for the aged and infirm, the long stay and the chronic sick and their ethos was still largely dominated by the less-eligibility philosophy of the Poor Law and custodial care.

This description of the pre-1948 hospitals is a general summary of the situation and its generalisation does not do credit to the particular situations. In the voluntary hospitals, many patients were encouraged to contribute towards the costs of their care and many were partly supported by insurance funds of one sort or another such as the Hospital Saturday Fund. Nonetheless, the 'Lady Bountiful' ethos tended to linger. The municipal hospitals were often large and fairly modern establishments which took in some general, acute cases as well as others that did not qualify for admission to voluntary hospitals. The public assistance hospitals, on the whole, were

1

restricted to non-operative cases, geriatric or chronic patients and those with little hope of cure or recovery.

The relationship between their respective nurses and patients was coloured by their different origins as was the status of the nurses. Until the implementation of the Rushcliffe Committee[1], salary agreements and conditions of employment varied markedly between the three streams. Similarly, the organisation of the nurses was different. In the voluntary hospitals, the matron was the recognised head of the nursing service and often reported directly to the board of governors. In the other hospitals, the matron reported to the medical superintendent who was the final authority and who reported only to the health committee or the medical officer of health.

The voluntary hospitals were on the verge of financial bankruptcy and were subsidised by central Government funds. They were, however, steeped in a tradition which had been little affected by the recent war and social changes. The other hospitals were largely funded through the rates (but also with government subsidies) and were therefore subject to political considerations. They had few comparable traditions but were more often in newer buildings, usually purpose-built for modern demands. Generally speaking, but certainly in the later ones, the municipal hospitals were better equipped, although this may have held truer in the wards than in the departments.

Municipal hospital nurses were more often non-resident, or even married, than were the voluntary hospital nurses, who had to resign on marriage and were usually discouraged from being non-resident.

There were, therefore, three very disparate streams of nurses who came into the National Health Service in 1948 and whose institutions were all thereafter subjected to national policies relating to the welfare state.

The Nurses Registration Act 1919 prescribed for the setting up of the General Nursing Council and a register of nurses. In the course of time, a mandatory syllabus and common examinations were established for general nurses.

The general register contained the names only of female nurses, and there was a supplementary part for the names of male nurses. There were also supplementary parts for mental and mental deficiency nurses, sick children's nurses as well as an open part for any other prescribed training. Fever nurses were subsequently registered on this part, until 1967 when their register was closed. All the registers had to do with primary, or basic, training. The GNC had no powers to control post-basic training until 1943 when the Nurses Act empowered them to register nurse tutors.

There was a problem, however, in defining the term 'basic training' or, for that matter, 'basic nurse'. Not everyone agreed with the GNC who claimed that the general nurse was the basic nurse and that all other hospital-based training should be post-basic, with the possible exception of sick children's, mental and mental deficiency nurses.

The Council for the Care of Cripples[2] and the British Tuberculosis Association also trained their own 'basic' nurses for their particular spheres of work. There were other special trainings including ophthalmic and ear, nose and throat nursing. Although the Royal College of Nursing and the GNC had both adopted a policy that all nursing should be based on general training and special training only given after registration, the reality was different.

In 1948, therefore, not only were there several very different streams of nurses from the different hospital organisations, but there were also many different trainings, not all of which were controlled by the GNC who maintained five registers.[3] In addition to the registers, the GNC also maintained a roll of nurses.

The NHS Act 1946 established 14 (later 15) regional hospital boards and 388 hospital management committees were set up. Each management committee was responsible for a group of hospitals consisting of several hospital units which were included in the group for either functional or geographical reasons.

In addition to the RHBs and HMCs, the act allowed medical teaching hospitals to retain their autonomy under their respective boards of management which reported directly to the Minister of Health.

Thus, only to a certain extent were the several streams of hospitals joined together in the health service. The prestigious teaching hospitals remained outside the regional hospital board organisation; other voluntary hospitals were taken into the RHB structure but, if they were big enough, the grouping arrangement might not have affected them. Alternatively, they would have become the central hospital within the group and so be able to dominate the other hospitals in terms of administration, organisation, policy making and planning. Seldom did the local authority hospital become dominant over a voluntary hospital except where these had been small cottage hospitals.

In many instances the public assistance institutions were taken over by the local authorities to serve as residential homes under the National Assistance Act 1948. In these cases, the nurses became social service officers or attendants: they were therefore not considered to be part of the national hospital service and were not subject to the Nurses and Midwives Whitley Council agreements.

3

This functional council was part of the general Whitley Council for the NHS and assumed, from the Rushcliffe committee (which was disbanded in 1948), responsibility for negotiating salaries and conditions of work for all nursing staffs in the health service.

The post-war shortage of nurses was described by the National Advisory Council on Nurses and Midwives.[4] Their report was introduced by the warning: '. . . the situation is extremely serious already. It is likely to become critical unless thousands of new recruits can be obtained quickly'. The study which this council made was in anticipation of a nationalised health service and called for substantial improvements in the treatment and training of nurses. Many of their recommendations, such as the combination of a number of small training schools into larger, more efficient and better equipped ones, were subsequently adopted. Many were echoed in the Wood report[5] and subsequently embodied in administrative or legislative changes.

Their report was supported by a mass of statistics which, since few had previously been available, became the foundation for planning the nursing service in the new NHS.

In June 1944, there had been over 30,000 vacancies for nurses and midwives, including trainees. There were over 11,000 vacancies for trained staff – 2,200 more than qualified each year for all parts of the GNC register. The advisory council also supported the need to recruit secondary school girls for nursing but conceded that more elementary school leavers should be accepted in order to make up the shortfall.

The way in which the Ministry of Health was to regard nurses in the new NHS could be predicted by a Ministry circular in 1948 entitled *Nursing and Domestic Staff in Hospitals: notes for guidance of HMCs*. In this circular, nurses and domestic staff were treated together with one or two hints as to those tasks which domestics, rather than nurses, should undertake. The Ministry, clearly, did not have a high regard for nurses and saw them more as pairs of hands or cover for the wards than as skilled workers. This attitude was to colour the way in which nurses were treated until the early 1960s.

The self-image of nurses, however, was sublime and was still supported by the mystique and ideology of the Nightingale era. If the nurses even saw the 1948 Notes for Guidance, they gave little appearance of perceiving any slight to their status. They entered the NHS like crusaders or missionaries, full of zeal, high hopes, fervour and good intentions:

In the last 30 years . . . the country's foremost brains have given more and more thought to sick and helpless people – young and

4

old ... Gradually the nursing profession has grown to be something of national importance, the Royal College of Nursing to be its mouthpiece.[6]

However, it must also be said that the professional organisations, as well as some nurses, were more taken up with discussions on the Wood report and the legislation that ensued from it. In the organisations, the coming of the NHS also brought power struggles. If the bulk of British nurses tended to be complacent, the RCN and its kindred organisations had already learned that they had to fight for every bit of power and every place in the new central policy making institutions.

In 1942 and 1943, the Horder committee had published the first three of its four reports.[7] In 1947, the Wood working party published its report.[5] There had been, therefore, a considerable amount of discussion about the need for changes in nursing (although it is remarkable how little comment was published concerning the Horder reports). If a small section of nurses and the nursing institutions were concerned, the correspondence columns of the nursing journals were more preoccupied with birdwatching, the profitable use of off-duty, the design of uniforms and the spirit of service to the patient.[8]

Nursing had been an institutional life since the Nightingale era, if not even before that. Almost all nurses lived in residences provided by the hospitals. Even the nurses working in the community – the public health nurses – lived in district nurses' homes. Only the health visitors were sometimes exceptions to this rule.

Before the war, nurses had to resign on marriage, and their hours of duty were so long that any life outside the hospital was difficult to maintain.[9] Their meagre salaries did not encourage any social activities and, certainly, did not allow them the luxury of non-residence.

The Wood report[5] complained of the cloistered life that nurses led and, particularly, pointed out the failure of nurses to respond to social changes and new social attitudes. The ethos of nursing in Britain was of dedication to their work. This precluded much concern or interest in outside life and most nurses were unaware of the changes taking place in the world surrounding them.

After the war, though, many nurses returned from the services or other war work and brought with them an awareness of the life that other workers led. Many had travelled, most had enjoyed better salaries and the companionship of non-nursing colleagues. Many service people entered nurse training after their demobilisation and were less amenable to the institutionalised life of student nurses. They were older and more experienced and had learned to look after themselves during the difficult and dangerous years of the war.

There was therefore a conscious, concerted, active and prolonged policy by the Ministry of Health and the professional organisations to drag nursing out of its nineteenth century institutionalism and plant it in the post-war Britain of the twentieth century.

At the same time there was the need to recruit more nurses and establish some machinery for nurse training for which the organisation of the health service, as set out in the NHS Act, so far lacked. Nurse education had to be grafted on to the health service, using, as far as possible, the existing institutions.

In 1948 nursing was a series of small groups of people working in a variety of local organisations such as hospitals and voluntary district nursing organisations. It was not nationally organised and it could not be recognised as a social system except within the hospital or local setting.

There was no observed need to adjust the nursing structure for the health service. Each hospital had its matron and those other posts that the Rushcliffe committee had defined remained. It was a simple, flat structure designed to run the nursing service of a single hospital unit. In the end, it proved to be entirely unsatisfactory, but this was not anticipated and not recognised for many years.

Few people gave any thought to the consequences of nurses entering a national health service except in terms of how to staff the empty beds.

Before the NHS, nurses had been the symbols of charity in the voluntary hospital or servants of the municipal ones. With the coming of the NHS, their status would be changed. Health care was to be the right of every citizen in the country and was to be delivered freely according to need. This was to change the status of nurses since charity no longer figured in health care. Health care became one of the cornerstones of the new welfare state and a new occupational status had to be found for the nurses.

Whereas, previously, nurses had been employed in small groups by a number of employers, with the NHS nurses became part of a national system. The function of nurses was rather taken for granted and nursing was assumed to be a unitary system requiring a common policy. Events were to show that this assumption was mistaken.

The nursing service, therefore, had to make adjustments to meet the needs of the new health service. These were understood to be increased recruitment, the organisation of nurses within the national negotiating machinery and the setting up of a modern nurse training system which would fit nurses for the needs of modern medical regimes and the new social climate.

Chapter 2/The post-war reconstruction of nursing

The post-war shortage of nurses could not be ignored as it threatened the government's plans for a national health service. At the end of the war, conditions in nursing were still far from satisfactory and there was much public anxiety about the need for reform.

Public concern had surfaced before the war and had partly been instrumental in the setting up of the Athlone committee in 1938. This committee had published an interim report[1] in 1939 but, because of the war, had not completed its investigations. The period 1939 to 1949 is characterised by a series of reports and investigations into nursing which were to have a profound effect over the next 20 or 30 years. Indeed, many of the proposals currently under discussion are derived from the Athlone interim report, the Horder reports[2] and the Wood report.[3] An analysis of these is therefore helpful in our study.

The Athlone interim report

The evidence given to Athlone and the other committees is of interest not only for its content but also as a clue to the priorities and attitudes of the various associations. It also has relevance to later sections of this study and, for this reason, it is given in some detail.

The Association of Hospital Matrons commented on the supply of recruits to nursing to meet the demand for nurses. It thought that there was a need for some sort of national survey to establish the numbers of nurses required annually for all branches of nursing.[4]

With regard to the student nurse, the matrons thought that there was a need for a minimum educational standard. They also felt that hours of duty were too long from the point of view both of the health of the probationer and of putting off possible candidates, so they recommended a 96-hour fortnight.

The matrons also felt that sister tutors should be certificated and that every training school should appoint one of these. There was an implied criticism of the quality of teaching of probationer nurses. They thought that probationers should be offered a training grant as were some other students, but were against giving them salaries. However, they advocated better residential accommodation and more relaxed discipline.

With regard to registered nurses, the association thought that their salaries, pensions and accommodation compared unfavourably with those of other female professions and should be improved. A progressive salary scale was needed for nurses in order to retain them in the profession, and their pensions should be transferable from one hospital to another.[5]

The matron of every hospital should have direct access to the governing body and should be able to give her own report.[6]

Ward sisters and staff nurses must have better status as trained nurses.

It is possible to detect here real concern for the nursing staff and for the profession. There is no doubt that improved career prospects, status and service conditions would help in the provision of nursing services for their patients, but the memorandum gave the impression that the welfare of the probationer and the registered nurse was the primary concern of the matrons. This is interesting because there is a gradual, but marked shift in the orientation of the matrons later in the period under examination.

The Joint Consultative Committee of Institutions responsible for the training of health visitors was composed of health visitor tutors, medical officers of health, local authority health committees and others. This joint committee felt that the general training of nurses at the time was too narrow and too much oriented towards cure of general medical diseases to be a suitable basis for training health visitors. They recommended that the training should be broadened to include aspects of sick children, infectious diseases, prevention of illness and infection. They also complained that the poor educational background of many candidates, as well as the poor teaching methods employed by sister tutors, gave rise to a suppression of individual powers of thinking, initiative and reasoning.[7]

Probationers should have student status and should be required to pass part I of the preliminary state examination before they started training.

Sister tutors should be qualified in teaching and should use modern teaching methods.

The Voluntary Hospitals Committee comprised representatives of the voluntary hospitals and could be described as employers of about half of the hospital nurses.[8]

They were concerned to maintain a minimum age of 19 but to fill the time between school leaving and training (known as 'The Gap') by pre-nursing courses. They wanted better publicity for recruits and a central recruitment and information centre. They were concerned at the rising popularity of the cooperative agencies, since those nurses received better salaries. Hospitals were often obliged to employ 'co-op nurses' in order to maintain their cover of patients. They wanted these agencies to be controlled.

They felt that training was too intensive and contained too much theory; that there was a continuing need for candidates without any educational qualifications, and that a simpler training was quite adequate. They asked therefore that hospital management committees should be represented on the GNC. They also agreed that there was a need to relax discipline and that there should be a 96-hour fortnight, a greater use of ward orderlies to augment the nursing staff and permission granted to nurses for non-residence.

We see here the employers' and the managers' concern for the maintenance of the nursing service in the hospitals and their prior economic considerations. There is no evidence of interest in nursing as a profession nor of any long term foresight. This joint committee memorandum highlights the little value placed on nursing qualifications and the attitude that untrained staff would be able to support the bulk of routine nursing with the minimum provision of trained nurses, who should supervise and control them. It was an attitude inherited from the past, before the institution of nurse training in the middle of the nineteenth century. It survived the formalisation of nurse training and survives in the United Kingdom today. It is of interest since it appears to enhance the evidence offered by White[9] and others that most patients are nursed by untrained staff and that trained nurses are used mostly for supervision or teaching.

The East Suffolk and Ipswich Hospital sent a memorandum very similar to that of the Voluntary Hospitals Committee. It criticised the syllabus of training for being too theoretical, proposed a heavier lay representation on the GNC, and viewed any proposals for enrolment of assistant nurses with alarm. This possibility, it said, was a consequence of the GNC setting the examination level for SRNs too high.[10]

The Society of Male Nurses wanted better status and more training schools for themselves and proposed that male patients should be nursed only by male nurses. It also proposed reduced training periods for male nurses who, trained in one speciality, wished to move to another speciality. They advocated the abolition of the Royal Medico-Psychological Association (RMPA) certificate for mental nursing since it was of a lower standard and outside the control of the GNC. They wished to have just the GNC certificate for registered mental nurses (RMN) which enjoyed a higher status.[11]

The GNC memorandum was long. It complained of inadequate

arrangements in some hospitals for teaching modern medical and surgical treatments. It wanted a minimum standard of education and a higher ratio of trained nurses to students. The hours of duty were too long, and matrons and administrative nurses were overworked. It reported that it had twice debated separating the preliminary state examination into two parts (as earlier recommended by the Lancet Commission in 1932) but that the council had on both occasions rejected the proposal. It promised that the recently elected Council would again debate the issue.[12]

It reported that there were few arrangements for the systematic teaching of students but, by then (1938), no hospitals were approved that did not have 'some sort of classroom and the necessary minimum equipment'. It regretted that progress was slow but explained that this was made necessary by the council's unwillingness to upset the hospital services. All sizes and shapes of hospitals took probationers and for many years very little inspection by the council had been possible but, by then, no approval was given to training schools without a visit. Withdrawal of approval could only be taken after sufficient time had been given to the hospital to effect the required improvement. There were 713 approved training schools. Thirty-eight hospitals had been removed from the list of approved training schools since the inception of the GNC.

The GNC described the conditions that were required for approval of a training school: experience for students in four main services – medical, surgical, gynaecological and children's diseases; there should be adequate staff for teaching the prescribed syllabus; at least one resident medical officer; the training should be of at least three years' duration, divided between surgical and medical experience. Other conditions included an appropriate number of beds and daily occupancy, numbers of nursing staff, types of cases, and so on.

In many ways this was rather a defensive memorandum and seemed to admit that conditions and standards of training were not as good as they could have been.

The Interdepartmental Committee on Nursing Services published its interim report in 1939 and was subsequently disbanded at the outbreak of war. The report was prefaced by a description of the extremely urgent problem of the shortage of nurses which had been manifested by the public through Parliament, the press and in private communications.

During the course of their investigations the committee had been hampered by the lack of reliable statistics for nurses and midwives but they had been able to glean some from the General Nursing

10

Council (GNC). These showed that in December 1937 there were 73,849 registered female nurses including 44,268 who had been placed on the register by examination since 1919.

In addition to those on the general register, there were on the supplementary parts of the register:

	Total	Including by examination
Male nurses	315	168
Mental nurses	5,073	1,202
Nurses for the mentally deficient	246	52
Sick children's nurses	2,716	2.053
Fever nurses	7,007	5,724
All registered nurses	89,206	53,467 (59.93 per cent)

Approximately 32 per cent of these registered nurses were members of the RCN.

The committee commented on the status of nursing as an occupation and said that it was time to recognise it as one of national importance. The radical changes in the social and industrial structure of the country made recruitment on the basis of a 'sense of vocation' unreliable and inadequate: in order to find enough recruits it would be necessary to improve the nurses' conditions of service and to make their salaries competitive with those of teachers. They recommended that salaries and pensions should be placed on a national basis, negotiated by a national committee and grant-aided by the government, since the hospitals were unable to afford a proper level of remuneration.

The report found an acute shortage of nurses and probationers, although there was no apparent falling off in the numbers of recruits. There was an 'astonishing wastage' of first year probationers (said by the Lancet Commission in 1932 to be 25–30 per cent)[13] and a further weeding out of probationers as a result of the state examinations.[14] The report therefore deduced that the demand for nurses had exceeded the supply. Nevertheless, in spite of pressures, the report recommended that the minimum age of entry should remain at 18, although this was not supported by regulation.

Recruits were mainly drawn from the secondary and elementary schools. The proportion between these was about half and half. The committee felt that there was a need to draw as many as possible from the secondary schools, the better educated recruits, but at the

11

same time it was bound to acknowledge that they would not be able to supply the numbers required, and recruits from the elementary schools should not be turned away. On the other hand it was thought that a possible cause of wastage in the first year of training was due to a lack of an educational standard.

The committee commented that the quality of the teaching given by nurse tutors to probationers was not always good enough. It recommended therefore that the usual route of entry to training should be through pre-nursing courses taken in secondary schools or, in the case of elementary school leavers, in the evening institutes. These pre-nursing courses should take the candidates to the level of part I of the preliminary state examination.[15] The report also proposed that all nurse training schools should have an introductory period for recruits, lasting about six weeks, in the form of a preliminary training school (PTS).

Reporting on conditions of work, the committee found that these 'were not always tolerable'. Up to 120 hours were worked per fortnight. A 96-hour fortnight was proposed. Better living conditions, a separate bedroom for each probationer, planned off-duty and four weeks' holiday per year were recommended. It was also suggested that a relaxation of the requirement for residence would be helpful. Discipline and rules, especially in off-duty hours, should be relaxed.

The committee found very little involvement of nurses in policy-making and proposed the setting up of nurses' councils with 'staff' and 'official' representation in order to allow grievances to be aired. It was thought that these local councils could be linked to a national council charged with the consideration of conditions of service on a broader basis.

The most significant section of the report came at the end when it discussed the problems of the assistant nurses. These were untrained and outside the control of any regulating body. They were felt by registered nurses to be a threat to the profession and to the public.[16] Athlone therefore recommended that they should be given a recognised status and placed under the control of the GNC who would be empowered to set up a roll. It was recommended that they should be given a short training of two years and required to take a simple examination in order to qualify for enrolment. The new enrolled nurses should always work under the supervision of registered nurses. They should be called 'assistant nurses', commonly 'nurse', and to distinguish them from the state registered nurse, the latter should commonly be designated 'sister'.

The four nurses on the committee signed a reservation against the title 'assistant nurse' and proposed 'registered invalid attendant' in order to make the distinction clear and to reserve the title 'nurse'.

The committee discussed the problems surrounding the protection of the title 'nurse' and the closure of the profession. It was thought that only state registered nurses, assistant nurses on the roll and nurses in training should habitually and for gain nurse the sick, but the problems of legislating for this were recognised as being too difficult to surmount.

The Athlone report is preeminent for its recognition of nursing as a profession. A high proportion of its recommendations were put into effect, probably because of wartime needs, which also brought the activities of this committee to an end, and no final report was published.[17] The College of Nursing had provided both oral and written evidence to the Athlone committee and in its subsequent comments, it generally welcomed the interim report. 'Altogether the report embodies many of the ideals for which the College of Nursing and all progressive nurses have been striving over many years.'[18,19]

It was a little anxious about two grades of nurse, as it felt that the public would not be able to distinguish between them and that the cheaper nurse would be preferred, especially in private nursing, which then gave a more remunerative form of employment to a significant number of nurses. On the other hand, the College recognised that untrained assistant nurses were already being employed as nurses in large numbers by the nursing agencies and in private nursing homes and that enrolment under the GNC would help to control this.

The College felt that not enough emphasis had been given in the report to the better educated girl, since to take all intellectual levels for registered nurse training would deter the more able and lead to frustration and boredom during training. Whilst accepting the principle of a roll, it resisted the proposed title of 'assistant nurse' and the use of the term 'nurse' for this second grade.

It accepted the idea of some central machinery for negotiating salaries but thought that the terms of reference should be widened to include conditions of service as well. Salaries could not be negotiated in isolation from conditions. It therefore preferred a body more akin to the Whitley Council than the Burnham Committee. It felt that it was imperative to close the profession to nurses on the register and roll.

In summary, therefore, there was general agreement that a single grade of registered nurse could not provide the labour force required, that conditions of work and salaries had to be improved, that nurse training should be improved by better qualified tutors and a wider training syllabus.

There was lack of consensus on the nature of the second level of nurse; whether she should be a nurse under the control of the GNC or an auxiliary; what training she should have; for how long it should be and whether or not there should be some sort of qualifying assessment or examination.

There was little discussion of the nature of the nursing that should be undertaken by this second grade but general agreement that, in hospitals, she should be supervised by the registered nurse. This point, though, was not thought through by anyone since there was a lack of consistent consideration as to which hospitals and which patients the second level nurse should work for. Was she to work in acute hospitals in which most registered nurses worked and almost all of which employed student nurses, or was she to work only in the chronic institutions which did not take student nurses and which had difficulty in attracting registered nurses? At the time, these institutions were almost entirely staffed by untrained assistant nurses.

The Horder report

The Royal College of Nursing was disappointed and worried by the disbandment of the Athlone committee and decided that it must take some initiative in reviving the enquiry into nursing. It therefore determined to institute its own. In order to make it as impartial as possible and to give it weight and status, the College decided to invite half of the committee's members from other organisations which had an interest in nursing. Lord Horder accepted the chairmanship of the Nursing Reconstruction Committee in 1941, and the joint secretaries were Miss Frances Goodall (general secretary of the RCN) and Mrs Hilary Blair-Fish (a long-time member and officer of the RCN).

The terms of reference of the Horder committee were 'To consider ways and means of implementing the recommendations of the Interim Report of the Inter-Departmental Committee on Nursing Services, and to recommend such further adjustments to the nursing services as the present situation and post-war reconstruction may demand'.[20]

Altogether the Horder committee issued four reports and a number of supplements:

I   1942 *The Assistant Nurse*
II 1943 *Education and Training*
III 1943 *Recruitment*
IV 1949 *The Social and Economic Conditions of the Nurse*

The Horder report was probably one of the most important so far produced in nursing. The crux of the report was lost in the welter of detail and recommendations and in the discussion that followed over the years.

Briefly, Horder found that there was a hierarchy of skills in nursing. These skills could be practised by a hierarchy nurses. There should be an 'officer' level of nurses whose general education and training should be at an advanced level. Their numbers should be smaller than the next level of nurse, the enrolled assistant nurse, who should be recruited from less educated girls and whose training should be a two-year course of instruction. The assistant nurse, Horder said, was 'pivotal to the reconstruction of nursing'. The committee saw her as 'one of the most stable elements in our national nursing service, an integral part of the profession and a person whose status offers the key to the improved training and employment of her senior partner, the State Registered Nurse'. Horder felt that only when the services of the assistant nurse had been defined and regulated could matters regarding the SRN be brought into line.

Horder wrote that the main target of the report was a complete nursing service. This orientation was different from that of the Athlone committee whose concern was to make recommendations to alleviate the shortage of nurses. Horder therefore looked at a nursing service as a structure and considered the parts of the whole in relation to each other.

Briefly, Horder's argument was as follows.

The supply of well-educated girls for registered nurse training was obviously not sufficient to provide enough nurses for all needs.

The training of SRNs (assuming student status which the report recommended) was very expensive and therefore it would be economically unviable to attempt to have the bulk of nurses trained to registration level.

The more routine tasks of nursing did not demand the intellectual level of a well-educated nurse and, indeed, to expect such a nurse to spend most of her time on these tasks would be to cause boredom and wastage.

The more skilled tasks of nursing, increasing with the growth of medical knowledge, would require more hours of the high grade nurse as time went on.

There was therefore a need for a hierarchy of nursing skills – and grades – to match the hierarchy of nursing tasks.

Horder therefore proposed a reversal of the proportionate numbers of SRNs and assistant nurses – more 'other ranks' and relatively fewer 'officer' nurses.

15

Whereas, at the time, most assistant nurses worked in the chronic and long-stay hospitals (the public assistance hospitals and institutions inherited from the Poor Law), Horder wanted them to be given a training to enable them to work anywhere, a recognised status and enrolment under the GNC. He wanted the assistant nurse to be the regular grade of nurse and the SRN to be the advanced grade.

For the SRN he wanted student status separate from the obligation to provide nursing services for hospital patients. He thought that it was vital to indicate the position which the nurse should occupy in schemes for any national health service. 'Given a liberal outlook and a careful, planned curriculum, the training of nurses in this country could be developed into one of the great national educational movements for women.'

Horder was critical of the training of nurses: 'In no other professional training is there so little periodic inspection, in none is the standard of entry so dependent on the demands for student labour, in none have the requirements with regard to teaching staff been so nebulous'. He thought that the demand for labour had led to the multiplication of training schools and to the lowering of educational standards for the entrants and the quality of the training.

He recommended that the future health service planned around regional bodies should include institutions to ensure an improved education for nurses.

He was severely critical of many attitudes regarding nurses. Nurses, he said, should know 'the why' as well as 'the how'. 'As the SRN responds to new requirements, so the Assistant Nurse should come forward to relieve her in suitable spheres.' University courses would be appropriate for post-registration training and, by inference, for basic training once the new structure that he proposed had been achieved. Until then 'there can be no real reform in nursing education till each school has an income independent of the hospital to which it is attached'. In the last report, 1949, Horder made an outright recommendation for a degree course in nursing.

Assistant nurses should have an apprenticeship training. SRNs should have a combination of studentship and apprenticeship such as the qualified engineers: studentship first, apprenticeship second.

Horder considered a number of alternatives to the two-stream model and argued against a one portal system, saying that it would deter the able candidate.

Other recommendations included the reconstitution of the GNC to make it more educational and to give a wider representation of teachers, both nursing and non-nursing; more frequent revision of the nursing syllabuses; a minimum standard for approval of training schools; better and more frequent inspection of training schools; school certificate level for entry to registered nurse training, with a later requirement for the higher school certificate so that the officer level of nurse could take her place with other professions in evolving a national health policy.

The Horder committee carried out a most comprehensive piece of investigation for the nursing profession at a time of radical social change. It reviewed demographic and educational changes and used these in its considerations. It anticipated changes and developments and its reports, as a consequence, were forward-looking. In contrast to this, the Athlone report could be said to have tried to improve the status quo.

The main recommendation of the Horder report – the reversal of the proportional numbers of SRNs and enrolled assistant nurses – has never been achieved. This can be explained to a large extent by the reluctance of the Ministry of Health to reinstitute the minimum educational level for nursing candidates which had been dropped for the war and was not introduced again until 1962. When it was reintroduced, it was set at a very low level, hardly comparable to the pre-war School Certificate which had by then been superseded by the General Certificate of Education. It was therefore possible for candidates with minimum educational qualifications to take training for the register and there was little incentive for candidates to opt for a subsidiary grade with lower status.

In spite of continuing attempts by both the RCN and the GNC to have fewer student nurse training schools and more pupil (assistant) nurse training schools, this goal was never achieved. Student nurse training was felt to have more appeal for recruits and hospitals consistently refused to change so long as they could qualify for approval by the GNC. The GNC found it very difficult to remove their approval, mostly because they were not able to rely on the support of the Minister. The numbers of SRNs have consistently been something more than three times the numbers of SEANs (SENs since 1961).

It is possible that Horder's retention of the existing titles, state registered nurse and assistant nurse, for greatly developed roles was another contributory cause. Had the existing SRN level of training been allowed to continue and a higher grade, possibly of a graduate level, been superimposed, his objective could have been achieved. As it was, legislation[17] had to be passed in 1943 to require the GNC to set up a roll of assistant nurses, thus 'legitimising' the second grade, but this did nothing to control the employment of untrained nurses. The enrolment of the assistant nurse created a vacuum which was immediately filled by the nursing auxiliary, still untrained.

Horder also recommended the closure of the profession to all but trained nurses but, once again, admitted the problems of drafting appropriate legislation because of the time-honoured practice of the use of the term in connection with nursery nurses, Christian Science nurses and others.

The Horder enquiry into nursing was searching and wide and was the first one instituted by the profession itself. It could be anticipated, therefore, that it would have provoked a great deal of discussion and interest. This proved not to be the case. The four reports came out over a period of years – 1942, 1943, 1949. On the occasion of each publication, there was a comment in the nursing press. This was usually, as was invariably so in those days, self-congratulatory (of the profession, the RCN and of the respective journal which claimed to have had many of its ideas reproduced) and uncritical. There was usually a later item reporting a speech made by a nursing or health dignitary on the report. There might have been one or two short letters in the correspondence columns about a secondary aspect of the report, normally about hours of work or salaries. There was nothing else.

This is quite remarkable, especially in the light of the interest that was provoked by the publication of the subsequent Wood report. One reason that may be put forward was the restricted circulation of the reports because of a wartime shortage of paper, but this might also have applied to the Wood report, which, in fact, had a much wider circulation. Possibly the Government made available supplies of paper for the Wood report which was a Ministry publication.

Another reason may be put forward: the profession was still, in 1948, a service very much based on individual hospitals. White[9] showed that nurses were regarded as 'local' and that they themselves reflected this in the orientation of their thinking. The focus of nursing attention was the hospital in which they served: their loyalties, ambitions and standards for comparison were parochial and very few gave any regard to wider nursing issues.

This may have tended to lead nurses to discount a report emanating from the profession itself. Athlone, Horder and Wood all flattered the profession (whilst at the same time criticising it quite severely) by acknowledging it as being of national importance. The Athlone and Wood reports were, however, government inspired and, as such, may have represented to the nurses, steeped as they were in an authoritarian tradition, tablets of stone. It was possible to regard the Horder reports more as pillars of salt.

Another observation must be made. There were many strong criticisms of the Wood report; nursing organisations and individual nurses had a great deal to say about it. There were many letters in the two weekly nursing journals and a number of memoranda from the institutions. Opinion was divided and comments were not inhibited. This tends to weaken the description of nurses as parochial, but Horder was concerned with a national service, and Wood was predominantly seen to be concerned with nurse training. Whilst Horder could, and possibly should, have been seen as proposing fundamental changes to the fabric of nursing, the point was missed. Wood, on the other hand, was clearly seen to be proposing changes and criticising the ritualistic elements of nursing in the form of routine procedures and ward organisation. Wood took the argument to the hospital level, even the ward level. Whilst Horder dealt with a concept which the nurses could not grasp, Wood dealt with practical issues which were within their experience.

The nursing profession was not yet used to having any say in its affairs and found the variation of emphases in the Athlone and Horder reports confusing. Both reports boosted the image of the SRN as a profession; both criticised the profession for rigidity and ritualistic practices. Both reports advocated a second grade of nurse. Athlone wanted to inject this assistant nurse at a lower level, whilst Horder preferred to lift the SRN to a higher plane in order to find space for the assistant nurse. Both reports insisted on the essential need to keep nursing at all levels on a practical base rather than an academic one, although Horder understood the need for theory.

It must be remembered that in the post-war years university education was still for an élite and was directed towards the production of graduates in the traditional professions. There was still then an emphasis on the arts and the humanities: science courses were of a secondary status. Social science courses had by then hardly taken much shape. University education was considered to be highly theoretical, to provide knowledge for the sake of knowledge rather than for the purpose of vocational or technical application. The Butler Education Act had been passed in 1944, but the Robbins report was not produced until 1965.

If Horder was aware of a growing technology, most nurses were not aware of any level between 'practical' and 'academic' and considered theory to be too remote from the everyday needs of the patient to be relevant. The majority of nurses did not possess the school certificate although those who did were more inclined to be in the decision-making levels and in the London teaching hospitals.

Talk of a minimum educational standard was therefore threatening to many nurses and talk of university courses or higher school certificates was too remote and threatening to be entertained by most.

Whilst Horder could look at and plan for a nursing structure, most nurses saw only the need for four grades: staff nurse, ward sister, administrative sister and matron. Hospitals were relatively small; the few with more than 1,000 beds were unusual, and most had fewer than 250. Therefore, where was the need for a more complex plan?

The Government was also undecided. There was a certain amount of agreement that the assistant nurse should come under some control. There was general agreement that the training of nurses should be improved and more modern methods of teaching should be introduced. Certainly, public pressure demanded improved conditions and better salaries. But the Government had never before been much involved in nursing and exchequer funds had not been used for nursing salaries nor for nurse training until 1943 when the Rushcliffe committee made its recommendations on nursing salaries.

The Wood report

There was, however, a nursing crisis, and the Ministry of Health recognised that it would become responsible for the nursing service in the new National Health Service. It decided, therefore, to set up a working party on the recruitment and training of nurses under the chairmanship of Sir Robert Wood, then chancellor of University College, Southampton.[3] Other members of this small working party included Miss (later Dame) Elizabeth Cockayne, matron of the Royal Free Hospital and subsequently chief nursing officer to the Ministry of Health; Miss Daisy Bridges, who later became executive secretary of the International Council of Nurses; Dr John Cohen, a psychologist then in the Cabinet Office, and Dr Inch of the Department of Health in Scotland. There was a steering committee consisting of officials from the departments concerned. The nursing organisations were not consulted and the original intention, subsequently modified, was to review the several published nursing reports and to make recommendations.

The working party report was published in 1947. A minority report, written by Dr Cohen, was published in 1948. The main thrust of the enquiry was directed towards five questions:

1 What is the proper task of the nurse?
2 What training is required to equip her for that task?
3 What annual intake is needed and how can it be obtained?
4 From what groups of the population should recruitment be made?
5 How can wastage during training be minimised?

The working party understood that it was required to take a long-term view rather than to look at immediate needs.

Wood tried to make use of the burgeoning scientific methods of social enquiry and 'to reach conclusions not resting solely on opinion but verifiable by reference to facts . . . not to form impressions but to discover the facts and let the facts speak for themselves'. There was therefore a mass of detail culled from statistics by previous reports and existing hospital sources.

On wastage, the report proposed that student nurses should be accorded full student status, and be more carefully selected on personality traits rather than on educational grounds. It found that senior nurses should be carefully selected and taught interpersonal skills in order to improve relationships on the wards, and that a three-shift system of duty should be introduced.

On training, it reported that the course should be based on the needs of the students rather than on the needs of the service, that the GNC should be reconstituted to give better regional representation and a stronger educational bias, and that the several GNCs representing the four countries of Great Britain should be incorporated into one council which might also absorb the Central Midwives Board (CMB).

On the assistant nurse, it found that this grade should not be perpetuated, that the roll established in 1943 should lapse, and that the one remaining grade of nurse, the SRN, should be supported by student nurses where practicable and, substantially, by a new grade to be called nursing orderlies, who should have a short in-service training for simple nursing duties.

The report is best known for its contentious finding that if student nurses were relieved of repetitive and non-nursing duties, they could be effectively trained in 18 months with a further six months, before registration, of concentrated study in a chosen field. This would be a single portal of entry for all who wished to train for nursing. The plan of training should be broadened to include experience and teaching in public health, obstetrics, psychiatric nursing and paediatric nursing.

This plan of training was for the first level nurse. Appendix VIII extended their model: 'We do not consider it unreasonable to assume that before a nurse proceeds to a post carrying new functions. . . . she should receive some training beyond that provided in the basic course'. The working party thought that this need should be met by an increasing number of university courses, as well as others. No nurse should claim to be a specialist until she had undergone 'post-graduate' training. Unfortunately, this appendix was overlooked in the ensuing debate.

21

Finance for training should be drawn from public funds, independent of hospital revenues. Students should be under the control of the training establishment and not the matron or the hospital. They should be given training grants.

The report was critical of the quality of teaching given to students and recommended that there should be adequate numbers and quality of teaching staff and that there should be composite and independent training units covering all fields of nursing with their own directors. Hospitals would be used for ward training purposes only. There should be regional nurse training councils to plan and coordinate training facilities, set entry qualifications and approve supervisors for the internship period.

The working party also proposed inspection of the training centres by the health departments, similar to the general education inspectorate.

In relation to the numbers of nurses required, the working party found that to give effect to the three-shift system and full student status there would have to be an additional 22,000-24,000 trained nurses and some 14,000 nursing orderlies, without allowing for any expansion of the health services.

The Ministry of Health invited comments on the report from the institutions.

The King Edward's Hospital Fund (KEHF) was an extremely influential trust which had, for many years, taken an active interest in hospitals in the London area and had, since 1944, run the Nursing Recruitment Advisory Centre in London. It is of interest to note that the secretary of the King's Fund at that time was also the secretary of the Voluntary Hospitals Committee. It published a memorandum which was highly critical of the Wood report. It attacked the proposal to broaden the training; it particularly disliked the bias towards public health nursing since, it said, there was considerable doubt that more public health activity would reduce the demand for hospital beds. The proper task of the nurse, it said, was to care for the sick and helpless under medical direction. Reforms in nurse training should tend towards greater skill in actual bedside training. Nursing was a practical art and required practical skills.[21]

It attacked the emphasis given to wastage of student nurses especially in relation to the working party's plans to reduce the shortage of nurses. It sought to demonstrate that it was the loss of nurses after training that was critical in this matter. It placed its own emphasis on the need to retain trained nurses and thought that Wood's proposal to make student nurses supernumerary on the wards would place extra pressure on an already inadequate number of registered nurses.

It admitted the need for a subsidiary grade of nurse but thought that these should be auxiliaries with a certificate given by the regional authorities rather than the GNC.

The King's Fund did not think that there was much wrong with the idea of student status so long as it did not entail their being supernumerary. It was ambivalent on the proposed selection tests and wanted selection by the matron to remain. It attacked Wood's proposal for a shortened period of training of two years. It thought that there was no evidence to show that this would increase the number of candidates but that, on the contrary, it would cut back on the quality of recruits by deterring the more highly educated girl.

A shortened course of training would only increase the output if the input was adequate. The KEHF was sure that, in nursing, there was the problem of an insufficient input.

Its comments and alternative proposals for nurse training were to be of considerable significance later (see chapter 3). The KEHF was concerned not to make sweeping changes in nurse training before experiments had been made. This referred specifically to the syllabus and to the proposal for independent training units with their own directors. The King's Fund did agree with, and had for some years advocated, training grants for student nurses, with free residential accommodation and tuition; a critical proviso of this idea was the need for a grant machinery analogous to that already used in the case of the universities. In addition, it insisted that the grant-giving body should be educational and not concerned with the provision of service for the hospitals.

Whilst the KEHF preferred the training school to remain in the hospital, it thought that there was need for much greater freedom and initiative than there had been. There was a place for pioneer training units and each candidate should be free to choose the school to match her own inclination and intellectual level.

Certainly the GNC should be reconstituted, but its powers, responsibilities and methods of control should be more carefully considered before this was done. There should be greater decentralisation.

The KEHF was scornful of the Wood (and Cohen) preoccupation with manpower planning. It felt this was irrelevant since 'direction into nursing is undesirable and direction out of nursing is unthinkable'.

It also attacked the premises underlying the statistical analyses in the report: 'Efforts to solve the nursing problem by reducing

23

wastage during training and to secure more favourable conditions for the student will not succeed if there is a failure to appreciate how short is the period of hospital life of many trained nurses and how wide is the gap between the numbers qualifying and the numbers [subsequently] entering hospital service'. It made no comment about Appendix VIII.

The RCN set up a subcommittee, comprising members of both the Horder and the professional advisory committees, to study the Wood report, and a draft memorandum was subsequently debated by the RCN council before its publication.[22] There was some coolness in the tone of its comments since the memorandum could only call the report 'timely', and the RCN council thought that its criticisms of nursing might be harmful to recruitment.

The RCN memorandum had been influenced by the Ministry of Labour's paper, *Recruitment of Nurses and Midwives to Training Institutions*[9], which called for a national survey of patient dependency needs. The RCN called for both an analysis in order to establish the need for nurses and a review of non-nursing tasks which an increased provision of domestics could take over. It repeated one of the Horder themes that a hierarchy of nursing tasks and skills should be determined in order to make more effective use of the different grades of nurse.[23]

There was considerable and significant disagreement between the subcommittee who drew up the memorandum and the RCN Council (consisting mainly of matrons) over the term 'student'. Whilst the draft memorandum insisted that the student nurse should be a student, in the same sense as that employed by Wood, working an academic year and with supernumerary status on the wards, the RCN Council could not accept this. Instead, it amended the draft memorandum, used the term 'student nurse' instead of 'student' and explained that the student nurse should not *primarily* be an employee. This shifted the emphasis considerably and was an important departure from the ideology put forward by Horder.

With regard to training, Council thought that the repetition of tasks, criticised by Wood as being excessive and a waste of student nurse time, was necessary for the development of skills. It was also doubtful that the shorter training recommended by Wood would be satisfactory.

The province of British Columbia had recently rescinded its reciprocal agreement with the GNC and would no longer register British SRNs automatically because, it explained, the standard of education of the recruit to British nurse training and the standard of the training itself were no longer considered satisfactory. This had been a real blow to the pride of British nurses who consistently considered themselves to be superior to all others. The RCN was therefore touchy on the subject and could not accept any adjustment which might be seen as an erosion of the quality of training. It therefore rejected the Wood proposal for 18 months' training and six months' internship and proposed instead two years and one year. The final examination should be taken at the end of the second year and registration be given at the end of the third year.

Even in this there was no consensus. The public health committee of the RCN thought that two years training was enough, especially as nurses wishing to become health visitors had, anyway, to take a further year's training for a midwifery qualification before they were eligible to undertake the health visitor training (increasingly becoming a one year course). On the other hand, hospital nurses insisted that three years was the minimum that they could consider. The general secretary (Miss F Goodall) said that whilst the RCN Council had supported the Horder proposals in principle, the needs of the community for more nurses might necessitate the shortening of the basic training and it was therefore necessary to make a compromise.

Council therefore agreed three years which was also to include experience in public health (preventive) nursing and communicable diseases. It did not include the Wood elective period. No mention was made of the comments included in Appendix VIII of the Wood report, which would, in fact, have given the RCN their 'officer class'.

It is interesting to note that their opinion was dictated more by the influence of the matrons who were responsible for maintaining a nursing service, by an altruistic sense of responsibility and international political considerations than by any objective criteria relating to the content of the training.

The subcommittee thought that clinical instruction of the student should be the responsibility of the school of nursing. RCN council wanted it under control of the ward sister.

The subcommittee and RCN Council both agreed that there should be a minimum education level for candidates and the reinstitution of the GNC test as an alternative. There was also agreement on the need for a reconstituted GNC. The subcommittee agreed with the proposal to have one nursing council for all the four countries of the United Kingdom (England, Scotland, Wales and Northern Ireland) whereas the RCN Council was afraid of over-centralisation and preferred to retain the three existing organisations (England and Wales, Scotland, Northern Ireland). Everyone liked the proposals for regional training bodies for the coordination of training in the new NHS regional hospital board areas.

One more significant disagreement is noted. The subcommittee, under the guidance of the RCN director of education, Miss M Carpenter, had drawn up a proposal for a scheme of training which was appropriate to full student status and which would allow considerable flexibility to the schools for experiment and to meet local needs. It integrated prevention and curative aspects, theory and practice, proposed modern techniques for teaching and for practice such as case assignment and case reporting; it offered blocks of experience in medicine, surgery and operating theatres, special departments, psychiatry, paediatrics, obstetrics and gynaecology as well as an elective period in which to study one area in greater depth.

Council could not entertain this and rejected the entire scheme out of hand. Instead it set up its own working party to draw up another one. The scheme that it eventually agreed was not very different from the then current one.

The published RCN memorandum incorporated, naturally enough, Council's views rather than those of the subcommittee. In addition to those already discussed, it made the following points.

There should be only one register for men and women.
The GNC should be reconstituted to include more educationalists, but not until three to five years after the institution of the NHS.
The matron must remain head of the school of nursing.
Assistant nurses should be retained, nursing orderlies were not suitable.

The GNC memorandum was no less disapproving.[24] It disagreed with the causes of student nurse wastage put forward by the working party. It felt that reinstatement of the minimum education requirements would ensure that recruits were suitable and able to cope with the training and examinations.

It agreed with student status and thought that improved working conditions and a 96-hour fortnight would help considerably.

It disagreed with the 18 months and six months training period. It was most anxious that too much emphasis should not be placed on the removal of repetitive tasks since, the GNC was sure, every patient was different and repetition was necessary to develop skills. The elimination of repetitive duties would only serve to rob the student of her ultimate job satisfaction derived from confidence in her skills.

Although it agreed with the content of the proposed training, the period of training should remain at three years. (The GNC originally proposed four years but compromised.) It also agreed that the supplementary parts of the register should be closed but thought that there should be a special part of the register for mental nurses.

The GNC had no comment on the independent financing of nurse training as it considered that this was not within its sphere of reference. It thought that student nurses could be supernumerary for the early part of their training but should later be included on the ward staff in order that they could learn to take responsibility. More trained nurses were necessary on the wards.

The GNC (also predominantly composed of matrons but including established sister tutors as well as Ministry of Health and Privy Council nominees) did not like the proposal for nurse education directors: the matron should remain head of the school of nursing.

The GNC did approve the proposal to establish regional nurse training bodies but stoutly rejected the proposal for the Ministry of Health to approve and inspect the training schools. Council was determined to retain these functions.

Whilst it did not reject the proposal for its own reconstitution ('it was open to the Minister to appoint whomsoever he pleases'), it did not think that this should be done until after the NHS had been in operation for some years. It did reject the idea of one GNC for the United Kingdom as being too unwieldy.

The GNC thought that it would be premature to close the roll of assistant nurses and proposed that this should be re-examined in three years. It thought that there was room for SRNs, SEANs and an auxiliary grade, although it did not like the title 'nursing orderly'. Once again, the GNC had nothing to say about Appendix VIII.

There is an inescapable feeling of disapproval emanating from this memorandum, a primness and a preference for the maintenance of the status quo.

One last memorandum must be noted. This was one which was privately printed and published and was produced by a group of ten leading nurses, many of whom held official positions and felt that they had to remain anonymous. They called themselves the Ten Group.[25]

The Ten Group considered that the nurse was a member of a team that provided the total needs of patients both in and out of hospital. The nursing group, controlled by professional nurses, should be prepared to assume the responsibility within the team for every kind of nursing for every type of patient. This statement was a reference to the resistance that many registered nurses felt towards nursing the chronic sick and the elderly. The voluntary hospital nurses were steeped in the ideology that acute cases only merited trained nursing skills and that the chronic sick should be looked after by a lesser grade of nurse, or a nurse with less professional status such as the former Poor Law nurses (White[9]).

The Ten Group proposed that the question posed but not answered by the Wood working party, 'What is the proper task of the nurse?' could best be discovered by the analysis of the many needs of all patients and by the employment of different categories of staff to meet those different needs. This was a reflection, of course, of the Horder statement describing the hierarchy of skills and the hierarchy of nursing tasks. It was an interesting precursor of the nursing process propounded some 20 years later.

The Ten Group then described the changing needs of patients arising out of medical developments. They suggested that with early diagnosis many more patients in hospital were ambulant and could look after themselves. Routine nursing tasks were, therefore, now less important than some other considerations such as nutrition and the composition of the health team therefore required reviewing, as did its members' training. They felt that the failure to differentiate between the categories of service demanded by the patient had blurred the line of demarcation between nursing service and domestic service. They offered, as an example, the difference between feeding the sick patient and taking meals to the ambulant patient.

The total needs of the patient, they said, could only be met by a team of nurses of different degrees of knowledge and skill. Since the patients were being looked after by numbers of people, the nurse had to be their point of reference and interpret to them what was going on. The nurse therefore had to be an interpreter, a hostess, a carer who provided the treatment ordered by the doctor, and someone who coped with emergencies until the doctor arrived to take over. She was also a health teacher. The Ten Group did not feel that there was a great deal of difference between the hospital nurse and the public health nurse in their functions: the needs of the patient would provide the foundation for the practice and the training of the nurse.

They recommended, therefore, that the roll of assistant nurses should be closed, that there should be a common basic training for all nurses, a recognition of the nurse as an expert in her own right and a distinction made between those duties that required her skills and those that were more properly within the purview of someone else.

The Ten Group thought that the working party had put too much emphasis on student nurse wastage and not enough on the need to retain trained nurses. Recruits should have a grounding in the basic sciences before they started training; there should be experimental forms of training, and the continuing use of auxiliaries. Promotion of nurses to more senior posts should be by virtue of further study as well as experience. If a university degree in nursing were possible, the two-year course for registration should be of a level acceptable as the first year of university study on which the degree course could be based. Alternatively, the basic course could be regarded as experience in the ranks, a prerequisite for officer status.

Other points made by the Ten Group were that the final state examination should be by assessment rather than by written examination, that there should be training for senior posts, and that there was an urgent need for good nurse teachers. Theirs was the only memorandum that appeared to have recognised Wood's proposals for advanced training.

Three major reports—two of them from committees set up by the Government whose primary concern must have been to achieve enough nurses to man the hospitals and to reopen some of the 50,000 unstaffed beds (in 1948), the third report stemming from the profession itself, concerned to improve the standard and the status of the profession but also seeking to be rational and forward-looking.

In response to these reports, we have noted the differing comments and opinions—most of them dissecting the reports and commenting on individual proposals or points. None of them appeared to examine the whole model or structure incorporated in any of the reports and the RCN Council, although it had accepted the Horder reports, was already losing sight of the principles adopted by him and beginning to erode them by slight shifts of emphasis. Furthermore, we are able to note that since 1939, there had been a considerable change of mood in the matrons. In 1939, they had been concerned for the welfare of their nurses. The difficulties of the war and the need to keep their service going during the emergency had changed this. By 1948 their primary concern was the need for labour.

The prior interest of this chapter is the reconstruction of nursing after the war, in preparation for the inauguration of the National Health Service. It is possible from this point of view to distil from this profusion of detail and comment three critical points: the question of how many levels of nurse there should be, the level of general education required as a minimum for recruits, and the question of the training for the registered nurse.

Athlone wanted two levels of nurse only, the SRN and the enrolled nurse. He wanted a three year training to the level then current for the SRN and a two year practical training for the SEAN. He stipulated a secondary education or an augmented primary education for the SRN. He was not specific about the enrolled nurse but thought that aptitude and inclination were important criteria.

Horder wanted most nurses to be enrolled after a two year training. The SRN was to be highly educated and highly trained. She should have first an academic training then an apprenticeship; he did not depart from the three year period for these nurses.

Wood wanted only one grade of basic nurse, supported by a band of auxiliaries with a short in-service training. The SRN should have a broad two year training and should be an all-purpose nurse with a mandatory supplementary training for advanced or specialist duties.

There is little doubt that the cost of training nurses has increased considerably since 1948. Salaries for both nurse tutors and student nurses have risen appreciably. Hours of work have been reduced by stages from the 96-hour fortnight to a 36-hour week. The numbers of learner nurses have increased from 49,055 students and 2,599 pupils in 1951 to 56,558 students and 22,258 pupils in 1979.[26] The syllabus of training for student nurses has been changed several times since 1949, as has that for the pupil nurse who now receives a training as comprehensive as the student nurse did in 1948. The student nurse by now is required to have more classroom hours and is no longer free to spend enough time on the wards to allow her to be anything more than a short-term member of the staff. Whereas in 1948 it was cheaper to employ student nurses as labour than it was to use auxiliaries, the position is now reversed and the auxiliary is the basic nursing member.

The overall ratio of trained nurses to untrained nurses is slightly higher now than it was in 1948, but a direct comparison is difficult to make as the form of collection of numbers and the categories have been substantially altered. It is quite clear, however, that the hospital service could not be staffed only by SRNs nor even by SRNs and SENs; it continues to rely on untrained nurses to a very substantial degree.

The demand from both the profession and the service for further post-registration training has increased substantially, to a point where it was considered necessary in 1970 to establish the Joint Board of Clinical Nursing Studies.

In 1962, the GNC was finally allowed to reinstitute a minimum educational level for recruits. This was then set at two GCE 'O' levels—a very low level. In succeeding years, it began to tighten up on its examination standards. Many hospitals imposed their own education requirements which were much higher than the GNC minimum. It is interesting to note that after 1962, over a broad period of time, recruitment rates increased, wastage rates dropped and pass rates for the GNC examinations improved. This applied to the general student nurse. The GNC was not allowed to set a minimum education level for student nurses in the psychiatric field until 1965, and there was no commensurate improvement until that happened. The many integrated training courses demanded a much higher education level, indeed some of the courses which combined general nurse training with health visitors' training demanded two or three GCE 'A' levels. These courses were all over-subscribed, and the health visitors' courses had four or five times more applicants than they had places.[27]

The position of the enrolled nurse has never been satisfactorily settled. Where there is a registered nurse, the SEN is subordinate to her, but where no registered nurse is available, the SEN may take charge of a ward. There are very few career prospects for the SEN, although she is the most permanent member of the nursing team. Today, the SEN is a respected member of the nursing group in nearly every area of nursing, but the demarcation between the SEN and the SRN is not clear and some investigations have failed to distinguish any difference in either the level or the quality of their respective work.[28]

The recruitment of pupil nurses for enrolment is still only about one third that of student nurses for registration and, obviously, the status of the registered nurse is more attractive. The registered nurse also has better career prospects. But there is still a deficiency of registered nurses with enough general education to provide a corps that is able to take the profession forward in conceptual or analytical skills. This deficiency was certainly felt in 1951 when the GNC had to find candidates for the newly formed area nurse training committees.[29] In the 1980s, there is still a problem in finding suitable and adequate candidates for key posts, especially those that require nurses to be capable of holding their own with other professionals and graduates.

The reactions of the profession during the negotiations for the Nurses, Midwives and Health Visitors Act 1979 were not dissimilar to the reactions manifested in 1948. Nurses are not educationally minded on the whole and resent groups within the profession whose level of education is higher than that of the general run of SRN. They did not understand, and certainly did not admire, the fight put up by the Council for the Education and Training of Health Visitors to maintain its standard of education and to resist being absorbed by those with a lower educational requirement.

Throughout the period reviewed by this book, nurses consistently confused skill for knowledge and common sense knowledge for theory. This confusion probably persists in many quarters today. This is a pity since it induces many nurses to persist in an inflexible but superficial knowledge which is inappropriate to the current state of scientific theory.

Athlone was satisfied with the level of the registered nurse and put the enrolled nurse below that level. That did nothing to enhance the status—or the recruitment—of either grade. Furthermore, as we have already shown, he miscalculated the position with regard to those workers who want to nurse on a more casual basis and who do not want to take a formal training. He ignored the auxiliaries, thinking that the problem would go away with the enrolment of the assistant nurse.

Wood wanted all trained nurses to be registered and for them to be supported by auxiliaries whom he wished to be called 'nursing orderlies'. He did not stress the need for an organisation or structure to support a national nursing service and therefore did not include in the main body of his report provision for advanced training for specialists and a nursing leadership. Although his remit was for a long-term policy, his recommendations were not of that order. He failed to anticipate the changing needs of the National Health Service which were to demand a growing number of specialists and administrators. By relegating his recommendations for further training for nurses to an appendix and by failing to work through the financial and organisational implications of that appendix, he gave undue emphasis to a shorter basic training. His model was not clearly stated and was not therefore understood by the institutions. Whereas it could be argued that his proposals were not too dissimilar to those of the Horder reports, he appeared to be down-grading nurse training and was seen by the profession to be doing just that.

On the other hand, a basic nurse training is still considered necessary as a starting point for further specialisation and the later proposals made by the Committee on Nursing[30] were a development on this Wood theme in which the nurse should receive blocks, or modules, of training after her first 18 months. The Wood model therefore was capable of development.

Horder wanted to improve the quality of the registered nurse, to establish her on a higher plane in order to place the enrolled nurse on a more realistic level. He accepted the increasing need for developed skills that medical science and technology would continue to demand. He also accepted the need for nurse leaders and policy makers. He wanted a corps of nurses, of a level something below the then registered nurse, to be the substantive body. He realised the cost of training and proposed for the enrolled nurse, who was to have a developed role, a two year in-service or apprenticeship type of training. This was the nurse who would staff the wards. He did not reject the auxiliary but, on the contrary, saw a real place for her in the support of the enrolled nurses. Whilst Wood stressed the general nurse, Horder placed his emphasis more on specialisation.

The relatively few registered nurses for whom Horder wanted a higher education were to be leaders, educators and policy makers. Briggs advised a corps of graduate nurses of about 2.5 per cent of the total and considered those to be essential if the profession was to develop and hold a place in the health service and amongst other professions. It is probable that a rather higher proportion than that is now needed.

With hindsight, we may detect that the arguments were about two issues: whether all nurses should be regarded as generalist or semi-skilled; or whether there should be a small élite group who would be educationally qualified to be called specialists and, secondly, models of care.

Athlone tended to regard the registered nurses as generalists but introduced an even less skilled element to support them. Horder, on the other hand, introduced the idea of an educational élite, leaving the newly created enrolled nurses as the generalists.

Wood differed from Horder only in that he chose to retain the SRNs as the generalists whilst selecting from them the better qualified élite. The Horder model was a closed system and the Wood model an open one.

This issue was not recognised and the arguments centred around how many grades of qualified nurses there should be. In 1948 the authorities had not yet come to understand the growing trend towards the division of labour and the development of a specialist élite in occupations. Given this factor, it really matters very little how many grades of statutorily qualified nurses there are since the increasing complexity of health care will require both the basic nurse and the nurse with advanced educational qualifications.

In the issue about models of care, all three reports discussed a team of nurses with different levels of expertise. All three reports appeared to consider only a ward team caring for all the patients as a single group. It was not until the Goddard report[31] that the proposal was made for ward nurses to be formed into several small teams each looking after its own group of patients (see chapter 10).

Chapter 3/The Nurses Act 1949

This chapter discusses the Act[1] and the negotiations which preceded it. For the first time, draft proposals are disclosed together with the reactions of the RCN and GNC to them. No attempt is made in this chapter to follow the Bill through the legislative procedure since that has already been done by other authors. Instead, we deal with the relationship of the Act to the nursing institutions and the major nursing reports which preceded it.

In the wake of the Wood report[2] and in preparation for the National Health Service, the Minister of Health (Aneurin Bevan) recognised that there was a need for changes in the organisation of the training of nurses.

The National Health Service Act, 1946,[3] provided a structure for the administration of the hospitals and those health services delegated to the local authorities. There was no provision in the Act for the training of nurses and no organisation within the NHS was charged with this responsibility.

Both the Horder reports[4] and the Wood report[2] had provoked a wide variety of responses. Many people were concerned with conditions of work and the need for improved salaries for nurses, but these matters could be dealt with by the Whitley Council for Nurses and Midwives set up under the NHS Act. The Minister's immediate concern in 1948 was to establish an improved system of training for nurses, and he had to find a path through the conflicting advice offered by the many institutions.

It is possible that the Government had not by then realised the deterioration that had taken place in the quality of recruits to nursing since the removal of the educational requirements. Both the RCN and the GNC had repeatedly asked for its reinstatement, but the Ministry was faced with an alarming shortage of nurses and was being pressed by the employing authorities to resist the profession's requests.

The BMA wanted more nurses of adequate skill and a capacity to follow doctors' orders; many doctors wanted the devoted assistant and handmaiden that had been available before the war; some doctors could foresee the increasing need for a higher grade of nurse to support the growing complexity of medical technology. The employing authorities were concerned only for cheap labour and were not concerned about skill or professional development.

The GNC wanted to develop a general corps of competent bedside nurses and to allay the criticisms made by the Wood report and the national press. It showed little appreciation of future technical demands that would be made on nurses, but it was concerned not to provoke the hospital authorities through whom it had to work. Its primary concern was for a minimum level of qualification.

The RCN was dominated by a Council of senior nurses who were concerned to preserve the image of the voluntary hospital ideal type: the dedicated, amenable gentlewoman. They were also concerned to preserve their control of the student nurses who Wood had proposed should be trained in independent nurse training colleges. The shortage of labour and the nationalisation of hospitals had made it very difficult to find enough staff to keep beds open and to maintain the service.

At the same time, there were on the College's staff a number of more forward-looking women who had been influenced by the advanced thinking incorporated into the Horder reports. Their ambitions tended towards setting up an élite band of nurses supported by a larger group of second grade nurses.

The Public Health Section also wanted better training for nurses. Many health visitors had received their training at centres of further education and appreciated the benefits of this. Furthermore, the tutors in the Public Health Section were aware of the difficulties generated by the narrow, rigid training given to student nurses. They appreciated that much of the general nurse training had to be countered or overcome before a health visitor student could begin to understand her new role. They had found that general nurse training was too narrow and hardly suitable as a base for their students, and they were therefore also anxious for a broader training. They considered that Wood's proposals for a two-year course would be a better start for their recruits: the shorter course followed by the one year elective training (which the future health visitor students could take in midwifery) would allow health visitors to qualify in four years instead of five or six years as was then necessary.

In September 1948, both the GNC[5] and the RCN[6] received invitations to attend the Ministry of Health for discussions on the Wood report and legislative proposals. Also invited were the National Council of Nurses, the Association of Hospital Matrons and the Society of Registered Male Nurses. At this meeting certain proposals for legislation were put to the nursing organisations, and these included the following notes:

1. Responsibility for nurse training currently rested with individual local units, the expenses of training were borne by the

hospital authorities. The new RHBs and Hospital Management Committees (HMC) were not appropriately designed as bodies suitable to be responsible for organising or financing nurse training and separate arrangements would be required.

2. There was a proposal to guide Exchequer money for financing training through a reconstituted GNC but the GNC should not have to deal with the budgets of all the units. This, together with the constitution of the training units, their grouping[7] and the supervision of their work might become the function of new regional bodies (discussed in para. 4). The actual training would continue to be done by the individual training schools and approval would remain the responsibility of the GNC.

3. *The Principal Functions and Constitution of the Reconstituted GNC*
    i.   Distribution to regional training bodies, on the basis of periodic budgets (say three to five years) of funds made available by the Exchequer for nurse training.
    ii. Prescribing the general curriculum for nurse training and the conduct of examinations. Where it is satisfied that the examinations and training of individual training units, or the regional training council, is equal to or higher than its prescribed standards, the GNC should have the power to recognise these and give exemption from the State examinations.
    iii. Registration.
    iv. Discipline.
    Details of the suggested new constitution are given in Appendix 1.

4. *Functions and Constitution of Regional Training Councils*
    i.   Constitution, grouping, financing and supervision of individual training schools. Items to be financed by the Regional Council would include salaries of tutors and buildings required solely for training purposes and, possibly, students' training grants.
    ii. Preparation and approval of schemes for training schools in the region on the basis of the general curriculum prescribed by the GNC.
    iii. Power, at some future date, to conduct examinations subject to the approval of the GNC.
    iv. The general promotion of training efficiency within the region.
    The general type of constitution of the Regional Councils would be prescribed by Statute. They would come into

being on the initiative of the Minister after consultation with the GNC.

Membership might include members nominated by the GNC, RHBs, Boards of Governors [of the teaching hospitals], local health authorities (LHA) and local education authorities (LEA).

Constitution of Training Schools

The hospitals forming the new training schools might be under one or more HMCs (in groups approved by the GNC) on the recommendation of the Regional Training Council, in association with the LEA and LHA.

5. *The Roll of Assistant Nurses*
   The Roll to continue but the Minister to be empowered to prescribe a date on which fresh admissions should cease, after consultation with the GNC. Constitution of Assistant Nurses' Committee [of the GNC] to remain as at present but to be varied by Rule with the Minister's approval.

6. *The Supplementary Parts of the Register*
   The Minister to have power to prescribe a date on which admission to any supplementary part of the Register should cease, after consultation with the GNC. (It is not contemplated that admissions to the mental or mental defective parts should cease before a considerable period.)

7. *Appeals under Section 7 (2) 1919 Act and Section 5 (2) 1943 Act*[8]
   The appeal to be no longer to the Minister but an independent arbitrator.

8. *List of Nurses, Section 18, 1943 Act*[9]
   Nurses who are within the provisions of the Nurses Regulations 1947 to be admitted to the List on application with a time limit for application.

9. *Reciprocity*[10]
   The GNC to have the power to register nurses trained abroad whose training is of equal standard to our own whether or not reciprocal arrangements are in operation with the country where the training was obtained.

The notes were dated August 1948.[5,6]

There was also a letter to the GNC with proposals for a mental nurses committee of the GNC.

These proposals, made by the Minister, were of considerable significance. In effect it was proposed that there should be independent training councils set up in each region to organise, supervise and fund the nurse training schools. The regional councils would have authority to design training syllabuses and conduct their own examinations and would be able to build their own nurse training schools and be the grant-giving body suggested by the King Edward's Hospital Fund and the Nuffield Provincial Hospitals Trust (see chapter 2).

This idea would have provided each region with an educational organisation independent of the hospital authorities. The regional councils would have had the freedom to design their own training schemes within certain criteria laid down by the GNC. They would have had the capacity to build their own training centres, staff them with their own nurse teachers and conduct the training centres as nursing colleges.

The GNC would have been set at a higher level, at a stage once removed from the local training units. Instead of dealing directly with each unit, it would have dealt with the several regional councils. It would have set a broad curriculum for the guidance of the regional councils, retained overall control of the councils by virtue of its control of finances and retained the final sanction, that of approval of the training units.

In many ways this plan was a reflection of the training of doctors, where the University Grants Committee (UGC) is the grant-giving institution and therefore oversees the courses. The GMC retains the rights of licensing medical practitioners.

Both the RCN and GNC discussed these proposals and drew back in some consternation. Neither appeared to have understood the far-reaching possibilities of this scheme. Neither appeared to have understood the concept and the professional independence offered by the plan. Both Councils nibbled at the separate paragraphs and made counter-proposals in a piecemeal fashion.

It is apparent from the discussions reported in the minutes of the GNC[5] and the RCN Council[6] that neither was familiar with the organisation of university funding or the workings of the UGC. Both Councils looked at these proposals and interpreted them from their own points of view, rooted in their own interests and values.

In discussing the Minister's proposals for legislation, therefore, the GNC felt threatened. It did not like the prospect of the powerful regional training councils and felt that these would undermine GNC powers and influence. They proposed that the RHBs should set up special nurse training committees instead of the independent training councils. They took strong exception to the proposal that the examination of any training school should give exemption from the Council's examinations. They felt that the setting up of regional training councils was an unnecessary proliferation of administrative machinery and that there would be enough difficulty in finding suitable nurses to sit on the RHBs without having to find more for the proposed training councils.[11]

The GNC did not wish training schools to be supervised by an intermediary body and insisted that these should remain under its own jurisdiction. They were suspicious of the proposals to give the regional training councils any say in the use of nurse training budgets and preferred to retain control of these.

They also resisted the proposal to establish independent training schools, separate from the need to provide labour for the hospitals. There are not many details relating to the discussion of this point and it must be deduced from the tone of the minutes, together with subsequent reports, that the matrons on the council feared for their power over their labour force if they lost control of training. They talked in terms of selecting 'suitable candidates', 'concern for the patient', 'the need to maintain standards', 'the importance of nursing being practical', 'the need to maintain a balance between practical skills and theory'.

There was a considerable amount of cross-membership between the GNC and the Council of the RCN. It is not surprising, therefore, that the discussion reported in the RCN minutes was similar.

The RCN Council was not in agreement with the proposed new regional bodies as this would be administratively wasteful. It would prefer that each RHB should have a nurse education committee.[12]

The RCN Council was against any major changes in the constitution of the GNC for at least five years after the start of the NHS, but it did agree with funding for nurse training to be routed through regional machinery. It did not agree that the examinations of training units should be accepted as an alternative to GNC examinations.

The RCN Council offered alternative plans for the regional training councils:

a the financial arrangements should be dealt with via the RHB finance committees;

b it accepted that regional plans for training schemes should be possible, subject to GNC guidelines;

c it did not agree that the regional bodies should have power to conduct their own examinations.

It rejected the proposal that the nurse education committees should be set up by statute.

Once again the service interests of the profession overruled the interests of education. Indeed, on this occasion, it can safely be said that the matrons' interests, which RCN Council adopted, were directly antithetical to the development of the profession and professional control.

It was only in 1919 that the profession had gained statutory recognition and the authority to organise the training, examination and registration of its members. Even by 1948 these powers were illusory since every substantial decision taken by the GNC had to be agreed by the Minister. Each time the GNC tried to withdraw approval from a training school, the hospital management (often backed by the doctors) could appeal to the Minister for a reversal of the decision. On more than one occasion, the Minister had upheld the appeal. Each time the GNC tried to alter the training syllabuses, it had to obtain ministerial approval which was withheld or delayed for years. The profession insisted that the lack of any minimum educational requirement for recruits had a deleterious effect on the recruitment of secondary school leavers and caused wastage of student nurses who were unable to cope with training, but the Government refused to allow the reintroduction of the minimum standard and discouraged inspection of training schools. Every advance that the GNC had been able to achieve had been in the face of government discouragement, procrastination and opposition. It is not surprising, therefore, that the GNC felt alarm at any prospect of having its powers apparently reduced by legislative proposals. Its defensiveness and suspicion of the Government unfortunately overwhelmed any appreciation of the opportunities offered by these proposals.

The meeting with the Ministry of Health took place on 5 October. After the meeting a letter from the Ministry dated 11 October was received by both the GNC and the RCN.[13] This letter summarised those discussions which appeared to have centred around the position of the state enrolled assistant nurse and the matter of the reconstitution of the GNC. The Minister, the letter said, was committed to drafting a Bill before the end of the year.

With regard to the organisation of training, the civil servants 'appeared surprised' at the RCN proposals that the new bodies should not be separate entities but should come under the authority of the RHBs. In their view, the present position of the conflict between service needs and nursing training would be perpetuated under such an arrangement.

The Ministry was disappointed that the RCN did not wish the GNC to handle training funds as the civil servants had wanted to establish a position similar to the UGC for grant-making.

The Ministry wanted to give a reconstituted GNC fuller powers than it had at the time with regard to the curriculum, the conduct of examinations and the nature of the examinations.[14]

It appeared that all the nursing organisations were unanimous in their desire to keep the assistant nurses roll. The Ministry was not happy with the position at that time: there were not enough recruits for training and most potential candidates appeared to prefer to work as hospital orderlies (later re-styled nursing auxiliaries). There was agreement that the training should be reviewed. There was some discussion as to whether the present qualifications for enrolment could be modified in order to allow existing auxiliaries to be included or, alternatively, whether the auxiliaries should remain outside the system of enrolment by the GNC. They could, for instance, be given an in-service training. It was, however, feared that this second option would result in the eventual disappearance of the SEAN and her replacement by an unqualified grade who was outside the control of the GNC.

The GNC held a special meeting on 16 October to discuss the meeting with the Ministry. Representatives from the Scottish GNC and the Northern Ireland council were invited to attend. The morning meeting was entirely taken up with discussion on the enrolled nurse.

One member, a doctor, felt that it had to be accepted that there had been a failure in the recruitment of pupil nurses. There were, at that moment, only 1,000 pupil nurses, compared with over 12,000 auxiliaries. He thought that the reasons for this failure were threefold: the poor salaries offered to pupil nurses, the lack of any career prospects for enrolled nurses and the GNC requirement that training for pupil nurses should be directed towards the nursing of the chronic sick.

He felt that there were only two options available: to maintain the two-year training for pupil nurses, in which case the roll would probably die and the care of the sick would revert to untrained people, or the reduction of pupil nurse training to a shorter period and the relaxation of the requirement for a compulsory period of training with the chronic sick. If this failed, the GNC would have to advise the Minister that it could do no more.

A member of the assistant nurses committee agreed with the reasons for the shortage of pupil nurse recruits but thought also that there were too few nurse tutors for the pupil nurse courses. He thought that potential recruits were put off by poor salaries and preferred to take posts as nursing auxiliaries where the salaries were higher without any need for training. The two-year training was too long for these women, many of whom were married and most of whom did not wish to leave their homes in order to take training. Every effort should be made to enrol the 12,000 auxiliaries by assessment only; the theoretical examinations for enrolment should be eliminated.

Dame Katherine Watt was the chief nursing adviser at the Ministry of Health. She thought that the training could be reduced to one year. She also felt that the supervision of pupil nurses in training was often very meagre.

Other speakers held divergent views of the theoretical teaching and the length of training. There was some agreement that the inclusion of the term 'assistant' in the title was unpopular and that there should be a prospect of promotion for enrolled nurses. Some members thought that it should be possible to train pupil nurses in the same wards as student nurses in the acute hospitals. Many members thought that there would be a continuing need for the third grade of worker, the auxiliary, who should receive some minimum training on an in-service basis but who should not enrol under the aegis of the GNC. Eventually, it was agreed that the roll should be continued.

There was then a resolution put to Council that pupil nurse training should be shortened, that the training should have only a minimum of theory and that it should be modified.

The voting was split – nine votes for and nine votes against. The chairman declined to give her casting vote. It was necessary therefore to advise the Minister that opinion was equally divided.

Several observations may be made about this meeting. One of the members had been prevented from attending but had written to the registrar giving her views. These were not reported, but it is possible that if she had been able to attend, there would not have been a tied vote.

It will have been noted that the resolution incorporated three proposals. Many members could have voted differently if each proposal had been put separately and if each had been more specific. As it was, there was a stalemate and the GNC lost the initiative.

The afternoon was taken up by a discussion of the meeting at the Ministry but only in relation to the proposed reconstitution of the GNC. Council affirmed the need to confirm its powers to control post-registration courses and the granting of specialist certificates such as for paediatric nursing, the possible forms for redistributing seats for the representation of specialties and geographical areas and the formation of a statutory committee for mental nurses. There was apparently no great disagreement about these matters and no further discussion about regional training councils.

In December,[15] both organisations received new proposals from the Minister and met to discuss these. The proposals included the following:

1. The training organisations should include (a) the GNC, (b) nurse training committees for each RHB, (c) nurse training schools.
2. The GNC should retain its present functions and, in addition, should be responsible for distributing funds for nurse training and have powers to facilitate experimental training schemes. The constitution of the GNC would be amended to include two places for the representation of Sister Tutors.
3. The Standing Nurse Training Committees should be responsible to the GNC and should be constituted by regulation. The members would be appointed by the RHB, GNC, Central Midwives Board (CMB) and by the Minister from the local health and education authorities and the university residing within the region. Each Chairman was to be elected by the committee members.
4. The Supplementary parts of the Register would at some time in the future be closed, at the request of the GNC, by the Minister.
5. Appeals from hospitals, approval of whose training schools had been withdrawn, were to be heard by independent arbitrators appointed by the Lord Chancellor.
6. The list of nurses (Sect. 18 of Nurses Act, 1943) was to be reopened for nurses who were within the provisions of the Nurses Regulations 1947. [This was specifically for nurses who had been prevented from applying for admission by virtue of being prisoners of war.]
7. Provision for reciprocal registration with the Dominions was to be repealed but the GNC was to have powers to register overseas-trained nurses.
8. There was to be a Mental Nurses Committee of the GNC.

Thus, the nurse training bodies were to be tied to the service organisations, the RHBs, and the status of these bodies had been down-graded from councils to mere committees.

Both organisations wanted the GNC to have powers to set up a register of sister tutors. Both organisations backtracked and commented that the title of the training bodies, proposed as standing nurse training committees, should be re-styled regional nurse training councils in order to avoid any assumption that they were under the control of the RHBs.

Both organisations wanted clarification of the details of membership of the training bodies. The RCN specifically wanted to ensure that the local health authority representatives were health visitors rather than medical officers who would have no familiarity with nurse education.

Discussions with the Ministry continued and the Bill was introduced in the House of Lords in April 1949 as an agreed non-party measure. This did not, however, ensure its swift and uncontroversial passage. Both the RCN and the GNC continued to lobby for amendments in order to achieve as much as they could of what they thought had been omitted.[16]

The RCN wanted to ensure a majority of nurses on the training bodies and continued to press for a change of name. The GNC was disappointed that there was to be no mention of post-registration courses in the Bill. They had no powers to organise, examine or grant certificates for these courses, including fever or tuberculosis nursing, without first prescribing additional parts to the register and then making additional rules. If the supplementary parts of the register were to be closed, the GNC anticipated that there would be difficulties in dealing with these nurses who had only specialised training and were not on the general register. On the other hand, the GNC was set against anyone qualifying only in one limited branch of nursing and wanted to close the supplementary registers. They had hoped to be able to institute post-registration certificates for these specialties but needed powers to do this.

An amendment to give the GNC powers to recognise post-registration qualifications was introduced in the House of Lords by Lord Webb Johnson, but he was persuaded to withdraw it by Lord Addison, on behalf of the Government. The Minister was against this proposal because, in pursuit of the Wood policy, he was seeking to achieve a broad training which would make this kind of specialisation unnecessary. It was hoped that, in the future, nurses would be judged on their post-registration experience alone. If statutory recognition of additional training were allowed, it was feared that the authorities would require further qualifications for higher appointments. This would lead to 'certificate hunting' by nurses.[16]

It had also been decided that the new training bodies were not, after all, to be allowed to pay training allowances to the student nurses. This decision had, it was said, been taken by the Ministry on administrative grounds since there was already machinery available for the payment of student nurses by the HMCs. Furthermore, if training allowances, instead of salaries, were to be paid, there would be problems with national insurance and superannuation payments. With regard to the constitution of the training bodies, the Minister did not wish to lay down any firm arrangements in the Bill; he preferred to make regulations on this matter in order to retain a degree of flexibility.

There were continuing discussions and much in-fighting about many points. The Government wanted to limit the number of matrons who might be elected to the GNC. The GNC was not happy to accept any restrictions for nominations or elections and retorted that any registered nurse was eligible to stand and the choice of members should be left to the electors.

There was a problem about how regional representatives could be elected, and a working party was set up to consider the mechanics of this.

In May, it was reported that an amendment had been carried to provide for the administration of the training funds by a hospital grants committee to be specially constituted, but this amendment was later negated by the re-insertion of the original clause.

In June, the Bill passed to the House of Commons, and the Minister's brief included the following passage:

Undeniably in the past student nurses have suffered in their training because it was too much subordinated to the staffing needs of the hospitals ... The new arrangements should ensure a proper balance between the needs of training and staffing with a proper opportunity for the student nurse to be properly trained.

He said that the finances for nurse training would be in the hands of the profession. A sign that a profession has reached the adult stage must be when it can be entrusted with the funds for its professional training.

The content and standard of nurse training are professional matters which should be settled by the professional bodies ... the Bill looks forward to a time when there may be a comprehensive training with provision for specialisation which will make it unnecessary to continue the present supplementary special registers.[16]

However, in July 1949, the BMA sent a memorandum to the Minister. It had seen the draft proposals in confidence and complained that they did not meet with the association's agreement.[16]

The BMA advised that whilst the finance of nurse training should be separate from hospital administration budgets, the GNC should not be responsible for distributing the funds; the training bodies should be advisory only, without powers to dictate how the funds should be used.

The BMA did not agree that nurse training should be separate from the staffing needs of the hospitals and the training bodies should not be empowered to dictate the numbers of student intakes to the RHBs or the hospital managements; nor should the GNC be put into a position of being able to impose its demands in respect of training in such a way as might dislocate the provision of hospital services. It would therefore be preferable to have an ad hoc body for the management of training funds such as that proposed by Lord Webb Johnson during the committee stage in the House of Lords in May.

The BMA also insisted that training allowances for student nurses should be paid by the hospital authorities in order that the student nurses were clearly recognised as employees and the hospitals known to be the employers, with control over the student nurses and responsibility for their actions. The Government should ensure medical representation on the GNC and the training bodies.

At the second reading of the Bill in the House of Commons, the title of the training bodies was finally settled as area nurse training committee (ANTC), and the Act went on to the statute book in November 1949. It was to be operative from 1 December 1951.

The final version of the Nurses Act 1949 contained, *inter alia*, the following provisions:

Section 1 The reconstitution of the GNC.
17. elected members including 14 general nurses elected by general nurses in the 14 health service regions of England and Wales; two registered mental nurses elected by registered mental nurses; one registered sick children's nurse elected by registered sick children's nurses.
12 members appointed by the Minister of Health including
    2 public health nurses
    2 nurse tutors
    1 male nurse
    1 ward sister
    3 hospital administrators
3 members appointed by the Minister of Education
2 members appointed by the Privy Council, one of whom was to represent universities in England and Wales.
Section 2 There was to be an area nurse training committee in each RHB which should have regard to the methods of training nurses, promote research and investigations in order to improve methods of training and advise and assist the HMCs, boards of governors and any other authority.

The RHB was charged with the duty of providing services for the committee.

Section 3 made provision for the GNC to authorise experimental courses of training.

Section 4 provided for the expenditure on nurse training to be defrayed by the ANTC.

Section 6 provided for the expenditure of the ANTCs to be defrayed by the GNC.

[It should be noted that capital expenditure was excluded in the Act.]

Section 8 provided for the appointment of a finance committee by the GNC.

Section 9 established a Mental Nurses Committee.

Section 10 provided for the registration of nurses trained overseas.

Section 11 made provision for the register of male nurses to be amalgamated with the general register and for the closure of supplementary parts of the register.

Section 12 made provisions relating to the approval of training institutions and the appeals procedure.

Section 14 made provision for admission to the register of people included in the list (those trained before July 1925).

Section 16 made provision for copies of the register, roll and list to be kept open.

Section 22 gave the GNC the duty to make an annual report to the Minister. The report was to be laid before Parliament.

Each of the ANTCs was to include persons appointed by the RHB, the board of governors of teaching hospitals, the GNC, the CMB, the LHA, the LEA and the university situated in the area.

The profession and the Minister had openly claimed great hopes for the Act, but events were to show that many of these hopes were to be disappointed. It is open to question how either the Minister or the profession could believe that nurse training could be separated from service needs by the form of the Act. Training grants or salaries were to be paid by the hospitals who would therefore continue to be in the position of hiring and firing students. The finances available to the ANTCs were restricted to funds for the salaries of the tutors and clerical assistants. Some small sums were available for teaching materials, but the original proposal for capital funds was dropped.

The finances for training were reputedly in the hands of the profession, but in fact were severely pruned by the Ministry each year to the point, in some years, where new schools could not be opened and extra tutors could not be engaged.

The content and standard of nurse training had, for many years to follow, to be approved by the Minister and there was considerable difficulty and delay before the supplementary register for fever nurses could be closed.

The GNC had many problems in finding suitable nurses to appoint to the early ANTCs and many of the nominees were matrons whose service requirements took precedence over the establishment of nurse education. There was, for many years, a shortage of qualified nurse tutors. In the following ten years, the ANTCs were obviously dominated by the non-nurse members, and the GNC often found itself in an isolated position.

Funds for research by the ANTCs were almost non-existent and, after a few gallant efforts, even the more ambitious committees appeared to abandon trying to set up projects.

Student and pupil nurses continued to be employees of the hospitals and never achieved student status, nor even student nurse status.

Probably the single, most significant development achieved out of the Act was the growth of experimental forms of training.

In studying the draft legislation which was so peremptorily declined by the RCN and the GNC we can see clear signs of the Wood report in its formulation.

Wood had advocated a reconstitution of the GNC in order to underline its educational function as contrasted to its disciplinary one. He had also recommended that there should be a United Kingdom GNC but that had been quashed by the nursing institutions. Nonetheless, the draft legislation (as well as the subsequent Act) did propose changes in the GNC.

Wood had also proposed regional training bodies, independent of the NHS, to coordinate the work of the new colleges of nursing, which, also, were to be independent of the health service. Both were included in the draft proposals.

Wood had proposed that the roll of nurses should be abandoned and this had been included in paragraph 6. Wood advocated that the cost of nurses' training should come from outside the health service and the draft had accepted that Exchequer money would be used for these purposes.

In the Act, only the reconstitution of the GNC followed the Wood report and then only partially. Apart from the provision for experimental schemes of nurse training, the professional bodies had successfully defeated the Wood report and, in so doing, they lost the goodwill of the Minister and the civil servants.

It may be seen that the changes introduced by the Act were piecemeal and left much to the administrative and educational discretion of the reconstituted GNC. Whereas each of the three major reports had offered an implicit or explicit model of restructuring for the nursing service which their proposed training schemes would support, the Act built on the existing structure and did very little to improve it for the future. Both the Horder and the Wood reports proposed a basic grade of nurse with a shortened course of training. The Wood report offered an open system for progression: the Horder report proposed a two-tier system with less (but some) opportunity for movement from the basic to the advanced level. The Act did not describe any movement from one level to another. Subsequent administrative regulations permitted movement but did not make that constructive in the sense that passage from the SEAN grade to the SRN grade offered salary improvements rather than specialist promotion.

The Act was a reflection of those changes which the nursing establishment (particularly the matrons) and the employers had permitted. It took no account of the critical recommendations made by the post-war nursing reports.

Change and restructuring of nursing itself was therefore to be more a matter of directives and relatively less for legislation. The Ministry had not shown itself to be reluctant to issue instructions to either the NHS authorities or the GNC; why then was the reconstruction of nursing seen to be a matter for a Nurses Act? In fact, the Nurses Act 1949 failed significantly to achieve any reconstruction.

Any answer to this question can only be a matter of conjecture. There is no evidence to offer a substantial reason for the choice of legislation as a single method of reconstruction. If the Act had been supported by appropriate directives, the recommendations of one or other of the reports (or some of both) could have been effected. As it was, very little was achieved.

The only clue that presents itself in the search for Aneurin Bevan's actions lay in the letter dated 11 October 1948 from the Ministry of Health to the GNC and the RCN.[12] This letter outlined the discussions which had taken place on 5 October between the institutions and the Minister, relative to his draft proposals for the new Bill. The Minister, the letter said, was committed to drafting a Bill before the end of the year.

Aneurin Bevan had shown great goodwill towards nursing in the form taken by his draft proposals; they were sweeping and extraordinarily ambitious for a hitherto subsidiary occupation. The proposals were in considerable contrast to the attitudes of the civil servants which had been manifested in the years before the White Paper of 1946. Whereas, prior to that, the civil servants had felt no inclination to discuss policy matters with the nurses and had not at first considered a standing advisory committee for nursing, their attitudes had shown contempt. Bevan must have had quite a struggle to persuade them to draft his proposals as they appeared.

After the profession's rejection of the draft proposals, the impression of contempt was once again evident in future developments. It is possible that Bevan felt considerably disillusioned and let down by the nurses. Having committed himself to a Bill, he followed it through but omitted to support it with further directives.

Bevan left the Ministry of Health soon after the Bill went on the statute book. It is not possible therefore to gauge his attitudes towards nurses after that. His successors at the Ministry certainly did nothing to further the restructuring of the nursing service: subsequent sections of this study tend to show that much was done to undermine it.

One of the most significant observations to arise during the passage of the Bill through Parliament was the Minister's refusal to allow the GNC to have powers to control post-registration training. Aneurin Bevan was set firmly against this because the proposed broad training would make it unnecessary. Bevan had noted Wood's comments about turning out a broadly based nurse, the generalist, who would be able to nurse all types of cases in hospitals. It appears, however, that he had misunderstood Wood's meaning or, alternatively, had failed to understand the significance of Wood's Appendix VIII.

Wood had written his report in 1947, before the nationalisation of the hospitals, whilst the three streams of nurses were still in existence. At that time, the hospitals accepted different types of cases: the voluntary hospitals dealt almost exclusively with acute cases, the municipal hospitals mostly with long stay cases, or those that the voluntary hospitals did not admit, and the public assistance hospitals took the senile, chronic and geriatric cases. The nurses trained in each category of hospital tended therefore to have experience only in these respective types of nursing. The voluntary hospital nurses had no experience of chronic or geriatric nursing; the municipal hospital nurses had little experience of acute nursing and particularly of modern surgical nursing; the public assistance hospital nurses had nothing but experience with the elderly, frail and senile patients. SEANs were trained only in chronic and geriatric nursing.

Wood's proposals were aimed at offering a broader training for all nurses in basic nursing. He did not envisage that these nurses would not need further training in highly specialised areas. On the contrary, his Appendix VIII specifically recommended that further training in these areas would be necessary.

Soon after the nationalisation of hospitals, the extra funds that became available to the former voluntary hospitals enabled them to extend their specialist activities and to put into practice the technology developed during the war in the USA and the services, which emergency conditions and lack of money had, until then, made impossible.

Consultants, junior doctors, trained nurses and technicians returned to the hospitals and introduced new techniques and regimes. New departments and equipment were quickly introduced. Specialisation in medicine and surgery became more pronounced; the former general physicians and general surgeons found themselves being overtaken by colleagues who dealt only with a particular body system. These consultants demanded specialist nurses who developed their own particular fields of narrow expertise.

In the same way, the municipal hospitals, brought under the RHB system, broadened their fields and undertook work not too different from that of the former voluntary hospitals.

Wood had anticipated this development and had, therefore, recommended the more broadly trained basic nurse. He was not against specialisation. Aneurin Bevan, on the other hand, apparently failed to appreciate the basis for Wood's wanting the broadly trained nurse and understood that she was to be a generalist without a need to specialise in the new fields that were appearing.

It was this policy, based on a lack of understanding, which made Bevan turn against controlled post-registration courses. He saw the nurse as a generalist and his civil servants shared this misunderstanding. From then on, the Ministry of Health, under succeeding Ministers, persisted in regarding nurses as general workers with consequences which will become apparent later in this study. It was not until 1970 that the DHSS agreed to a central system for post-registration specialist training and, even then, they preferred to set up a separate board, the Joint Board for Clinical Nursing Studies, rather than to give it to the GNC. The United Kingdom Central Council for Nursing, Midwifery and Health Visiting, set up in 1979, is to take over post-registration training, as well as the several statutory bodies, in 1983.

Chapter 4/The matrons

This chapter examines the authority structures that resulted from the inception of the National Health Service and how they affected the role, function and status of the hospital matrons. In particular, it discusses the contraction of the matron's functions, her relationships with the group hospital management committee and its other officers, the nursing hierarchical structure and the Bradbeer committee's[1] recommendations for the administration of the nursing service.

The chapter first gives a brief description of the central policy-making and advisory bodies and the policy-making and management components of the NHS. After this, it describes the position of the matrons in the hospitals prior to 1948, and the changes brought about by the coming of the health service.

The chapter concludes that there was a considerable contraction of the matron's functions, which generated defensive anxiety amongst these nurses. Whereas before the nationalisation of hospitals they had been part of a team which was responsible for policy decisions, under the new arrangements, they were distanced and kept separated from the policy-making centres. The inappropriateness of the flat hospital nursing structure added to the matron's difficulties, since she was not able to create new types of posts required in response to the changing function of the hospitals, the new NHS organisation and burgeoning medical technology. These difficulties were exacerbated by the inflexibility bred into nurses by the pattern of their training and selection.

The central policy-making and advisory bodies

The Central Health Services Council was constituted to advise the Minister upon general matters relating to the services provided under the Act and any matters referred to the council by the Minister.

The machinery of the Central Health Services Council (CHSC) also included a number of specialist standing advisory committees. One of these was the Standing Nursing Advisory Committee on which there was a number of nurses and whose chairman was also a nurse. Not all the members of the standing advisory committees were members of the Central Health Services Council and the committees were free to elect their own chairmen and regulate their own procedures. The committees could be asked by the council to investigate topics of interest but were also free to institute their own investigations. All the members of the CHSC and the standing advisory committees were appointed by the Minister.

Also at a central level was the NHS Whitley Council and its seven functional councils, including one for nurses and midwives. The Whitley Council was composed jointly of official and staff representatives and provided machinery for negotiation on conditions of service affecting the several occupational groups in the National. Health Service. Negotiating machinery for separate sections of the service was provided through the various staff associations which the employees (including the nurses) were encouraged to join. The staff side of the Nurses and Midwives Whitley Council was composed of the professional organisations, including the Association of Hospital Matrons and the Royal College of Nursing, and the trades unions, including the National Association of Local Government Officers (NALGO), the Confederation of Health Service Employees (COHSE) and the National Union of Public Employees (NUPE).

The management side was comprised of representatives from the Ministry of Health, the Welsh Board of Health, the Department of Health for Scotland, the employing bodies in the NHS and also the local authorities.

After 1948, the Labour Government attempted to establish locally based joint consultative committees in the hospital groups. These were to provide means of consultation between the hospital staff groups and the hospital management.

The hospital and specialist services were administered by 14 (later 15) regional hospital boards. The teaching hospitals were allowed to keep their boards of governors who became directly responsible to the Minister of Health. With the remaining hospitals, responsibility for policy formation and planning passed into the hands of the regional hospital boards, the management of each group of hospitals being vested in a hospital management committee.

The total number of hospitals that passed into the National Health Service was 2,835 with 388,000 staffed beds.[2] Over half these hospitals had fewer than 200 beds, however, and the first major task of the regional hospital boards (RHBs) was to form the hospitals into groups under hospital management committees (HMCs). The grouping of hospitals was originally designed to offer a coherent service for all categories of hospital patients, but the geographical distribution of the different types of hospitals – general, chronic, infectious diseases, psychiatric, mentally handicapped, and so on – was such that that plan was eventually compromised by considerations of convenience and accessibility for the officers and members of the HMC.

The matrons

In order to understand the changes which the National Health Service brought to the matrons, it is necessary to understand their positions in the hospitals before 1948.

The title 'matron' was just as imprecise as the term 'nurse'. Looking at the hospital scene before nationalisation, we find many grades of matrons who came from different types and sizes of hospitals with an equally diverse number of authority systems.

The matrons of the former voluntary hospitals were responsible to their boards of governors but, contrary to conventional opinion, most reported through the house governor or secretary. The matrons of the teaching hospitals more often reported directly to their boards, and thus had greater authority and status.

The matrons of the former local authority hospitals, on the other hand, had relatively less authority, since they were responsible to the medical superintendent and had no contact with the health committee of the local authority. These health committees were responsible for the regulation of the local authority health services and the medical officer of health was their chief officer. The hospital's medical superintendent usually reported to the medical officer of health. The chain of communication for the local authority hospitals was, therefore, much longer than for the voluntary hospitals, especially the teaching hospitals, and on this chain the matron occupied a correspondingly lower place.

In the mental hospitals, frequently a chief male nurse was responsible for the male nurses and patients, dividing the nursing authority with the matron, who was responsible for the female nurses and patients. The matron invariably took precedence over the chief male nurse since she was also head of the nurse training school.

When, in 1951, the Bradbeer committee was set up to investigate the internal administration of hospitals,[1] the King Edward's Hospital Fund (King's Fund) described the 'traditional principles of hospital administration' with considerable insight.[3] It pointed out how a new concept of the place of the nurse in the voluntary hospital had taken shape during the Nightingale era, having been grafted onto the already well-defined partnership between the governing body and the medical staff. The medical care of patients had originally been entrusted to the visiting physicians and surgeons (and their assistants), who acted as an advisory group to the governing body. The governing body, primarily concerned with an 'enlightened pursuit

54

of economy' without prejudice to the requirements of the sick, delegated its function to the chairman, the house governor or other officers acting in conjunction with a weekly or fortnightly executive or house committee. Florence Nightingale's reforms had admitted the matron as a third party to the partnership between the governing body and the medical staff. The nursing care, as well as the control of the training school, was entrusted to her. She was also responsible for all female staff which included those working as domestics, in the catering departments and in the laundries. Where there were therapeutic or diagnostic departments (such as massage, physiotherapy and X-ray), these female staff also came under her authority.

The hospital, therefore, came to be regarded as a tripartite organisation: the governing body, the medical committee and the matron. The King's Fund was of the opinion that this was a sound organisation and that it had contributed very largely to the advances that had taken place in the hospitals since the 1880s. The King's Fund paper, however, admitted that the principles of this organisation had been variously interpreted and that the functions of the matron had changed. With the increasing scale of some hospital departments it was no longer either practicable or desirable for her to be head of all the women employed, and with regard to the local authority hospitals, many patterns of organisation seemed to have developed. The respective local authority committees were *de jure* the governing bodies of the hospitals, but they had little *de facto* control over the financial expenditures, the buildings or the use of stores. As their authority was exercised at a considerable distance, the medical superintendent was very powerful in his domain, leaving the matron with only day-to-day control of her nurses and the school of nursing.

After 1948 the position of the matrons was affected by a complex series of developments, each reacting on the others, which may be discussed under three headings:

1 Hospital groups and the position of the matrons in these.
2 Loss of territory over non-nursing staff, problems caused by grouping schools of nursing and the rising specialism of nurse tutors.
3 The nursing structure.

Hospital groups and the position of the matron

The far-reaching changes introduced by the National Health Service Act of 1946 included basic alterations in the chain of command which, in many cases, had the ultimate effect of diminishing the authority of the matrons.

Each hospital management committee had an administrator called a group secretary, and each hospital within the group, a hospital secretary or unit administrator. Each hospital also had a matron, but there was no provision for any nurse equivalent to the group secretary. The matron thus shared authority with the hospital secretary, but both had to report to the HMC through the group secretary. No formal provision gave the matrons routine access to the HMC meetings and, in fact, most did not even receive the papers for these meetings.[1]

Two other group officer posts were established, those of the group finance officer and group supplies officer. No provision was made for a group medical officer, but statutory provision had already been made for medical representation on the RHBs and HMCs. The doctors set up medical staff committees at hospital level and medical advisory committees at group level. Some committees were already in being when the Bradbeer report was published and others proliferated after that. The medical profession was therefore well placed to influence policy and the respective chairmen of the two medical committees were able to act as spokesmen for their colleagues.

The management committees set up their own sub-committees such as the finance and general purposes committee. Sometimes they set up a nursing advisory committee, but Bradbeer reported that these were usually constituted of lay people. The HMCs also sometimes set up house committees for each hospital in the group. These were responsible for local concerns, including nursing, but had no executive functions and could not make policy. Where these house committees existed, it was possible for the matron to meet or work with their members but even that access was not routine.

The organisation of mental and mental deficiency hospitals was similar to that of the general hospitals with the important exception that the medical superintendent preserved his legal responsibility for the patients and reported through the group secretary to the HMC. After 1948, the medical officer of health was no longer involved in running these hospitals, nor, indeed, was the local authority. The HMCs did, however, often appoint a mental sub-committee which frequently included representatives of the old local authority mental committees who had valuable, specialised knowledge and experience.

Whereas, therefore, some matrons had previously enjoyed close contact with their governing bodies, the position of most matrons after 1948 was considerably weakened, particularly in the RHB hospitals. Only the matrons of the teaching hospitals retained their direct link with their boards of governors as the structure of these hospitals remained substantially intact. In these instances the position of the matron remained strong.

The matrons recognised that they were cut off from policy-making, but considered that this was due to their lack of representation on the RHBs and HMCs. They did not recognise that the lack of a nursing post at group level was significant until much later in the period, towards the early 1960s. Their efforts at redressing this situation were, therefore, directed in the main towards obtaining more nurse representation on those committees. It will be seen later in this paper that the matrons were actually hostile towards any proposal to establish group matron or principal matron posts.

The Royal College of Nursing and the trade unions pressed the Minister to appoint nurses to these regional and hospital committees, but there was considerable resistance by both the Ministry and the RHBs. Throughout the period 1948–61, there were frequent comments in the RCN Council minutes about representations made to the Minister on this matter, and the issue was frequently raised at the RCN branches standing committee meetings. Most RHBs did eventually have one nurse member appointed by the Minister. It was, however, the responsibility of each RHB to appoint members to their own HMCs, and the Minister had no power to direct these.

The unions, too, strongly urged the Minister to appoint nurse representatives to the RHBs and HMCs. In June 1948, C F Comer (general secretary of COHSE) wrote to Aneurin Bevan, the Minister of Health, complaining about the composition of RHBs and HMCs which had 'excluded junior members of nursing staffs'. The private secretary replied that the Minister had no powers to order the nature of the members appointed by the RHBs to their HMCs; the Minister's appointments to RHBs were made after consultation with the various organisations.[4]

In September, COHSE wrote to the Minister to say that they were not satisfied with his reply and that 'great resentment' was felt by the trade union movement at the situation. This was followed in November 1950 by a letter from the general secretary of the TUC, Sir Vincent Tewson, again complaining about the composition of the RHBs and HMCs. There was particular concern after the publication of circular RHB(50)150 which expressed the view that RHBs should not appoint HMC officers as members even of other HMCs by which they were not employed. Since senior doctors were employed by the RHBs, they were not HMC officers, even though they worked in the hospitals. The circular therefore effectively excluded them and appeared to be aimed at the nurses, debarring them from the opportunity of serving on any HMC.

Sir Vincent reported that this had been discussed at the recent TUC Congress at which a resolution had been passed regretting the position and asking for the Minister to receive a deputation. He pleaded with the Minister to relax these regulations. There followed a minute from the private secretary to a senior Ministry official, Mr John Pater:

> As you know, the Minister holds decided views on this question of the appointment of hospital staff as members of Hospital Management Committees. Such evidence as we have suggests that they do not always make very satisfactory members and our recent suggestion to Regional Boards in RHB(50)105 that they 'should not appoint management committee officers as members even of another committee unless there are exceptionally strong reasons for doing so' was made at the request of the Boards themselves and with the personal concurrence of the Minister.[4]

The Minister, however, agreed to receive a deputation from the TUC and, in preparation for this, asked for the numbers of doctors, dentists and nurses in HMCs.

The information was not readily available, and a count had to be made. In order to save time and effort, only two regions were examined: the North East Metropolitan and Birmingham. No reason was offered for this choice, and they did not claim that this was a representative sample:

HMCs of North East Metropolitan RHB:	doctors	19%
	dentists	2%
	nurses	3%
HMCs of Birmingham RHB:	doctors	23%
	dentists	1%
	nurses	7%

It was also said that the Ministry staff may not have counted all the nurses because their only means of identifying them was to look for the initials SRN after the names.

In January 1951, there was a further minute from the private secretary to Mr Pater, the Ministry official, saying that the main objection to the appointment of hospital employees was 'the general objection of syndicalism'. The Minister had, however, advised the boards to avoid an excessively large professional element in the constitution of HMCs. The minute went on to admit 'we have always ourselves opposed the appointment of nurses as members of Management Committees . . .'[4]

Soon after this, the Minister met the TUC delegation and was persuaded that employees should not be excluded from sitting on other HMCs. He asked that the instructions should be appropriately modified.

Before this could be done, there was a change of government, and the Conservatives took office. Mr Iain Macleod became Minister of Health in January 1951. There was some discussion at the Ministry as to whether or not the new Minister would want the policy altered, and it was known that the RHBs would not welcome any change since they had 'regretted appointing junior officers as members even of other committees'. In the end, the civil servants decided that Mr Bevan's had been a clear commitment and must therefore be honoured. This resulted in another circular, RHB(51)20, which referred to RHB(50)105 and said:

> . . . the Minister does not wish this to be interpreted as an absolute ban on such appointments where officers who are suited for the work by their personal qualities and experiences are recommended to the board.

The nurses were effectively kept away from the governing bodies by distancing them from the group administration, by denying them positions on the HMCs and by the neglect to set up and give formal voice to any form of nursing advisory committees.

Loss of territory

This separation of the matrons from policy making was not their only loss in power and status: they had also lost part of their empire. The grouping of hospitals had bureaucratised the administrative structure and had brought about further divisions of labour. Lay administrators and specialists were increasingly assuming responsibility for the linen rooms, laundries, female domestics, catering and other departments. The matrons found themselves left with responsibility only for the nurses and training schools.

Responsibility for these extra-nursing departments had taken the matron into areas outside the wards and the nursing service. She had had power over a large section of the hospital's employees besides the nurses. The matron had had control over the running of the wards, departments and most services relative to total patient management: she had had control over the patient's environment. Release from these responsibilities took that away and reduced her field of influence to the nursing service alone. It diminished the matron's power in the management of the hospital and increased the power of the hospital secretary. As a consequence, the nurses' stature and authority were also diminished, and the nursing service had to rely more on the administrators. The nurses were responsible for the patients, but the administrators had become responsible for the environment in which the nurses had to function.

These factors generated a considerable amount of insecurity in the matrons which was compounded by the lack of any form of job description or terms of reference. The boundaries between the functions of the matron and the hospital administrator were blurred and shifting, and matron's position in regard to her own nursing service was also in question. Very often, a satisfactory negotiated order was achieved between the lay administrator and the matron, but there were numerous instances where this was not possible and friction developed. In these cases, the group secretary was in a position to present the problem to the HMC and, commonly, the matron lacked the opportunity to defend her point of view.

In 1948, the Royal College of Nursing set up a labour relations committee which received many complaints about the relationships of matrons with administrators and hospital committees, as well as the employment of specialists to relieve the matrons of non-nursing duties.[5] There were reports of matrons who had been sacked by their HMCs and who, without references, were unable to obtain other posts.

The RCN sought to reinforce the matrons' position by setting out a form of standing orders which, they proposed, should be adopted by the management committees. They had little cooperation and only a few authorities adopted them, or, indeed, any contract of employment. The matrons were beset by difficulties and assaulted from many quarters by opposing interests.

On the one hand, a series of enquiries such as the Nuffield Provincial Hospitals Trust job analysis[6] and the Dan Mason research reports[7] criticised the frequency of non-nursing tasks undertaken by nurses and complained of the misuse of nurses' time; on the other hand, there was a shortage of domestic staff and a reluctance on the part of many authorities to employ more for the relief of nurses. There had also been a change in the functions of hospitals from being centres of treatment and recovery to being centres of diagnosis and more sophisticated forms of therapeutic intervention.[8]

At the start of the NHS, most nurses had been trained for the care of infectious diseases in which, failing an effective pharmacopoeia, the need for bedside nursing care of the patient was paramount. The change in the use of hospitals, in the patterns of morbidity and mortality and the use of new drugs and treatment routines rendered this devoted bedside nursing obsolete. The nurses were not prepared for this shift and found that their skills, which had once been acclaimed, were being adversely criticised as unprofitable, repetitive duties which less well-trained staff should take over. Furthermore, the doctors were persistently relegating more technical tasks to nurses who were not trained for them and who felt that, by accepting them, they were neglecting their own duties.

Another difficulty facing the matrons was the shortage of recruits for nurse training. There was no minimum education requirement for recruits since this had been abandoned in 1939. The HMCs, who relied on student nurses for labour, pressed the matrons to increase their numbers of students. The matrons had no objective criteria for the screening and selection of candidates and relied on their own judgment.[9] The lack of an objective standard made it difficult for the matrons to withstand pressure from their authorities, and their aspirations to maintain 'professional standards' often succumbed to bureaucratic priorities.

The combination of these opposing pressures, their removal from policy-making in the HMC and their lack of settled terms of reference made it difficult for the matrons to take a strong stand although some did and paid the price. More often, however, the political ingenuousness and social inexperience of the matron enabled the doctor or administrator to out-manoeuvre her too easily. The dominant ideology of nurses, inherited from pre-war days, made them adopt the dependence and pliant credulity of the gentlewoman of the Victorian era. This ideology too often failed the matrons in the new social environment which the coming of the NHS had underlined – the difficulties were not overcome until they began to learn more appropriate moves and a new generation of senior nurses graduated through the ranks in the late 1950s and early 1960s.[10]

The matrons had responsibilities but an indeterminate degree of authority. This produced structural problems and affected the whole nursing service in two critical areas: the lack of an official, recognisable nurse leader within the hospital group and the indeterminate position of the matron with regard to her nurses. Each of these two problems appeared to act upon and enhance the other.

In the grouping of hospitals, each constituent hospital had its own matron, but there was no generally accepted method by which the matrons could be represented at the HMC meetings – if indeed they were invited to attend. There was, therefore, no coherent nursing voice and, often, the nursing voice was divided. Sometimes the matrons formed themselves into a committee whose chairman might attend management committee meetings. Sometimes the chair was taken by each matron in turn, so that there was little continuity. Sometimes the nursing committee spoke for the matrons even though it consisted predominantly of lay people.[11] The matrons had inherited strong territorial feelings and defended their authority within their respective hospitals against what they might consider to be intrusions by their colleagues.[12] It was not difficult, therefore, for others to overwhelm the nursing voice by the system of divide and rule.

The problems raised by this became especially evident where the nurse training schools were also grouped. The General Nursing Council (GNC) had a policy to encourage the closing down of smaller schools and the establishment of larger ones on grounds of economy in the use of trained tutors and more competition and stimulation for the student nurses. These group schools were established either by incorporating all the schools into a large one, in one of the hospitals, or by maintaining most of the training schools under the control of one senior tutor and a pooled tutorial staff. The former method seemed to be the more common. In either case, however, the hospitals continued to recruit their own student (and pupil) nurses who received their tuition with those of the other hospitals but worked on the wards of their parent hospital. It was, though, often necessary to move the students to other hospitals for specialised experience. The shortage of nurses often made the student nurses' stays on the wards very short. Menzies[13] reported that 30 per cent of the student nurses moved after less than three weeks and 44 per cent after less than seven weeks. A study in 1957 by the South East Metropolitan Area Nurse Training Committee showed a similar picture.[14]

The students of each hospital owed prime allegiance to their respective matrons but also had to acknowledge the authority of another when they were working on her wards. Thus their loyalties were divided, and the corporate loyalty to one hospital and its matron was diminished. Their adherence to the traditions, customs and particular procedures of their own hospitals was similarly reduced.

From the matron's point of view, this mixing of students brought further problems since each matron had her own criteria for selecting suitable candidates.[9] The students from another hospital would not necessarily measure up to these. There was also an inevitable rivalry between the matrons in the recruitment of candidates from a common pool.

Furthermore, by GNC regulations, one matron had to be nomin-ated as head of the school of nursing. she became responsible for the training of the students but had little control over their ward teaching in the other hospitals. The other matrons lost their status as head of the school of nursing, lost the salary differential and lost control of the teaching of their own students. This made for much ill-feeling and jealousy and further reduced the cohesion of the matrons' group.

The second important problem arising from the matron's lack of terms of reference was the indeterminacy of her own position with regard to her nurses. The King's Fund[3] described this very clearly. There were too many people sitting as members on the HMCs who did not sufficiently understand how the old pattern had worked. Some were used to the pattern adopted by the voluntary hospitals, some were used to the pattern used by the local authority hospitals. Attempts to combine the two patterns in the HMC were liable to lead to friction. Those with no previous experience of hospital management, and they were many, knew no pattern. It was clear that little thought was given to this matter, and the profession was slow to identify the problems that had been thrown up uninten-tionally by the nationalisation of the hospitals.

The King's Fund identified two areas of responsibility inherent in the administrative duties of the matron: first, she exercised a profes-sional function as head of the nurse training school and the nursing service. In this she was responsible for providing and maintaining the nursing services for the hospital. Her authority was derived primarily from responsibility delegated to her by the governing body. In this sense she was a professional head rather than a depart-mental head.

> The extent to which the availability of skilled nursing care throughout each 24 hours is a main reason for the existence of hospitals serves to indicate the true professional status of the head of the nursing service as contrasted with the somewhat superficial claims for 'status' put forward on behalf of matrons by profes-sional organisations.[3]

Secondly, in her professional function the matron might act in an administrative capacity. The fact that she was quite often the chief resident executive officer meant that she had to take decisions or action outside her purely professional capacity.[15] In these non-professional functions, the matron was acting not as the professional head but as a third partner in a 'firm combining administrative, medical and nursing interests and that in matters of policy outside her own speciality she would of course recognise the authority of other heads of the firm'.

These two separate aspects of the matron's role were not clearly distinguished by either the nurses or the authorities, and the confusion created further problems. If the matron was part of the tripartite management structure was she not a 'head'? If so, why should she have to report to a lay administrator? If she were not a 'head', how could she be responsible for the nursing service?

The matrons argued it one way and the administrators argued it the other way. It was a circular argument and could be picked up at whichever point best suited the case. The argument further undermined the matron's position with her nurses since, if the matron were not a head, the head of the nursing service, what powers of hiring and firing did she have? Furthermore, was the matron the spokeswoman of the nurses or was she a manager and a representative of the employing authority?

Traditionally, in the voluntary hospitals, the more powerful matrons had had powers of both hiring and firing. The less powerful matrons and those in the local authority hospitals had had powers to hire only. They had to seek authority from the house governor or medical superintendent for firing. Some had powers only to suspend.

Nursing Times[16] in 1953 commented on the difficulties that matrons were experiencing because of their lack of standing orders. It reported the results of a survey of Scottish hospital matrons which had been undertaken by the Scottish Board of the RCN. Of 163 responses, only 48 had standing orders. Of these 48, 33 pre-dated the NHS and five were based on the RCN proforma. All the matrons responding to the questionnaire reported that they had some or complete responsibility for appointing nursing staff and selecting student nurses. The majority reported responsibility for appointing domestic staff. One hundred and thirty two appointed auxiliary staff.*

Sixty six reported direct responsibility for dismissals of staff; 101 for various grades of nursing staff; 102 for various grades of domestic staff; 79 for auxiliary staff.

Fifteen had power to suspend and report; 44 carried out dismissals only in consultation with a medical consultant.

Forty two received written instructions regarding appointments and dismissals; 109 had none.

Only 50 per cent of those who exercised responsibility for

---

*No amplification of this term was given. It is not clear whether it refers to medical auxiliaries such as physiotherapists, or to nursing auxiliaries.

dismissal of staff possessed the protection of written authority to
do so.

It is quite clear, therefore, that the position of the matrons with
regard to the ultimate sanction was ambiguous and insecure. The
matron may have been the head of the nursing service, but too often
she lacked final authority.

The matron had always been regarded by the authorities as
the spokeswoman for her nurses. Matrons had been elected or
nominated as representatives of nurses to all the principal institutions set up after the 1946 Act: the staff side of the Whitley Council,
the Central Health Services Council, the Standing Nursing Advisory
Committee. They were on the Council of the RCN and they were
members of the GNC as nurses in their own right.

Often, as nurses themselves, it was reasonable that they should
represent their professional colleagues. On the other hand, the
matrons also had strong management and service commitments, and
their priorities could not fairly have been described as being representative of nurses working on the wards or in the community.[17]
White[18] described the absorption of bureaucratic values by nurse
managers and how this process affected their decision making. The
period after the coming of the NHS was one when this process
began to become evident.

The questioning of the matron's right to represent her nurses was
received as a blasphemy that added further to her insecurity. If she
was not accepted as part of the policy-making group and was not, on
the other hand, considered capable of representing nurses, what was
her position? In fact, what was she doing? There was a very present
danger that the position of the matron was degenerating into a
merely administrative one, subordinate to the lay administrator and
isolated from the nurses. This was work for which the current
matrons had neither training nor taste.

The ambiguous position of the matrons and their changing status
with regard to their nurses was further reinforced by the setting up
of the joint consultative committees (see chapter 12). When a constitution for these committees was laid down by the Ministry of
Health, the matrons were placed on the management side and their
nurses began to view them as employers rather than as their representatives. The 'us' and 'them' division between the matrons and
their nurses was institutionalised.

Although the matrons did not generally recognise the need for a
post at group level, some hospital authorities found the lack of one
to be the cause of organisational difficulties. Early in 1949, the Mid-
Herts Group HMC advertised in the nursing press for a principal

matron to be employed at group level as a coordinator of their unit matrons. This advertisement was brought to the attention of the RCN Council who discussed the title in particular.[19] They did not like it, as it had associations with the nursing services of the armed forces and provoked ideas of compulsory drafting of nurses.

Direction of labour had been a reality during the war years, and nurses were still apprehensive that a nationalised health service might use this as a means of coping with the acute nursing staff shortages. The shortages were more acute in some regions than in others; in some hospitals (particularly the teaching hospitals), there were even waiting lists for candidates to take their training. The question of compulsory drafting had been mentioned once or twice and the Ministry of Health, with the RCN, had had to run a publicity campaign in 1948 to reassure nurses that this device would not be used.[20]

The RCN Council, therefore, disliked the proposed title, principal matron, but had little to say about the principle underlying the advertisement.

The problems of the matrons were not the only organisational ones that the National Health Service was experiencing and in 1951, the Central Health Services Council, at the behest of the Minister, set up a committee on the internal administration of hospitals under the chairmanship of Alderman A F Bradbeer.[1] The Bradbeer committee invited evidence from interested institutions, and the King's Fund was one which took this opportunity. Its evidence, published in 1951, expressed the opinion that the position of the matron in the HMC organisation often fell short of the part assigned to her in the Nightingale pattern. This resulted from the grouping of hospitals.[3]

In respect of the question asked by the Bradbeer committee: 'To what extent should administrative duties be undertaken by nursing staff?', the King's Fund found that there were two issues: firstly, to what extent the matron was regarded as carrying a share of the general administrative responsibility, or as a departmental head responsible to the chief executive officer; secondly, to what extent members of the nursing staff should undertake duties which did not make full use of their nursing qualifications, for example, home sisters, sister housekeepers or those working as receptionists, and so on in hospital departments.

As far as the matron was concerned, the King's Fund pointed out the two areas of responsibility borne by her as a professional head (and therefore a member of the tripartite management) and as a resident executive officer. The King's Fund pointed out that as the matron was the professional head of the nursing service, the nursing committees set up by some hospitals (which, unlike the medical committees, were not composed of members of the professional staff concerned) should have acted in an advisory capacity rather than that the matron should report to and receive instructions from them. Where there was a medical superintendent (as in the mental hospitals), the King's Fund thought it might be natural for the matron to accept guidance from him in her professional work but that, on his part, he should accord her the courtesies due to a professional colleague.

The Fund hoped that the forthcoming Bradbeer report might help to clarify the confusion about these two aspects of the matron's responsibility which, it pointed out, had been a common cause of friction between matrons and chief executive officers.

In the second issue, that relating to nursing staff and administrative duties, the King's Fund considered *inter alia* that some administrative posts were necessary to train nurses for higher posts, but that suitable candidates should be selected and given appropriate training.

In all fields of work which were concerned with the environment of patients and welfare of nurses, the King's Fund thought that the lay departmental head should be responsible directly to the matron and only through her to the chief executive officer. The matron should always be bound by the 'old tradition, lost sight of in the increasing complexity of hospital administration, that the matron is "mistress of the household"'.

The Bradbeer committee did not publish its report until three years later (1954), however, and in 1951 the Minister asked the Standing Nursing Advisory Committee (SNAC) to advise him on the general desirability of establishing posts for principal or group matrons. He set out the problem in terms of rates of remuneration rather than as a structural problem, and he described the existing situation only as it related to nurse training schools. His memorandum to the SNAC made very clear his own feelings on the matter.[21]

The SNAC dutifully considered the matter as it was presented to them and stuck closely to the form of the Minister's memorandum. They restricted their study to the problem of how to have one matron, in a group, act as head of the nurse training school, and the administrative adjustments that would be necessary. They made no mention of other more important advantages that might have accrued to a group nursing post and evidently failed to consider these.

The SNAC drew up a draft reply which they sent to the RCN, the Association of Hospital Matrons and the Royal College of Midwives.

The RCN set up a sub-committee to consider this and Council ultimately gave general approval to it. Council did also add a *caveat* that the SNAC report should be advisory rather than directive.[22] When the SNAC had received these replies, it sent an amended draft to the Bradbeer committee for further comment and then once again amended its report.

Ultimately the SNAC replied to the Minister[23] in 1952. In January 1954, before the Bradbeer report was published, the Minister issued circular HM (54) 4, *Hospital Matrons with Extended Responsibilities*.

The Bradbeer committee had been set up by the CHSC, of which the SNAC was a standing committee. The members of both committees were appointed by the Minister. It has been shown that the SNAC consulted the Bradbeer committee prior to finalising its report. All the parties concerned, therefore, including the Minister, had made up their minds in concert and the ministerial circular was published before the Bradbeer committee had finalised its report. As the SNAC had closely followed a line of deliberations set out and circumscribed by the Minister, only what he had described had been debated. This closely followed the circular method of policy making described in the Acton Society report 1958.[24]

In his memorandum to the SNAC[21] entitled 'Principal Matrons and Group Matrons', the Minister had written:

1 The Departments are asked from time to time to advise on various questions connected with the appointment of 'Principal Matrons' or 'Group Matrons' of a group of hospitals. The question most often raised is the rate of remuneration. The Whitley Council has not agreed any scale of salary for such appointments and in any case the precise functions of the officers in question are not uniform nor are they always very clearly defined.

2 The types of appointment seem to fall into the following four main groups:

a) A single matron is appointed for several hospitals which, although previously run as separate hospitals, are now to be run as a single hospital made up of several units.

b) One matron among those employed by a Hospital Management Committee is selected to advise the Committee on general nursing questions.

c) One matron in charge of a hospital is given certain administrative responsibility for other hospitals which are under their own matrons.

d) A matron with no hospital of her own is appointed to carry out certain general duties for a group of hospitals.

3 It appears to the Minister that there can be no objection to appointments falling in class (a) provided that:

i) the hospitals forming the group are so situated in relation to each other that the day to day administration can be carried out by a single matron – this will depend on the circumstances in each case and no fixed criteria would seem applicable – and

ii) one matron only is appointed for all the units which are to form the new hospital, each separate unit being in the charge of an assistant matron or sister-in-charge as the circumstances require.

4 Appointments falling in class (b) are probably an inevitable development. It seems to the Minister that a Hospital Management Committee may reasonably expect to be able to look to one person for advice on general nursing questions and he does not think that objection could reasonably be taken to such an arrangement provided that the matron concerned has no administrative responsibility for hospitals other than her own and is in regular consultation with the other matrons of the group.

5 Appointments falling in class (c) and (d) seem to the Minister to be much more open to doubt.

6 The issue is frequently complicated by the formation of group training schools incorporating a number of hospitals which may or may not cover a whole HMC group.

In its report to the Minister, the SNAC[23] advised that

1 As a general rule each hospital should have its own matron . . . and the type of appointment referred to in paragraph 1(a) above should accordingly be discouraged.

The report discouraged the inclusion of mental hospitals with other types of hospital under the same group matron and continued:

The hospitals should be so situated in relation to each other that the day to day administration can be carried out by a single matron. This will depend on the circumstances in each case, including the experience and qualifications of the matron concerned, and no fixed criteria would seem applicable.

This referred to paragraph 3(i) of the Minister's memorandum and virtually reproduced it.

In respect of the complications introduced by the formation of group training schools, the SNAC advised that the matron of one of the hospitals in the group should be made responsible; the matron of each of the other hospitals should retain full administrative responsibility for her own hospital; the ...

> Matron and Superintendent of the Nurse Training School should be given full facilities for visiting the other hospitals in order to satisfy herself of the standard of training given; she should be consulted about the engagement of staff who would take part in nurse training and there should be an education committee consisting of all the matrons, the tutors and appropriate ward sisters.

The SNAC also recommended that the Whitley Council should be asked to fix a suitable salary for the matron and superintendent of the nurse training school.

The SNAC felt that no case could be made for the type of appointment described in paragraph 1(c) of the Minister's letter.

> The Committee is unanimous that the creation of a 'Principal Matron' grade is unnecessary and undesirable. The type of appointment visualised in paragraph 1(d) above appears particularly undesirable.

They recommended that the matrons should nominate their own representatives to attend HMC meetings as necessary.

When the Bradbeer report was published, it reinforced the position of the group secretary as a coordinator, the head administrative officer and the person responsible for securing policy from the governing body.

As far as nursing administration was concerned, Bradbeer's comments were selected from the advice given him by either the King's Fund or the SNAC. He commented that the functions of the matron had been wider a generation previously than they were then. The matron had been 'the mistress of the household' who supervised virtually all aspects of the hospital. He observed that 'recently' numbers of specialist posts had been created to minimise the complexity of hospital administration in areas such as cleaning, the laundries and catering. Whilst agreeing with the rationale of this, he felt that it should not allow the position of the nurse in the partnership of officers to be minimised. The matron and her staff should still be responsible for the establishment of the 'atmosphere', comfort and contentment of the hospital (para 144).

Bradbeer found (para 146) that grouping hospitals had placed the matron in an 'obscure' position, since she was much less in contact with her governing body than previously in the voluntary hospital system. Her position had become more akin to that obtaining in the old local authority system. He thought that as a member of the tripartite administration she must be regarded as being directly responsible to the governing body of her group, but then he continued to say that, in practice, this might be more easily achieved through the house committee of her own hospital, although she should have the right of access to the HMC.

Bradbeer agreed that each hospital should have its own matron and that one of these should be responsible for the nurse training school. He also agreed that a grade of principal matron with no hospital of her own would be undesirable (paras 147, 150).

He accepted the idea that, for the matron, there was a dichotomy of administrative responsibility and that for part of her executive responsibility she should be responsible to the group secretary. He listed the content of the matron's responsibilities:

1 nursing and welfare of the patients
2 training the nurses
3 recruitment, interviewing, appointment, control, welfare of the nursing and domestic staff
4 the nurses' home
5 the health of nurses and domestic staff
6 general cleanliness of the hospital
7 linen room
8 supervision of the equipment and furniture of the nurses' home
9 cooperation with the chaplaincy services
10 hospital chapel
11 relations and visitors
12 day to day administration of the wards
13 good order and conduct of the patients
14 spread of infection
15 obstetric flying squad

It will be noted that he did not discuss the problem of firing staff. Although he had earlier accepted the employment of 'specialists', he left many of these departments within the matron's purview. He proposed that the matron should continue to take an interest in these areas and that the domestic superintendent should be responsible to her, and emphasised the need for the matron to shape nursing policy and for the governing body to seek advice from her. He expressed shock at the discovery that this was not always the case.

In the mental hospitals, he observed that the matron was responsible for the nurse training school as well as the female staff and patients.

This gave a salary lead to the matron over the chief male nurse, but as the training school usually catered for both female and male student nurses, he wondered why this convention should persist. He had ascertained that the GNC did not have any particular policy in the matter so long as the nurse in charge of the training school was appropriately qualified. He considered therefore that there was no reason why the convention should not be varied.

He confirmed that both the Association of Hospital Matrons and the RCN had proposed that there should be standing orders for all senior hospital officers in order to reduce friction. Bradbeer objected to this proposal and declined to recommend it although he did not give his reasons for this decision.

Bradbeer also discussed the committee system. No officer, he said, had the right to attend meetings of the governing body. The group secretary and finance officer should normally attend, the chairman of the Medical Advisory Committee should attend if he so wished and so should the chairman of the Nursing Advisory Committee. All officers should receive advance copies of the papers. Unit heads, including the matrons, should attend if matters affecting them were to be discussed and should receive all papers of the house committee. Copies of Ministry circulars should be sent to all officers.

He said that he did not believe that officers should be nominated as members of their own, or any other, governing body (except for the case of the doctors) as they were bound to suffer from divided loyalties.

Bradbeer considered that every hospital should have a medical staff committee which should include all doctors. This committee should generate hospital medical policy and accept responsibility for medical administration. He also proposed that there should be a medical advisory committee at each group, such as had been proposed in the Ministry's circular RHB(53)91.[25]

Bradbeer criticised the constitution of nursing advisory committees as he had found that these were usually of lay people. He proposed that they should be constituted from all the matrons in the group, together with representatives of the ward sisters. There was, he said, a need for the collective advice of nurses to be articulated to the governing body, and nursing advisory committees should be formed in all groups. One of the matrons, or some other nurse, should be the committee's chairman and spokesman and should represent the senior nurses at group level. The governing body should regard the chairman of the nursing advisory committee as the spokesman of the nurses.

Bradbeer also considered that there should be a nursing staff committee at each hospital, similar to the medical staff committees.

A similar structure should be established in the mental hospitals and, the report said, the supervision of the medical superintendent over nursing should be 'discreet and minimal'.

The Bradbeer committee was not sufficiently clear on how they considered the two levels of professional committees should work. They envisaged that the medical and nursing staff committees, at hospital level, should be something of a representative committee for local professional consultation, along the lines of the joint consultative committees. They probably saw the advisory committees, at group level, as bodies offering professional advice on wider policy issues.

The Ministry also accepted this interpretation for the doctors and issued RHB(53)91 recommending and encouraging the institution of medical staff and medical advisory committees where they were not already in being. The Ministry issued no similar circular for the nurses.

The nursing profession had been in trouble since 1948 with their representative councils at hospital level, and the RCN Council thought that the proposed nursing advisory committees could very well replace these as an avenue for professional discussion in such matters as nursing procedures. The Ministry rejected the idea.[26] Council asked to meet representatives from the Ministry Nursing Division to pursue this proposal, but its approach was ignored. The Ministry thought that joint consultation was a Whitley Council matter and any such proposal should be put through the staff side.

It appears, from the evidence available, that the Ministry adopted a double standard for the doctors and the nurses but also that the request made by the RCN to the Ministry was misleading in its phraseology, since the letter seemed to emphasise joint consultation rather than professional discussion.[27] The RCN labour relations committee later reported that it had again met Dame Enid Russell Smith, under-secretary at the Ministry, who had again repeated that this was a matter for the Whitley Council.[28]

From the nurses' point of view, the Bradbeer report was something of a let-down. It described the major problems experienced by the matron; it emphasised the need to establish her position in the tripartite structure, and then it offered recommendations that left her more or less where she had been before. It did not insist that she should attend HMC meetings since it had proposed, as an alternative, that her contact might be through the subordinate house committee. It did not confirm her loss of control of the domestic

73

departments but offered an unsatisfactory compromise by giving her responsibility without authority. It further emphasised her already insecure position as spokesman for the nurses by proposing that the chairman of the nursing advisory committee, who need not be a matron, should be recognised as the representative of the nurses. It failed to confirm her position as a manager, or head of the nursing service, by offering her only a possible opening as chairman of that same committee. Furthermore, the report failed to clarify her boundaries by refusing to recommend terms of reference. The unsatisfactory *status quo* had been reaffirmed.

The RCN working party to consider the Bradbeer report reported in February 1955.[29] In general it agreed with the content of the report, especially its comment about the matron's position in the tripartite organisation and the recommendation against a principal matron grade. It regretted that Bradbeer had advised against standing orders and therefore it considered that the matrons should have power of suspension of student nurses and domestic staff only. In order to safeguard her position, she should suspend other grades only in consultation with the chairman of the appropriate committee. It had nothing to say about how these limitations on the authority of the matron might affect her position.

The RCN Council made little attempt to analyse the report and failed to perceive its weaknesses and ambiguities. Instead, they concentrated on the blandishments which the report had offered to the matrons, particularly its comments that the matron was an equal partner in the tripartite system, that the matron's position needed to be upheld and that she must be directly responsible to the HMC. They were gratified that the report accepted the need for the matron to be able to shape nursing policy and for the governing body to seek advice from her, but they failed to notice that the report had done nothing to ensure these.

Council failed to recognise that what the report had said should be, could not be supported by its recommendations. How could the matron shape nursing policy if her contact with the HMC was to be through the impotent house committee only? How could she be an equal partner if she alone of the tripartite organisation did not, of right, attend HMC meetings? How could she be directly responsible to the governing body if she had to report through the group secretary?

Unfortunately, the report did little to resolve (or to diagnose) the severe problems that were building up for the matrons and their service.

There were persistent complaints after 1955 that matrons were excluded from, or, at best, not invited often enough to, HMC meetings. It was reported from South Wales that many HMCs, composed mainly of union members or officials, voted to exclude the matrons from their meetings and took decisions on nursing matters after discussion with the stewards, who usually represented the unqualified staff, rather than the trained nurses.[30]

In 1957, the RCN branches standing committee resolved that the Minister should be advised that the matron's attendance at HMC meetings was essential to efficiency and effective working relationships. It was also reported that Ministry circulars, which were sent to the group secretaries *en bloc* for circulation to officers, were not forwarded to the matrons.

Even the Ministry of Health began to appear to have lost control of the situation. By 1960 it had sent out four circulars to the NHS authorities[31] and a leader in *Nursing Times*[32] declared:

> Ever since the Bradbeer Committee urged that the matron should be directly responsible to the governing body of her group of hospitals and should have direct access to it, the Ministry of Health has several times reminded hospital authorities that matrons should be kept informed about matters of policy, attend house committees, Hospital Management Committees and Boards of Governors and have an opportunity to comment on developments and changes of policy .... We in the nursing profession are fully aware that, up and down the country, many matrons are still refused access to their governing bodies and, indeed, in some instances, are only aware of changes in policy when they read of them in their local papers.

In fact, the obstruction appeared to be the regional boards and HMC administrators who were encouraging their authorities to keep nurses off their committees and matrons out of their meetings. By doing this, and by maintaining control of the nursing budgets and most information (including papers circulated by the GNC), they had effectively achieved power over the largest body of employees in the NHS, the nurses.

In 1958, the situation began to come to a head. 'Wrangler' wrote in her weekly column, Talking Point, in *Nursing Times*:[33]

> The NHS has brought about a change of status to many within its ranks. It is generally agreed that whereas the lay administration has grown in stature, the matron and the doctor have lost status. There are hospitals where the tripartite conception works extremely well and there are hospitals where it leads to internecine warfare.

On 13 June, 'Wrangler' returned to this theme and quoted a speech made at the recent meeting of the Institute of Hospital Administrators:

> There should be no doubts in the minds of any of the staff as to who is the Chief Administrative officer in the hospital and if the hospital secretary does not enjoy that status then the problem of staff management will be increased in number and magnitude.

'Wrangler' paraphrased the rest of the speaker's message: he did not like the tripartite system which envisaged three equal partners but the hospital secretary had to be more equal than the other two.

These articles evoked much correspondence in the following weeks. On 27 June (page 751), a letter from a matron, signed 'Militant', commented that she wholly agreed with 'Wrangler': the administrator had 'snatched' power since the inception of the NHS and the whole policy of the health service played into his hands. The RHBs, she continued, communicated with the administrator about nursing problems rather than with the matron. The administrators talked about 'My hospital', and 'My Matron' and 'My Doctors'.

Another letter from 'Matron' (page 783) said that the HMC often failed to consult the matron. This was due to an ignorance on the part of the members about the nature and scope of the matron's responsibilities which was fostered by the chairman of the HMC and the group secretary. 'Matron' continued rather ingenuously:

> It is hard to appreciate how any administrator can be so conceited as to consider himself more important than the matron who is responsible for the administration of considerably more than half the staff ... Unless the nursing profession makes an effort to maintain its position ... the public will consider them [the Administrators] more important than they are.

By this time the changes brought about by the grouping of hospitals and nurse training schools caused yet another encroachment on the functions of the matron. As the schools became larger and the numbers of sister tutors increased, it had become necessary to establish a teaching hierarchy. More senior tutors, and even principal tutors, were appointed in the larger group schools. The training of these tutors had been changed to include more educational psychology and educational methods. The tutors were becoming educationalists and looked for greater control over nurse training in the hospitals. In doing this, they were challenging the traditional authority of the matron over the nursing schools.

Many influential nurse tutors had visited the USA since 1948 and were clearly impressed by what they had seen in the American nursing schools. At the annual conference of the RCN Sister Tutor Section in 1954[34], Miss M M Springer, the principal tutor at Hull Royal Infirmary, said that the American Society of Superintendents of Training Schools stressed the importance of the development of the nurse as a person. At the same meeting, Miss B N Fawkes, then the principal tutor at the Middlesex Hospital, reported on some aspects of American nurse training that she had noticed. These included lectures in sociology, group work with ethnic minorities in the community, case studies, discussion panels with teachers and students and the involvement of students in curriculum development committees.

Later that month, the RCN report on the *Function, Status and Training of Nurse Tutors*[35] proposed posts for 'directors of the nurse education department'. There were evident difficulties being experienced by tutors who complained that they were not allowed time for preparation of their classes and lectures and lacked the support of their clinical colleagues.

At the winter conference of the tutors section this report was discussed.[36] Miss M G Lawson, the deputy nursing officer at the Ministry of Health, considered that there should be adequate scope in the tutor's job. Miss D L Holland, principal tutor at Guy's Hospital, whilst agreeing that the matron had overall responsibility for nurse training, also confirmed that the tutor planned the curriculum and allocated the students to their wards for clinical work. She complained of the way in which student nurses were selected and felt that the tutor should have more responsibility in her own professional arena.

In defence of the matron's position, Miss G Ceris-Jones, matron of the London Hospital, said that the education of the nurse must be more than mere preparation for examinations: it had to include the development of practical skills. 'It seems to me quite unpractical for the principal tutor to take any part in the . . . allocation for practical experience.' At her hospital, her office was responsible for that. The principal tutor might be a very important person, but the matron must be head of the training school.

> One of the main principles of the Nightingale system is the pre-eminence of the matron in the Nightingale School and her full control of the nursing staff throughout the hospital. In my view this is essential – it would be utterly damaging to British nursing and prestige if this structure were changed.

She felt 'quite unable to agree' with the proposed new title of director of the nurse education department.

But in the large group schools, there was a committee of matrons, and the principal tutor answered to the head of the school who was only one of that committee. Once again, therefore, there was a dangerous weakness in the matron's position.

As the group schools grew progressively larger, the senior member of the tutorial staff grew more authoritative within her own sphere. The matrons were powerless to defend their position since the further division of labour and the growing specialisation of nurse training once again demonstrated the inability of the matron, trained as a general nurse, to retain her professional authority in this new department.

The nursing structure

In fact, the position of the matrons deteriorated progressively until the institution of the Salmon grades after 1966.[37] For a long time they were substantially penalised, financially, from two points of view: firstly, because the differentials between the matrons' scales and the lower scales were held down as a matter of economic policy;[38] secondly, the matron's point in the scale range depended on the number of beds in her hospital. As wartime emergency beds were closed and new treatments and admission policies allowed an increased turn-over of patients, bed numbers (particularly in mental hospitals) could be reduced. Thus the matron's salary was reduced, notwithstanding the increased workload generated by the faster turn-over of patients and the concurrent establishment of the day hospital system. The latter did not qualify for any improvement in the matron's salary as there were no 'beds'.

The invidious position in which the matrons found themselves, the frequently ignominious treatment which they received and the financial penalties imposed on them were not lost on the profession at large. Candidates for promotion to the higher administrative grades were insufficient to fill the deputy and assistant matron posts. The increasing complexity of the bureaucracy and the changes in the work of the hospitals were demanding more posts, but different from the traditional ones.

The nursing hierarchy was characterised by descriptive posts such as staff nurse, ward sister, home sister, assistant matron, deputy matron and matron. These had been established during the nineteenth century and had later become formalised by the Nurses Salaries Committee (the Rushcliffe committee) from 1943 onwards. The grades designated by that committee were taken over by the Whitley Council in 1948. After this date, it had proved very difficult to establish new nursing posts within the existing structure. As the hospital departments, such as the outpatient departments and the operating theatres, proliferated and increased in importance, it had become necessary to try to fit new posts, such as departmental sister or theatre superintendent, into the established hierarchy. There were also situations where the established posts had outgrown their old capacity and enlarged posts had had to be set up, such as night superintendent.[39] Since these posts were neither predominantly clinical nor fully administrative, difficulties were encountered by the authorities and the Whitley Council in defining them and in slotting them into the structure.[40]

The traditional structure was a flat one and, increasingly, failed to reflect the vertical bureaucratic organisation of the NHS. There was therefore both an inhibition on the growth of administrative and clinical nurse specialists and a corresponding failure of the nurses to be able to respond to the new needs of the NHS.

The nursing structure became complex and untidy; salary grades were too specific and restrictive to allow much flexibility and the nursing service could not grow or expand. The complexity of the salary structure was not so much that there were innumerable different posts, which there were not, but that there became too many sub-bands, attached to each band or job-title, in the attempt to accommodate these new jobs and, at the same time, to maintain differentials and comparability, often with quite unrealistic expectations. The attempts to keep the salaries of nursing auxiliaries at least comparable with those of the ward orderlies (in the Ancillary Staffs Council), without paying them more than the staff nurses, was a constant source of difficulty.[39] Another example of these problems, and at the other end of the scale, was the difficulty of paying a reasonable differential to the deputy matron of a student nurse training school without paying her more than the matron of a pupil nurse training school.

The extraordinary contortions that were necessary to enable recruitment of male mental nurses, who were paid a salary suitably depressed for both females and nurses, was another example of the inflexibility and complexity of the system.[39]

In 1959 the position became worse, and both the RCN Council and the Ministry were concerned.[41] Council took the decision to revive an earlier agreement to inaugurate an administrative section in the College and to hold a conference in the autumn of 1959 (this was later deferred to the spring of 1960) at which the problem could be discussed. Pending this, it was decided to set up a working party 'to study the present position in the field of nursing administration, with particular reference to the shortage of suitable applicants'. The Nurse Administrators Group was launched in March 1960.

In March 1959 Council also decided to set up another working party to examine the salary structure of nurses. Job descriptions, drawn up by nurses themselves, were to be obtained as a basis for a questionnaire. This questionnaire was to be used to try to evaluate and rank the various jobs in a new hierarchy.

The concurrent working party on nursing administration was pursuing its own line of enquiry and had enlisted the help of the statistics department at the Ministry of Health. They planned a two-part report including both a statistical survey and a descriptive section incorporating quotations from the nurses' expressed opinions.

In March 1961 the Nurse Administrators Group was given section status and re-styled Hospital Nurse Administrators Section. The section celebrated this by the presentation of a report to Council offering its opinions on the need for prerequisite experience and qualifications for nurse administrators before appointment to senior posts. They asked for a diploma course to be arranged in conjunction with a university, similar to the Diploma in Nursing which had been established by the University of London in 1929.[42]

As this work continued, the BMA held its annual representative meeting (December 1962) and passed a resolution to the effect that the time had come for an impartial review of all matters relating to nursing, recruitment, training, housing and remuneration.

The RCN did not disagree with the need for this. It already had two major projects in hand: the review of the salary structure and its review of basic and post-basic nursing education.[43] It felt that there was a need for an independent review body to consist of doctors, nurses and lay people appointed on a personal basis. The College hoped to be able to attract the sympathetic support of the Minister of Health. It therefore proposed to send these background details, with its proposals, to the BMA to see if they were interested to proceed along those lines.

In February 1963 it was reported that the BMA council had agreed to the proposals, and the terms of reference were settled –

... to review all matters relevant to the provision within Great Britain of an adequate number of suitably prepared and qualified nurses to meet the demands of the nursing service and to ensure a high standard of care.

But, unknown to the profession, the Minister of Health had already decided to set up his own committee to advise on the senior nursing staff structure.[37] A letter was received by Council advising the RCN of this decision. In July 1963 Council decided to suspend any further action on the proposed independent review and the salary structure whilst it waited for the Salmon committee to report. It would continue with its review of nurse education.

This account of the matrons and their difficulties during the period 1948–61 helps to clarify the background to the Salmon Committee on Senior Nursing Staff Structure.[37] The committee was set up by the Minister because both sides of the Whitley Council agreed that the structure had become unwieldy and too complex.[44] There were problems of assimilation, differentials, leads and shortages of certain categories of nurses. No standard job descriptions were issued. There were particular difficulties with certain senior grades, such as night superintendent, departmental sisters and assistant matrons. Jobs had to be fitted to grades but the jobs, as they arose in the hospitals, were all more or less ad hoc and great confusion arose during salary negotiations.

The Noel Hall report[45] had been published in 1957 and had recommended a more simple salary structure for the administrative and clerical grades. All those involved in the negotiations of salaries for nurses and midwives believed that something similar could be done for them.

Until the public records become available it is possible only to infer what other reasons there may have been for instigating a committee to examine the nursing structure.

The shortage of senior nurses was a matter of common concern; so were the difficulties with the ad hoc grades. The Ministry of Health wanted a new structure but did not think that any alteration of the hierarchy was required, nor, in fact, did they think that the Staff Side was interested in structure or relativities. They thought that the nursing organisations were interested only in rates of pay.[46]

The evidence on the Staff Side is more fragmented and it is complicated by inter-organisational gamesmanship. Certainly, one factor which influenced their agreement on the need for a structural review was the problem of salaries for mental nurses who consisted of a much larger proportion of males than was the case for the general nurses. The male nurses could not keep their families on their salaries and family allowances were not sufficient to bring their incomes up to a satisfactory level. The Confederation of Health Service Employees (COHSE) was especially aggressive in this difficulty since the mental nurses were more usually members of that union.[47]

The RCN also wanted a review of salaries and, as we have already seen, a review of the structure and the introduction of job descriptions. Their interest lay in the difficulties that the matrons were experiencing with the lay administrators and the shortages of recruits for the senior posts.

The matron's job had been changed by the coming of the NHS, but there is little evidence that the profession was especially aware of this. They were preoccupied more with the decline of her status and authority in the hospital organisation. They were aware of the reduction of her territorial boundaries and they were resentful of the increased power of the administrators, but they failed to observe the growing importance of the nurses in the health service as an occupational group. They therefore failed to understand the compensating power that the matron, as the professional head of the hospital nurses, was beginning to have.

In 1950, a leader in *Nursing Times*[48] observed that the matron's job was changing: whereas it used to be based on housekeeping duties, it was becoming much more administrative: ' ... within the hospitals, nursing administration as a specialist's task is developing rapidly and being recognised as having an important part to play in the future'. But the matrons, beset by problems of shortages of staff and difficulties of recruitment, preferred to take a more pessimistic view. They saw, mostly, the loss of their territorial authority and their power in the hospitals; the apparent decline in the social prestige of nursing as the numbers of nurses increased; and the decline in their economic status compared with teachers in particular but also with other occupations opening up for women.

Mary Farnworth[49] wrote in *Nursing Times* that nursing was no longer favourably considered by certain classes who preferred teaching and secretarial work. With increasing specialisation in the health field, she observed, nursing was being considered as relatively unspecialised and the nurse a subservient member of the health team.

The matrons had been used to being considered as highly knowledgeable nurses who were heads of their nursing staffs. They found it difficult to come to terms with being administrators whose technical knowledge of nursing was of less than secondary importance. In this, their lack of standing orders was particularly important. They were used to a highly structured life and found the uncertainty and ambiguity of their changing jobs difficult to handle.

At the same time, even those matrons who did perceive the changes in their jobs and who wished to meet these, were hampered by the grading structure of the nursing hierarchy.

The growth of the administrative role of the matron also had the effect of distancing her from her nurses. She had been used to working directly with them; she had dealt with them on a face to face basis. Each morning, the night sister had reported to the matron on the patients; each day, the matron had made her rounds of at least some of the wards. Each student nurse in trouble on the ward had been reported to the matron and personally interviewed. In many hospitals, it had been the custom for nurses to report to the matron personally on their return from leave or sickness absence. With increasing bureaucracy and administrative duties, these personal contacts could not be sustained. Deputy matrons and assistant matrons were more frequently appointed and came between the matron and her nurses. It was a change in the style of management and, as Sofer [12] found, required new personalities to meet that change.

Even the matron's position as head of the nurse training school was affected by the grouping of schools and the appointment of more senior tutors. The matron became more of a coordinator or figurehead. It had become the function of the tutorial staff to interview and select recruits, to allocate the students to wards and to coordinate school work with ward teaching.[50]

These changes obscured the difficulties that were caused by the flat structure of the nursing organisation within the vertical organisation of the NHS bureaucracy. It did not appear that anyone anticipated the need for the radical changes in the senior nursing posts which the Salmon report recommended. Nor is there any evidence to show that the Ministry might have consciously wished for checks or balances on the power of the lay administrators. In fact, this was one of the outcomes of the new Salmon organisation which not only gave the nurses powerful posts at group level but also formalised the changed role of the matron.

There are reasons for understanding that these factors were not specifically considered before the Salmon committee was set up.

The responses of the RCN and the matrons to the possibility of establishing principal matron posts were clearly hostile: they did not want a post above that of the matron grade.[48]

In 1959, the Ministry of Health provided a package of restructured salaries and grades which was put to the Staff Side.[51] This package provided for new salary scales for all existing grades, made new proposals for grading matrons' posts and attempted to deal with differentials. The proposals eliminated some anomalies and improved nurses' salaries, but were not a new structure.

It must be considered that the Ministry was influenced by the regional boards and HMCs. These clearly did not want, and did not see the need for, any nursing influence in their policy deliberations. They went out of their way to block any steps taken by the profession to enforce the nursing voice.[52] It must, however, be asked why the RCN and the matrons did not accept the idea of principal matron posts which, to the outsider, would appear to have opened up to the profession paths to greater influence.

When the Salmon structure was imposed in the later 1960s, one chief nursing officer post was established at each group. In addition there were principal and senior nursing officer posts at unit levels. Some of the former matrons were promoted to CNO grade, some were appointed to PNO and some to SNO grades. Clearly, the matrons of many of the lesser hospitals were afraid that they would lose their status, as in fact they did.

Another solution might have been that the matrons were not sufficiently well educated to understand the power politics that had taken over the administration of the health service. This was largely so, not so much because the matrons lacked a general education, but because the education of women had been such as to lack the development of these powers of perception and analysis. Until the middle 1950s, matrons in posts were the product of the prewar education for women which concentrated on the arts but avoided the sciences. The matrons had also been subject to the prewar requirement of the GNC for School Certificate qualifications for student nurses and must, therefore, have had a certain level of general education. Others would have gained entry to nursing via the GNC education test. It was the succeeding generation of matrons, after the middle 1950s, who entered nursing with no educational qualifications. The matrons, at the time of the Bradbeer enquiry, can be said, therefore, to have had a general education but one which sought to develop 'feminine' qualities rather than 'masculine' qualities geared to the pursuit of power.

The matrons in posts after nationalisation were nurses who had been trained during the time when voluntary hospitals had to rely on voluntary donations in an ethos of the 'Lady Bountiful'. Nursing then was part of the system that provided medical attention from funds graciously given and graciously received. The donors received in return a social status and privilege: the nurses were the gracious supplicants on behalf of their charity patients. So strong was the ideology of the voluntary hospital system and so powerful was the status of the voluntary hospital doctors and nurses that the municipal hospitals, funded from local authority budgets, sought to simulate the same ethos. But this ethos was geared towards the feminine values of caring, sacrifice and a subsidiary status. These qualities were not appropriate to the new climate of managerialism and the pursuit of power.

Sofer's[12] theory seems to help in this question. He studied the reactions to the administrative changes brought by the NHS and the staff relationships in three hospitals.

He found a formal system of administration in the hospitals and an informal code of behaviour which enveloped a variety of status groups, sub-groups and informal groups. Each hospital had a rigid structure and valued traditions which had accumulated over the past years.

There was little mobility between the separate occupational groups, each of which had its own value system. There was a high degree of formalisation in the relationship between the occupational groups, with corresponding tensions.

The authority and status systems facilitated swift decision-taking and unquestioned obedience. The institution was built around the doctor's skill, but this provoked resentment and envy in the other staff. There was particular tension between the medical and lay staff, and the distinctive lines of authority for the medical, lay and nursing staffs led to a lack of a unity of control.

Under the NHS, Sofer found that the interaction between the groups was still geared to the prior rules and was underpinned by the old established values.

The new HMC was a superimposition of external authority, and the old responsibilities of the hospital officers for advising on policy had been taken over by the group organisation which included the group medical advisory committee. In addition, there was further centralised policy and salary decision-making deriving from the Whitley Council.

The matron had lost more responsibility by the loss of authority over the non-nursing departments and, later, the schools of nursing. There was therefore competition for control over the patients' environment and non-nursing staff. Whereas the staff had been used to obeying the matron, they were now under the control of the administrators. Habits and customs were slow to change, and the decision was ultimately made by the individual. The complexity of the new organisation had brought about the loss of a personal touch and slow decision-taking.

Sofer found that there were changes in the formal rules without a corresponding change in the internal social structure and culture of the hospital: the informal relationships were out of gear with the new formal relationships. The changes were resented and there was a mutual antagonism felt towards the individuals (the lay administrators) who were seen as the agents of change. The shift of power to the administrators had been reinforced by their control of information, specifically that relating to policies.

The changes were perceived as a reassessment of the social value of the services of each occupational group. The matrons, perhaps more than others, had much circumstantial evidence to feel that the value of their services was being undermined.

Sofer described how specific ideologies were attached to roles which bounded the obligation and responsibilities of the incumbent and legitimised his behaviour. Specific and highly functional ideologies were also attached to social structures as a defence and in order to unify the members of the group. When the key roles changed, existing incumbents were often not able to adapt and different personalities were needed.

Sofer also described how the world of the hospital remained bounded by the traditions and customs of that hospital. With the grouping of hospitals there was no compensating widening of its horizons. The groups therefore remained a set of individual units and did not become a corporate body.

In applying this theory to the matron, we can understand that there was a strong value system in the nursing group and that the ideology attached to her role included the belief that she was the spokesman and representative, as well as the matriarch, not only of the nurses but also of all the patients and female staff. After the NHS, this ideology was attacked from many quarters: by the removal of the female staff from her authority, by the superimposition of the group organisation and central committees and also by the Bradbeer committee's recommendations for the nursing advisory and nurse education committees. These appeared to the matron to compromise the unity of the nursing group and her role position in that group. With her position in the nursing group apparently undermined, there was a corresponding increase in the tensions between the nurses and other occupational groups, specifically the administrators.

Given this process and given the bounded horizons of the hospitals, it is not surprising that the matron did not look beyond, to the advantages she might have gained by accepting a principal matron post at group level. The assaults on her position were already so damaging that the idea of becoming subordinate to another nurse manager was rejected.

Similarly, the ideology attached to her role, which related to her position as spokesman of the nurses, was too strong for her to change easily. She was not able to perceive her ambiguous position and was not ready to abandon her professional orientation in order to enhance her management status.

The RCN was strongly influenced by the same ideology and the voice of the matrons was powerful on the Council. If the matrons rejected the principal matron post, it was not surprising that the Council would adopt the same line. It was only later, when many of the original matrons had retired and a new generation had taken over (Sofer's different types of personalities), that there was a change of heart demonstrated by the profession's enthusiastic acceptance of the Salmon proposals.[53]

Menzies[13] found that the insecurity identified in the matrons was endemic in the nursing profession. Her research confirmed much of Sofer's in that she too described the formation of a social organisation as a defensive mechanism against the anxieties generated by the nature of the nurse's work.

She gave as examples of this social defence system, the stern discipline and the attempt to eliminate decisions by ritualistic behaviour, the reduction of the weight of responsibility by checks and counterchecks and the involvement of others in decision-making. She elaborated this by describing the collusive social redistribution of responsibility (usually to superiors) and a purposeful obscurity in the formal distribution of responsibility.

Change was avoided in the operation of the social system of the defence system. Anxiety inhibited constructive and realistic planning and decision-taking. The rapid changes then taking place needed greater flexibility but had been handled with increased prescription and rigidity. She found that nurses had little capacity to confront anxiety situations or to tolerate the objective reality; they avoided the challenge of change and of devising successful strategies for it. Menzies did not add, as she might well have, that each successful attack on the matrons further exacerbated such behaviour.

The traditional organisation of nursing was such as to make it difficult for nurses to take effective decisions. Their social system inhibited their capacity for creative or abstract thought and conceptualisation; it interfered with judgment and provoked mistakes. Menzies found that the proportion of more intelligent or better educated girls was high amongst the student nurses, but the rates of wastage amongst these were higher than amongst the less well endowed. The system drove away the very people who might have been likely to remedy the inadequacies of the system.

Many nurses have an acute and painful awareness that their profession is in a serious state . . . there have been many changes in the peripheral areas of nursing . . . one is astonished to find how little basic and dynamic change has taken place. Nurses have tended to receive reports and recommendations with a sense of outrage and to react to them by intensifying current attitudes and reinforcing existing practice.

Needless to say, she also found that the system did nothing towards enabling or encouraging the maturation of the individual. The matrons were the product of their training and of the system and therefore inherited its defects. If they had learned as students and junior nurses to involve others in decision-taking and to delegate responsibility upwards, it can be anticipated that they would look to the doctors and administrators: who better then than the group secretary? If they had been taught discipline and if their training had deterred constructive thinking, can it be wondered at if they received their terms of reference from the Minister or the HMC and obediently followed those directions? If the usual method of coping with responsibility was the purposeful obscurity of its distribution, how better to achieve that than by refusing the need of a new post of group matron? It was not therefore only the traditional ideology of the gentlewoman that enforced pliancy and dependence, it was the whole structure and system of nursing, especially the methods of training, the lack of a minimum education standard and the priority given to service needs to the detriment of the students. Until the system could accept the thinking nurse and adjust its social organisation to tolerate, or even use, nonconformism, it would continue to breed 'the matrons'. However, as Maggs[9] showed, the matron was the person responsible for the selection of recruits on a very subjective and uncertain basis and directed towards the selection of like-minded individuals into the occupation. The process of socialisation could be relied upon to mould the trainee further into the 'ideal type'. Shortage of recruits made it necessary to admit 'less suitable' candidates but, as both Menzies and Maggs found, the system ensured the wastage of most of those.

The lack of a minimum education requirement for nursing recruits compounded the problems by denying the matrons an objective test of suitability and rendering them more vulnerable to the pressures of the health service bureaucrats. It also deterred the more able from entering the nursing service. Thus the circle was completed, and its vicious effects on nursing were to be felt for many years to come.

Chapter 5/The minimum education level

Before the 1939 war the GNC insisted on a minimum education level for recruits to nurse training. The standard that had been set was that of the School Certificate but, since many girls' schools did not prepare their students for this, the GNC offered an alternative test education examination.[1]

In September 1939 the test education examination was suspended, as was any other qualification: any girl could be accepted for nurse training. The hospitals, however, were free to set their own criteria for recruits and many did so. The teaching hospitals continued to ask for some educational criteria, usually the School Certificate standard, but sometimes matriculation level.[2] The levels of candidates therefore began to differ widely between hospitals. Some hospitals, short of recruits and heavily dependent on student labour for their wards, swept in any candidate. Others, often with waiting lists, were more selective.

This chapter examines the profession's attempts to reimpose the minimum education level for candidates for nurse training and the consequence that their failure in this had on the development of nursing.

By 1949 it was clear that the intelligence or educational levels of student nurses had declined significantly and the profession was anxious to rectify the situation.[3] The Horder report[4] considered that

> ... the education of student nurses will necessarily be governed for some years to come by the standard of intellectual attainment represented by the applicants which in some cases, it must be admitted, is grievously low.

And the headmistress previously quoted[1] had to remind the profession that

> ... the girls now starting training at 18 years of age have had a difficult upbringing. It is frequently forgotten that they were born in 1935 and during the war they were in primary schools, if at school at all.

During that period there had been shortages of routine, schools, books, and teachers. Many had not mastered the three Rs, 'the effects of the war years will be felt for some time.'[1]

It would have been a relatively simple matter to reintroduce the minimum education level by GNC rule but this required the acquiescence of the Minister. The shortage of nurses, however, was a matter of considerable concern to the Minister, who was also very much influenced by the hospital authorities. Their argument was that the institution of an educational level would automatically screen out many recruits and leave them short of student nurse labour: this must be the 'common sense' consequence of imposing a standard.

The profession, too, was divided. Whilst both the GNC and the RCN officially claimed a policy for the restitution of the education level, both organisations had members who did not wholeheartedly support that policy.

The RCN Council was composed of a number of matrons whose responsibility was to staff their wards with nurses. The GNC was in a similar position. These matrons shared with their authorities the 'common sense' response.[5]

It is indeed possible that immediately after the war, given the immense disruption to education between 1939-1945, there would have been insufficient candidates with a School Certificate. There would, however, have been more candidates who could successfully have taken the GNC test.

The Ministry's attitude was less straightforward, however, when it is judged alongside its concurrent policy to recruit as many state enrolled assistant nurses (SEAN) as possible. These pupil nurses took a two-year practical training which culminated in a practical test of proficiency. Their training included very little book work and their educational requirements were fewer than those of the student nurses studying for state registration.

Both the GNC and the RCN urged that candidates who failed the minimum education requirements, if they were reimposed, should be steered into pupil nurse training. It was, after all, policy that there should be more SEANs and fewer SRNs.

The hospital authorities feared that their appeal to recruits would be prejudiced if they opened pupil nurse training schools which enjoyed less prestige than did student nurse training schools. The matrons also preferred to retain student nurse training schools, not only for the prestige, but also because they, as heads of these schools, earned a greater salary than did their colleagues in charge of pupil nurse schools and, furthermore, the three years' training was of more value on the wards than the two years of the pupil nurses.

In 1945 the GNC asked the Minister to reinstate a test of education. The Minister, advised by the National Advisory Council for Nurses and Midwives, refused the request because of the shortages of nurses. The British Hospitals Association supported the Minister. The GNC was, however, allowed to appoint their first two full time inspectors of training schools.

In 1946, the GNC proposed to enforce its conditions for the approval of training schools. It wished to set a minimum number of occupied beds, and was concerned that some training hospitals had too few for the adequate provision of clinical experience for students. It was reported that some hospitals had an average bed occupancy rate of only 20-54 per cent.[6] In this the Minister also thwarted them.

In 1947, the GNC used a letter from the Registered Nurses Association of British Columbia to support a further request to the Minister for an education test. The GNC had had, for many years, reciprocal agreements with the British dominions through which the respective trainings could be accepted by each country for registration. The letter from British Columbia cancelled this arrangement with the GNC on the grounds that nursing education in Britain had failed to keep pace with British Columbia in respect of both the minimum education qualifications and the quality of nurse education itself.

Council members who had visited North America could confirm that British standards had slipped but qualified this by remarking that the standards set by the GNC were only a minimum level and better levels were available in some schools.[7]

At this time Aneurin Bevan was considering the recently published Wood report[8] and promised to bear in mind the Canadian letter. He added that he would not mind if the GNC experimented with a test examination, as well as a revised syllabus, on a voluntary basis. The GNC had to remind him that they had no powers to experiment with the syllabus.

The Wood report was something of a disappointment to the nursing organisations since it did not recommend a minimum education level. It was primarily concerned with the recruitment and training of the basic nurse and considered that a two-year course would be adequate so long as it was a training rather than a service oriented course. Tucked away in Appendix VIII, however, it did explain that the two year training was not intended for functions over and above those normally carried out by a staff nurse in hospital or for a first level public health post:

... consequently, we do not consider it unreasonable to assume that before a nurse proceeds to a post carrying new functions ... she should receive some training beyond that provided in the basic course.

These further courses should, in many instances, be provided by universities and no nurse, including ward sisters, should be entitled to call herself a specialist until she had completed a 'post graduate' training. The Wood report therefore envisaged an open system of progression with the better intellects rising through post-basic training. Mainly because of this, the working party felt able to recommend the closure of the roll.

Statistics provided in the Wood report gave some indication of the educational level of nurses up to 1945.

Table 1. The educational level of nurses up to 1945

	Voluntary general hospitals	Municipal general hospitals
Candidates with matriculation level or above	36%	15%
Candidates below matriculation level	64%	85%

In intelligence levels, their tests had shown the following:

(A = highest level, E = lowest level)

	Voluntary general hospitals	Municipal general hospitals
A	26.5%	19.2%
B	31.0%	27.9%
C	33.0%	33.9%
D	7.2%	14.6%
E	2.2%	4.4%
Wastage rates:	35%	43%

Total student intakes:

	Voluntary general hospitals	Municipal general hospitals
1937	7,950	3,800
1938	7,850	3,400
1939	8,500	4,700
1940	8,600	3,600
1941	8,800	3,600
1942	10,150	4,900
1943	10,300	5.100
1944	10,200	3,750
1945	10,050	4,050

The voluntary hospitals therefore had the edge over the municipal hospitals in the upper two grades of intelligence and a considerable margin in educational standards.[9] From the statistics it might have been argued that the lower wastage from the voluntary hospitals was due to these two factors. Instead, the working party argued that educational levels did not equate with intelligence levels and neither of these factors were critical in the making of a nurse. They considered that wastage was a reflection of the interpersonal relationships within hospitals and the abundance of repetitive duties demanded from the students.

The profession's demands for a return of the minimum education level was therefore deflected and, instead, the main thrust from all quarters in the next ten years was aimed at improving interpersonal relationships, reducing discipline and removing non-nursing duties, as they came to be known after the Goddard job analysis.[10]

The question of training was further complicated because, in the eyes of the profession, the length of training was a measure of the social status of the nurse. In this matter nurses had a confused and equivocal sensation that the NHS was depressing the prestige or socio-economic status of their occupation.

The social status of nurses had, before 1948, been signalled more by the hospital in which they trained or worked than by any recognised ranking of the occupation. Thus, the nurse training or working at a London teaching hospital could feel secure that she was working in a profession. In contrast, the nurse working in a provincial non-teaching hospital often felt that her status was inferior to that of her colleagues in London. This had something to do with the educational standards demanded by the different hospitals as well as the quality of training. It must be said, however, that the training of the more prestigious hospitals was not always better and, sometimes, was not as good as the 'smaller' (that is, in status, if not in size) hospitals.

Although the Wood report did not find any significant difference in socio-economic levels between the students in voluntary hospitals and those in municipal hospitals, the fact was that the London teaching hospitals could be far more selective in their recruitment than could the other hospitals, either voluntary or municipal.

The social status of nurses was therefore a matter of ascription, a reflection of the prestige of the hospital in which they trained or worked.

The NHS, with its policy of regionalisation and hospital grouping, had quickly removed the honorary status of former voluntary hospitals. Each hospital would henceforward have to earn its status in the eyes of the public by a more realistic set of values related to quality of care and the way in which it could engage the respect and affection of the community. Nurses working in these hospitals could no longer feel separate from, and therefore superior to, nurses working in former municipal hospitals.

The exception to this trend of equalisation was the teaching hospitals who remained outside the regional hospital board structure until 1974. Nurses working in these institutions continued for many years to feel apart from their colleagues. Indeed, in many instances, their working conditions were better, there was a higher nurse/patient ratio and they were often treated with greater courtesy by other disciplines. Since their hospitals could be more selective, recruits could continue to be from the same social or educational strata: there was greater cohesion.

The equalisation of the RHB hospitals, however, did appear to many nurses to have the effect of reducing the social status of the occupation. There was a strong feeling that the professional status of nursing was diminished. Added to this, the loss of the minimum educational level had indeed brought into nursing a greater number of girls from the lower socio-economic classes.[11]

There was therefore some justification for the nurses' fears that their occupational status was being depressed. In 1948, in pressing for improved salaries for nurses, the RCN had compared these rather unfavourably with wages paid to ward maids. There was an immediate outcry from nurses that the College should have put the two occupations alongside each other, for whatever purpose.[12]

In 1952, Mary Farnworth, a graduate nurse, published a report of a survey she had made in *The Social Prestige of Nursing*.[13] In this she found that nursing was no longer favoured as a career for their daughters by certain classes. The public appeared to be more biased against nursing when it was compared with teaching and secretarial work. This was a surprising reversal of attitudes compared with the report of Box and Croft-White.[9]

In fearing for their diminishing social status, the nurses sought to maintain the length of their training as well as to press for the return of a minimum education level. The battle to retain a three-year training was not hard to win since it accorded with the economic priorities of the service. After the Nurses Act 1949 had been passed, the GNC was able to revise the syllabus of training which, in 1952, confirmed the three-year course. The nurses continued to fight for a minimum standard of entry but two factors militated against their efforts, in addition to the continuing opposition of the Ministry and the hospital authorities.

In the first place, by 1949 there was a majority of nurses without a secondary education. These nurses were defensive about raising the educational standard and, not unnaturally, did not support it as a policy. They argued that they had successfully completed their training and passed their examinations and asked why a GNC test was necessary when they had demonstrated that they could manage without.[14] These nurses failed to observe that the national standard of education was rising as a consequence of the Education Act 1944 and that nursing was being left behind. They also failed to note the growing professionalisation of occupations, all of which were demanding additional educational qualifications.

In the second place, most nurses were complaisant about the standard of British nursing. Their counter to the letter from the Registered Nurses Association of British Columbia and to the rising academic ambitions of the American nurses was that British nursing was rooted in practical skills and should remain so:

> . . . skill comes to the craftsman by constant practise. Is our young nurse only learning to pass examinations? . . . Let us beware of the example of those countries that, in former years, over-developed the student aspect of the nurses' training, almost to the exclusion of the art of bedside nursing and the gain of a daily increasing sense of responsibility.[15]

And, some years later;

> Unfortunately . . . the really brilliant girls have the wrong temperament for the work. Their alert, quick, intense minds accompany impatient and intolerant natures, and being rather excitable and erratic people they are the types prone to panic.[16]

Years later, Crow[17] was to demonstrate that undergraduate nurses were able to develop a wider understanding of patients' problems and, potentially, a greater armamentarium for use in problem solving.

The professional organisations were pressing for a better educational level for inappropriate reasons. They were seeking a better status for nurses rather than better nurses; they wanted a minimum education standard because they wanted 'aptitude' which would serve to help nurses pass their qualifying examinations and so increase the available numbers of nurses.

This extraordinarily equivocal attitude was present when the GNC approached the National Institute of Industrial Psychology to design a test of candidates for training. Their wish was for a tool which would eliminate those who were totally untrainable, rather than to select those who were most trainable. They chose this approach because they were concerned that any test should not screen out candidates wastefully.[18]

95

It was only after they had started their discussions with the National Institute that they discovered, to their intense annoyance, that a small office committee at the Ministry of Health had also begun to investigate possible tests.

The Minister was able to smooth the ruffled feathers of the GNC by telling them that he had not known about the office committee's activities. He invited the GNC to meet the office committee who proposed to undertake a study of selection procedures. Three hospitals were to be chosen, an ex-voluntary hospital, an ex-local authority hospital and a teaching hospital. A psychologist and the respective matrons were each to interview and select candidates for a 'batch follow-up' for comparison of the results. The office committee sought also to discover causes of failure rather than to search for suitable qualities but, during the experiment, both approaches would be used. As with the GNC, the office committee was concerned lest screening out candidates might result in the loss of too many potentially suitable candidates. It was agreed that both the GNC and the Ministry would continue with their separate projects.

In November 1948, the GNC and Aneurin Bevan agreed that the SEAN training should be shortened from two years to one, with a second year of supervised practice before enrolment. It was also agreed that their training should not be restricted to the chronic sick but could be given at any approved hospital. This was a manoeuvre to try to increase recruitment which up to then had been minimal. The GNC continued to be most anxious to retain the roll.

The years 1948 and 1949 were very much taken up with considerations of the forthcoming legislation. The GNC badly wanted some control over post-registration training: if the supplementary parts of the register were to be closed – and it was envisaged that those for fever and tuberculosis nurses would be – there would be a problem with those nurses who had only their specialised training. As it was, the GNC had no power to organise, examine or give certificates except by first prescribing additional parts of the register and then making new rules. The Council was against anyone qualifying in a limited branch of nursing and would have preferred a system by which nurses could take their general training first and then move on to a special training.

The Ministry wrote to them in February 1949 confirming that it did not intend to deal with that problem in the Bill. During the passage of the Bill, an amendment was introduced in the House of Lords, to allow the GNC to authorize post-registration qualifications, but it was later withdrawn at the request of the Government.

Later in 1949, the GNC began discussions about what level and what subjects taken for the new General Certificate of Education (GCE) should be accepted as a minimum, if and when this might be re-instated. The GCE examination was about to replace the School Certificate. There were two levels of GCE examination, the ordinary level ('O' level) and the advanced level ('A' level). The former was a school-leaving qualification and the latter was the university entrance level.

The GNC members and staff were obviously not completely familiar with the ramifications of the new examinations and sought the advice of the Association of Headmistresses. They asked two specific questions: could certain GCE subjects exempt candidates from part I of the preliminary examination and, secondly, what GCE subjects should be accepted as a requisite standard of education for entry to nursing in place of the School Certificate.

During these discussions, a curious misunderstanding occurred. The GNC failed to realise that the GCE subjects could be taken serially, unlike the School Certificate which was taken as a con-solidated examination. It is not clear whether the headmistresses explained this to the Education and Examination Committee with-out making the significance clear, or whether they were so familiar with the arrangements that they took them for granted. It may have been that they did not understand this arrangement themselves.

With regard to the first question posed by the GNC, many girls' schools had been giving pre-nursing courses to their students and preparing them for part I of the preliminary examination which could be taken at school. It was agreed between the GNC and the headmistresses that this practice could continue and that anatomy, physiology and hygiene would cover part I requirements.

In the second question, the headmistresses explained that they considered that the GCE would be of a higher standard than the School Certificate. They were anxious that the GNC should not demand more than two subjects, including English. The GNC wanted three subjects, including arithmetic. The headmistresses countered that it was unlikely that arithmetic would be available as a separate paper and, anyway, the standard would be higher than the GNC needed. Besides, even if the girls only took two papers, they would have been prepared to GCE level in at least five subjects. This later proved to be untrue. Eventually it was agreed, on that basis, that the GNC should require a minimum of two passes from history, geography, religious knowledge and, compulsorily, English literature or English language.[19]

The matter was again raised with the Association of Head-mistresses in 1952. During the interim period the GNC had been asked to widen the list of subjects which they would accept. As a result the GNC and headmistresses jointly agreed that two 'O' levels would be required, one of which should be English (or Welsh) language and that a certificate should be furnished by the headmistress that the candidate had satisfactorily completed a five year grammar (later changed to secondary) school course during which she had reached a satisfactory standard in at least five other subjects.

When it eventually turned out that not all school leavers would be prepared to take five subjects and that each subject could be examined serially, the GNC found that they had accepted a much lower level of entry qualification than they had intended.

In 1950, the GNC received an interim report from the National Institute of Industrial Psychology. They had tried out a test of general intelligence and educational attainment on 2,376 student nurses, including some 128 overseas nurses and 155 males. The test had been followed up between six and fifteen months later by a verbal report from the respective matrons which was based on the subjects' ward reports, marks obtained at the preliminary training school and other observations. Reports for 93 students had not been obtained: it was thought that some of the subjects might have discontinued training but the Institute warned that there might be a possible distortion of results as a consequence.

The matrons' reports posed the problem of assessing subjective judgments since no common standard was used. The comments tended to be contradictory and unreliable: a student described as 'brilliant' at one stage had subsequently left 'because she could not make the grade in theory'. Very few of the subjects had yet sat for the preliminary examination, normally taken at twelve months.

The reasons reported for the students' leaving were intellectual inferiority, unsuitability, health or vague and extraneous reasons. The scoring distribution was as follows:

Score	Number of students
200–215	5
180–199	39
160–179	106
140–159	195
120–139	364
100–119	425
80– 99	398
60– 79	334
40– 59	230
20– 19	112
0– 39	40
Total	2248

The Institute had felt it necessary to treat the foreign students separately.

Taking 40 as the critical score,

5 per cent of candidates would have been eliminated,
10.9 per cent of candidates who left between 6–15 months would have been eliminated,
5.8 per cent of candidates who had remained would have been excluded.

The percentage of each score who had discontinued was as follows:

Score	Percentage discontinued	Original total
0– 9	75	12
10–19	51.4	23
20–29	39.8	48
30–39	33.3	61
40–49	30.6	85
50–59	29.7	118
60–69	27.9	133
70–79	25.6	187
80–89	25.6	193
90–99	24.9	178
100 and over	21.7	1084

The results were still indeterminate and a further report was promised.[20]

It was received in June and reported that:

2,221 tests and reports had been made (excluding foreigners)
1,041 subjects had taken the preliminary examination.

There was no further news, on this account, of 610 students.

570 (21 per cent) of the total 2,221 had discontinued,
1,541 (74.3 per cent) continued in training.

The Institute had decided not to use the matrons' reports in their main analysis as they were not sufficiently reliable although they had been useful in augmenting the data on those who might have been rejected as a consequence of the screening.

On the whole, the value of the screening tool showed a slight correlation between continuity of training and success in the preliminary examination: less so for continuance, more so for success in the examination. No detailed examination of the top 60 per cent of candidates had been made.

Taking 40 as the critical score, after screening there would have been a 3.5 per cent loss of candidates who had passed part I of the examination or 3.4 per cent of those who had passed both parts of the examination. On the other hand, the Institute reported, screening would have eliminated 20.9 per cent of the examination failures and 12.6 per cent of those who had discontinued.

Naturally, the higher the critical score was set, the greater would be the number of candidates who were successful in the examinations and who continued their training.

In the graph which accompanied the report, the critical score appeared to be 45–50 where the success rate made a marked upward curve. The Institute evidently considered that 40 would be an economic and satisfactory point but the GNC decided to set it at 35. Council also agreed with the Institute that the tool would make a satisfactory test for recruits and proposed to recommend it for universal use.

When this was discussed at the meeting of the General Council the Ministry representative, Mr Milne, raised strong objections to the proposal that the test should be instituted on a national level and suggested that it should be offered to authorities on a voluntary basis.

The Institute was concerned that its haphazard use might make the test unreliable. In the end, it was agreed that it should be made compulsory for all candidates without formal qualifications but that it should also be phased in over the period of a year. The Minister, though, continued to refuse to allow its mandatory use until he had seen the Institute's final report.[20]

The Minister received this in May 1951 but it was not until February 1952 that he got around to writing to the GNC to say that his study of the results had demonstrated that he still could not agree to the return of the minimum education level. He asked that any discussion on the matter should be deferred for at least a year. In the light of this the Education and Examination Committee asked the National Institute to make a further analysis of the data incorporating that which had been collected since June 1950.[21]

The last report was received from the Institute in the autumn of 1953. They had analysed the results through to the state finals and provided an up to date record of discontinuance:

48.3 per cent had continued to the final examination,
13.7 per cent were still in training,
38.0 per cent had discontinued, and of these,
25.8 per cent before the preliminary examination,
12.2 per cent after.

The Institute confirmed that the relationship between the test score was significantly positive: the higher the score, the higher was the percentage of successful nurses and the smaller was the proportion of failures.

If the critical point was taken as 30, this would reject 10 per cent of the failures; the test would help to eliminate the majority of those candidates who, for one reason or another, would be unable to compete satisfactorily.

The Education and Examination Committee recommended to Council that the Minister should be asked to allow the test to be adopted experimentally for two years. Council wondered if it would be worth all the time needed to use the test for each candidate if the pass mark were set only at 30. But the Education and Examination Committee was supported by the Mental Nurses Committee who also hoped to use it, and the Minister was again approached. Again, the Minister refused; this time on the grounds that the test would not be suitable for general use by the hospital authorities.[22] The Minister's letter was dated in December.

The timing of Iain Macleod's refusal is rather strange since he had received, in November, a report from the National Advisory Council on the Recruitment of Nurses and Midwives. This council, it will be remembered, had published quite a comprehensive set of reports in 1945, backed by a range of statistics unusual at the time since there was no central collation of data. For the purposes of this report, it had continued its survey of nurses, concentrating on student nurse wastage between 1948–1953.[23]

The GNC had allowed the council to use its student index and the study had included 18,000 entrants of all categories. The report showed that:

46.3 per cent (8,350) had passed the final examination,
38.2 per cent (6,900) had terminated,
15.5 per cent (2,800) were still in training.

Of those who had terminated

3,800 left in their first year
1,800 left in their second year
1,000 left in their third year
300 left in their fourth year

Approximately 15 per cent had left for educational reasons.

The wastage rate was lower than the figure given by the Wood report in 1947.

The highest number of leavers were under 18 years;
the lowest number of leavers were over 26 years.

The report concluded that the best age of entry was 18 years of age and found that a substantial number of candidates had left after four years, having either failed the final examination or failed to sit it.

The figures showed that about 31 per cent of students left by their second year during which time they should have taken their preliminary examination. Assuming that those remaining after the second year stayed to take the final examination, 10.48 per cent of the remnant failed or failed to take the final examination.

The Minister was evidently not impressed by this evidence; or success in completing their training was not his prior interest. His comments on the matter were few and not very revealing. All he had to say was that whilst the work in hospitals was increasing, there was also a 'notable increase' in the numbers of nurses and the number of staffed beds. But there was a shortage of student nurses and the numbers had declined since 1951.[24] His 'notable increase' in the numbers of nurses related only to untrained nursing staff: the numbers of trained nurses were being more and more diluted.

In fact, the Royal College of Nursing was complaining that untrained nurses were being employed as staff nurses and were giving out drugs. The College was also convinced that the Ministry and NHS authorities were more concerned with recruitment of student nurses for labour than they were with the training and final qualification of these young recruits.[25] Many of the recruits to nurse training were so educationally unfit that they were reported as being unable to calculate drug dosages and lotion dilutions.[26] The College had vigorously supported the GNC in its efforts to reinstitute the entrance test but had been equally rebuffed:

> ... the Minister admitted that there was some apprehension among Boards of Governors and HMCs in the effect on staffing if such a test were introduced.[27]

The College was consequently very supporting when the Florence Nightingale Memorial Committee funded a research project, in collaboration with the Dan Mason Research Fund, to investigate basic nurse education, methods of training and nursing techniques.[28]

In 1954 the GNC again decided to approach Iain Macleod about the use of the test devised by the National Institute of Industrial Psychology. At the meeting the Minister confirmed that his primary concern was staffing the hospitals and that the standard of training was only a secondary consideration. He did not consider the Institute's test suitable and reported that its use was meeting with the greatest opposition from the hospital authorities who were responsible for staffing their wards.[29]

The College Council received reports, at the same time, that many matrons were under considerable pressure by their HMCs to recruit even unsuitable candidates; included amongst these were overseas recruits who were barely literate and could hardly speak English.[30]

In the meantime, there was a desperate shortage of nurse tutors and a committee set up by the GNC, the Ministry of Health and the Department of Health for Scotland had found that whilst there was no real shortage of recruits for tutor training, many of them were educationally unfit and others were put off by the poor quality of students whom they would have to struggle to teach. Conditions for tutors were also considered to be poor and they were allowed little scope in their work since the attitudes of the hospital authorities were hostile to nurse training.[31] In desperation the GNC determined to disseminate the test to hospitals for their voluntary use.[32] In 1956 they raised the pass mark from 35 to 40.

No one, except possibly the GNC, even bothered to deny that the practical training of student nurses was poor in the hospitals. There was so much evidence to substantiate this, and the lack of involvement shown by most hospital authorities – as well as the Ministers as they came and went – was so manifest, that it became an accepted fact in the NHS.

The Wood report had criticised nurse training in 1947. The several reports of the Horder Committee had been equally critical. In 1953 the Goddard report [33] found that work allocation in hospital wards depended very much on the number of student nurses and domestics available to do the jobs. It concluded that theoretical considerations about what practical work student nurses should be doing in each year of training had to be abandoned when the balance of the various grades and types of staff altered. It found that there was little formal teaching on the wards for the students who learned more from each other than from the trained staff. They seldom had an opportunity to study the patients' case notes. There were many complaints from students about the inadequacy of their ward experience, although they formed the bulk of the labour available for the work. They were students in name only and training was subordinated to service needs.

At the time, the GNC defended the position by affirming that student nurses needed to perform repetitive duties in order to develop their skills. In addition, the GNC claimed, students had to be given time to do the more mundane tasks in order slowly to develop a sense of responsibility.

But in 1957 another report, also produced by H A Goddard, was published under the auspices of the area nurse training committee of the South East Metropolitan RHB.[34] The later report found that there was a wide variety of patterns and policies in the several hospitals that it had studied for the allocation of nurses for ward experience: it could find no common factor by which to measure the quality of nurse training except, in the end, by examination results. Although there was a tendency to build up the student's experience from 'basic nursing' to 'technical nursing' over the three years of training, the major factor was the day-to-day staffing situation.

The GNC did not lay down minimum requirements of practical instruction and experience but published schedules of techniques or activities. Some students had not received instruction in more than half of these prior to taking their preliminary examination, or in more than one third of those required before taking their final examination. Practical instruction on the wards was almost non existent and there were unequal periods of experience in the different specialties. Only 13 per cent of the students' time was given to theoretical teaching which the tutors and students all considered inadequate.

The report concluded that, without doubt, the training arrangement for students was subordinated to service convenience. The report also published a number of comments by student nurses which were almost universally unfavourable and sometimes quite bitter.

The GNC then felt obliged to agree that some changes should be made, specifically to the way in which records of practical experience were kept. They again defended the use of student nurses for repetitive duties and considered that some of the tasks which Goddard had described as non-nursing did have a nursing component.

Council also agreed that some thought should be given to evaluation of the training received by the students, and that some way of combining theory and practice should be found.[35]

In ten years, since the Wood report, the findings and criticisms had not changed much, nor had the syllabus.

It may be of some interest, at this point, to review the published views on nurse education made by members of the profession. Nurses were not notably vocal in their professional journals until the late 1950s; the published views cannot be taken as representative, therefore, but they do offer opinions which may be contrasted with those of the nursing institutions.

In 1955 Joyce Akester wrote a paper which discussed the education of the nurse. She complained that nurses were losing status compared with other professions and quoted the World Health Organization's third report of the Expert Committee on Nursing. This had said that nurse education should be established on a sound basis which, in Britain, would require a university education on the same lines as other professions. Akester considered that there would not be enough secondary school girls available for all nurses to receive this level of training. There was, she said, an anti-education prejudice in the profession and an over-emphasis on practical training. Consequently, she proposed a two-tier system for the practical nurse and for the advanced nurse. For the latter, she argued a case for a four-year integrated form of training but feared that there would be difficulties in funding these courses.[36a]

In the following weeks, there was a commendable amount of response to Akester's paper. At first there was support for her views, specifically her proposals for university based courses. But on 23 September Lilian M Darnell complained of Akester's use of the doctors and social workers as comparisons. She cited the International Council of Nurses' paper *The Basic Education of the Nurse* which had described nursing as 'a separate profession with its more distinct functions and organisation'. She thought that nursing's preoccupation with status was dysfunctional and that a university degree or a School Certificate would not impose prestige where it had not been earned by the individual.

Darnell did, however, agree that there should be two groups of nurses, the leaders and the basic nurses but emphasised that there should be an open system. Only the potential leaders should have a university education but whatever changes might be made should be designed for the improvement of the service rather than for status reasons.[36b]

A few weeks later Akester returned to the attack at a public health section meeting when she complained that nursing leaders were insufficiently educated. She considered that the basic training of nurses was defective and that there were too many chiefs [SRNs] but not enough Indians [SEANs], the basic workers. Her message was that the basic nursing course should provide the all-purpose nurse who did not require supplementary training and that training was confused with experience, hence the unnecessarily long three-year course.[36c] Other nurses appeared to agree that they lacked prestige compared with their colleagues in the hospital team.[36d]

At the joint conference of the Association of Hospital Matrons and the RCN Sister Tutor Section, the views expressed by matrons and tutors remained rather bland and non-specific. Most comments generalised the needs of all nurses although they accepted that a wide range of skills and abilities was required. The exception to these conservative views was Miss M Houghton, the education officer of the GNC. She anticipated the need to revise nurse education in the light of rapid developments, new nursing functions and new responsibilities. She considered that all forms of nursing would require specialised preparation.[37]

This was, perhaps, the first official intimation of a change of philosophy which moved from the all purpose nurse to the basic-plus-specialised training concept. It will be noted, however, that these views were not reflected in the proposals made by the ad hoc committee in 1957 (see page 108).

In October 1956 the RCN published a major policy document, *Observations and Objectives*, which sought to build on the Horder report now some ten years old. The preamble explained that the policies set out aimed to be realistic rather than idealistic. It called for both horizontal and vertical expansion: it described a team of nurses led by a 'fully qualified leader'. The SRN was to be the leader and the enrolled nurse was to be 'the stable element in the team'. Learner nurses (the term included both pupil and student nurses) were to be part of the team only in so far as their training required. The vertical expansion would demand increased educational opportunities including university qualifications in teaching and administration.

Part III of the RCN publication reiterated the need to reduce the numbers of registered nurses and increase the pupil intake. The two trainings would need distinct standards of admission and methods of recruitment. The return of educational qualifications would be necessary, as would post-registration training, for specialists and leaders.[38]

At a conference to discuss *Observations and Objectives* RCN speakers explained, again, the ideas underlying the model and Miss Houghton discussed international trends in nursing. She seemed to be introducing what has since become known as 'situation learning' and suggested that classroom teaching should be subordinated. She reminded the audience that the 1953 WHO conference in nursing education (Technical report series No 60) had worked out a graded pattern to afford a progressive series of learning situations which were calculated to teach the student how to meet the needs of a particular patient. She also repeated the Wood report's recommendation

106

for independent schools of nursing so as to separate education from service needs.[39]

Other correspondents in the nursing journals were complaining, at this time, of poor bedside nursing, too much 'technical nursing' and too many specialised techniques.

The doctors, too, became embroiled in the debate. The *British Medical Journal* was against degrees in nursing unless it was for clinical nurses to advance the practice of nursing. It was fearful that an élite of teachers and administrators would be out of touch with the ordinary working nurse.[40]

Dr Ritchie Russell wanted only one grade of nurse, that of the enrolled nurse.[41]

Dr Thomas Anderson was concerned that an élite of nurses would result in patients being nursed by aides and auxiliaries. He considered that much of the training of student nurses was more appropriate to junior doctors. He was particularly incensed because he and his medical colleagues had recently been displaced by nurses as lecturers in the school of nursing. He called for another Lancet commission to 'allow the medical profession to redefine in the terms of the 1950s the kind of nurse this country requires'.[42]

Dr Ronald Macbeth observed that the academically oriented American nurses spent most of their time at their desks:

Many of us have noticed with concern a growing lack of acceptance by senior members of the nursing profession that they belong to an auxiliary service which must be subordinate to the doctors and which cannot have an independent existence.[43]

There were other letters, many of them very sarcastic, about higher educational standards for nurses. Some, taking their perspective from the other side of the Atlantic, anticipated that patients in Britain would be abandoned by a nursing élite to the care of untrained staff.

Nursing Times commended the fair, constructive and encouraging editorials from both medical journals but regretted that the correspondents had not, apparently, first studied *Observations and Objectives*. The editor asked these critics if they would disagree with the WHO report that the kind of nurse needed was

... one who is prepared through general and professional education to share as a member of the health team in the care of the sick, the prevention of disease and the promotion of health.[44]

It will be observed that there were two principal groups of opinions and a major misunderstanding about the term 'leader'. The

RCN used the term to mean leader of the ward team, the ward sister or staff nurse type of figure who would direct and supervise the care of patients given by their nursing team made up of basic nurses. Other critics took the term to mean administrators and teachers, or nurses removed from the patient care setting.

Opinion was generally divided between those people (including doctors and nurses) who wanted a single level of qualified nurse who was broadly competent and skilled in basic nursing techniques, and others who recognised the increasing complexity of medical regimes and technology and realised the need for nurses with intellectual attainments that would allow them to support doctors in these, or to assume some of the established medical routines.

There was a very small third group of people who recognised, but could not specifically describe, the growing complexity of nursing as an occupation in its own right. Social changes and the patients' enhanced expectations, as well as a better understanding of psychology and sociology, were making the work of nurses more demanding and more complex. But this trend, although it was felt by some people, had not been articulated. It was not until the nursing process was described in the 1970s that the change in nursing could be specifically identified. (see chapter 11)

There was therefore confusion about the role of nurses and about how the basic nurse and the more highly trained nurse should function. The nursing process has offered greater clarity and has allowed us to understand that the advanced nurse, or nurse leader, should diagnose patient needs and plan nursing care whilst the basic nurse may carry out the nursing care plans. This provides for a highly trained nurse to have a valuable function in patient care: it also provides for fewer of these nurses but a greater number of basic nurses. Surely a more effective and economical use of all levels of staff.

Late in 1957 an ad hoc committee including the GNC's Education and Examination Committee, the Association of Hospital Matrons and the RCN Sister Tutor Section made proposals for revised conditions of approval of hospitals for nurse training purposes. Two papers (A and B) were drafted.

Paper A included a lengthy discussion on the current problems of nurse training and the solutions which the ad hoc committee considered to be desirable. It set out a fresh basis for training registered and enrolled nurses and proposed a reversal of the relative numbers of these two grades.

It recapitulated all the difficulties that nurse training had experienced over the past years, the difficulties of some hospitals in providing enough clinical experience of the right sort, the lack of recruits with a satisfactory educational standard and the paucity of recruits for nurse tutor training. It reiterated the need to reintroduce a minimum education standard and repeated the findings of reports that many nurses were academically unfit for student nurse training. It made the point that only Britain, Luxembourg and Northern Rhodesia did not require a minimum level for nurses.

In discussing the preliminary examination it reported that many students had no hope of passing this; it was a waste of time and money (as well as disconcerting for the tutors) to try to push these people through. Most of these students would be much better taking pupil nurse training and would make much better nurses at that level. Many people considered that the examination was out of date as it militated against patient centred teaching. They thought that a system of continuous assessment followed by a more comprehensive final examination would be preferable.

Some people still felt, as the Wood working party had, that a single portal of entry was preferable and that training should last two years with a third year of supervised practice before registration. Against this opinion was the problem of mixed abilities and the probable frustration of the more able students. Many of the best training hospitals would resist this model and, in addition, there was the problem of winning international recognition for British nurse training.

The ad hoc committee considered that a two-tier system would be preferable with more pupil nurses and fewer student nurses.

For the future, the committee wanted to see a raised standard for both registered and enrolled nurses, better selection and guidance into the two forms of training and better preparation for service in any field. In order to achieve these, the committee proposed to revise the existing conditions of approval of hospitals, raise the minimum standard of entry, effect a reduction in the number (but an increase in the size) of schools, make better educational use of the first eight weeks of preliminary training, look at the possible elimination of the preliminary examination and try to have more pupil nurse schools. Given these aspirations, they set out their minimum conditions for approval of training hospitals in their second paper.

Paper B set the minimum number of beds at 300 in addition to provision of necessary departments. There should be adequate clinical experience, which the paper described; there should be an approved curriculum of training and clinical instruction; there should be at least one registered nurse tutor who should have enough assistant tutors and clinical instructors. The ratio of tutors to students should not be below 1:50. Amongst the other provisions, the committee stipulated that the school should have no fewer than 100 students with an annual intake of 35–40.

The GNC approved the report and sent it to the Association of HMCs, the RCN, Ministry of Health and area nurse training committees.[35]

The tone of this paper was remarkably firm and gave opinions and clear indications which had not been evident in previous GNC reports.

The paper put forward a model for training which was to shape nurse education for many years to come, possibly until the new model put out by the United Kingdom Central Council for Nursing, Midwifery and Health Visiting during 1982. It is doubtful, however, if the GNC ever fully understood or appreciated the full implications of the changes it was proposing. It is fairly clear, too, that neither the professional organisations nor most of the nurses themselves understood what the model would effect. They saw only the explicit changes that the ad hoc committee proposed and failed to perceive the implicit changes in their implications. Once again, too, the profession took each separate proposal and debated it as a discrete matter: they failed to treat the proposals as a rational, integrated package. This was, and appears still to be, the only way in which nurses were able to deal with policy making.

Taken as a model for the future, the paper proposed a two-tier (or three-tier if nursing auxiliaries were included) system of nursing. The SRNs would be the leaders of a team – the 'officers' suggested by the Horder report – and the SEANs would be the 'other ranks'. This would have restructured the nursing service as well as nurse education. If it had been implemented, it would have been a more economical use of nursing and educational resources and would have opened out a career structure for clinical nurses, which was lacking at the time. It could also have developed a leadership for the profession which did not become available until the implementation of the Salmon report.[45]

The paper depended heavily on the reintroduction of a minimum educational standard for student nurses. Whilst this was missing, there was no reason for recruits to elect for pupil nurse training which lacked prestige, since they could just as well take student nurse training. SEANs had a very limited career structure but SRNs could progress through the hierarchy if they so wished.

The paper also had four major deficiencies. There was no clear distinction in the training standards between pupil nurses and student nurses. Even given the return of an educational test, the theoretical (or academic) training of student nurses was considered to be necessary only in so far as might be required for them to learn procedures. The profession persisted in its anti-education sentiments and in its insistence that nurse training had to be practically based.

There was no clear differentiation between the role and function of the SRN and the SEAN. Since the ad hoc committee had failed to perceive the implications of its proposals, they failed to make this distinction and to work through the significance of their ideas.

The paper implied a new service structure but this was not made explicit. If there were to be officers and other ranks, there would have to be some form of team nursing and the hospital authorities would have to be involved in the reorganisation of their nursing structure. Failing this, SRNs and SEANs would lack recognisable roles and hospital authorities could employ either level as they preferred. In fact this happened and later investigations into nursing were unable to determine any difference between the work or skills of SRNs and SEANs.[46]

Lastly, the paper described two distinct levels of nurses (which already existed) but failed to discuss the possibilities of the SEAN moving up to the SRN level. It also failed to deal with the professional development of SRNs for specialist work or, even, with building on their basic training. The nursing organisations were still stuck in the groove which believed that the SRN qualification provided the basis for all nursing with one or two notable exceptions. In other words, there was an element of stasis in the model for both the SEAN and the SRN; instead of visualising these qualifications as the starting point for further training and development, the ad hoc committee saw them as the final goal.

There was general approval for the proposals: the ANTCs seemed to like them as did the RCN. The College would have preferred a higher educational requirement than the two 'O' levels specified by the paper.

The Ministry agreed with the plans to cut down on student nurse schools and increase those for pupil nurses; they also agreed with a revision of the system of training but they would not agree to a minimum educational level until the conditions of approval (Paper B) had been completed.

The GNC and the RCN pointed out that the whole scheme depended on the educational entry requirements and could not work without it. The Ministry would not budge.

The Education and Examination Committee therefore proposed

that the test should be applied from 1 January 1959 but that, for two years after, schools need not reject candidates purely on the results of the test. Hospitals and schools were notified of this. The committee also proposed that the revised conditions of approval should be effective from 1 January 1962 for existing schools. It wrote to the Minister, quite firmly, advising him that the GNC 'intended' to enforce the test (as an alternative to two 'O' level results) and hoped that he would 'assist' them by circulating hospital authorities at the same time as the GNC published its plans.[47]

In December, the Council heard that the Minister had agreed to the GNC intentions but wished first to discuss them with the hospital authorities.[48]

The Ministry and regional authorities met together to discuss the training proposals in January 1959 but no report of their discussions is yet available. There had been a report from the National Consultative Council on Recruitment of Nurses and Midwives late in 1959 which confirmed that an important factor in student wastage was the educational unsuitability of the candidates.[49] This report may well have helped the Minister in these discussions. There was no further movement until June. In July, the Minister finally confirmed that he would allow the test to be reintroduced with effect from 1 July 1962. In September, Council received a post scriptum from the Ministry to say that the educational standard would only apply to general students: no standard would be applicable to mental nursing students. There is some evidence in Council's records to make it seem possible that the Minister had reneged on the agreement which the GNC had always intended for all students.[50]

The statutory instrument was laid before Parliament in April 1960 and in spite of a complaint that it did not include mental nurses, it was successfully carried.

Some late findings of the voluntary use of the test were reported to the GNC in July 1960:

Grade	Score	% completing	% discontinuing
A	113–167	67.9	25.9
B	92–112	64.2	31.0
C	61– 91	59.4	33.7
D	41– 60	38.6	50.3
E	40 or less	33.3	59.5

The Education and Examination Committee wanted to set the critical score as high as possible but feared that by being too ambitious they might risk the compulsory implementation of the test which could still not be imposed until 1962. They agreed to make a middle D (a score of 50) the cut-off point on the understanding that this minimum could be raised later and that hospitals would be free to make their own levels higher if they so chose.

Another consideration swayed them: all nursing groups were very disappointed that the mental nurses could not be included in this new rule. They felt that their status would once again be depressed, that the level of their training must suffer and that a minimum entrance level would stimulate recruitment in both numbers and quality: all the studies had demonstrated this in the general field. It was remarkable that the hospitals who set the higher selection criteria had the least trouble in recruitment. If, therefore, the GNC criteria were not too high, the mental hospital authorities might be more easily persuaded to adopt them in the future.[51]

In fact, some mental hospitals were already using the test voluntarily and in 1961 the GNC made a survey of their results. A questionnaire was sent to 119 hospitals recruiting female staff and 117 returns were received. Eighty hospitals used the test and some others used it partially. Nine others used another type of test, most requiring a higher level than that of the GNC.

One hundred and twenty hospitals recruiting male staff were also surveyed and 116 replies were received. Seventy-five used the test; many others used another type of test or used the test as a part of the selection procedure. Most required a higher score than the GNC minimum. A similar picture was presented by hospitals for the mentally deficient. On the basis of this information, the GNC decided to make another approach to the Minister.[52]

The Minister was adamant that he could not allow any educational standard in the mental field until an alternative training was available for enrolled nurses. It was not until 1964 that the GNC was finally permitted to widen training for the roll to include pupil nurse schools in mental hospitals. In the same year the minimum educational standard for mental nurse recruits was promulgated to take effect from 1 January 1966.

There remained the matter of examinations. In some years there had been complaints about these in terms of their content and their marking. Their questions had been criticised as being too medically oriented. 'Give the signs and symptoms of a peptic ulcer', or 'Outline the treatment that might be prescribed for a patient suffering from a peptic ulcer'. Doctors who helped to mark the papers considered that a nurse's understanding in these matters must be too superficial to be of any use. Nurses marking the papers were sometimes criticised as being out of date in their knowledge. Other nurses considered that examinations should test nursing rather than medical knowledge. A further problem had arisen because of the time that was needed to mark the essay-type answers and the disparity between the many examiners' standards.

Miss Houghton, the GNC education officer, retired at the end of 1959 and was asked to stay on to undertake a study into the method of examining student nurses and the syllabus of training.

In September 1960, an experimental use of objective tests, with some additional conditions, was discussed and in 1962 changes in the final general examination were introduced.

The new syllabus was prepared during 1960 and 1961. It anticipated the forthcoming changes in conditions of approval of training schools and the reinstitution of a minimum educational standard and was introduced experimentally in 1962.[53]

In the meantime, many nurses, including the RCN, were thinking that nurse education was in a mess and needed a fundamental change. The new syllabus and examinations could only make minor improvements but would not resolve the growing problem of the respective roles of the SRN and SEN.[54] In 1959, the College set up a working party on nurse education to prepare a fresh policy for nurse training.

The College had reviewed existing training schemes in all their diversity and found it difficult to give precise meanings to terms such as 'basic training', 'integrated training', and 'comprehensive training' as these varied from one school to another. They thought that there was a need for a better level of registration in all parts of the register and for a more discriminating selection of candidates. They also considered that there would be a need for one common first level training with further specialist training, but they felt that other options should be considered.

The current system of specialist training was not sufficiently flexible to allow a response to rapid advances in medical and scientific knowledge or changing patterns of disease and need.[55] The form taken by current specialist training did not allow much mobility and overlap between areas; much of it was not under professional control and, often, the several trainings seemed to duplicate or repeat elements already included in the basic training. The College considered that a system should be devised in which blocks of training could be built on each other.

There must also, the College thought, be a better understanding of how the SEN and SRN could work together as a team rather than as alternative forms of nurses.

After a certain amount of work by the working party, Council decided that the College should set up a prestigious, multi-disciplinary committee along the lines of the Horder committee. In 1961 they were able to announce that Sir Harry Platt, emeritus professor of orthopaedic surgery at the University of Manchester had agreed to be the chairman of the committee on nurse education. The first meeting of the Platt committee was in February 1962 and the Platt report was published in 1964.

For thirty years the Ministry of Health blocked the profession's attempts to revive a minimum education standard for nurse recruits. In the early days one might have sympathised with the common sense view that it would depress recruitment. But the strength of this opinion was diminished and exposed by research findings and we need to ask what other reasons there may have been for the Government's intransigence.

It will have been noticed that the problem was interwoven with other considerations. After the period covered by this study, it became clear to some people that a resolution of the problem of educational standards would dispel the other factors: they were not so much interwoven as dependent. With hindsight, we may understand that the educational standard was the single most influential factor in the history of nursing after the second world war.

Between 1948–1961 there were six Ministers of Health.[56] From 1948 to 1950 the Labour Party was in power; for the remainder of the period the Conservative Party was in power. Their policies for the NHS differed but the nurse staffing situation was always difficult and their treatment of the problem was consistent.

There seem to be four areas that may usefully be discussed: the value attached to nurses, the lack of differentiation between the functions of the SEAN and the SRN, the insistence of the profession that nursing must be rooted in a practical training and the concommitant anti-education ethos expressed by the profession.[57]

Prior to 1948, whilst the form and structure of the new health service were being widely discussed, the nurses were not considered as significant and they were not included in early consultations. It is true that several nursing organisations insisted on offering their opinions but there is little evidence that much notice was taken of them. The 1944 White Paper which set out the Government's plans for the NHS gave a single sentence to nurses: it said that a district nursing service should be available freely to all patients in the community.

In 1948, Aneurin Bevan showed a surprising degree of goodwill towards nurses when he drew up draft proposals for the forthcoming Nurses Bill. He offered them independence for nurse training and suggested a system which would have allowed them control over their own educational affairs. The negative reactions of the profession must have astonished and dismayed him and, after that episode, there was no further sign of the same respect or willingness to give them much rein.[58]

The attitudes of the civil servants are difficult to estimate. What evidence there is shows that they had little respect for nurses and viewed them very much as ward labour. Their possible contribution towards policy making was almost totally discounted.[59] Nurses were not welcome on HMCs and no plans to appoint regional nurses were made in the original RHB staff structure.[60] During the drafting of the 1949 Bill there was an exchange of information between the Ministry and the Treasury. If full student status were to be given – as it was then intended – there would be financial implications.

T J Bligh, a senior officer at the Treasury, wrote:

> ... the effect would be that the hospital domestic staff would have to be increased, and that the cost per bed (the over-all cost) would by the amount of the wages for the extra staff be increased ... This seems to be rather a luxury in these days. Instead of learning as they work, the student nurses will merely learn and somebody else will have to do the work which was done by the student nurses before they became students ... I regard the Bill with misgivings.[61]

At one point there was a chance that the Chancellor, on the advice of his senior civil servants, might have vetoed the Bill because of the difficulties of funding more domestic staff and the probable need to pay more trained nurses if the wastage of student nurses were reduced.

Another minute from L L H Thompson, in the Treasury, asked what are the students going to do all day if they are not going to be allowed to do domestic duties?

> Will it be possible for any student nurse to refuse to flick a duster at the bedside table on the ground that this is domestic work from which, by Act of Parliament, she is entirely free?[61]

Aneurin Bevan had a hard fight before he could draw up his draft legislation. When the profession rebuffed him he could understandably have felt rather sore: the civil servants had had the last laugh.

The attitude of the regional and hospital authorities was similar to that of the civil servants.[59] They had the responsibility to staff their wards and the nurses had always been their ward labour. If they saw

116

nurses as being solely the carriers of bedpans and the flickers of dusters, what need was there for an educational standard? If they were willing to recruit students with minimal intelligence, why bother to try for the better educated candidates? The Ministry circular *Nursing and Domestic Staff In Hospitals* (1948) had set the tone and had established the level for nurses. Given enough repetitive training, an imbecile could give out a bedpan as well as a grammar school girl and would probably be more amenable to discipline and poor salaries.

The insistence of nurses that their training must be practical, and their anti-education sentiments, only helped to emphasise the attitudes of the authorities. Whilst the College and the GNC declared the need for a better training, they were at the same time saying that there should not be too much theory. There was little appreciation amongst nurses that theory should form the basis of practical skills: nurses were there to do what they were told, they were not there to think. Nurse training was founded on procedures which could be learned by rote: there was little attempt to teach by principles. When some nurses began to campaign for better educational standards their aim was to achieve a better social status for nurses rather than a better understanding of nursing or higher standards of patient care. For many people, education was for the nurse administrators and teachers rather than the clinical nurses. Whilst nurses talked about practical skills they remained unaware of what these were: skills were for performing tasks rather than for caring for the person of the patient, managing patient care or for communicating.

Given this anti-education sentiment, the emphasis on practical training and the completion of tasks, there was very little that the SRN could do which the SEAN could not do as well. The lack of differentiation between the two grades further emphasised the official attitude that nurses did not need to be educated. If you could teach an uneducated girl in two years what it took three years to teach a better educated girl why bother with School Certificates and 'O' levels? The only reason why student nurses were more sought after than pupil nurses was that the former gave three years of service whilst the latter gave only two years or, later, only one year.

The RCN was perfectly justified in saying that there was lack of definition in terms such as 'basic training' or 'basic nurse'. We have seen earlier that there were many different understandings of the term. Both Wood and Horder used similar expressions to mean first level training for the general nurse. In addition, there was the SEAN who was a basic nurse and also the specialist fever nurses,

117

cripple or orthopaedic nurses, tuberculosis nurses and so on. These were basic nurses without general training, as were the mental nurses. The Briggs report[62] recommended a common core of first level training for all nurses on which could be built modules of further, specialised training. Not all nurses might take the further modules and these would, presumably, constitute the basic nurses. The point to be demonstrated is that the term 'basic nurse' has become clarified as has the term 'specialised training'. This has been possible since the recognition that nursing is more than giving bedpans and flicking dusters and since the understanding that the general nurse must be as much of a specialist (in medical, surgical nursing, and so on) as are the mental, paediatric, district nurses or health visitors.

Once the education test was returned, there was the beginning of a differentiation, at least for selection of recruits.

The profession's insistence that education or intelligence levels were not totally the right objective criteria for selection further muddied the waters. These feelings were obviously influenced largely by Florence Nightingale's antipathy towards examinations for registration and further supported by their anti-education emotions. The matrons wanted to retain control over their recruits and preferred to rely on their own intuition.[5] They overlooked or ignored evidence of their fallibility. Furthermore, many were under considerable pressure from their management committees to fill the available student places. An objective test would have undermined their own positions in all these areas. In fact, even after the imposition of the minimum education level, many nurses continued to complain that education and intelligence were not the critical attributes and that reliability, kindness and motivation were more important. It seemed to them, apparently, that intelligence precluded the more desirable factors or that these more desirable factors were not compatible with education.

It was not until Scott-Wright[63] and Pomeranz[64] reported the results of their research that the profession appeared to abandon subjective criteria and adopt educational criteria as a major measure.

It may be of interest, finally, to show that the employing authorities and the Ministry were mistaken in thinking that an educational standard would deter recruitment. Apart from their contempt of nurses and their lack of interest in the standard of care for patients they ignored the psychology of potential recruits. The minimum education level, when it was finally introduced, offered a certain status to nurse training even though the level was set very low.

The evidence shows that the Government was influenced by the employing authorities and the doctors more than by the nursing profession and research studies. It is quite probable that the politicians were influenced by their civil servants who had consistently tried to restrain any attempts by nurses to develop the profession or to improve working conditions. None of these parties demonstrated any interest in the standard of care received by the patients: their primary concerns were to achieve greater efficiency in the use of financial resources and to nurse their patients as cheaply as possible.

After the introduction of the test more students were recruited and there were fewer withdrawals. The GNC annual report for 1963 reported 'a surge of applicants' and the intakes were only limited by the amount of money available for training. The same reaction was evident after the reintroduction of the education test for mental nurses.[65] The numbers of pupil and enrolled nurses also increased but the ratio of SRN to SEN has not yet been reversed.

There were complaints after 1962 that the education level required of student nurse candidates was not sufficiently high. An increasing number of girls stayed on at school to take 'A' level GCE examinations and many training schools set their criteria much higher than the GNC minimum without prejudicing their intakes.

After 1948 the profession took 14 years to regain any entry standard. The lack of an educational test did untold harm to the occupation and its effects linger on. Many nurses in posts of authority today were the recruits of the days of free entry. There remains an anti-education ethos and graduate nurses are still regarded with suspicion and considered to be more suitable for administration or education in spite of much evidence to the contrary. The status of nursing was also depressed, particularly when nurses were compared with other similar occupations such as teachers and social workers whose vocational training was situated in mainstream education institutions.

Probably, the most serious casualty of the post-war free entry years was the development of nursing itself. Nursing techniques, procedures and regimes continued with very little change even into the 1970s. Whilst other occupations were analysing their own work and premises, nurses were locked into rituals. It is only recently that nurses, too, have been able, and academically prepared, to challenge their own beliefs and sacred cows and to try to introduce much needed changes.

Chapter 6/The mental and mental deficiency nurses

Until 1948 the mental institutions were maintained by local authorities under the central authority of the Board of Control. The hospitals were subject to the control of medical superintendents who were responsible for the business side as well as the medical and nursing regimes. Unlike the general hospitals, the medical superintendent had a hierarchical authority over his medical staff who reported to him for their clinical work. The medical superintendent, then, was a very powerful person.

After 1948 the mental institutions were incorporated into the National Health Service and became part of the general health service of the country for the first time. Although the erstwhile stewards of the mental hospitals became known as hospital secretaries and reported to the group secretary, the medical superintendents retained their clinical control and, in most instances, their administrative authority as well.

The first experiment in a mental nursing curriculum is cited by Walk[1] as being in 1854. This was a course of thirty lectures, primarily for officers and attendants, given by W A F Brown at the Crichton Royal Asylum. 'In these lectures', Brown wrote,

> mental disease was viewed in various aspects; the relation of the insane to the community, to their friends and to their custodians were described; treatment, so far as it depends upon external impressions and the influence of sound mind, was discussed; and it was attempted to impart attraction by illustration and narrative and by examples from the actual inmates.

Walk pointed out that this curriculum was chiefly concerned with human relations, and the methods of teaching included visual aids and clinical demonstrations.

This was followed in 1870 by a letter, signed 'Asylum Chaplain', in the *Journal of Mental Science* advocating the systematic training of attendants. The suggestion was that the Medico-Psychological Association[2] should issue a simple catechism embodying what was required of an efficient attendant. Novices were to be tested and, until they passed that test, they were to be known as probationers.[1]

The Medico-Psychological Association published a handbook for mental nurses in 1855. In 1822 Cambell Clark of the District

Asylum, Bothwell, started classes for his nurses and was impressed at the enthusiasm and self-teaching that these generated. In 1886, Shuttleworth, at the Royal Albert Institution, reported that he was giving his staff some elementary training. By 1888 classes were being held at Haywards Heath, Dundee, York and Morpeth.

In 1889, at their annual meeting, the association appointed a committee to consider systematic training, examination and certification of mental nurses. The committee decided that training should extend over two years, to include 'exercises' under head nurses and clinical instruction in the wards by the medical staff, as well as lectures, of which only twelve were compulsory. Examination papers were to be set centrally but their marking and the conduct of the practical examination were left to the medical superintendent and an assessor from another hospital.[1] The scheme was adopted in 1890.

In 1908 the curriculum was extended to three years and it, as well as the fifth edition of the handbook also published in that year, was 'arranged on speciously logical lines'. The syllabus and book both began with anatomy and physiology and progressed through bodily diseases (second year) to psychiatry and mental nursing (third year) 'after almost every other subject had been exhausted'.[1]

Walk pointed out that this 'unusual arrangement' derived from the imitation of the medical students' course in general hospitals at the time when there was considerable enthusiasm for approximating the methods of the asylum to those of the general hospital.[3]

At this period, general trained nurses were brought in as matrons of asylums or, in preparation for promotion, as assistant matrons. In many instances, especially in Scotland, they were given charge of both male and female patients. Female nurses also began to take over the nursing of male patients.

The shortage of male staff during the 1914–18 war led to a still wider use of female nurses and by 1925 there were few hospitals in which females were not nursing some male patients.

The RMPA was closely associated with the nurse registration movement and at the select committee[4] Professor White and Dr Shuttleworth described the nature and scope of its training and examinations. The committee recommended that state registration should be instituted and that the Medico-Psychological Association's examinations should be recognised as qualifying for registration.

When, in 1919, the Registration of Nurses Act was finally passed, a supplementary part of the register was formed of nurses trained in the nursing and care of persons suffering from mental disease.

Nurses of mental defectives were to have a separate division in the mental nurses register, and a special standing committee was set up to consider their registration. It was agreed that the certificate of the Medico-Psychological Association should be accepted for admission to the mental register.

The General Nursing Council was concerned, however, that mental nurses should have the same treatment as their general nurse colleagues and that all registered nurses should share the same standard. It was embarrassing that there should be both a training and a certificate which admitted nurses to the register but over which the council had no control. In 1925 it was announced that the GNC would no longer recognise the RMPA certificate for the purposes of registration but the RMPA announced that it would continue with its training and its own certification.[5] In this way two streams grew up for mental nurses, with those undertaking the GNC training sitting the same preliminary examination and a similar final examination as the general nurses.

The two streams of training were based on different principles and opinions as to their respective merits were divided. On the one hand, there were those who considered that the RMPA was a medical body, dominated by the powerful medical superintendents of the mental institutions. The RMPA training was therefore controlled by the doctors under whom the trained nurses would continue to work.

On the other hand, there were those who argued that the GNC was dominated by general nurses who had little understanding of mental nursing and who were seeking to raise the status of mental nurses by moulding them into a general nursing or physical illness model.

The issue was rather more complicated than this. Under GNC regulations, student nurse training had to be under the control of the matron who was nominated head of the nurse training school. Furthermore, examiners for GNC students had to include nurses, whilst the practical tests had to be examined by nurses alone. Under the RMPA regulations, the examiners were medical superintendents and the school of nursing did not need to be controlled by a trained nurse.

Furthermore, the GNC set provisions for approval of hospitals as training schools which were not matched by the RMPA. Until 1939 the GNC laid down minimum education standards whereas the RMPA did not. Recruitment of student nurses to mental hospitals, under GNC regulations, was therefore more stringent than it was under RMPA regulations.

In 1944 the GNC set up a sub-committee to revise the examination of mental and mental deficiency nurses. In 1945 the GNC and the RMPA met again to discuss the unification of mental nurse training. In 1946 the Athlone sub-committee published its report on mental nursing and recommended the amalgamation of the two training systems.

The RMPA was prepared for the GNC to take over all examination of mental nurses providing there were representatives of these nurses on the Council and providing a section on normal psychology was included in the syllabus. As the preliminary examination incorporated questions relating to bedside nursing which were not suitable for mental nurses, the RMPA asked that alternative questions, open to all candidates, should be included in the future.[6] These proposals were submitted to the Minister of Health.

The Athlone mental sub-committee report proposed one accepted qualifying examination for the mental nurse, the establishment of a mental nurses sub-committee of the GNC and a higher diploma to be established for more advanced training for some mental nurses.

There was considerable agreement between all the institutions on these proposals and in August 1946 the RMPA announced that no further candidates would be accepted for training after 31 December 1946. Those holding the RMPA final certificates would be entered on the appropriate parts of the GNC register, and the GNC would, in future, be responsible for approving those schools of nursing previously approved by the Association. The final date for applications from holders of the RMPA certificate to be placed on the GNC register was eventually set as 31 March 1952. In over eighty years the RMPA had issued some 48,000 certificates in mental nursing and some 47,000 in mental deficiency nursing.

The Athlone mental sub-committee had proposed, also, that the GNC register should be in three parallel parts for general, mental and mental deficiency nurses and that all registered nurses should be designated SRN with appropriate letters of their specialty in brackets. The sub-committee pronounced itself to be strongly against the introduction of an assistant nurse grade to mental nursing.

This last item is of some interest for two reasons. In the first place, the parent Athlone committee had been responsible for the establishment of the roll of nurses in 1943. The sub-committee went against this idea, not so much because it was opposed to assistant nurses in the general field, but because it considered that the standard of mental nursing at the time was not high enough to allow a second grade below the registered mental nurse. In this it was influenced by the medical superintendents. The sub-committee, in 1946, appeared to have agreed with the Horder reports[7] which had recommended that advanced levels of training should be given to registered nurses to fit them for leadership roles. Hence their recommendation of a training at diploma level for mental nurses.

In the second place, their disfavour of enrolled nurses in the mental field reinforced the mental hospitals' refusal to admit those nurses until the Nurses Act 1964. The sub-committee went further; it proposed that mental hospitals should be staffed only by trained and student nurses.

In its comments on the sub-committee's report the Royal College of Nursing wrote that this last proposal was 'so unlikely of fulfilment as to be beyond the realm of practical politics'. The College considered that all the circumstances which the Athlone sub-committee feared as a result of recognising assistant mental nurses were already present: the need was to regulate the position by recognising assistant nurses in mental hospitals and by restricting recruitment to mental nurse training schools to suitable candidates.[8]

The Nurses Act 1949 made provision for the establishment of a Mental Nurses Committee of the GNC which was to be responsible for their training and registration. It was to consist of twelve persons: six appointed by council, two elected by registered mental nurses, four appointed by the Minister. The Council itself was also reconstituted and the first schedule of the Act made provision for two places to be reserved for mental nurses (one male and one female) elected by registered mental nurses.

Post-war developments in nursing were substantially delayed pending the passage of the Nurses Act 1949, and the RMPA felt obliged to write to the GNC, in August of that year, to express its concern at the situation in mental nursing. Recruitment was almost at a standstill and most nursing fell to untrained personnel; there was a serious shortage of mental nurses qualified to take senior posts and the association anticipated a dangerous position developing in the future.[9] There was an estimated shortage of 25 per cent to 50 per cent of trained mental nurses and at times orderlies had to take over from them. The association felt that there was, by then, a need for some sort of 'sub-nurse' who could receive a form of training without the need to sit examinations. Training for mental nurses needed to be improved, as did their salaries. They recommended that mental nurses should be encouraged to accept a secondment for general training and that general nurses should be persuaded to take mental nurse training.

The GNC responded by agreeing that there was a grave shortage of mental nurses as well as suitable candidates for promotion. Council also agreed that a second grade was needed in mental nursing but explained that mental hospital authorities had vetoed the grade of assistant nurse: if the authorities had changed their minds they should say so. Council could not accept the association's ideas for a 'sub-nurse' as, according to statutory restrictions, someone was either a nurse or not a nurse. Council confirmed that every effort was being made to encourage the hospital authorities to improve their training standards in order to attract and keep student nurses and that the GNC requirement for the establishment of preliminary training schools was to come into effect in January 1950. They disclaimed any capacity to influence salary matters which were the province of the Whitley Council and were currently under discussion; they did, they said, encourage secondments, and general nurses were allowed a reduction of one year if they undertook mental nurse training. The GNC felt that the most effective means of encouraging recruitment was to raise the standards of mental nursing.[10]

In fact, the Ministry of Health was concerned at the shortage of mental nurses as well as all other categories of nurses. It reported gross overcrowding in the mental hospitals and, paradoxically, many beds which could not be used for the lack of nurses. Bed space of a recognised standard in 1948 was for 55,590 male and 69,121 female patients but the number of patients actually in residence was 56,372 males and 75,097 females. This represented overcrowding to the extent of 8.1 per cent on the male side and 17.1 per cent on the female side.[11] This picture, together with the shortage of nurses continued until about 1957 when recruitment of mental nurses began to pick up.

The shortage of nurses was exacerbated by compulsory national service for all males, including male nurses. Most male student nurses were eligible for deferment of their call-up until they had completed their training but many enjoyed the better pay and working conditions which they experienced in the services and were reluctant to return to mental nursing. The salaries of male nurses were augmented by family allowances but, even so, these were too low for most males to be able to keep their families at anything much above subsistence level. At the end of their national service many male nurses preferred to find alternative work, usually at better rates of pay and, certainly, with shorter hours. There was, therefore, a particular shortage of trained male nurses.

By 1950–51 the approval given by the GNC to former RMPA

training schools was coming to an end. Many of these hospitals declined to accept the conditions set by Council for re-approval and their schools were faced with closure. In some instances conditional approval for one year was given whilst negotiations continued.

The shortage of mental nurses and of students for mental training became critical. The slow rise of student nurses and trained staffs in other fields was not reflected in the mental field where over-crowding of patients continued and sometimes increased. In 1953 it became 11.6 per cent on the male side and 19.1 per cent on the female side. The patient/nurse ratio in the mental hospitals was 6.7 : 1 and in the mental deficiency hospitals it was 6.9 : 1.[11]

The Ministry of Health urged a speedier discharge rate for patients but found that this policy was blocked by the large numbers of psychogeriatric cases and mental defectives. The Ministry had also become aware of the mismatch between the training of mental nurses (which was geared to custodial care) and the more progressive, therapeutic regimes quickly introduced to the mental hospitals after the war. Although more nurses and students were urgently needed, the poor physical conditions in the hospitals were a deterrent. The Ministry earmarked an extra one million pounds for these hospitals[11] and asked the Standing Mental Health Advisory Committee to investigate the training of mental nurses.

The standing committee's report[12] found that the need for a double qualification for promotion to senior posts detracted from the career prospects of many nurses, especially males, and gave the appearance that mental nursing suffered from an inferior status. There was no need for a complete revision of the training syllabus but they recommended that the course should be broadened by the inclusion of three months' secondment of all students to a general hospital. The Standing Nursing Advisory Committee agreed with the report but went further and recommended more facilities for secondment of general nurses to mental hospitals, the provision of administrative courses for mental nurses who might wish to take senior posts and the institution of experimental schemes of training which would combine both general and mental nurse training.[13]

The Royal College of Nursing was clearly dismayed by the report. Council concluded that it was more directed towards the recruitment of labour than the improvement of training. They considered that the report was out of date in its concepts and understanding of modern needs and that it had neglected to take account of trends in psychiatric medicine. Council complained of the poor buildings and amenities available to mental institutions and reiterated the observations made by the Horder committee, relative to mental nursing

126

staff and matrons, who lacked 'the professional strength and solidarity which have been developed in other branches of nursing'.[14] Council considered that many problems in nursing could be laid at the feet of the autocratic medical superintendents: too much emphasis was placed on economy, the training of nurses was poor and there was too little professional development of the staff. Too many uneducated recruits had been imported from Ireland who were untrainable and they thought that the 80 per cent wastage rate of students was a consequence of this policy.

The College therefore reiterated its policy for mental nurses which included the need for better selection of student nurses, a revised curriculum of training, the recruitment and training of assistant nurses, a better use made of registered mental nurses by the employment of more domestic staff and better working conditions. The College also considered that the long-stay cases should be separately accommodated, away from the acute cases.[15]

After receiving the standing committee's report the Minister issued circular RHB(53)4 without any consultation with the nursing organisations. In this circular he asked hospital authorities to consider the immediate need to recruit more nursing assistants who should have a 'systematic training'. There should be more careful selection of student nurses in order to reduce wastage and consideration should be given to removing the requirement for double qualifications before promotion.

In its overall review of mental nursing the Ministry also examined what part salaries played in the shortage. It soon decided that the current salary claim for mental nurses should be dealt with in such a way as 'to make improvements as economically as possible at the points where improvements are likely to do most good'. These included rises for nursing assistants and student nurses. In the case of the latter, the Ministry proposed to the Whitley Council that the basic allowances should be left unchanged but that proficiency allowances, payable after successful completion of both the preliminary and final examinations, should be enhanced.[16]

The Ministry considered that no case could be made to improve the pay of qualified staff and that there was no evidence that the current salaries were a cause of loss of staff after they had qualified. They had found that the ratio of trained nurses to untrained nurses was higher in the mental than in the general field. They therefore advised that the mental hospital authorities should take the same action as had been taken in the general field: to engage 'pairs of hands' to relieve the nurses and enable students to be properly trained. They further emphasised that there was a need for a considerable number of staff trained to a lower standard than that of the registered nurse.[16]

In the end, the salary claim for mental nurses went to arbitration. In putting its case to the industrial court, the Management Side pleaded that there was no advantage in giving a general rise to the students since this would precipitate a flood of unsuitable applicants. The Management Side considered that there was no case, either, for an increase in the pay of trained nurses. If the Staff Side claim for a lead in pay for all mental nurses were allowed, this would give a lead to senior nurses for the first time. The Management Side did not consider that increased salaries would profit the service nor would it help in maintaining the levels of trained nurses. Salaries for senior nurses had reached parity with their equivalents in the general field but their superannuation conditions were more favourable since mental nurses could retire at an earlier age.

The industrial court eventually awarded increases in salaries to all grades of trained nurses.

The GNC was also concerned at the staffing situation in the mental hospitals and was most aggrieved by the lack of consultation before publication of RHB(53)4. The shortage of recruits and the indifferent training was, the GNC felt, exacerbated by a shortage of qualified tutors. One of the problems in this respect was that mental nurses could not return to the field as tutors after their tutor training without losing out in their superannuation benefits and earlier retirement age since they were no longer classified as mental nurses or mental health officers.

The GNC asked the Minister, in 1950, to rectify this position in order to encourage an improved supply of trained tutors.

The GNC had also taken steps to encourage the secondment of student nurses to mental hospitals and the establishment of both post-registration and combined training schemes.

When they protested to the Minister, Iain MacLeod, about the publication of the circular in 1953, they were advised that he did not see that it had anything to do with them.

The GNC, however, was anxious that the increased use of untrained staff would dilute the ratios of trained nurses and, in this way, make approval of hospitals for training purposes that much more difficult. Needless to say, a reduced proportion of trained nurses would also deleteriously affect the training and supervision of student nurses.

Another clause in the circular also concerned the GNC. In seeking to make the selection of student nurses more stringent, the circular had made no mention of steering the less acceptable candidates into an alternative training. The GNC would have liked to set up enrolled nurse courses in the mental field but the hospital authorities remained adamantly opposed to this. As a consolation, the GNC forwarded a suggested scheme of training for the nursing assistants.[17]

There was little doubt that the anxiety felt by the GNC and the RCN for the quality of training was substantiated. In 1952 the Oxford Area Nurse Training Committee had made a study of the recruitment and training of mental nurses in their region and reported 'that student nurse training in the majority of mental hospitals had been merely a token affair'.[18] The Mental Nurses committee (of the GNC) considered that one of the chief reasons for the wastage of student nurses in the mental field was the unsuitable level of candidates and, until a minimum educational standard for entry could be re-established, the wastage would continue.[18]

Indeed, the situation continued to deteriorate and the numbers of students declined.[19]

Numbers in training at:	Mental hospitals	Mental deficiency hospitals
31.3.51	5,083	1,225
31.3.52	4,614	1,161
31.3.53	4,439	1,080
31.3.54	4,299	1,040
31.3.55	4,103	916

A Statement by the Relatives and Visitors Association of Menston Hospital, a mental hospital near Leeds, was published in 1953.[20] This article described the poor conditions in which the patients lived. In one ward of 103 patients there were five lavatories. In some wards there were five rows of beds, and mattresses were laid on the floors at nights. Whereas the hospital was approved for under 1,900 patients, there were currently 2,500; one ward designed for 30 patients housed 112, with beds less than twelve inches apart. On wards in which there should be six nurses, there were only two.

The article continued: the total patient population had increased by 50 in each year since the war; there were growing numbers of mentally ill people requiring admission but a continuing shortage of nurses. Whereas the hospital nursing establishment was 250, there were in post only 94 whole-time and 95 part-time nurses.

A debate in the House of Commons discussed the failure of recruitment of mental nurses. Mr Mellish (Bermondsey) declared that their hours of work and salaries had not kept up with those of other occupations since the war: the salary scales were too long and it took seven years to reach the maximum of a grade. Trained nurses could not afford to keep their families. The nursing profession had to realise that it had to compete with conditions in industry and the rest of the labour market. Advances in the field of mental health could not be exploited because of the shortage of nurses.

Mr Shepherd (Cheadle) found that at one trained nurse for seventeen or eighteen patients staffing levels were extraordinarily poor. He considered that the status of mental nurses had never been raised and a better appreciation of their work might be achieved if more general nurses were made to work for a period in the mental hospitals.

The Parliamentary secretary to the Ministry of Health, Miss Pat Hornsby Smith, explained that the problem had been exacerbated by the rise in the number of patients. Whereas in 1949 there had been 47,040 (with a waiting list of 5,316), in 1953 there were 53,066 patients and 9,300 on waiting lists. It was hoped that the additional £1 million allocated to the mental side would provide an extra 1,200 mental deficiency and 800 mental illness beds. Two other schemes in train would provide a further 800 beds.

She felt that apart from accommodation the main problem was the shortage of beds. In addition to the steps that the GNC was taking, the Ministry of Health had appointed two mental nursing officers and the Whitley Council would have to make nursing salaries more attractive.[21]

Early in 1954 the RCN held one of their nation's nurses conferences, this time in mental nursing. Rather surprisingly, one of the country's more progressive mental nursing matrons, Miss P Loe, of St James' Hospital in Portsmouth, praised RHB(53)4 as both realistic and refreshing. Mr Milne, assistant secretary at the Ministry of Health (who also sat on the GNC) confirmed that policy was against the introduction of assistant nurses in mental hospitals since experience in the general field had shown that there were insufficient candidates.

Dr Sawle Thomas, the regional psychiatrist on the North Eastern Metropolitan Regional Hospital Board, considered that well educated nurses were not required in mental nursing, particularly with the chronic patients. He preferred understanding, sympathetic people to the scientific approach. He, therefore, found the need for an enrolled nurse in preference to the nursing assistant.

Another matron, Miss W Davison, of Moorhaven Hospital, was at pains to demonstrate that the mental nurse was achieving the same status and functions as the general nurse. She described the training as including tasks similar to those of general students, such as recording urinary output, temperature, pulse and respiration, giving daily enemata, tepid sponging etc.

A chief male nurse, Mr P M Lloyd of Rainhill Hospital, evidently did not agree with Miss Davison and thought that mental nurses should not be cast in the same mould as general nurses, nor that the GNC syllabus was suitable for mental nurses. He also thought that enrolled nurses should be trained in the mental field.

Other speakers also complained of the training. Miss B A C Michell of St John's Hospital, Stone, felt that the needs of the service should not over-ride the needs of training. Older staff also needed professional development and, she agreed, the mental nurse was a psychiatric nurse rather than a 'half-way general nurse'.

Mr Keith Newstead, principal tutor at Bracebridge Heath Hospital, Lincoln, asked how anyone could teach students who were forbidden to see their patients' case notes. He, too, complained about the organisation of training which did not allow time for formal classes. He thought that the GNC should be stronger in its control over student training: it made recommendations but did not ensure that these were implemented.[22]

The conference demonstrated a division of opinion. There were those who wanted mental nursing to remain as it was and who seemed to wish to take it nearer to general nursing in function, training and status. On the other hand, others were dissatisfied with the state of things and wished to develop mental nursing into a more up-to-date system of psychiatric nursing, with its own ethos, syllabus of training and identity.[23]

In the meantime, although one matron may have found circular RHB(53)4 refreshing and helpful, nationally it was beginning to backfire. The last salary agreement for mental nurses had produced anomalies which were difficult to remove without producing more discrepancies. The policy, set out in the circular, to employ 'pairs of hands' had succeeded to such an extent that student nurses were leaving to take up positions as nursing assistants at a better salary. Other students were beginning to refuse to do non-nursing duties which they considered were the province of the better paid nursing assistants. The hospitals found it cheaper to employ students than nursing assistants and had, consequently, further lowered their selection standards. In the case of the trained staff, ward sisters were now able to earn more than unqualified tutors, assistant matrons and deputy matrons. The management side was beset with complaints and considered that there should be an immediate review of salaries in order to adjust the anomalies. To add to their difficulties, the Staff Side was demanding enhanced overtime rates of one and a quarter time for the first two hours and, thereafter, one and a half time.[24]

Iain MacLeod wanted more time to experiment with his new policy and did not allow the Management Side's request for a salary review. But, in the meantime, a further problem arose regarding the salaries of senior nurses (matrons and chief male nurses) which were linked with the number of occupied beds in their hospitals. In many progressive hospitals, patients were discharged more quickly to receive care as day patients or in outpatient clinics. This new regime allowed a reduction in the number of occupied beds even though the patients continued to receive treatment from the hospital. Thus, the senior nurses were being financially penalised. One HMC (Mapperley) had written to complain about this anomaly and had proposed that the senior nurses' salaries should more fairly be based on the total number of patients. This proposal was resisted by the RHB (Sheffield).[25]

Shortly after this, the management side received data, collected from hospitals through the country, about nurse leavers. This showed that many students discontinued their training because of educational unsuitability. It also confirmed that the payment of proficiency allowances on which the Minister had pinned his hopes, was not working as he had planned. The Department was still unwilling to increase student nurse, and other, salaries. They proposed, instead, to offer enhanced dependants' allowances (which mostly would have affected the male students) or, alternatively, to give to employing authorities the option of paying third year student nurse rates to all students. The civil servants thought that the advantage of this alternative was that the option could be withdrawn when the emergency had abated. Also, those authorities who might not be suffering from an acute shortage of students need not take up the option.

During the discussion, the chairman (H A Goddard) voiced his opinion that dependants' allowances were a separate issue and should not be treated as part of a salary. Other points that were raised included a discussion on the chances of winning a favourable decision if the matter went to arbitration, the fact that many regional and hospital authorities were urging an increase of salaries, and that a large proportion of senior nurses were due to retire and would have to be replaced. There was also evidence to show no shortage of recruits in those larger hospitals where nurse training was well organised. It was said that nothing less than an extra £100 would enable mental hospitals to compete with industrial wages. Some members thought that the Minister's proposals to give hospital authorities an option to pay all students at the third year rate would remove control from the Whitley Council. The Management

Side thought that the picture drawn by the Staff Side was exaggerated but that 'the present critical situation in the mental field could not be ignored'. Some of the Management Side thought that they should take the Staff Side into their confidence and try to find the right solution without worrying about tactics. Others considered that the only logical solution was to allow an increase in training allowances which would give all mental nurses the same lead over general nurses.[26]

The last opinion was accepted. Although the Management Side persisted in trying to justify their previous stance, that of paying proficiency allowances to students in order to try to encourage them to complete their training, this new decision effectively annulled circular RHB(53)4. The problem of the matrons' and chief male nurses' salaries was not resolved however and dogged the NHS until the implementation of the Salmon structure.

Although the circular may have been nullified as far as the Minister's pay policy was concerned, the policy put forward concerning the training of nursing assistants continued. There was disagreement between the Standing Advisory Committee for Mental Health (in which the medical superintendents had control) and the Standing Advisory Committee for Nurses (SNAC). By 1954 the SNAC changed its mind about the need for enrolled nurses (possibly because its advice in 1953 had been so severely criticised by the nursing organisations) and now advised the Minister that enrolled nurses, trained in the mental field, would be helpful. The Mental Health Committee (SACMH), on the other hand, continued to veto the idea. The Minister therefore asked the Central Health Services Council (CHSC) to investigate the matter. The CHSC found that state enrolled assistant nurses (mental) would have a useful place, but that they could not help in the immediate difficulties since their institution would require legislation,[27] the drawing up of a syllabus of training examinations, and the approval of hospitals for pupil nurse training. The CHSC also repeated the point that the number of pupil nurse recruits in the general field was too small to allow hopes of adequate recruitment in the mental field. The CHSC therefore recommended that nursing auxiliaries (nursing assistants) should receive training under government control for not less than six months. No examination should be set but a certificate of proficiency should be awarded by the HMC and the matron.[28]

The Ministry drew up circular HM(55)49, *Courses for Instruction for Nursing Assistants*, and sent copies to the GNC and the RCN three days before it was due to be published.

This circular had been drawn up by an advisory group of medical and nursing experts under the chairmanship of Dr Sawle Thomas. The training for nursing assistants, which the group proposed, was to be simple and practical and should take not less than six months. No nursing assistant should be compelled to undertake the training and there should be no examination although a certificate might be awarded.

The group proposed that the matron or chief male nurse should organise the training and that nurse tutors and doctors might give the teaching. The course should offer instruction on the simple care of patients, and ward sisters should give clinical training in their wards.

The Mental Nurses Committee of the GNC agreed that some training would be useful but did not like the idea of awarding certificates. They were anxious that these might encourage some abuse of the title 'nurse' by the nursing assistants and employing authorities and thought that the project might detract from the training of nurses since there was already a shortage of nurse tutors. They anticipated that certificated nursing assistants might be used in responsible positions in the wards.

Whilst the nurse members of the GNC were alarmed at the proposals, the non-nurse members, who had been appointed by the Ministry or Privy Council, took a cooler view of the affair. They reminded their nurse colleagues that there was a staffing crisis, that the medical superintendents wanted a lower grade of nurse as long as they were not enrolled nurses. They felt that there was a need for a complete review of mental nurse training to take it away from the general nursing model and make it more oriented to the real needs of mental nursing. They considered that in the short term, a programme of training for the numerous nursing assistants would be helpful and serve a valuable purpose. They considered that the Mental Nurses Committee (and the Enrolled Nurses Committee who had also reacted negatively) had been too emotional in their response.[29]

At a later meeting with the Minister, the GNC told him that the circular had abused the title 'nurse' and that this would mislead the public. In response, the Minister said that he had not meant to mislead anyone but that the employing authorities felt strongly that mental nurses were being too highly trained. The proposed training of assistants would enable student nurse training to be improved.

Further discussion took place and the GNC complained at the lack of consultation before the circular was framed. The Minister said that he had had a great deal of conflicting advice from a number of people: if he had consulted the GNC he might not have been able to take their advice and would have run the risk of upsetting them. The GNC representatives replied, rather sourly, that they were used to his not accepting their advice.[29]

The GNC had, in fact, been working on a new syllabus for mental nurses and, in September 1956, sent a draft to the RCN as well as other interested bodies.

The RCN were mostly in favour of the new approach incorporated in the syllabus. They felt, too, that it would be a suitable base for a shortened general training for mental nurses.[30]

The Minister, Robert Turton, gave his approval to the new syllabus in 1957, on the basis that it was an experimental scheme to last for five years. The documents were circulated in March 1957. A similar review of the mental deficiency syllabus took place later in the same year.

The new syllabus embodied the concept of the mental hospital as a therapeutic community and emphasised the educational principle that learning was most effectively carried out if it was directly related to the practical situation. This required closer liaison between the school and the wards and the formulation of a nursing education committee.

The subsequent success of this syllabus led the way for the revision of the general nursing syllabus in 1962.

In his report the chief medical officer discussed the uncertainty about the role of the mental nurse which had been shown up by the Liverpool RHB study (and one published in 1959 by the Manchester RHB). The new syllabus would include aspects of community health and visits by students to the homes of their patients.[31]

Changes were also being made in the mental hospitals and some improvements could be reported even if over-crowding continued. The Ministry's chief medical officer could begin to boast that there was increasing recognition of the patient as a member of society: that lockers and clothes hangers were being provided for them. Male and female patients were no longer strictly segregated and could meet each other in the day wards and departments; male and female nurses looked after the patients jointly.[31]

In 1958, St Crispin Hospital HMC published a review of their hospital during the first ten years of the National Health Service.[32]

Like many beneficiaries, these committees were at first more than doubtful about their inheritance ... their authority would be curtailed, their place in the service bound by legislation, their pathway paved with ministerial memoranda.

However, time had allowed changes.

135

... old buildings have been modernised, and old fashioned practices have given place to newer methods. The goal we seek no longer seems so far away.

The physician superintendent's report demonstrated an impressive increase in both admissions and discharges:

	Admissions	% Non-certificated	Discharges
1948	280	66	320
1950	282	66	350
1952	417	87	480
1954	579	88	570
1956	672	93	640
1957	824	96	870

In 1953 he reported an epidemic of typhoid and three carriers were discovered amongst the patients. In the same year there had also been a problem with pulmonary tuberculosis to such an extent that a sanatorium had had to be built in 1957.

In 1954 and 1955 there had been outbreaks of Sonne dysentery and 31 female patients had been affected; 1957 had produced an outbreak of scabies in two female wards.

Since 1956, when the allowances had been increased for mental patients' meals, they had been able to improve the diet.

He discussed the progressive extension in the range and variety of treatments which allowed a higher turnover of patients. Improved diagnosis meant that earlier diagnosis and treatment was possible, more treatment could be given and there was better recognition of emotional factors in mental illness and the problems of ageing, all of which increased the work for doctors and nurses. Treatments that were current at St Crispins included psychological and psychotherapeutic sessions, electro-convulsive therapy, insulin coma, electroplexy, tranquillising drugs and a few pre-frontal leucotomies. Malarial and penicillin treatments were used for syphilitic infections of the nervous system. Prolonged narcosis, abreactive techniques and narco-analysis were also used.

The NHS had enabled the hospital to acquire a hairdressing salon for their female patients, a psychiatric social worker, a pathology laboratory, X-Ray department, dental surgery, hospital pharmacy and a chiropody service. Occupational therapy included a library (for patients and staff) as well as art classes, a music group and a patients' social club.

Outpatients' facilities were increased and clinics were also held in neighbouring hospitals.

Retirements and the lack of recruits had made the nursing position increasingly difficult. More nursing assistants had had to be employed and many part-time nursing staff were now in post.

The financial report was also interesting.

Item	1949–50	1951–52	1953–54	1955–56	1957–58
Average number of patients	1411	1360	1231	1230	1132
Total weekly cost per patient	£2.2.9	£3.5.9	£4.12.3	£5.5.9	£7.1.1
National average	—	£3.19.1	£4.10.5	£5.6.6	—
Central administration	£252	£336	£416	£414	£444
Salaries and wages	£116,548	£127,764	£159,239	£182,544	b237,136
Provisions	£33,509	£46,142	£56,177	£56,298	£63,067
Drugs, dressings and equipment	£3,430	£5,537	£6,325	£7,830	£11,987
Maintenance	£4,597	£9,003	£18,747	£26,147	£32,297

Day hospital facilities had been developed in many units quite quickly after the setting up of the NHS. In 1951 there was an early report of one which had been set up because of shortcomings in hospital facilities and in orthodox psychoanalytic treatment. In this particular experiment, a wide variety of patients were accepted for therapeutic treatment oriented towards social psychiatry.[33]

By 1958 it was clear that treatment of mental illness had progressed beyond the provisions of existing mental health laws and the recommendations of the Royal Commission[34] very quickly resulted in the Mental Health Act 1959. The Ministry of Health annual report for 1959 called it

> ... a major event in the history of the health services in England and Wales. It completes the revision of the mental health laws which was started by the National Health Service Act 1946.[35]

The 1946 Act had repealed the Lunacy and Mental Treatments Acts 1890–1930 and the Mental Deficiency Acts 1913–38 relating to the administration of hospital and community services for mental patients. Since 1948 these services had been part of the NHS. The new Act completed the process by repealing the remainder of the two early Acts, the parts which dealt with certification and compulsory detention and other special provisions that applied only to mental patients over and above the NHS Acts.[35] In particular the new Act coincided with important developments in the general pattern of hospital and local authority services, particularly the shift of emphasis to services for patients living outside hospital.

The movement to community care, which had taken place since 1948, mirrored the growing acceptance by doctors that, for many patients, treatment was likely to be more effective if their links with their own home environment could be kept intact. There was an increasing trend to providing treatment on a domiciliary basis, or through day hospitals and outpatient departments. There were, therefore, more discharges and a consequential need for an expansion of all forms of community services, residential homes, training and occupational services, and so on.

In future, the Minister anticipated that general hospitals would provide facilities for screening all types of mental illness and for the active treatment of short-stay patients. Hospitals for the medium stay and psychogeriatric patients would have more contact with the general hospitals and the community; the elderly might be rehabilitated preparatory to returning to the community, including local authority residential homes.

The new Act also dissolved the Board of Control whose duties were assumed by the NHS.

The new direction in mental health, given statutory recognition by the 1959 Act, made it all the more important that both the standards and numbers of mental nurses should be enhanced. In spite of all the rhetoric and national recruitment drives for these nurses, the numbers of trained nurses in 1959 were not much more than they had been in 1949.[36] There had, however, been an increase in the number of student nurses which brought the figures up to something only just above the 1949 statistics but which represented a significant rise over those of the intervening years. In 1959 the Minister finally gave in to the professional institutions and authorised the re-institution of a minimum education standard for general nurses only. He excluded mental nurse recruits from this concession in spite of strong protests from both the GNC and the RCN.

After the re-introduction of the education standard, figures for general student nurses and pass rates for the final examinations made a steady climb upwards. The figures for mental nurses did not show an equivalent improvement until after 1964 when the Minister authorised the imposition of the minimum education standard for mental nurses.

The lack of a minimum education level for mental nurses (they became more generally known as psychiatric nurses after the 1959 Act which altered the designation of mentally ill patients) made the success of any scheme to train enrolled nurses problematic. It was not until the Nurses Act 1964 that the GNC was empowered 'to make Rules for the Enrolment of persons experienced in psychiatric nursing . . . '

The shortage of psychiatric nurses persisted therefore as did the anomalies in their salary structure. The mental nurses were very dissatisfied with the way they thought their problems were dealt with by the Nurses and Midwives Whitley Council. It was their view that the Whitley Council did not have enough expertise on the Management Side to be able to understand the needs of the mental nursing service. On the Staff Side, a mental nurses staff committee had been set up which tended to formulate and negotiate salary claims and working conditions on behalf of the whole staff committee. There was a preponderance of union officials on the mental nurses staff committee although the professional organisations had a majority on the Staff Side. Relationships between the union and professional representatives were strained and it sometimes seemed that more time was spent in inter-organisation rivalry and politics than on discussion of salaries.

In 1955 it had been agreed that mental nurses with a single qualification should be allowed to take senior posts. The RCN wanted to level up the salaries of female nurses with those of the male nurses and achieved this in 1955. At the same time the mental nurses staff committee was pressing for a complete review of salaries because of the anomalies and problems of overtime rates.

The discontent felt by the mental nurses was so serious that they demanded a separate functional council. There were those on the Management Side who were reported to have some sympathy with these views.[37]

A complete review of the nurses' salary structure was considered by both sides to be needed; the general nurses' salary structure was also in disarray. But whereas the unions wanted a simple review of salary ranges and some reorganisation of grades, the RCN was anxious to have a more profound revision in order to restructure the nursing service. The College had started work on this but the project took longer than they had anticipated. The RCN representatives had, therefore, to stall on the Staff Side and in doing this they generated considerable exasperation from the union representatives.

The changes in the Management Side that were made after the Guillebaud report[38] helped to delay any further negotiation on a separate mental nurses functional committee for the time being.

Whilst the RCN was pursuing its enquiry into staff structures, the Ministry of Health , unknown to the Staff Side, was also working on a similar scheme. Salary negotiations for all nurses between 1957 and the early 1960s became something of a game: each side sought to achieve some sort of satisfactory settlement which would not be so fundamental as to compromise any possible outcome from their several reviews. The mental nurses were not alone in being trapped in their anomalies during the intervening period and the problems were not resolved until the implementation of the Salmon report.[39]

Although the mental nurses were the first to have a revised syllabus of training, the lack of a minimum education requirement mitigated the benefits that could have been anticipated from it.

When the Bradbeer committee on the internal administration of hospitals reported in 1954[40] it found that the control of the medical superintendents of nursing was still pervasive. It recommended that this should be relaxed to become 'discreet and minimal'.

Sofer[41] found a rigid structure with a high degree of formalisation in the relations between the medical, nursing and administrative groups. In the mental hospital he found that the coming of a hospital management committee had made relatively little change in the conduct of authority except that the hospital secretary, as well as the medical superintendent, had become responsible to the HMC. He diagnosed that the old relationships had not changed very much and were out of gear with the new structure: the old roles persisted. He considered that this would continue until new personalities took over the key posts and changed their roles.

For these historical reasons, the matrons and chief male nurses remained under the authority of the powerful medical super-intendents, as, in many instances, did control of nurse training.

Mental nurses continued to suffer from a second class status, and the findings of the working party set up by the RCN in 1958 confirmed this. The working party report[42] discussed the lack of professional development for ward sisters and charge nurses and the need to develop a better therapeutic climate. It considered that mental nurses were falling behind general nurses in the adoption of modern methods both in the clinical areas and in administration.

The medical superintendents still held sway in mental hospitals, and matrons and chief male nurses continued to defer to their authority. Medical and service priorities suppressed the needs of the nurses and students until the introduction of the Salmon hierarchy, when a chief nursing officer was appointed to each hospital group and could manage the mental nurses as part of the total nursing service.

The influence of the medical superintendents in mental nursing and training persisted until after 1946 when the two streams of training were joined under the control of the GNC. The training given under the auspices of the RMPA was criticised as being medically oriented which, to many people, meant that the nurses were prepared for work as assistants to the doctors. The educational standard of the nurses so prepared was never as high as those who took their training under the GNC.

This factor, combined with the isolation of mental hospitals (even after 1948) and the stigma previously attached to mental illness, did much to give mental nurses a second class status.

The mental hospitals had suffered in status from being local authority institutions, and even those nurses who were registered with the GNC were not on the main register but on a supplementary part.

As the hospitals were absorbed into the health services of the country, and as nurse training was slowly freed from medical dominance, mental nurses still failed to win an identity. This was because they veered away from their old roots and fell into the general nursing mould. Their fall from the frying pan into the fire was further enhanced by the requirement for a double qualification as a prerequisite to promotion. Furthermore, the hospital authorities' refusal to allow enrolled nurse training and the critical shortage of nurses in the mental field tended to encourage them to seek relief by secondments to and from the general area. This, too, tended to emphasise their attempts to gain a better status by modelling themselves on the state registered nurses.

The shortage of trained nurses and the authorities' policy of recruiting 'pairs of hands' in the form of nursing assistants led to a continuance of custodial care. Although medical treatment of mental illness had veered towards therapeutic care, the nurses were not able to respond to this change because of staffing and educational policies.

The mental nurses were the first to have a new training syllabus but were not able to exploit this until they were subjected to the minimum education standard. It was only after this that they were able, in any way, to compete with their general nurse colleagues.

The treatment afforded to them by the Ministry of Health – and mirrored by the Management Side of the Whitley Council – was not any different from the treatment given to other nurses. All nurses were seen by the Ministry as 'pairs of hands' with few skills of any importance. The need for nurses was never seen as being of any relevance to the standard of care or the treatment of patients: it was simply a matter of work to be done and cover for the wards.

The mental nurses were, however, important in Whitley Council affairs because of the large numbers of males in the nursing service and because, conventionally, male nurses cared for male patients in

141

the mental hospitals. Whereas female nurses could be paid the lowest possible salary and be relied upon to live in, male nurses had to be paid something near a living wage in order that they could support their families. It was this factor, and the later equal pay policy, that helped to raise salary levels for all nurses at the end of the 1950s.

The mental nurses had traditionally belonged to trade unions and were not so professionally oriented as their female colleagues. Their opportunities for promotion into the higher echelons of the hierarchy were also poor. They were therefore more inclined than most female nurses, or nurses in the general field, to be militant and to look to the industrial world for peer group comparisons in conditions of work and pay. The mental nurses had traditionally been paid for overtime whereas the general nurses had not. If industrial workers received enhanced rates for overtime, the mental nurses could be expected to demand the same treatment. Their expressed dissatisfaction with the workings of the Whitley Council and with their rates of pay was a major factor in achieving salary rises for all nurses at the end of the 1950s. Their receipt of overtime payments was to lead to changes in payments for the general nurses in the mid 1960s.

Bellaby and Oribabor[43] have pointed out that there are two methods of fighting proletarianisation: unionism and professionalisation. The general nurses chose professionalisation but prevented the mental nurses from taking the same option by keeping them out of the professional organisation until 1960 and ascribing to them a second class status. It was not until they were received as members into the RCN that they had an opportunity to acquire a more equal status and to take an active part in the professional affairs of nursing. Even then, however, many mental nurses preferred not to join the association that had for so long spurned them. Those that did join often took with them their militancy and played an active part in unionising the College.

Chapter 7/The district nurses

The 1944 White Paper outlining proposals for a National Health Service[1] mentioned only one section of nurses, the district nurses. The health service was to be a comprehensive one for all, based on the personal relationship between the patient and the doctor. The general practitioner service was to be designed around the concept of group practices and 'a full home nursing service must be one of the aims of the new organisation . . . all who need nursing attention in their own homes will be able to obtain it without charge'.

District nursing has a long and honourable history. The first recorded venture was in 1863 when William Rathbone employed a nurse to visit women in their homes in Liverpool. When the Liverpool Royal Infirmary set up its nurse training school, Rathbone helped with funding on condition that half the nurses should work in the district, supervised by lady superintendents. In the years to come, these lay workers were superseded by 'district matrons', but the ladies continued their work on 'social and reform aspects'.[2] Most of the work of the nurses was described as 'relief' rather than nursing, since it included guidance and provision for debility, malnutrition, destitution, drunkenness, housing problems and bad sanitation.

In 1889, the Queen's Jubilee Fund endowed the Queen Victoria Jubilee Institute for Nurses which later became the Queen's Institute for District Nurses. The institute designed a specific training for district nurses which lasted six months.

During the early part of the twentieth century, the district nurses became more involved with public health which was the responsibility of the local authorities. Many voluntary agencies organised district nursing services and, after 1929, some county authorities also began to establish their own services for infectious diseases. Until 1936 they had no power to provide a comprehensive service although they could provide some financial help for the voluntary societies.

In 1948, therefore, there was a variety of organisations for district nursing: some counties employed their own nurses, some relied on voluntary agencies, some used the Queen's Institute as their agent. Most of the voluntary agencies were affiliated to the Queen's Institute.

Under the National Insurance Act 1911, only workers were eligible for medical assistance; their families could not get financial help for the payment of medical fees or expenses. The district nurses were therefore more heavily concerned with non-workers: the old, women and children. Their work involved the care of infectious diseases, the chronically ill, terminal cases and, often, the daily administration of insulin.

After 1948, every man, woman and child was eligible to register with a general practitioner and to receive his care and treatment 'free' under the National Health Service.

Provision of community nursing services, including the domiciliary midwives and the health visitors as well as the district nurses, became the responsibility of the local health authority, under the control of the medical officer of health. At first, the local health authorities tended to leave the organisation of the district nurses as it had been, but they quickly put forward proposals for the expansion of home nursing services which the Ministry readily approved. Sixty local health authorities (LHA) provided their own nursing service, 56 LHAs used voluntary agencies (including the Queen's Institute) and 13 LHAs used a mixed system. As time went on, however, more local authorities took over provision of their own arrangements and many of the voluntary agencies ceased functioning. Half of the district nurses had no district training and there was no express duty for the LHA to employ district trained nurses.[3]

Training, in the main, was obtained through the auspices of the Queen's Institute. The institute did not, itself, train but provided supervised courses through the affiliated associations or through local authorities which had joined the institute as member organisations. Generally, the duration of training was six months, but a shorter course of four months was allowed to health visitors, midwives or district nurses with 18 months' experience.

The Queen's Institute inspected and approved the training courses and examined the candidates, of whom the successful ones were allowed to have their names placed on the roll of the QIDN. On the other hand, some local authorities preferred to arrange their own training and certification. There was, therefore, no national syllabus and no standard examination and qualification. Not everyone was convinced of the need for special training and some considered that a general nurse training should be sufficient for the work.[3]

During the run-up to nationalisation, the Queen's Institute was very anxious to gain overall control of training and inspection in the new NHS. The Ministry was not in agreement with this because too many other organisations were also involved and they proposed to give the local authorities a statutory responsibility for home nursing services. The Ministry hoped to put district nurse training under some form of central control and inspection.[4]

In 1944, further discussions about district nursing involved the Queen's Institute, the Ranyard Mission and the Royal College of Nursing. It was agreed that a common standard of training was necessary and that a central council of some sort would be helpful. Agreement on training was deferred.[4]

Other matters discussed at this time included the question of payment for the district nursing services. The nursing organisations asked for a national agreement on salaries and conditions of service. This was subsequently settled by the Rushcliffe Committee on Nurses Salaries.

The Queen's Institute continued to press for responsibility for training and stimulated a considerable campaign to lobby the Minister and Members of Parliament.[5] There were, however, enough letters putting forward different views to persuade the Minister to postpone any decision.

The policy of the Queen's Institute was, unfortunately, not consonant with that of the RCN. The College had, in 1944, confirmed its policy that there should be a statutory qualification for district nurses. It also believed that all post-registration qualifications should be controlled by the profession, preferably the General Nursing Council. Council was not happy, therefore, at the decision to establish another central council for district nurses and refused to ratify it.[6]

In 1947, the Minister of Health wrote to inform the organisations that any decision on district nursing would have to wait for the *Report of the Working Party on Recruitment and Training of Nurses*.[7]

The Wood report[7] resulted in the Nurses Act 1949 which legislated for a reconstruction of the GNC which was given certain additional functions. As these did not include post-registration training, the GNC could no longer be considered a suitable body for the training and control of district nurses and the RCN had to reconsider its policy in this matter.

In the meantime, the Queen's Institute was very anxious to find some place for itself in the new central machinery which was being set up for the NHS. They wrote in 1948 to the management side of the Nurses and Midwives Whitley Council asking for representation. This was refused. They wrote again in 1949 but were once again denied a place.[8] Following this, the institute wrote to the Staff Side and claimed a place as representatives of district nurses.[9] This was refused on the grounds that the institute had not been a negotiating body.

When the Central Health Services Council was set up, the general superintendent of the QIDN, Miss E J Merry, was appointed one of the two nurse members.[10] Other Queen's officers were appointed from time to time on the Standing Nursing Advisory Committee.

In the years after 1948, there was a significant change in the work of the hospitals and an increase in the turnover of patients. This meant that patients were discharged to their homes more quickly and returned to the care of their own doctors. The general practitioners were able to recruit families to their lists and their work changed too. More women and children could seek the help of the GPs who were able to refer their patients more easily to hospitals for clinical tests and specialist opinion. These changes allowed patients to be diagnosed and to receive treatment initiated by hospital consultants who then sent them back to their doctors for follow up supervision. Earlier discharge from hospital meant that more acutely ill patients had to be cared for at home by the district staff. The work of the district nurses was, consequently, radically changed and increased.

The local authorities were not able to recruit enough district nurses for a variety of reasons. There was a housing shortage which prevented nurses from moving easily either from one district to another or from hospital work into district nursing. Part-time nurses were increasingly recruited but these were not available in sufficient numbers and often did not live where the posts were available. The hours which the nurses were required to work involved being on call for 24 hours each day, including their nominal day off. Many nurses lacked transport facilities and time was wasted as they waited for public transport or bicycled to their patients. Few had telephones.

In order to meet the shortage of staff and the increasing case loads, LHAs resorted to employing state enrolled assistant nurses (SEANs).

A further cause of the shortage of district nurses was the problem of living on their salary. Nurses' salaries had been based on the assumption that they lived in hospitals. There was slow progress in agreeing the value of the so-called emoluments (board, lodging, uniform and so on) which was eventually set at an artificially low level. Non-resident nurses were paid a gross salary, including the cost of emoluments as a living out allowance.

Since the salaries were low and the non-residence allowance nominal, the total income of district nurses was such that those who did not live in the district nurses' homes could hardly afford to keep themselves. Furthermore, although the hospital nurses had received some increase in their salaries in 1948–49, there had been undue delay in settling those for the community nurses. The Ministry representatives on the Whitley Council had asked the Management Side not to pursue the matter in the face of the Government's wage stabilisation policy. Most of the Management Side was considerably discomfited and concerned about the resultant anomalies and repercussions on recruitment.[11] The local authority representatives, however, supported the Ministry as they were anxious about a following claim from the teachers.

By 1953, some element of stability was becoming apparent in the district nursing services. A slow improvement in housing and salaries encouraged a small rise in the numbers of district nurses. This allowed the Ministry's annual report for 1953 to discuss the general practitioner's function as 'the clinical leader of a domiciliary team'. The report also discussed the need for a growth of preventive and after-care services as an essential part of this new team which would help to reduce the demand for institutional treatment.

The numbers of visits paid by district nurses had increased in 1952 by over 3.5 per cent and in 1953 by over 3.7 per cent compared with 1949; the number of patients visited increased by 8.6 per cent and 9.46 per cent respectively; more children were nursed at home and because of the increasing use of antibiotics, the number of visits for injections had also risen. Some LHAs had started surgeries at the district nurses' homes for ambulant patients, but there was also a complaint that some doctors were taking advantage of the nurses by requiring them to attend at their own surgeries in order to do dressings and other treatments which they would otherwise have done themselves.[12]

The report also disclosed that fewer nurses were willing to live in the district nurses' homes. Local authorities were having to supply accommodation for their staffs, especially the married ones and the male nurses recently introduced to domiciliary work.

The question of training was once again raised. Local authorities had to pay for training courses and some were wondering if this was a worthwhile cost. Where the Queen's Institute functioned as agents, they refused to use nurses without district training. Other local authorities, employing nurses directly, could manage to recruit staff without that financial burden. The Minister, Iain MacLeod, therefore decided to set up a working party to consider the matter. The chairman was Sir Frederick Armer, deputy secretary at the Ministry.

The Queen's Institute gave evidence to the Armer Committee and described its system of training. There were 55 training centres in Great Britain, served by 18 lecture centres. Between 600 and 700

SRNs trained every year and 25 more were trained by the Ranyard Mission, a district nursing association in London. There was a total capacity for 913 students but not all those places were filled owing to the shortage of candidates.

The shortage was due, the institute thought, to the reluctance of nurses to undertake the hard work, long hours and travel in all weather. Furthermore, trained nurses had to take a drop in their salaries during their training, as they received only a training allowance. Once qualified, the district nurse received £35 per annum less than domiciliary midwives or health visitors.

After giving details of the length of training, the institute said that their courses prepared nurses to work 'under the direction of the patient's own doctor'. They took care of sick children, the aged sick, advanced carcinoma patients, incontinent and crippled patients and tubercular patients. They performed skilled nursing procedures such as the irrigation of sinuses and wounds and changed pessaries, in-dwelling catheters and drainage tubes. The district nurse also had to deal with social problems. The institute urged six months' training in order to give the hospital nurse time to learn these skills and to reorient her attitudes from task assignment to dealing with the whole patient.

The cost of training a district nurse was approximately £90, and this was paid by the LHA to the institute.

The institute considered that a national central body was needed for training, examination, certification and control of district nursing. The Queen's Institute should be that body.

They thought also that SEANs should receive district training and could be allowed to work as members of home nursing teams, under the supervision of a Queen's nurse.

The Royal College of Nursing evidence took into consideration the recently broadened syllabus of training for student nurses which included some public health and social medicine content. They did not entirely agree that hospital nurses were still task oriented, as they felt that case assignment, a current favourite topic of discussion, helped the student nurse to view the patient more as a 'whole patient'.

Under the new syllabus, district nurses would need less, rather than more, training in future, and the College did not support the institute in its stand for a six months' course.

They recommended that there should be experimentation in integrated nurse training and that there should be a central body for district nurse training. There should be fewer but bigger training centres located in universities where better teachers and fieldwork could be made available. The course should be educational rather than instructional and fieldwork training should be controlled by the training centre.

Students should be supernumerary to service needs; courses should be evaluated and the training centres, rather than the local authorities, should select students.

Better educational methods should be employed in the courses which should aim to integrate theory with practice. There was a need for a national examination standard.[14]

There was therefore a clash of opinion between the institute and the College, essentially about the length of the training.

Miss E J Merry. general superintendent of the institute, and Dr Struthers, a member of one of the institute's committees, were the representatives on the working party. They were given a free hand by the institute to voice their own opinions but, in fact, they worked very closely with the institute's ad hoc committee which had been set up to deal with the working party. The institute started by wanting one representative body to standardise the training, examining and certificating procedures. Naturally it would have liked to be that body, but it did not think that it would press the point too strongly.

The institute was already concerned that some LHAs would ask for a reduced period of training. They had previous experience of authorities who did not accept the need for specialised training in the work. Furthermore, the LHAs had until then been subsidised by the voluntary associations in the training of district nurses. It was only then, when they were required to meet the full cost of training, that LHAs were demanding a shortened course. The primary goal for the institute was to preserve the standard of district nursing as it had sought to do since its inception.[15]

It became clear that the working party was going to recommend a shorter training of four months, or three months for health visitors and nurses with additional qualifications or a minimum of 18 months' experience in district nursing.* The general executive committee of the Queen's Institute therefore reviewed its policy on training in the light of the growing opinion against them.

The majority of nurses who took their training actually only took the four months' course since most of the district nurse students had extra qualifications. The Queen's training consisted of one part

* This will be referred to as 'four + three months' training'. The institute's training, on a comparable basis, will be referred to as 'six + four training'.

theoretical and two parts practical. Out of a total of 747 hours on the course, 249 hours were spent as a student and the rest involved working with selected cases (selected for a breadth of experience) under supervision.

The lectures were designed to widen the nurse's knowledge and general nurse training and included lectures on public health and social legislation (12), district nursing (8), environmental hygiene (2), special diseases (5) (these included tuberculosis, infectious diseases and other conditions with which student nurses were not familiar), nutrition and diatetics (3), prevention of accidents (1) and one lecture each on health visiting, geriatric nursing, occupational health, occupational therapy and physiotherapy.

The general executive committee did not consider that the newly introduced GNC syllabus would provide an adequate foundation for district nurses without the addition of all those topics. In any case, the nurses trained under the new syllabus would not be coming forward for district nurse training until 1957 or 1958. They did not feel able to change their general policy on the length of training but did agree to a small amount of flexibility.[16]

The following month, they heard that the working party was indeed to come down on a four + three training. Sir Frederick Armer asked the chairman, Mr A H M Wedderburn, to meet him to discuss the possibility of a compromise. Mr Wedderburn was told at this meeting that the working party was probably going to recommend a central executive body which would take over all the institute's functions regarding training. Sir Frederick hoped that the institute could find a compromise.

Mr Wedderburn replied that the institute would be prepared to accept a four months' training and that they would be prepared to provide those courses. Registered nurses without further qualifications would be given their district nurses' certificate but if they wished to be placed on the Queen's roll they would be required to take an additional month's training before beginning the course. Sir Frederick rejected the proposal.[17]

Miss Merry had reported to the general executive committee that only six of the 18 bodies represented on the working party had wanted a shorter period of training and that there had been a considerable amount of 'direction' from the representatives of the Ministry that the training should be reduced. She also reported that she had been put under considerable pressure.

The working party did not want a minority report which Miss Merry and Dr Struthers were on the point of writing. The Ministry officials made it clear that the institute would suffer if they refused to concede the shortened course, but that if they did agree to the four + three formula the LHAs would continue to use them for training.

Miss Merry thought that the working party might agree to an experimental period of three or four years for the four + three course. If the institute agreed this, they had been promised two places on the advisory body. If there was a minority report, the institute would be left out of the central body.

The institute noticed that the working party had conjured the four + three training period out of the air, without a syllabus. They therefore told the Ministry that they would review the four + three formula if it was accompanied by a syllabus.

They also decided to obtain expert opinion on their own syllabus to see if it could be taken in three months without lowering the standard. If it could, the institute would accept a shortened period of training. Mr Wedderburn had asked Sir Frederick why the working party were insisting on a shortened period of training but had not been given a reply.

Three professors of education were consulted from centres spread about the country. Each of them examined the institute's syllabus and each pronounced that it needed more than six + four months to cover properly. One of the academics, Professor Lauwerys, professor of comparative education at the University of London, wrote that the field to be covered was extensive, the skills to be developed were complex and there was a need for a subtle adjustment of attitudes. He did not believe that anything could be left out of the Queen's syllabus and thought that an additional two or three months would be beneficial. He said that there was need to emphasise the psychological and sociological aspect and for time to digest the content of the course. He thought that the working party's proposals to cut the period of practical training and supervised work was wrong.

It is surprising to me that a proposal to shorten the period of training for district nursing should be seriously considered at a time when the general tendency in all professions is to extend the length of training in view of [the] growing complexity and technicality of the knowledge and skills to be applied. The pity of it is that this is being proposed at a time when the extremely high cost of hospitalisation makes it increasingly desirable to extend the amount of home treatment.

To shorten the period of training required for a profession lowers its general social status and prestige. Thereby it adversely affects

151

recruitment ... it will be taken as an evident straw showing that the establishment of the National Health Service leads to a lowering of professional standards.

The general executive committee thought that they should stick to their policy as it was now backed by these experts' views. Unfortunately, their ground was a little bit cut away from them by the London superintendents who, in 1954, had agreed with their London County Council masters that five months was an adequate period for training.[18]

They advised Miss Merry and Dr Struthers to prepare their minority report just in case and agreed that the expert reports should be attached.

In June, Miss Merry told the general executive committee that the working party had refused to allow the attachment of the three expert reports and that there had been some unpleasantness. The working party members had accused the institute's representatives of breach of confidence in showing the report to the academics.[14,19] In fact, Mr Wedderburn had earlier received clearance for this, in a general sort of way, from Sir Frederick.

Negotiations continued between the institute and the Ministry all through the summer of 1956. In April, the RCN asked to meet with representatives of the institute to see if the latter would accept a compromise of four + five (which the institute had already proposed to Sir Frederick and had had rejected). The institute felt that it could not very well enter into discussions with a third party whilst it was negotiating with the Ministry and felt obliged to decline.[20]

During the summer months, the institute prepared a new syllabus to cover five months, still hoping that the Minister would accept a compromise. It had four fewer lectures than the Queen's syllabus and three more than the Armer majority report proposed. Supervised practice and practical demonstrations were also slightly reduced. This syllabus was subsequently rejected by the institute's education sub-committee which reverted to a hard position on the six months' course.[21]

In October, the Minister asked to see representatives of the institute in order that he could announce his decision to the institute's annual meeting, which he was to address, at the end of the month.

He told the Queen's nurses and members on 30 October that he had decided to accept the majority report. The four + three model would be laid down as a minimum standard and authorities could opt for longer training if they wished.

Mr Wedderburn had to give the vote of thanks, which he did politely but very coldly. He told the Minister that

> ... he has indeed sounded the death knell of one of the most cherished ideals of the Queen's Institute ... Our earnest hope was that as in all other branches of the Public Health Service, there should be officially recognised a single and high national qualification for the district nurse.

He considered that there would, from then on, be a grade two certificated district nurse, 'a semi-processed article'.[22]

The majority report[3] discussed whether or not a district nurse needed further training and concluded that she did. The trained district nurse gained an acceptable degree of efficiency more quickly and required less supervision. Nurses needed to learn to adapt hospital techniques to home nursing where, in addition, they were likely to encounter different kinds of illnesses. District nurses needed to have some knowledge of their different and additional responsibilities since they worked on their own; they also needed to know about the various social services that might be available to their patients.

The pattern of training for these nurses would be affected by the new GNC syllabus for student nurses which became compulsory in 1954 and which widened the scope of general nurse training by the inclusion of some aspects of social and public health. The district nurse trainee would, additionally, have to be given some experience in nursing the chronic sick and the elderly, lacking in her general training.

The majority of the working party considered that four months would be a suitable period of training (three months for health visitors) and that there should be a national standard for the examination.

The report also considered that there was no need for a statutory body to control the training. The Queen's Institute and the LHAs should continue to be responsible. A central committee should be set up to issue a syllabus and set examinations. Schemes of training should be sent by the LHAs to the Minister for vetting and the central committee should advise him on these. A national certificate should be issued.

There was, however, disagreement about the length of training, and a minority report was published. The Queen's Institute and the Ranyard nurses were not able to agree to what was, by their standards, a shortened training. They considered that four months was not long enough. Nurses needed an adequate period of supervised

153

experience in order to make certain that the advice they might give to their patients was sound. They needed more time to adjust to working in people's homes, alongside other community workers. The new GNC syllabus was not generous in the amount of public health content (four lectures) – work in hospital was task oriented, they argued, and in the district nursing field was patient orientated. Furthermore, in people's homes there would not always be facilities such as running water, lavatories and drainage that hospital nurses took for granted.[23]

The minority report did not accept the assumption that a shorter training would attract more recruits or that untrained district nurses would more readily take the shorter training. They argued that the shortened training would prejudice the prestige of district nurses in the eyes of their professional colleagues and patients, and the pro forma syllabus, provided in the main report, lacked essential details.

The working party consisted of five Ministry officials (including three nurses), four LHA representatives, five medical officers of health (one was the chairman of the training sub-committee of the Queen's Institute) and three nurses (one RCN, one QIDN, one Ranyard nurse). Of the 17 organisations submitting evidence, nine wanted a one year training, four wanted the candidates to be very experienced SRNs. Details of the 17 organisations wanting a long training are not known. It would be difficult to identify 17 different organisations who were all interested in district nursing. On the evidence that was available for the QIDN campaign organised in 1946 it may be considered possible that these were voluntary agencies in membership with the institute. These agencies would have tended to concur with the actively promulgated advice given to them by their parent institute.

The Ministry and the LHAs had a responsibility for both the financial implications of their recommendations and the management and provision of a service. It is not surprising therefore that they preferred a shorter training on purely service grounds.

The Queen's Institute and the Ranyard nurses, on the other hand, did not have this direct responsibility. Their priorities, therefore, were unmitigated by political considerations and were for the preservation of a standard of nursing. Many of their arguments were sound and in later years the training was fixed at six months. At the time, however, the general trend for all nurse training was to cut it as short as possible.[24]

The district nursing organisations had good reason to be suspicious of another move to cut nurse training, especially in the face of the expert opinion which supported their stand.

In the main, the other nursing organisations and the BMA wanted no change in the training period; the College of General Practitioners wanted a longer period; the Society of Medical Officers of Health, the Association of Hospital Matrons and the employing authorities all wanted a shortened training.

The Public Health Section of the RCN considered that the timing of the report had been unfortunately premature since little account could yet be taken of the new GNC syllabus for general training or of the various experimental courses which had been started for a combined general and district training.

They were also dissatisfied with the composition of the working party which had included too many doctors and only two experienced district nurses. Furthermore, they wanted the membership of the proposed central committee to be more detailed so as to ensure that there would be an adequate number of experienced district nurses. Any SEAN working on the district should be supervised by a state registered nurse and should not be given an area of her own.[25]

Augusta Black, education officer at the Queen's Institute, wrote in *Nursing Times*[26] that the recommendations of the majority report would produce a lower standard of district nurse. The working party had ignored much evidence and she believed that the decision to have a shorter training had been taken prior to examining the evidence rather than as a result of it. The minority group, she claimed, had offered to discuss a compromise period of training but this had not been taken up.

Both reports, she wrote, agreed a syllabus which was similar to that of the Queen's Institute but the shorter period would allow less supervision of the nurse and make the Queen's system of case assignment impossible.

A proposed central body with a four months' course would result in two standards: the Queen's six months' course and the local authorities' four months' courses. She promised that the institute would continue its longer training.

Her article was taken up in the correspondence columns. One writer felt that, under the majority recommendations, nurses would get at least four months' training: most were not getting even that at the time. Nurses, she thought, should not argue about the difference in course length when the patients were so many and the district nurses so few: 'Our first duty is to our patients'.

Another correspondent, J M Akester, thought that Miss Black was confusing training and experience and, because of that, nurses had for too long made their training too lengthy: 'training or education should be the preparation for experience but should not attempt to include it'.[27]

Another article also discussed the question of training time. This writer, Mary Witting, considered that no profession showed such a wide range of ability as did nursing. The range spanned from the 15-year-old school leaver to the School Certificate or GCE girl. Both the four months' and six months' courses were therefore needed. She criticised the Queen's Institute syllabus for having too much repetition: there were doctors and nurses lecturing on the same subject and much overlap with the basic SRN course. She was doubtful if district nurses needed to know anything about public health or social legislation, or about the work of the health visitor, or about the normal infant.[28]

Apart from these few articles and letters, the district nurses were remarkably mute about their own affairs. In the field of the general nurses, it was more usually the sister tutors and matrons who were vocal about their problems. The same grades verbalised for the mental nurses. In the field of health visitors, it was most often the lecturers and tutors, or the medical officers, who spoke out and discussed the future. In the field of the district nurses, there was very little public airing of their problems. There was some discussion in the Public Health Section of the RCN but the tutors and nurses had nothing much to say for themselves.

By this time the Guillebaud report had been published.[29] It hardly mentioned the nursing services but discussed the pros and cons of reorganising the NHS so as to integrate the community services with those of the hospitals. Some people recommended the appointment of statutory *ad hoc* health authorities to ensure that the hospital, family practitioner and home health services were organised in a more efficient and economical way; others considered that this manoeuvre would create another division between the community medical services and the other local authority social services. They considered that this might be as unfortunate as the current divisions in the NHS since it would 'drive a wedge' between the home health services, provided by the LHA, and their welfare services, provided under the National Assistance Act. They proposed, instead, active steps to ensure better cooperation between all services.

The Guillebaud report discussed the LHA services but, again, did not review the community nurses. It did consider that the slow progress in building health centres 'may perhaps be fortunate' since the committee considered that more experimental schemes should be evaluated before further capital investment was made. The report generally found the NHS to be working well and recommended that it should be given more funds in the future.

A minority report signed by E J Maude, discussed the divorce between curative and preventive medicine and considered that the dominant prestige of hospital medicine would lead to the preventive and social aspects 'falling into the background'. He preferred that responsibility for the hospital as well as the community services should be taken by the local authorities who would need to be reorganised beforehand.

This report did nothing for the nurses but did focus more attention on, amongst other things, the community services.

The annual report of the Ministry of Health for 1958[30] celebrated ten years of nationalisation with a review of the health service. In its review of the home nursing service (page 156) it described the changes in the duties of the district nurses and commented that more types of illness were recognised as suitable for nursing at home. More visits were made for giving injections; pre- and post-operative care and preparations for x-ray examinations were given at home. More patients could be discharged earlier, more children could be nursed at home and the care of the aged was more often left to the district nurses.

The nurses more usually preferred to live in their own homes, and local authorities had been able to provide accommodation for them.

Training was mostly afforded through the Queen's Institute, but a few local authorities ran their own schemes. Some authorities still did not recognise any need for special training.

The annual report for 1958 also mentioned that an integrated course for general, district and health visitor training had started at the University of Manchester for candidates possessing the usual university entrance requirements (page 175f).

The recruitment of home nurses had been fairly steady, but many still did not have special training. By 1958, almost all LHAs had taken over responsibility for running their home nursing service which still, largely, gave care to the chronic sick, elderly and children. State enrolled assistant nurses were sometimes employed and had been found very useful. The report made no mention of male nurses, but there was, in fact, a rather slow growth in numbers of these too.[31]

During the previous ten years, the report claimed, there had been an improvement in personal transport facilities, the provision of telephones and of comfortable living accommodation for district nurses. However, there was still a lack of sterilising facilities, and lack of storage space for equipment and record-keeping by district nurses needed further attention. There was almost no provision for the central sterilisation of syringes and dressings.

The Ministry of Health was probably prompted by the Guillebaud report to set up another advisory committee to study the training of district nurses.[32] The chairman was to be D H Ingall and out of 12 members there were to be five nurses, four of whom were district nurses.

The Ingall committee recommended that the model syllabus for four months' training put forward by the Armer committee should be adopted; schemes of training under this syllabus should be submitted for approval to the Minister. There was to be a national committee for district nursing and a panel of assessors set up to examine these schemes and to advise the Minister. Ministry nursing officers should make periodic inspections of the training courses; there were to be both oral and written examinations and a national certificate would be awarded. There was also to be a panel of examiners set up for the use of the training authorities.

In 1960, the RCN heard that the Minister had decided to accept the Ingall committee's recommendations for the training of district nurses. He was planning to set up a panel of advisors and had already appointed a number of members to the National Council for District Nursing. The Public Health Section of the RCN agreed with the proposals.[33]

There was very little change in district nursing after this time until the report of the working party to advise on senior nursing posts in the community, in 1969.[34]

During the period under review, there was evidence that the local authorities were not, generally, either constructive or even very fair with their nursing staffs.

Although salaries were regulated by the Whitley Council, their terms of employment were inferior to those for other local authority officials. The nurses therefore suffered a loss of status compared with welfare workers and teachers.[35] There was little opportunity for the nurses to attend professional conferences, refresher courses or study days; often nurses who were very keen to join these were obliged to take annual or unpaid leave. Few local authorities would second their nurses for administrative or tutor training courses, with the result that trained district nurse tutors were rare. In the same vein, district nurses, who had to pay into local authority superannuation schemes, also suffered. Transfer from one scheme to another was sometimes actually blocked by an LHA so that movement to another authority was either very difficult or involved the need to terminate one scheme and start anew with another. Some authorities who accepted transfers refused to credit the nurse with the full years of service that she had worked.

There were even cases where some LHAs refused to implement Whitley scales of salary and conditions of work. In rare instances, the nurses were paid more, in order to attract staff and to bring their salaries up to the level of staff of equivalent standing. Often the LHAs delayed giving their nurses the improved salaries recently agreed.[35]

The district nurses always felt that they were unfavourably compared with both ward sisters and health visitors; indeed, there was some substance to this as their salaries were less and their training was clearly inferior in length and depth when compared with that of the HV. There was invariably a greater shortage of health visitors than there was of district nurses and LHAs were much more willing to give HVs equal status with social workers.[35]

The local authority nurses were responsible to the medical officer of health who frequently delegated the organisation of the nursing services to an assistant medical officer. In 1959, of 39 local health authorities only 23 had appointed superintendents of district nurses.[36] The nurses had to work through intermediaries therefore and their problems and needs were often interpreted by an officer of another discipline. There was little professional support available to them.

Certainly the nature of their work was perceived as being of less value than that of other nurses: they were considered as generalists performing rather routine tasks in the patients' homes. Many authorities continued to reject the need for special training.

Whereas nursing had, after the Nightingale era, grown up with ladies in charge, by 1948 the district nurses were the only ones who remained subordinate to these voluntary workers. Even after 1948 the ethos of the ladies was retained by the Queen's Institute whose dominant values were the care of the patient and the social bearing of the Queen's nurse. All other nurses had become responsible to senior colleagues or, in fewer cases, to doctors.[37]

In the face of the rationalisation and centralisation which the NHS had introduced to all areas of health care, the Queen's Institute stood out as a voluntary organisation, a paradox in the heyday of nationalisation, and an irritant to the central planners.

The RCN Council accepted the shortened course of training although its own Public Health Section was opposed to it. It accepted a central body for the training and examination of district nurses in contradiction to its own policy of seeking professional control over post-registration training. It accepted the idea that district nurses would require less rather than more training in the future – the sentence of generalism rather than specialism for district nurses. In doing this, it went along with the Ministry of Health and continued to establish its position as the accepted representative body of nurses, the body accepted by the civil servants and the government.

The Queen's Institute opposed the Ministry with rational arguments, supported by expert opinion, insisting on the preservation of standards of training and long-term objectives. It failed to come to terms with the process of centralisation and nationalisation and precipitated its own death knell as a training institution, eventually withdrawing from all training in 1967.[38]

Eventually the district nurses suffered too, since their training fell into the hands of the local authorities who were responsible for organising the service and for whom training was of only secondary importance. Over half of all district nurses lacked specialist training and their generalist status persisted until the Nurses, Midwives and Health Visitors Act 1979 made provision for mandatory training in the future. It will not be until that comes into effect that district nurses can begin to recover their position alongside other branches of nursing.

Chapter 8/The health visitors

Health visiting is concerned with the principles of healthy living, the prevention and detection of ill health and building up families' and individuals' personal resources so that they can better cope with the normal crises of life.[1] Its history is better documented than many other branches of nursing even though there was no statutory body for education and training until 1962.

In fact, the roots of health visiting were not primarily in nursing, since the first recorded visitor in 1862 was 'a respectable working woman' employed by the Salford Ladies Sanitary Reform Association.[2] Later, health visitors were drawn from women doctors, sanitary inspectors, midwives and teachers, as well as nurses, all of whom were considered to have an appropriate background of training for the work.

Although the early health visitors were primarily concerned with sanitation, they became more involved with the maternity and child welfare movement by the 1914–18 war. The London County Council legislated for professional qualifications for their health visitors in 1909, and ten years later, the Ministry of Health prescribed their general professional requirements.

By 1907, there were several alternative training schemes designed both for those with a medical or nursing background and for those without. The Royal Sanitary Institute (later the Royal Society for the Promotion of Health) offered a short course for the former candidates, and both Bedford College for Women and Battersea College ran longer courses of two years for the second type of recruits. The Ministry of Health and Board of Education also ran one year and two year courses after 1919. The longer courses lapsed in 1944.

In 1943, the duties of health visitors were outlined by their training institutions in order to facilitate the formulation of a syllabus. These included maternity and child welfare (M & CW), school medical duties, tuberculosis visiting, control of infectious diseases, social work and caring for the family as a unit.[1]

If the list had not changed noticeably from their earlier duties, the emphasis had. The health visitor was part of the nineteenth century public health movement which, with the improvement of social conditions and the control of infections, was already on the wane.

After 1928, there were two methods of funding the training of health visitors. Some authorities advanced the student's salary for a six months' training. This was repaid during a further six months' service after qualification. Other authorities appointed students as probationary health visitors and paid them 75 per cent of the qualified visitor's salary during a course covering not less than three academic terms. The health visitor was subsequently required to work for the authority for a contractual period of time.[2]

The training of health visitors was different from that of other nurses in two important aspects. Firstly, she was educated in social health and social policy, building upon scientific principles. In contrast to this, other nurses were trained in curative medicine by didactic methods which concentrated on procedures rather than principles.

In the second place, from the earliest days, health visitor education was given in local authority or educational establishments rather than in schools of nursing. Their training therefore had roots in mainstream education.

In 1945, the Royal College of Nursing started a one year full-time course for HV tutors which included educational psychology and teaching methods as well as training school management and professional development. By 1950, practically all HV tutors were qualified and eligible for the roll of HV tutors which the College set up in 1952. This preparation enabled the tutors to take over for themselves the management and planning of their courses, and the teaching of health visitors quickly improved.[1]

In 1948, new regulations made qualifications for all health visitors mandatory, including part-time workers and those employed by voluntary agencies who had previously been exempted.[3] Some exemptions were made for those working in triple duty posts (district nursing, midwifery and health visiting).

The National Health Service Act 1946 gave local health authorities (LHAs) responsibility for providing health visiting services 'for the purpose of giving advice as to the care of young children, persons suffering from illness and expectant or nursing mothers, and as to the measures necessary to prevent the spread of infection'.[4]

In 1948, the Children Act removed from health visitors their responsibility for child life protection and transferred it to social workers.

The work of the health visitor was, therefore, only loosely defined by the NHS Act which was seen to have substantially broadened her sphere of activities. The amalgamation of the mental health services in the main body of the NHS and the creation of care and after-care powers were thought to have further extended her work. The trend of health and welfare activities towards the well-being of the family as a whole, brought the health visitor into contact and, sometimes, conflict with other workers in these fields. These other workers, such as the school attendance officers and the social workers, did not usually have medical backgrounds and, indeed, commonly lacked any form of training.[5] Often their work was as ill-defined as the health visitor's, and there was bound to be some competition.

The health visitor had always formed part of the staff of the medical officer of health and the NHS did not change this traditional organisation. However, whereas previously she had worked almost exclusively with medical officers and had very little contact with general practitioners, the new health service brought a reversal of this pattern.

Prior to 1948, few women and children could afford doctors' bills and relied on advice from the voluntary agencies or local authority services. After 1948, 95 per cent of the population registered with a general practitioner and were able to receive medical care freely. This slowly drew clients away from local authority clinics and made it necessary for health visitors to have more contact with the GPs.

The free availability of GP services also encouraged people to ask advice from their doctors on a host of minor health problems which they had previously taken to their HV. Whereas the doctors were still not much concerned with, nor yet very skilled at, preventive health work, the health visitor lost a convenient opening for the pursuit of her other work.

In half the counties and more than half the county boroughs, some health visitors undertook specialist duties, such as visiting tubercular patients, the aged, chronic sick, mentally ill people or premature babies. Some health visitors specialised in visiting diabetic people, unmarried mothers or children who were attending paediatric clinics.

All HVs were involved in M & CW duties (except the specialists); most did school health and tuberculosis visits. Many counties, especially the rural ones, had combined posts which included midwifery and/or home nursing duties. In the county boroughs, the HVs were more usually involved in infectious diseases, control of venereal diseases, care of aged and infirm persons and after-care. In some counties, the HV visited mentally ill patients, and in most authorities they were involved in providing health education to groups of people and the promotion of immunisation and vaccination programmes. Medical officers of health who were interested in epidemiological studies or other research often used their health visitors as data collectors.

There was obviously a great diversity in the work and role of the

163

health visitor but little evidence of the development of successful working relationships with the general practitioners who did not respond to the approaches of authorities or individual health visitors.[6]

After the war, the social security and housing measures greatly mitigated the living conditions of the poor. The National Insurance Act and the supplementary benefits scheme helped to alleviate the extreme poverty that had characterised the 1930s. The housing programme helped to obliterate many of the slum dwellings and bring more modern amenities to many people living in overcrowded and unsanitary conditions. Infectious diseases had almost been controlled and the newly labelled behavioural diseases were coming to the fore.

But the new social climate, whilst it had wiped out many adverse conditions, brought new problems. The removal of the younger generation to their new homes separated them from their parents and deprived them of parental support. The break-up of communities in the redevelopment areas could not be quickly compensated for by the building of new housing estates. The alienation of the young nuclear families was accompanied by the isolation of the older generation.

Needs in the 1950s became more related to mental health. These new developments were perceived as social problems which health visitors were not trained to cope with. The consequences of unresolved social problems were usually manifested as mental illnesses which the health visitors were not trained to handle. Their clients were better educated and came from a wider social spectrum than hitherto and the new social climate was helping to raise the expectations of the populace.

Health visitors were already fully occupied with mothers and young children, and it is not surprising therefore if they did not go out of their way to confront the new challenges.

It was clear to many, however, that if the new generation of health visitors were not equipped to handle the needs of modern society, their future would be short. Already GPs were taking more interest in mothers and young children. It was not outside the bounds of possibility that health visitors might be squeezed out of a viable function.

Some health visitors could see further significant shifts in the emphasis of their work and many thought that the syllabus of training needed to be broadened. The integration of the mental health services into the NHS and the already visible trend towards more care for these patients in the community would require some psychiatric training.[7] Furthermore, the shift from environmental conditions to concern for the general health of all age groups in the family unit would have to be reflected in a new syllabus.

But whilst the health visitors might have foreseen the need for radical changes in their function and training, they were still under the control of the powerful medical officers of health whose roots were deeply planted in public health. The MOsH were not willing for the health visitors to divorce themselves so entirely from their old role: it had, after all, been the health visitors who had given the personal services whilst the sanitary inspectors had given the environmental service – the twin pillars of the public health movement. If the health visitors moved over to medico-social work, they would be undermining the power base of the medical officers of health.

This consciousness of change was more evident in the health visitors than in other fields of nursing. They responded more quickly to the new social climate but they had little support from their colleagues in nursing and the public health field.

The majority of nurses were hospital based and steeped in the glamour of caring for sick patients. They were inclined, therefore, to discount the work and skills of the health visitors. They were, in any case, preoccupied with restructuring nurse education in hospitals. Since the basic nurse training was the foundation on which health visitor education had to build, this was also of concern to the public health nurses, but the small numbers of health visitors were not sufficiently important to the hospital nurses to encourage them to give any weight to the needs of health visitor training.

The health visitor had always been on the staff of the medical officers of health, rooted in the public health mould. The medical officers of health were primarily concerned with the environment and, therefore, the physical aspects of disease. They were slow to convert to social aspects of health and many failed to recognise the changing function of the health visitor.

Consciousness of change was mostly felt by health visitor tutors, many of whom were employed in educational institutions. Service health visitors were dominated by the medical officers of health and most shared their environmental values. Although health visitors acquired superintendents to manage their service more quickly than district nurses, the superintendents often retained their public health roots. In any case, the superintendents were answerable to the medical officers of health and did not attend the local authority health committee meetings.

Before health visitors could reorientate their functions and training, therefore, they had to free themselves from the dominance of the medical officers of health.

The problems of the health visitors fell into several categories. First, there was the question of what was the job of the health visitor. What direction should she take in the future? Next, there was the need to revise the training syllabus in order to meet the needs of her job. Thirdly, there was the problem of recruitment.

With regard to the work of the health visitor, there appeared to be three camps. One camp wanted her to be a general-purpose visitor, much as she had always been. She should continue to care for mothers and young children, do health education and advise on home safety, and help mothers to optimise their home conditions and raise their young children. These were the traditional environmentalists and the main proponents were the medical officers of health and the Royal Sanitary Institute.

Secondly, there were those who wanted the health visitors to turn more towards social medicine: to provide a follow-up service for patients newly discharged from hospital and a care and after-care service as loosely described by the NHS Act, and to continue to be responsible for building or encouraging positive health.[7]

Thirdly, there were the more ambitious people who wanted one general-purpose worker, a medico-social worker who should combine the work of the health visitor and the social worker.

The proponents of this new concept were principally the health visitor tutors, especially those working with university-based courses.

At a conference of the Royal Sanitary Institute, Patricia O'Connell, tutor to the HV course at Southampton University, advocated that the medico-social needs of people should be met by one basic medico-social worker, a new-style health visitor.[8] She anticipated that this worker would take an integrated general nurse/health visitor course based at a university.

Mary Davies, tutor to the health visitor course at the Welsh National School of Medicine, also wanted a medico-social type of health visitor to deal with complex social problems. She saw the need for a two-tier structure with general purpose health visitors and specially prepared people working at an advanced level. She found that the medical orientation of the health visitor's training was not an appropriate base for social case work and that existing case loads were too heavy to allow enough time for dealing with family social problems.

The advanced worker should function as a consultant to the general worker in dealing with complex problems. This arrangement could also help to offer some sort of promotion to health visitors which did not take them out of field work. There would have to be a suitable course for the advanced worker which would be academically approximate to the graduate social worker.[9]

Both O'Connell and Davies wanted a specialist level of health visitor with an academic education to compete with the graduate social workers. There was so much overlap between these two occupations that many nurses feared a take-over of their work.

Although social workers had relatively few graduates in their numbers, they derived a prestige from them which the health visitors lacked. Professor Crew, speaking to the conference of the Royal Sanitary Institute, voiced the feelings of some health visitors when he said that HVs, who could not claim the *cachet* of a university education, had become disadvantaged when compared with kindred workers in the social services who could.[10] However, whereas O'Connell and Davies both wanted a specialist grade for health visitors, Professor Crew did not. He considered that they should avoid specialisation and remain as generalists. All these speakers, however, realised the need for a new arrangement in the training and certification of health visitors.

The Royal Sanitary Institute was the body which organised the training and examination of these workers and it was very much dominated by the medical officers of health. Whilst the training schools had been able to introduce a new syllabus in 1950, they had not been able to influence the form of examination. The new syllabus included more social medicine and social policy but the examination remained environmentally oriented. There was therefore a gap between the training and the examination. Furthermore, whilst the nurses, specifically the Royal College of Nursing, wanted all nurse training to be controlled by nurses and all specialist training to be taken after basic nurse training, that of the health visitors remained under the control of the Institute.

In the meantime, recruitment of health visitors was poor and they were not, apparently, extending their role to take up the functions described for them in the NHS Act.[11]

It seemed to many that they were performing too many duties which less skilled people could adequately cope with and that they were spending more time in clinics. There was little agreement on the size of the work-load that health visitors should have and, with the agreement of the College, the Ministry asked the Nuffield Provincial Hospital Trust to undertake a job analysis on the work of public health nurses. This was completed in 1954 and covered district nurses as well as health visitors.[12]

167

About 40 per cent of all nurses worked in the public health field and they came out very well from the study: there was 'a wealth of good-will and expert knowledge whose potential in the organisation of the NHS ... is clear'. The GPs were criticised for a lack of cooperation with the health visitors with whom they had difficulty in forming links.

The study concluded that caseloads were still geared to the historical use of HVs and made no allowance for their extended duties. In any case, they were still based on the recommendation made in 1944 by the Ministry of Health for wartime conditions. The average case load was 980 children aged 0–5 years against a recommendation of 400 from the Department of Health for Scotland, the RCN and the Women Public Health Officers Association. The Standing Conference of Training Centres for Health Visitors, 'the only body known to have given detailed consideration to the matter' since the inception of the NHS, had recommended in 1950 a caseload of 665, not allowing for any extended duties, or 400 allowing for two-fifths of time to be spent on extended duties.

The report also proposed better organisation of clinics and a delegation of the HV's duties to other nurses and voluntary helpers.

In discussing the shortage of health visitors, the report agreed with Dr Fraser Brockington (West Yorkshire MOH at the time) that specialist HVs should not be encouraged, and that HVs should extend the range of their general duties. It also found that a three years' general nurse training in curative nursing could be excessive as a base for health visitor training. The integrated training schemes were commended.

School health duties should be given to school nurses, and ante- and post-natal care should be taken over by midwives in order to reduce the load on health visitors.[13]

The report commented on the wide variation of times given for clerical duties but did not provide a breakdown of these. The researchers probably did not appreciate the inclusion under this heading of liaison calls to other social service departments, the GP, teachers etc. The range given was one hour to $19\frac{1}{2}$ hours per week. The researchers criticised the old-fashioned method of recording visits and commented that the use of prescribed headings misrepresented the health visitor's work and workload. A specific heading, for example, 'First Visit', might conceal a discussion of multiple problems simply because of the original intention of the visit.

This report may be compared with one done in 1948, *Before the Appointed Day*, by B M Langton.[14] She was superintendent in Salford and had been concerned about a possible misuse of her health visitors' time. Unfortunately, her headings differed from those of the NPHT, but from her study she reasoned that a reasonable caseload was generally thought to be 500 children under the age of five years (allowing 10–12 minutes per visit). She contrasted this with the national average of something like 1,000 children aged under five years.

Both Langton and the NPHT had reported very high caseloads of 0–5 years. Their recommendations for a reasonable caseload were also similar, although both studies acknowledged a range of opinion. Clearly, however, with caseloads based only on under-fives and double the recommended numbers, health visitors had little chance of accepting the wider duties offered them by the NHS Act. There was an additional factor in the constraints experienced by the health visitors. The local authorities had a statutory duty to visit all new-born babies within one month of birth. They had delegated this duty to the HV whose priority it became. Thus any wider selection of work by the health visitor was virtually pre-empted since once a mother and baby had been visited, they would be on the HV's list and would have to be followed up. It was in this way that policy helped to prevent health visitors from extending their duties.

Recruitment, too, was less than satisfactory. Recruits had to come from the hospitals who selected them for clinical nursing. Hospitals had little regard for preventive work and did nothing to encourage their newly-trained nurses to leave for health visitor training. In any case, recruits had first to take some midwifery training before they were acceptable. There was therefore a further hurdle to overcome. Altogether a health visitor had to complete nearly five years' training before she could qualify.

There was very little opportunity for promotion once a nurse became a health visitor. The few superintendent or tutor posts that there were did not offer the able health visitor much opportunity for promotion and the job came to be seen as a dead-end one.

Most health visitor schools had high educational criteria which made many nurses unsuitable for acceptance. As the standard of recruit to nurse training deteriorated after the war, the health visitor schools experienced greater difficulties in filling their places.

In 1957, the first integrated course for nurse/health visitor training at a university was announced jointly by St Thomas' Hospital and Southampton University. Students spent their first year in the Department of Social Studies with other students, their second to fourth years in hospital where they received a general training and a special three months' obstetrics course, and then returned to university for their last six months' training as health visitors before taking the HV examination.[15] The numbers were small with only 39 students over five years, and the course was long, but the success rate was high, and the total wastage was only 8 per cent.

Almost at the same time, a second experimental integrated course was announced by the Hammersmith Hospital, Queens Institute of District Nursing and Battersea Polytechnic. This course was planned to train students for general and district nursing, Part I midwifery and health visiting.

The Ministry reported 'a flow of candidates with suitable educational qualifications' to be coming forward for these experimental courses.

But the 1950 syllabus and the problems of the examinations were continuing to cause anxiety in the profession.

The Public Health Section of the RCN wanted to place responsibility for training on the universities in order to ensure a sound educational background for new health visitors. They wanted to remove the training from the control of the medical officers of health and to make the GNC the registering and supervising body, rather than the medically dominated Royal Society of Health.[16,38]

Prompted by these proposals, Council agreed to ask the Ministry for an enquiry into health visiting. The Ministry decided to await the results of the NPHT job analysis and did not go ahead until 1954, when it announced that it was to set up 'An Inquiry into Health Visiting'.[17] This was to be undertaken by a working party under the chairmanship of Sir Wilson Jameson, a former chief medical officer at the Ministry. Other members were to be a Birmingham general practitioner, the chairman of a local health authority, a county nursing officer (Scotland), a county nursing officer (England, county borough) and a medical officer of health. No tutors were included.

There was also to be a powerful steering committee whose function was to act as an advisory body. The members of this were largely civil servants, local authority representatives, members of the RSH and the Standing Conference of HV Training Centres. Professor Titmuss and Miss Eileen Younghusband were also included. The former was an eminent social administrator who had been very influential on the Guillebaud committee.[18] The latter was an equally well-known lecturer in social work who was later appointed chairman of the twin working party on social workers.[5]

During the time when the Jameson working party was sitting, difficulties in health visiting seemed to become more pressing.

The RCN estimated that the shortfall in 1952 was 2,345. The Public Health Section reported that there was no likelihood of the extended duties being taken up until the acute shortage was dealt with.

The problem of overlapping duties between health visitors and social workers was more marked. Some authorities complained of too many professions visiting the same family; others seemed to find that families in need slipped between the professions and were missed altogether.

Relationships with general practitioners were not improving and some doctors were recommending that health visitors should be replaced or made redundant. At the same time, a few GPs who had taken the trouble to learn to work with HVs were apologising for their colleagues and asking for more.

The Public Health Section adopted Mary Davies's plan[9] for the establishment of a consultant grade of health visitor and asked Council to recommend it to the Ministry. Council referred the matter to its education committee since the consultant health visitor would need a new advanced course. Whilst this committee thought that the University of London could set up an appropriate course, as they had diplomas in nursing and nurse education, they considered that 'at the present time such a course would be premature', and the scheme collapsed.

The College believed that where there was an overlap of work between the health visitor and social worker the former was better qualified to take over. They believed in a two-tier social worker system with graduates and aides, but did not welcome the idea of a general social worker.[9]

The College also wanted more psychiatric social workers who, they thought, should be responsible for following up mentally ill people in the community. They believed that health visitors could continue to look after mental defectives living in the community.

Until then, health visitors and moral welfare workers (who were employed by the voluntary agencies) had looked after unmarried mothers, and the College saw no reason for social workers to enter this field; nor did they see a place for them as duly authorised officers and home help organisers. Responsibility for the disabled was also claimed by the College for health visitors who should be the key workers in the field.

Clearly, the College was protecting the health visitors' territory. The health visitors had earned a well accepted and respected role in the community during the inter-war years when the public health movement was still strong, but there was little evidence that they had done much work in many of the areas which the College was now claiming, such as among blind, deaf, and disabled people.

On the other hand, the social workers were rather disorganised and fragmented. The Younghusband report[5] found that 89 per cent of social workers in local authority services were untrained and described it as an unrecognised career. Whilst there were some graduates in social work, they were not all vocationally qualified: social science qualifications were academic rather than professional qualifications.

The health visitors had a good case when they argued that their nursing background gave them greater maturity and professionalism, but their case was not so sound when they argued that it also gave them greater experience in dealing with people and human problems. The general nurse training of the day was still grounded in hierarchical authority and was strongly oriented towards tasks and nursing procedures. Nurses in the community continued to be deficient in skills of inter-personal relationships. Nor did the general trained nurse have any knowledge, training or understanding of mental illness. Few student nurses had experience in nursing chronic illness, geriatric, blind or deaf people, and rehabilitation was not included in their syllabus.

Many health visitors accepted the idea of a combined worker; others proposed that health visiting should hive off from its medical ties and become more pronounced in its social orientation. The strained relationships between health visitors and the GPs probably tended to fuel this.

Lobbying by the health visitors continued: they were more vocal and articulate than most other nurses. Mary Davies provided another paper for *Nursing Times*[19] in which she said that the shortage of funds and recruits made development of health visitor training unlikely. 'There are indications that in the official view the health visitor is not a wholly satisfactory and self sufficient person in the field of social work.' She cited the Ministry of Health Circular 27/54 and the Minister's address in May 1954 to the County Councils Association and, in February 1955, to their welfare conference. It seemed that the official view was that health visitors had too wide a range of functions to be expert in every branch of their work and that they were not seen to be equipped for social case work.

Most health visitors agreed that they were held back by, and suffered from, the superficial and poor training given to nurses. J M Akester considered that basic nurse education was defective and that nursing was a profession by courtesy only. The lack of any university education for nurses caused nursing opinion to be discounted and undermined the comparative prestige of health visitors. The nurse was not recognised as a specialist in her own sphere.[20]

At a later conference, Ilse Windmuller[21] complained that the authoritarian and didactic attitudes developed during nurse training were not an asset to casework or health visiting. If health visitors did

172

not enter new fields of activity, others would; almoners and other social workers were ready to enter health departments and the health visitors would have lost a great opportunity.

The following week the Jameson report was published.

The working party had taken evidence from a wide range of organisations. They collected local professional views, used much data provided in the NPHT study and from government statistics; they analysed diaries specially kept by health visitors in six selected areas and obtained observations on the work of HVs which were made by three independent people – a lecturer in education, an almoner working in a university department and the headmistress of a girls' high school. Their observations had been steered towards the possibility of the health visitor being a general purpose family visitor; otherwise, what should she do?

The working party recognised the need to talk in generalities whilst admitting wide variations. Their terms of reference had confined their considerations to the health visitor's role, but they did not feel able to anticipate new needs which would require new methods of working or new types of worker (Chapter IX).

This apologia appears to demonstrate that they felt confined to the discussion of a current worker in a current role. They were discussing the status quo and, presumably, trying to optimise it. Similarly, it appears that they felt unable to consider a different and amplified role which might meet future needs. Their review and recommendations appear to support this deduction.

The Jameson report recommended that the health visitor should be a generalist 'teaching and guiding individuals and families to become physically and mentally healthier by their own efforts, to accept the family responsibilities and to fit into the community of which they are a part' (Chapter I).

In order to accomplish this, the working party made recommendations for the recruitment and training of health visitors, accepting as a base the registered nurse's training with the addition of some obstetric training. Candidates should have at least a School Certificate, but this was realised as being less than students required for a university based social science course.

The training itself should be linked with, or based at, a university and should have more intensive studies in aspects of social and mental health, child development and supervised field work experience. The Royal Society of Health was proposed as the central body for training and registration for the United Kingdom, and the local authorities were given responsibility for professional development and further training.

In the matter of the respective roles of health visitors and social workers, the report considered that the former should be the case finders and the latter the caseworkers. The health visitors should make routine visits for this purpose and it was anticipated that the social workers would make selective visits.

The health visitor should become the family visitor, whilst retaining her interest in mothers and young children and health education.[22] To these ends her caseload should be geared to a total population of some 4,300. This would require an addition of 10,300 trained staff to be reached in ten years, representing an additional 400 students each year.

The social scientists in the working party were most vocal and their evidence appeared to carry much weight. Instead of being a medico-social worker, the health visitor was to be biased towards health care. In the discussion on how much socially oriented work the new breed of health visitor could undertake, the agreed boundaries went very close to those proposed by the almoners' and psychiatric social workers' evidence.

Three independent observers had studied the work of a selection of health visitors. Two of these were academic social workers whose comments reflected the trend then developing in social policy: the absolute rights of the individual, casework, the divorce of psycho-social work from the domination of the medical model and the development of specialist fields. Social theorists disliked authority roles which health visitors represented and preferred counselling techniques to advice-giving in almost all situations.

They criticised the superficial level of work by health visitors and their failure to follow up cases; they criticised the tendency of health visitors to see problems as stemming from health or environmental causes rather than from personality or emotional roots; they disliked the tendency of health visitors to distance themselves from their clients rather than to reach out to their levels.

The report also recommended a new post of group adviser, who would remain in the field to train and advise her younger or newer colleagues and help with teaching students. This was a post rather similar to one later proposed for social workers and rather broader than that proposed by Mary Davies.

The report should be compared with the later Younghusband report for social workers (see page 176). It based many of its recommendations on the assumption that general nurse training would sooner or later be changed according to the model put forward by the Wood report.[23] But that did not occur. It optimised the status quo rather than foreseeing future social needs. It anticipated a structured social worker service composed of qualified candidates, and that failed to materialise. It proposed implicitly, rather than explicitly, a two-tiered health visiting service: there would be the general worker and the advance worker, but that did not materialise. It failed to ensure either continuing education or advanced training, as it left these in the hands of the local authorities who had already been shown to be recalcitrant. It failed satisfactorily to determine the boundaries of the health visitor's work.

Its proposals to make the Royal Society for the Promotion of Health the central training and registering body were extraordinary. The idea suggests that the working party had not thought through this recommendation since the RSH was not a training body and, as a voluntary agency, could not have maintained a statutory roll, nor could it have satisfactorily dispensed central or local authority funds for training purposes since it could not be properly responsible for public moneys.

Many of these weaknesses were rectified in the 1962 legislation. Many of the remaining weaknesses were neutralised by the Council for the Training of Health Visitors which that legislation embodied.[24]

The RCN produced two reports in response to the Jameson report, both of which were sent to the Ministry.[25,26] They were universally suspicious of the proposal to use the RSH as the central training body: the society had no experience of training and education and had not shown itself to be sufficiently forward-looking or flexible since 1948.

Both papers criticised the recommended content of the group adviser's post and wanted to keep education, supervision and field work training in separate compartments with a specialised training for each.

Nursing Times[27] called it an 'admirable report' but observed that since all HV students first had to take nurse training, the matrons would remain responsible for selecting the health visitors of the future. Of course, this was substantially true.

It also anticipated that some disappointment would be felt in the report's recommendations for training. This also was subsequently proved to be true.[28]

At the RCN Scottish conference, Miss E W Himsworth, a member of the working party and chief nursing officer of Midlothian and Peebles, told her audience that she did not agree with the idea that group advisers should have to rely on compulsory further training (for the diploma) before being considered eligible for promotion.

175

Although she thought that the diploma would be useful for group advisers, tutors and administrators, she knew of no other profession that insisted on further training for promotion. The acceptance of such a condition would impair the prestige of health visitors.[29]

Dr I A G MacQueen, medical officer at Aberdeen, thought that the special courses for group advisers would depress the status of general health visitors. He considered that there was still the danger that social workers might displace health visitors. Miss S M McGaw of Stirlingshire also supported this view.[29]

In the following weeks, there was a flurry of correspondence discussing whether or not health visiting included casework. This was started by a letter from Evelyn Davison (lecturer in social work, University of Southampton) who considered that health visiting was an advisory service and social work was casework (26 October). Miss I Windmuller (Salford) described a scheme in her authority which included integrated policies of casework, consultation and selective visiting (2 November). Other letters took exception to Davison's discrimination and considered that she was accusing health visitors of having only a superficial contact with their clients. Phyllis M Scott (tutor in social studies course, University of the Gold Coast), in a well argued letter, supported Windmuller against Davison. Using the latter's points and definitions, she refuted her arguments and pointed out that casework principles and skills were not the prerogative of social workers (page 1179).

At the health visitors conference in 1957, the deputy chief nursing officer at the Ministry of Health (Edna Jackson) gave the presidential address. She was looking forward to a revision of the HV syllabus: 'I hope we shall cease to refer to the course as training and consider it as education'. She thought that there was a strong case for university courses for senior grades of staff in which nurses could learn with other students so as to bring to the profession 'the kind of people we need' and help to develop better working relationships with other disciplines.[30]

The Ministry of Health waited for the Younghusband report to be published before it made any public moves in response to the Jameson report.

The Younghusband working party was set up in very much the same way as was the Jameson working party: they both had the backing of a steering committee and both were multidisciplinary. There was, however, one significant difference, that of the chairmen.

Sir Wilson Jameson was by training a medical officer of health, a former chief medical officer and a retired civil servant. He had all the attributes of those roles as well as all their biases. He was not a health visitor. Eileen Younghusband, on the other hand, was an experienced social worker, a former lecturer at the London School of Economics, adviser to the National Institute for Social Work Training and the principal officer for education and training to the National Association of Girls Clubs. She was very much a social worker.

Whilst the Jameson working party had included social workers and had invited evidence from them, the Younghusband working party did not feel the same way about nurses. They refused, at first, to see the RCN who wanted to give oral evidence and had to be persuaded by the Ministry to receive their written memorandum.

The Younghusband report found that social science qualifications, such as degrees, diplomas and certificates, were not qualifications for the practice of social work. Eighty-nine per cent of social workers in the employment of the local authorities were not trained. Although some practical work was included in social science training, this was not recognised as vocational training and many candidates went straight into a social worker post without further preparation. Of the welfare officers, 60 per cent had no qualifications, nor did 93 per cent of social workers. Over 50 per cent of social workers were males.

The report found that the twentieth century had brought about a change in the understanding of the causal factors of disease from the mechanistic approach, in which every disease process had a cellular pathology due to some causal factor, to the reactive approach, in which disease is seen to be a reaction of the individual to some causal factor which might be pathological, social or multifactorial (para 182). The social work element in some services had altered during the preceding years owing to changes in medical treatment, better facilities for rehabilitation or shorter periods of incapacity. There had been changes in understanding and new attitudes (para 550). Social work orientation had shifted from relief of human suffering to the prevention of suffering, the promotion of healthy living and the maintenance of independence.

Social services were provided under sections 28 and 29 of the NHS Act 1946 and also under the National Assistance Act 1948. Under the NHS Act, they were subject to the direction of the medical officer of health;[31] the 1948 Act also included domiciliary and residential services for elderly people, and services and residential accommodation for handicapped persons, all of which were subject to the general oversight and responsibility of the medical officer of health. Seventy-five per cent of local authorities had separate welfare committees: the others had a special welfare sub-committee of the health committee.

The working party considered that this sectionalisation of services was no longer sensible and that there should be a more general approach with the social worker meeting the needs of clients. Most of those needs were probably common to all or many of the clients.

They described the functions of the social worker as being to assess the disturbance of equilibrium and to give help to clients in adjusting, to support clients in emotional, psychological and material disequilibrium, to study the situation, assess the need and plan how to meet the need (para 615).

There were three levels of need and the working party proposed three levels of worker. There should be a welfare assistant (with in-service training), a general purpose social worker (with a two-year training) for the middle level of need and a professionally trained and experienced worker (who should have a social science or other qualification and vocational training) to take the highest level of cases (such as those requiring casework), to advise and supervise other social workers, to make initial assessments and to provide in-service training for the welfare assistants and social workers. The function of this third level worker was similar to that proposed for the group adviser in the Jameson report. They considered that the social worker with two years of training would be the general worker and take the main range of work (para 24).

The professional worker was to have university based courses; the general worker should have a general course of training outside universities; the welfare assistant would receive some in-service training only. There should be a national council of training, a national vocational certificate and a national staff college. This college should act as a forum for research, pioneer new types of specialist courses (group work for instance), offer intensive training in casework and supervisory skills and be a forum for discussion.

The working party found that social workers in hospitals, who were subject to Whitley Council scales of salary, had lower rates than did their colleagues in the local authorities, under the national joint committee arrangements (para 756). They recommended that salaries should be commensurate with the training received and the degree of skill and responsibility demanded of the workers: 'Those who chose this way of serving their fellow men should not be at a disadvantage compared with those who chose other opportunities for service, for example in education or administration' (para 756).

Grant aid should be available to students undertaking social work training. This should be derived from local education authorities, state scholarships via the Ministry of Education, awards from the Home Office and exchequer bursaries awarded by the Ministry of Health.

The report also discussed social worker relationships with related workers. The shortage of social workers had tended to extend the work of health visitors beyond their original functions. Health visitors and social workers should provide a complementary service: proper delimitation of functions should be worked out (part IV).

The working party considered that some of the claims made for health visitors in the Jameson report were over-statements; for example, they cited the expressed need for a nursing qualification in order to gain the confidence of families, admission to homes and an intimate knowledge of all families in the district.

The working party discussed the need for referral of some cases by the health visitors to the social worker. This was always in terms of referral to the professional social worker, the case worker: they viewed the general social worker as the equal partner of the health visitor, and they disliked Jameson's use of the term, referring to health visitors, of 'general family visitor'.

Both Younghusband and Jameson laid claims to work with mental care and after-care, with care and after-care of the sick, problem families, unmarried and unsupported mothers, the home help service, and domiciliary care of elderly and physically handicapped people.

Neither report made any specific differentiation in the work that their respective workers would do. There was therefore considerable potential for continuing overlap, particularly between the general social worker and the health visitor. This became more important as Jameson's recommendations for a higher level of health visitor, to match Younghusband's professional worker, failed to be implemented.

Whilst the social worker could progress from the general grade into the professional ranks, because her certificate had educational currency, there was no equivalent progression for the health visitor because nursing qualifications lacked educational merit, even though a number of HVs took their vocational training in universities.

Problems of territory and overlap continued to stem from the ill-defined and general nature of the work of both the social worker and the health visitor and also because the shortage of workers of both categories demanded that each had to fill in as need arose. Later there was the problem of returning the client to the other worker, sharing the work or withdrawing.

The function of the health visitor was confined within a statutory service and a vocational certificate required by regulation. The social worker operated in a service with no such well-defined boundaries and no previous training had been established. Whereas the health visitor was restricted by law and her own professional boundaries, the social worker lacked these restraints and was able to enjoy greater flexibility.[32]

The social workers started with the distinct advantage of already having graduates in recognised positions. Graduates were therefore accepted as a recognised grade and all further grades fell into ranks below them. In contrast, there were few graduates amongst the health visitors and the SRN qualification was the accepted level. No higher grade was achieved and there was therefore no higher level of functioning recognised for health visiting.

Another observation may be made: social work was based on an accepted theoretical framework including social policy, sociology and psychology. Theoretical understanding and discussion was very evident in the Younghusband investigations as well as in the report; no similar base was evident in the Jameson report which was framed by a medical officer and a civil servant whose attitudes towards a nursing service were recognised as conventional. Health visitors were described as 'willing horses' by the Jameson report; social workers were described by Younghusband as 'providing a statutory service of great intricacy . . . which frequently involves much mental and emotional strain in the worker'.

There were no reports in the RCN Council minutes of negotiations or discussions with the Ministry of Health concerning legislation for health visiting. In 1960, the Ministry's annual report announced that two training councils were to be set up for health visitors and social workers: they were to be separate but associated.[33] There was to be one chairman for both councils, some common membership and a shared administration and premises. The councils would function independently and would cover the United Kingdom.[34]

The Public Health Section was not happy about the proposal for a joint chairman but would agree if he were neutral and well-known. They were also unhappy at the coupling of the health visitor with the general purpose social worker. They considered that the long, three-part training of the HV merited a higher ranking alongside that of the professional social worker.[34]

When the legislative proposals were published, the Public Health Section's comments showed an extraordinarily reactionary frame of mind. They did not consider that the time was ripe for fundamental changes in the organisation of HV training: there had been a change in the examination procedure and a new syllabus was under consideration. These should be given a chance to develop, and the Royal Society for the Promotion of Health should not be rejected as the controlling body. The recent interest shown by the GNC in new forms of nurse training and integrated training, indicated the need for links between the GNC and the HV training body. They reiterated their doubts about linking the HV training body with that of the social workers who would only have a two-year training. They therefore recommended to the RCN Council that legislation should be deferred for five years.

In an annexe to their paper they wrote that they had subsequently discovered that the Women Public Health Officers' Association (WPHO) did not agree with their observations and asked Council to delay asking for a deferment of the legislation until the following January (1961) by which time they hoped that they would have reached some agreement between themselves.

The Ministry proposed to appoint all the members of the two new councils. The Public Health Section was most suspicious of the ultimate composition of the health visitors' council and sought reassurances from the Ministry that it would include at least 50 per cent of HVs. They continued to resist a joint chairman and the twin councils. They considered that if two chairmen were to be appointed, it would be unlikely that the more eminent would be given to the health visitors' council which would consequently suffer a secondary position. Council asked the section to be 'less categorical' in its discussions with the Ministry and WPHO.

In March, the section reported to Council that the Ministry had not been able to promise an equal membership of health visitors on the new council but had promised to consider the inclusion of a GNC representative.[35] The public health tutors' group told Council that they felt very strongly about this point and intended to take private action by lobbying their Members of Parliament.

In May, the Public Health Section reported that the Ministry had included a representative from the GNC but had, at the same time, increased the numbers of local authority representatives by two. The health visitor tutors had always questioned the need for any employer representatives on a training council and were dismayed at this action. There were also problems of representation for Scotland, since only names from the Scottish Health Visitors' Association had been considered. No RCN members were to be included.[36] They had come to the conclusion, however, that further lobbying would be counter-productive and did not propose to fight the matter further.

The Health Visiting and Social Work (Training) Act 1962 eventually went on the statute book in the autumn. Twelve members of the Health Visitors' Training Council were health visitors; seven RCN nominations had been appointed. The first chairman of the Council for Training of Health Visitors (CTHV) was Sir John Wolfenden CBE, Vice Chancellor of Reading University. The first meeting of Council was in October 1962, and the first chief professional adviser was Miss Elaine Wilkie, who had been lecturer to the integrated nurse/health visitor course and diploma course in community nursing at Manchester University.

It was noted by RCN Council that whereas the Ministry of Health had appointed one of their civil servants to the Council for Training Social Workers, no similar provision was made for the CTHV.[37]

Training, examinations and registration of health visitors were therefore removed from the Royal Society of Health.[38] The CTHV was responsible for determining training and professional development courses for health visitors but had no say in relation to the practice of HVs, nor was it given any disciplinary powers. It was the only statutory nursing body with responsibility for all four countries of the United Kingdom until 1981.

In 1962, when the CTHV was set up, there were 27 health visitor schools, 19 of which were organised by the employing authorities. In some cases, these schools were linked to universities or technical colleges but staffed by local authority personnel. There was no system of regular inspection of the schools. Most candidates were sponsored by local authorities, and in many cases, training was related to local service needs.[32] Recruitment was mostly from nurses trained in hospitals who had been selected for clinical needs and trained in the medical model.

Whilst the Jameson and Younghusband working parties were making their investigations, events in the field had provoked some innovations aimed at coping with the changing nature of health care.

Oxford County Borough and Hampshire County Council had set up experimental arrangements for placing health visitors to work with groups of family doctors. Other authorities were also planning to extend this experiment in their localities.[39]

Early discharges from hospitals were producing many families in need of help and support, but continuity of care was endangered by the lack of communication between hospitals and the community nurses, including the health visitors. This had given rise to the attachment of health visitors to some hospitals to facilitate a better flow of information.

The 1958 annual report of the Ministry of Health made a ten-year survey of the NHS.[40] It described the three-fold effects of the health service on health visiting:

1 The local health authorities had been given a duty to provide a health visiting service.
2 Regulations had laid down the need for a specific qualification.
3 The range of HV services had been extended to provide advice to all persons 'suffering from illness . . . and as to the measures necessary to prevent the spread of infection'.

There was still a shortage of health visitors and, although the Jameson committee was not in favour of it, specialties had appeared to deal with groups such as elderly persons and physically or mentally handicapped people. Prevention of physical illness in children had become a less overriding factor and problems associated with poverty had become less acute. The content of health visiting had changed to become more social and less to do with simple health teaching.

Selective visiting was replacing routine visiting; more health education was given to groups, in schools and to mothers' clubs.

Having made a nostalgic review of the health service in 1948, the next year's annual report was directed towards the future ten years. It hoped for a period of improvement and development with increasing emphasis on prevention of ill-health. There was a trend towards more community care, more early discharges and, consequently, the need for further developments and expansion of the domiciliary services.[41]

There was some reorientation of work in the child welfare services 'to meet modern needs': more GPs were attending the centres (instead of local authority medical officers) or holding clinics in their own surgeries with health visitors in attendance; clinic staff were advising mothers about child development for the 1–5 age group, as well as the 0–1 age group, and were monitoring the children's progress.

These last observations represented significant movements. Before this change had taken place, the M & CW movement had involved a close working relationship, in the mothers' and children's clinics, between the medical officers and the health visitors. Once the medical officers dropped out of these clinics, the health visitors tended to lose contact with them and worked instead with GPs, 'in attendance on them'. The change marked the growing interest of GPs in well babies.

The Cranbrook report[42] had recommended greater involvement and additional payments for general practitioners in the maternity services. The recommendations of this committee not only partly displaced the midwives and tended to medicalise childbirth, but also had repercussions on the health visiting services. They confirmed the movement of doctors into areas that impinged on the territory of health visitors, such as the replacement of local authority doctors by GPs in ante-natal and post-natal clinics.

The annual report[41] also discussed the rising number of home visits and clinic sessions and proposed that local authorities should review their staffing needs in order to get more realistic establishments.

In 1963, the CTHV decided that only registered general nurses with five or more 'O' level grades and obstetric training would be accepted for health visitor training. In doing this they eliminated all other candidates from the supplementary registers, as well as non-nurses, and health visiting became firmly rooted in nursing.

The CTHV was soon to change the health visitor training syllabus and to include much more theoretical content. Health visitors were the first nurses to receive a training in centres of higher education and became the best educated section. Their entry into the centres of higher education paved the way for future courses for other nurses and eventually opened up a route to nursing degrees.

In the community, the health visitors were the only nurses who had not been supervised or organised by voluntary workers – the lady superintendents or the voluntary agencies. After 1948, they soon came under the control of health visitor superintendents but remained within the MOH empire. This development should be contrasted with the lingering influence of the county nursing associations and the Queen's Institute over district nurses.

Whereas the Queen's district nurses failed to make concessions for the changing social climate and the centralisation of health care after 1948, the health visitors recognised their problems quite quickly and tried to take firm steps to meet them, both through their training and their organisation, but were thwarted by the institutions. In this they had to contend with the power and interests of their medical officers of health who remained environmentalists. They had also to contend with the anti-education ethos of general nurses who had no interest in social medicine and little respect for nurses working in preventive health.

The education committee of the RCN refused to set up courses in medico-social work or casework techniques for health visitors, and the grade of group adviser never became established.

The transition of health visitors from the paradigm of infectious diseases to behavioural or social diseases was a path fought on the one hand against the medical officers of health and on the other against the nursing establishment. In this they were never entirely successful. As they clung to their traditional role, looking after mothers and young children, the GPs edged them out. They became family visitors but were never really able to accept their potential role of caring for the elderly (a growing age group with many needs) and the family, partly because of policy decisions made by the Jameson working party and partly because the organisation of their work and their heavy caseloads did not permit this.

In a period of growing specialisation, the Jameson report confirmed the broad, general nature of their work. They remained 'the willing horses'.

Chapter 9/Teachers of nursing

However else they differed, the several reports on nursing all appeared to agree that the quality of nurse training was poor. The Athlone interim report[1] had said that the quality of the teaching 'was not always good enough'; the Wood report[2] complained of the extravagant wastage of student nurses, their failure in examinations, the harsh discipline and the poverty of relationships. Horder[3] commented rather stringently:

> In no other professional training is there so little periodic inspection, in none is the standard of entry so dependent on the demands for student labour, in none have the requirements with regard to teaching staff been so nebulous.

The RCN report[3] made extensive recommendations for the education of nurses, including a tutor:student ratio of 1:50, and that tutors should be regarded as specialists.

Courses for tutors had been started in the late 1920s at various colleges who awarded certificates to candidates that had successfully completed their studies. By 1943 the GNC recognised courses run by the Royal College of Nursing, King's College, Battersea Polytechnic, Bedford College, and Leeds and London universities. The Nurses Act 1943 allowed the GNC to make rules to grant or approve certificates, prescribe training and approve courses. After this, London University agreed to set up a diploma course for sister tutors.

The rules made by the GNC for candidates laid down that they had to be registered nurses, have had four years post-registration experience (two of which had to be as a ward sister in an approved nurse training school), and to have completed a two-year sister tutor course at an approved institution (temporarily, a one year's course was deemed to be acceptable). Successful candidates were granted a GNC certificate.

After approval had been given to the sister tutor diploma course at the London University, the GNC gave similar approval to the universities of Birmingham, Manchester, Hull and Leeds.[4]

In spite of these measures, there was no absolute requirement that schools of nursing should employ qualified tutors. In fact, many did not and some employed only one as the head of the school. This deficiency in the terms of approval of nurse training schools was probably at the root of the complaints by the various nursing reports.

In October 1948, Miss A Russell-Smith, a senior civil servant at the Ministry of Health, wrote to the GNC. The Minister, she said, had been thinking about the training of sister tutors, the content and length of the course and wanted to set up a small expert committee to discuss these matters. She invited the GNC to join and asked for their cooperation.[5]

When the meeting took place in December, Miss Russell-Smith asked the GNC to discuss with London University and the other training colleges the content of the course and whether it should be purely a teaching course. She asked to know how much longer the university felt that they had to supplement the basic scientific knowledge of the tutor students as she wanted to reduce the period of training. The GNC agreed to put these points to the university and to draft proposals for a shortened course.

In March 1949 these proposals were sent to the Ministry and a further meeting with them took place a couple of months later. It was then agreed to convene a meeting with the universities, the RCN, the Ministries of Health and Education, the local education authorities and representatives of training hospitals.[6]

In September 1949, the University of London submitted proposals for their two-year course. The GNC agreed that all parts of the course put forward by the university were essential since students had to receive training in both content and methods of teaching.

The Ministry was put out by the GNC's proposal to agree the two-year course at the university as they considered that the whole topic should first be discussed by the ad hoc group. The GNC replied that they had taken advice from other bodies and had subsequently made their decision. The Ministry wrote back to say that the GNC should have convened the meeting of the ad hoc group before taking a decision. They were concerned, as the Wood report had recommended, that the shortage of tutors should be overcome; therefore they wanted first to seek the best type of training. Since hospitals had to second students for training, the Ministry felt that they should ensure that the period of secondment was as short as possible.

Another meeting with the Ministry took place at which no decision as to who was to convene the ad hoc meeting was reached. They did talk around the subject of tutor training and opinions were expressed about the need for wide terms of reference. They also decided that the group should investigate the function of the sister tutors, their training, relationships with other teachers (such as doctors and ward sisters), the organisation of nurse teaching and the probable numbers of tutors that might be needed in the future.

187

The GNC later decided that the terms of reference were so wide as to take the matter out of their hands. They therefore decided that the Ministry should organise the ad hoc group.[6] There was no further mention in the minutes of either the GNC or the RCN about this matter until 1953.

In the meantime, in 1950, the Staff Side of the Whitley Council wrote to the Management Side. The letter was from Frances Goodall, the chairman who also happened to be the general secretary of the RCN. She was evidently seeking to follow up the proposals made by the Horder committee, since she described the current difficulties in recruiting suitable candidates for tutor posts and proposed that tutors should be removed from the hierarchy of hospital staff and included in a separate educational branch of nursing. She described the need to render tutors comparable with other professional teachers. The drift of tutors away from teaching into administrative posts because of their poor career prospects was, she said, wasteful of their training and unsettling for the schools of nursing and students.

The Staff Side had earlier asked for tutors to be graded as assistant matrons and Frances Goodall again asked the Management Side to consider that. There was, at the time, a discrepancy of about £100 between the Staff Side claim for tutors and the decision of the Management Side.[7] The Management Side was not sympathetic to these proposals and nothing came of this letter.

In September 1952 the GNC received a confidential copy of the ad hoc group's report, *The Function Status and Training of Nurse Tutors*.[8] It was published in the following year. Part I of the report was a general survey which described the growth of the need for tutors and the current shortage. This was due not so much to a fall-off of candidates as the unsuitability of many of those who would have liked to take the training (due to poor education), the lengthening of the tutor training, the wastage of tutors from the teaching field and the poor use made of them in the hospitals.

In 1946–47, 140 tutors had qualified; 94 had responded to the questionnaire sent out by the ad hoc group. Of these 81 were still teaching and 72 of these were with the NHS. Eight of the NHS group were contemplating leaving and the report considered that the non-respondents had probably also left the NHS.

Most of the respondents felt dissatisfied with their jobs because the hospital authorities did not understand their function and status, or they were not allowed enough time for non-teaching duties such as preparation of lectures, marking, reading and studying and contact with patients.

188

The report commented that tutors should have more scope in their work and that there should be a better career structure for them. Tutors should have more opportunity to use their skills more effectively; wastage should be reduced by better cooperation from the ward sisters so as to allow more teaching on the wards, better status in the hospitals and opportunities for promotion.

Part II related to the function and status of tutors. They should be regarded as educators rather than as people who pushed student nurses through examinations. They should be encouraged to make contact with the general field of education and to integrate theory with practice.

The principal tutor should have more influence in the allocation of students for ward experience, should be regarded as an expert in her field and should be involved in all policy decisions relative to nurse training. The group thought that, as the title principal tutor had been degraded, there should be a new title, director of the nurse education department.

Part III discussed the schools of nursing. Grouping of schools would help to make better use of tutors, raise the standard of training, possibly reduce the numbers of tutors needed but, also, offer an avenue of promotion.

Whilst the general responsibility for nurse training should remain with the matrons, the group thought that the director of nurse education in a large hospital could cooperate with her in planning and organising it. Where there was a group of hospitals, one of the matrons should be designated head of the joint schools of nursing. Where there was a single group training school formed from several hospitals a committee of matrons should be established to work with the director.

Small groups or individual units would not be of sufficient size to warrant a director of nurse education. In these cases there could be a principal tutor, or tutor in sole charge, who should be responsible to the matron.

Group schools should be staffed by qualified tutors; there should be a nurse education centre in a separate building and the ward sisters should be used as clinical instructors in the wards. Tutors should have more opportunity to specialise in a particular field.

Part IV discussed statistics. In England and Wales there were about 54,000 student and pupil nurses. In 1952 there were 854 full-time and 50 part-time qualified tutors; there were 390 full-time and 97 part-time unqualified tutors. This gave a total teaching staff of 1,244 full-time and 147 part-time. The ad hoc committee estimated that there was need for 1,455 qualified tutors. At the time, about 33

189

per cent of tutors were unqualified. The current ratio of tutors to students was within a wide range of 1:21 to 1:184. The committee thought that a desirable ratio would be 1:40 or 50.

Part VII considered the training for tutors, candidates for which were already mature and experienced. They thought that courses should be associated with a university and whilst one year's training was too short, two years was probably too long and would only exacerbate the shortage. They therefore proposed a course of five academic terms, 20–22 months, which would produce a basic grade of tutor rather than a specialist. The ad hoc group thought that tutors in mental hospitals would continue to waste unless the educational standard of student and pupil nurses improved.

Selection of candidates for tutor training should be the responsibility of the training institutions; no obstacle should be placed in the way of suitable candidates and the GNC should register tutors only after three months of experience in teaching.

Two academic educationalists in the ad hoc group were unable to agree to the five term training. They considered that two full years were necessary if nurse tutors were to take their places alongside other trained teachers. They added a rider to the report:

> [It is] so important that nursing teachers whose training will put them alongside other branches of education, that we should like to see the Departments of Health approach the Education Departments of British universities to see if at least one of them would not offer a full-time internal course to academically qualified students, as an alternative to the London extra-mural diploma.

They added that the proposals of the report for shortening the training were educationally retrograde.

The GNC commented, on the report, that they welcomed the 'schools of nursing' proposals although they did not like the new title of director of nurse education: they preferred the title principal tutor. They did not consider that it would be feasible to give ward sisters special training in ward teaching as the report had suggested and they doubted if the London university would consent to a five-term course. Although they thought that the proposal of three months' supervised teaching before tutor registration was sound, they did not think that it was practical.[9]

There was very little further discussion about the report and the GNC decided to make no further alterations in the prerequisites demanded of tutor student candidates for the time being. When the Aitken report was published, *Nursing Times* reported it but made no comment.

190

In 1955 the College's Sister Tutor Section held a conference with the report as its main topic. Dr Janet Aitken and Miss M G Lawson, deputy chief nursing officer at the Ministry of Health, both spoke. They had nothing much fresh to say but the ensuing discussion was revealing.

Miss Holland, principal tutor at Guy's Hospital and a member of the Aitken committee, talked about the lack of influence allowed to tutors in hospitals. She said that many hospitals had no nurse education committees, some nursing committees had no nurses in them and some had only the matron as the nursing representative. Tutors often had a difficult, unrewarding job because the training of the student was given such a low priority and so many students were so poorly educated. She asked for much greater influence for the tutors in education and training policy making.

Miss Ceris Jones, matron of The London Hospital, had also been on the committee. She absolutely rejected any idea that tutors should have any part in student selection or allocation. She insisted that the matron should retain a dominant role in the school of nursing. There were differences of opinion on other issues too, including the role of the ward sister as the clinical teacher.

Miss Houghton, education officer at the GNC, offered the opinion that the ward sister was the key person in clinical teaching. But Miss Le Quesne Mitchell, ward sister at St Thomas' Hospital, did not think that many ward sisters had the knowledge to pass on to the students.[10]

In 1955 the nurse teaching unit at Edinburgh University was announced. The unit was to offer a tutor's certificate only as they did not foresee enough suitably qualified candidates for a diploma course. The certificate course was to be 18 months.

The RCN Sister Tutor Section's comments on the Aitken report, published later that year (1955), were rather lukewarm as, evidently, the section thought that too many poorly educated candidates were being pushed through.[11]

An educationalist writing in *Nursing Times* evidently agreed with the section since he lamented that 'these women are not required to have wide education or academic qualifications and their talents are not always equal to their opportunities'. Neither did he have much of an opinion of the GNC syllabus which, he wrote,

... includes no general subjects, but a recent addition called 'Psychology in Nursing' provides a quasi-scientific formulation for the homely explanations about what it feels like to be ill.[12]

In 1956, the GNC, prompted by the College, successfully sought approval from the Minister to require four years' post-registration experience, including two years as a ward sister, as a condition of tutor training. Time had shown that some candidates lacked nursing experience. The more stringent conditions were to take effect in 1958. In the same year the GNC reported that tutor courses at the Universities of London and Hull were of two years' duration, but they had the discretion to approve shorter courses.[13] The following year, a two year diploma course was set up at the Edinburgh University. The Hull course ended in 1959 because of a lack of applicants.

All was not well and the tutors themselves continued to grumble. Since the hospitals had to second candidates they were in the position of screening applicants, even if the selection of student tutors was ultimately left to the training institutions. Clearly, they preferred to retain the services of competent ward sisters but might welcome the opportunity to rid themselves of unpopular staff. 'Junius', writing in *Nursing Times*, thought that 'all those who have not quite the physical strength or mental equilibrium to support the strain of a modern general ward' were found suitable for secondment[14] and 'Vigilante' agreed that there was cause for concern with the educational standard of tutors; 'the . . . calibre of nurse tutors shocks and worries me . . . Many of these men and women are really nice people but because of obvious educational handicaps are quite unsuitable to teach our future nurses'.[15] Her letter was attacked the following week as a 'foolish and wounding letter' which did not present a true picture. Another correspondent wrote to say that there would be a greater shortage than ever if the educational level for tutor students was raised. A third writer thought that 'Vigilante' was a snob. The editor defended 'Vigilante's' qualifications for giving such an opinion and described her as 'an experienced and informed member of the nursing profession'.

The discussion continued and *Nursing Times* organised a 'symposium' of anonymous contributors seeking their views: '. . . as far as we know all these contributors are unknown to each other; yet there seems to be a common theme running through all their replies'.

A ward sister thought that tutors lived in an ivory tower, away from the wards. If she were asked to undertake a two-year course 'learning physics and chemistry' she would refuse, but she would not mind taking a short course to be a clinical instructor.

'Sister tutor I' would have liked to be able to teach her students on the wards. 'Administrative sister' wondered what the real problem was. She asked if the tutors missed contact with the patients.

'Ex-teacher', now SRN, thought that nurse training failed to extend the nurses' minds, that there was a deep-rooted uncertainty in the nursing profession with no sense of direction. She, too, thought that her sister tutors would have liked to give up teaching and return to the wards. A principal tutor thought that tutors should be able to specialise in a subject. 'Sister tutor II' thought that candidates with a teaching certificate should be allowed to teach nurses without having to re-qualify as a registered nurse teacher.[16]

Nursing Times failed to offer their ideas of the common theme which they detected in these comments, but it seems that the contributors were unanimously dissatisfied with the system of training, whilst several of them wanted to have greater contact with patients.

The Ministry of Health, during this period, had nothing much to say about the problem of tutors except to report their shortage. Nonetheless there was growing concern and the Management Side of the Whitley Council discussed the problem in 1961. They appeared to centre their discussion around the question of tutors' career development. One member thought that there should be a career ladder but that the matron should continue to be head of the nurse training school. Another member disagreed and thought that the tutor should be head: they should encourage a small select band of highly prestigious tutors. The chief nursing officer disagreed with this: it was not wise to follow the American ideas on this question; the matron had to be in charge.

The Management Side recognised that teachers had much better salaries than nurse tutors and some tutors preferred to work in educational establishments. Unfortunately, if the tutors were given enhanced salaries they would start to overlap the salary scales of the deputy matrons and create further anomalies.[17]

At this point, the College published its own paper, *The Nurse Tutor: a new assessment.*[18] It bemoaned the low level of the recently-introduced minimum educational level for student nurse recruits which would not go far enough towards making the tutor's job more satisfying. One of the causes of dissatisfaction expressed by tutors was the ineducability of some students. Other causes were described as the failure of the hospital authorities to give enough consideration and emphasis to the training of students, the paucity of opportunities for tutors to further their own professional development, the attitude of the GNC towards the tutors (the GNC insisted on communicating with the group secretary and the matron), inadequate career prospects, poor salaries and the need for better selection of tutor candidates.

The College proposed a hierarchy for tutors ranging through three levels, separate from the administrative hierarchy, and recommended that there should be a reduction in the continuing employment of unqualified tutorial staff.

They thought that many authorities still regarded the function of the tutor as pushing students through qualifying examinations. Instead, the tutor should be allocated to a group in order to give them a sense of belonging and continuity, especially in group schools where the student was moved from hospital to hospital. Students should be required to spend less time at formal classes and be given more time for reading and studying on their own. There should be greater use of discussion methods and the tutor:student ratio should be reduced to 1:30 or, in mental hospitals, to 1:20. The tutor student should be required to have a minimum of three 'O' levels.

When the Management Side discussed this report, they came to the conclusion that it was too biased and that it presented only the tutors' point of view. They decided against the proposal to have senior posts as director of nurse education and they had been advised that the College did not immediately intend to press that point. They did not agree that tutors should be placed on the Burnham scales and Mr Willis, of the Ministry of Health, thought that nurse tutors should take their place in the nursing structure rather than be separated from it.[19]

Recruits to the tutor courses continued to decline in numbers. The GNC and London University became concerned at the lack of applications to the three London courses at the RCN, Queen Elizabeth College and the Battersea College of Technology. They talked to several of the nursing organisations and concluded that most of the reasons already put forward still held good. They also thought that the first year of study was proving very heavy for nurses who were not used to studying. The Ministry of Health refused to pay London weighting to candidates from other areas because they had not worked in London prior to starting their tutor training. The GNC appealed to the Whitley Council who, for once, disagreed with the Ministry and reversed their ruling.[20]

In 1963 the Tutor Section of the RCN reported that the drift of tutors into administrative posts or technical colleges (where the salaries and conditions were much better) was accelerating. They offered no figures for this assertion but a study made by the GNC in 1975–76[21] showed that 28 per cent of the respondents (registered nurse tutors) had moved out of schools of nursing and a further 15 per cent planned to move out of their current posts (seven per cent planned to move to colleges of further education). There remained a feeling of instability within the schools of nursing, where morale was low.

The problem of nurse teachers has not yet been resolved. The Salmon structure failed to offer them a separate educational career avenue and their salaries are still tied to the general nursing structure.

The GNC report in 1975–76 found that nurse teachers were still contending with a conflict between nurse education and service, that they still lacked control over student education and that there was still conflict between the teaching of students in the schools and ward practice. Nurse teachers continued to feel that ward staff failed to cooperate with them or to afford them enough status as experts in their own field; few teachers of nurses were encouraged to specialise in a particular field. Bendall (1975)[22] reported a continuing anti-education feeling which believed in 'an inverse relationship' between academic and practical ability.

The Aitken report should be seen in the light of the negotiations that preceded the publication of the Armer report on the training of district nurses[23] and the later Ingall report on the training of district nurses.[24] All these reports were dominated by the Ministry of Health and all flew in the face of expert advice from educationalists. All sought to reduce the period of training of the nurses concerned, not for educational reasons but to produce a 'semi-processed article' to meet a current shortage.

The Ministry of Health, during the 1950s at least, was considerably influenced by its civil servants in its attitude to nurses and nurse training. It refused to acknowledge the need for an adequate preparation and was concerned only with quantity, never quality. As with all the other special areas of nursing and, indeed, with the general nurses themselves, every effort that the profession made to raise the level of training was denied and the generalist nature of their work was emphasised.

Chapter 10/The Goddard report[1]

When the Wood working party was set up in 1946, it was asked to look into five specific questions:

    a What is the proper task of the nurse?
    b What training is required to equip her for her task?
    c What annual intake is needed and how can it be obtained?
    d From what groups of the population should recruitment be made?
    e How can wastage during training be minimised?[2]

Its report was published in 1947 and a minority report, written by Professor John Cohen, was published in 1948.[3] The main report complained about the total lack of reliable statistical data necessary to give background information showing the composition and structure of the existing nursing profession.

It recommended a two year training for the first level nurse and commented that this period of time would be quite enough if student nurses were relieved of domestic work and repetitive nursing duties. The working party was not able to answer the first question and also found it difficult to give a good answer to question (c) without better understanding of the nation's manpower resources.

The minority report was more emphatic about planning the future needs of nurses and considered that further research was required. There was, it said, an absence of any objective method of assessing optimum staffing standards, and it proposed for this purpose a study of patient stay as a test for nursing efficiency. Cohen adapted the industrial model and defined the function of the nurse as 'to reduce the incidence and duration of sickness'. He offered a provisional formula using numbers of nurses against length of patient stay to reach a satisfactory standard of staffing.[3]

One of the first goals of the Ministry of Health, after 1948, was to tighten up management efficiency in the hospitals and to achieve a better use of beds by speedier turn-over of patients. The use of an industrial concept for increasing efficiency in nursing was therefore welcomed and by 1949–50 the Minister was able to announce that the Nuffield Provincial Hospitals Trust (NPHT) had set up a job analysis under the direction of H A Goddard.[4]

H A Goddard was a director of a management consultancy firm; he was also chairman of the Management Side of the Nurses and Midwives Whitley Council and was consequently well placed to undertake such a study.

It was perhaps opportune that the Royal College of Nursing was already interested in job analysis as a new tool for administration[5] and that the superintendent health visitor of Essex County Council had recently analysed the work of her staff. This survey had shown her that they were spending too much time doing clerical and unskilled work at clinics.[6] The RCN was therefore very happy to ask the Ministry for a second study to be made by the NPHT team, on the work of public health nurses.[7]

The Goddard report on the work of nurses in hospital wards was published in 1953 and immediately set up reverberations throughout the nursing world. For some reason, possibly because most nurses knew about it only at second hand, it is the most misunderstood and misread study of any that was made during the period 1948–61, with the possible exception of the Wood report itself. It is interesting that in its misunderstood form, it survived and had more influence than most others. Its misrepresentation was even perpetuated in the Royal Commission on the National Health Service, 1979.[8]

The report is commonly held to have proposed that nursing work should be divided into three groups in rank order: technical tasks, basic nursing and non-nursing duties. Furthermore, Goddard is purported to have proposed that these tasks should be performed by senior nurses, junior nurses and untrained staff respectively. This misunderstanding caused a storm of protest at the time and has coloured much subsequent research and organisation since.

In fact, Goddard wrote that it was observed by the research team that nurses had themselves already divided their work into basic and technical tasks and that they were already allocating these tasks to junior and senior nurses (chapter 5).

Goddard continued by saying that this presented a danger to the patient since both kinds of tasks arose out of each other and reacted upon one another. Moreover, he said, nurses admitted that it was not possible to treat these needs in isolation. He observed that little time was given to dealing with emotional needs by talking to patients:

... the idea of unity of nursing [the whole individual rather than tasks] as a service for patients should not be sacrificed until the alternative [patient assignment] has been tried.

Goddard felt very strongly that bedside nursing was the task of the state registered nurse. Thus, he said, the respective spheres of the nurse and other grades would be determined by bedside and non-bedside functions. The SRN should see to the patient and leave others to look after the non-nursing functions.

Goddard defined non-nursing functions as being, *inter alia*, ward administration, maintenance of equipment and supplies. He had found the reverse in his job-analysis. Nursing tasks took 59.8 per cent of the total nursing hours (including physical, medical and social needs); ward administration took 23.5 per cent of time and domestic work 16.7 per cent. In these proportions, basic nursing took two-thirds of all nursing time.

He identified a difference in dependency needs for different patients, a difference in staff/bed ratios in different sized wards, the effects of the number of staff on time given to basic nursing, and the effects of equipment and ward design on basic nursing. In some wards there were no bedpan sterilizers, trolleys or sterilizers: nurses had to burn methylated spirits in bowls in order to sterilize them; often nurses had to go from one ward to another in order to borrow equipment. Technical nursing took less than one-third of nursing time and was less influenced by the patient dependency factor.

Between 16–34 per cent of total time observed was taken up by ward administration. Some relationship with the size of the ward was evident. Giving and receiving reports consumed 2 per cent of this time, ward organisation took 11 per cent. Between two and three hours were spent in writing and giving reports but on only six of the 24 wards observed did all the day staff receive a report.

He also found a wide variation in the composition of staff: all but two wards had a full time ward sister on day duty; all but seven wards had one or more full time staff nurses on day duty; only five wards had more than one full time staff nurse on day duty. Seven wards were without a staff nurse and in these a student nurse acted as sister's deputy. Student nurses were left in charge of their wards for 22 per cent of their time on day duty. Student nurses formed 48–78 per cent of the ward staff; on only one ward did he find a state enrolled assistant nurse. Of the other staff, the nursing orderlies were mostly ex-service people, and most of the others had no certificates at all; 14.8 per cent of the nurses were SRNs; 60.8 per cent were student nurses; 2.4 per cent were other nursing staff; 21.9 per cent of the total staff were domestics; 0.1 per cent were voluntary workers. These figures gave a ratio of one SRN per four student nurses. For every 100 beds there were seven SRNs, 31 students, one other nursing staff member and 11 domestic staff.

He found, surprisingly, that student nurses did relatively little domestic work: at most, 35 minutes per day. But they did 18.7 per cent of all recorded domestic work. The patients also did a lot of domestic work but they were not recorded.

Goddard observed a lack of distinction between the work of

doctors and nurses: lines of demarcation were drawn mostly by policy decision. Often nurses prepared and cleared up for doctors.

The distinction in the work of nurses and domestics was also vague and subject to local policy. Some orderlies did more domestic work and others did more nursing work. The picture was no different for 'medical auxiliaries'. Allocation of work to the several grades depended on the numbers of student nurses and their seniority; therefore all theoretical considerations about what practical work the students should be doing in each year of training must be abandoned when the balance of the staff was radically altered.

Only two of the wards used the system of case assignment; all the others used task assignment. There was little teaching given in the wards and neither the sisters nor the staff nurses spent much time with the students. Student nurses learned more from working with one another, but they seldom studied case notes, except on night duty.

Responsibility for allocating students to wards rested with an administrative sister, not the tutors. There were many complaints from students about the inadequacy of their ward experience and it was evident that service needs took priority over teaching needs.

Goddard reported that the complex administrative system of hospitals (since 1948) and developments in medical science had made new and increased demands on nursing time. These were further emphasised by a rise in the general standard of living and a change in the social class of many patients in the wards. He found a 'gulf' between the 'present' and the 'proper' task of the nurse. The traditional view of nursing was derived from Florence Nightingale's perceptions and was based on bedside care of the patient. The present tasks of nurses had become more technical.

In fact, this was an important observation and highlighted the change in the functions of hospitals since the 1939–45 war, and the move from the old domination of health care by infectious diseases to the newer paradigm of behavioural diseases. Before the advent of a scientific pharmacopoeia there were few remedies for infectious diseases and the recovery of patients depended heavily on good nursing. It was during this period that British nursing had developed and nursing techniques, procedures and traditions were, consequently, keyed to these needs. The change from infectious diseases to behavioural diseases, as the major factor in morbidity statistics, had not been recognised in nurse training nor in the nursing function. British nurses were therefore trying to ride two horses: they were trying to maintain their old traditions of bedside care whilst, at the same time, being pushed by the new practices in hospitals into more responsibility for technical procedures.

Shryock[9] described these changes: in 1860 the main tasks of nurses were to see to the ventilation of sick rooms, to provide the correct diet, clean rooms, maintain the patient's hygiene and give thoughtful care. In 1948, he found nurses were taking blood pressure readings, performing lavages, helping with blood transfusions, applying suction to surgical wounds, maintaining tracheostomies and chest cavities. They performed tidal irrigation, irrigated eyes, drained wounds, cleaned colostomies, applied sterile compresses, painted lesions, catheterised patients and gave injections. They tested urine, gave out drugs and medicines, helped with lumbar punctures and packed cavities.

Nurses needed to know each instrument and procedure, to detect toxic reactions and undesirable developments and to take appropriate action or modify their treatment.

Nurses were having to abandon their former skills, which had made British nurses famous and in which they had been taught to take such pride, to untrained staff. They had to learn new skills in which they received no training and for which many of the experienced nurses had little inclination.

Goddard found that basic nursing took up to 75 per cent of nursing time and dictated the framework of the ward routine. It was, he said, mostly repetitive. Technical nursing absorbed 30 per cent of nursing time and took priority over (and often interrupted) basic nursing. He reasoned that this set of values, which reflected those of the other hospital departments, caused a division of labour, with senior nurses doing the higher status tasks and junior nurses doing the lower status ones.

This system was one that the Horder report[10] had more or less advocated and was similar to the trend in the USA. It was seen to be more economical in the use of skilled workers, made a better use of all levels of recruits and offered greater prospects for better nurse training (since it appeared to increase the professional status of nurses) and the chance of full student status for learner nurses.

Shryock (1959) came to a similar conclusion and described the growing demands for improved educational programmes in the US, increased specialisation, standardisation and university education for higher status nurses.

Goddard offered arguments against the system. He considered that a nurse's usefulness was based on observing and reporting to the doctor. This required her to spend more time, not less, at the bedside. He did not think that technical tasks could be the basis of nursing and was very anxious that the patient should be nursed as an individual. He more or less implored nurses to maintain the unity of nursing until, at least, the alternative (patient assignment) had been evaluated. If this were to be so, the division of nursing labour should be made between bedside and non-bedside nursing functions, which have already been described as administrative duties and maintenance of supplies and equipment etc.

Goddard found that the student nurse was 'the nurse' and that, once qualified, the staff nurse's aim was to gain promotion. The ward sister, he found, had three functions: care of patients, ward administration and teaching the students. He did not believe that she could do all these. If she were to manage the ward, the other two functions had to be delegated. He therefore proposed a new model for the organisation of patient care and training.

He proposed that this should be done in units of about 50 beds (subject to further studies). Each unit should be in the charge of a ward sister. The patients should be divided into groups, with a staff nurse in charge of each and a small team of nursing staff to help her. The team should consist of 'nursing auxiliaries' (including enrolled nurses) supplemented, from time to time, by student nurses. He quoted the Horder report (Section IV, 1949):

... where there is a choice of two tasks, the student nurse should be given the task which builds up her knowledge and skill rather than the one which is unnecessary to her learning but is necessary to the service needs of the hospital.

The staff nurse should give personal care to her patients and the nursing auxiliaries should work under her supervision. Nursing care by the teams should be independent of students who should be able to supplement it, working in conjunction with the trained staff; but this must be planned in accordance with their training needs. In other words, the student was to be supernumerary. In this way, Goddard proposed that all nursing should be in the hands of trained nurses who might get advice and guidance from the ward sister.

The ward sister should have a personal assistant of an appropriate calibre. Goddard insisted that this would be a secretarial post and should not be a clerical assistant or errand boy.

The ward sister would be in a key position at the hub of the unit. She would be responsible for domestic staff, supervise the practical training of student nurses, be responsible for the management of the unit (assisted by her personal assistant) and monitor the nursing teams:

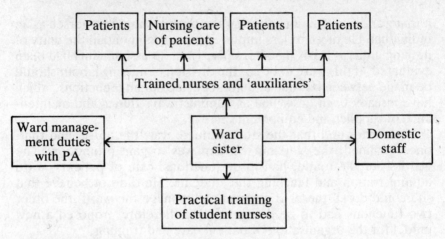

The advisory panel, appointed to support the study, approved his recommendations and confirmed that nursing care of patients should be given by trained nurses.

The GNC was not obviously impressed with the report and did not take up its criticisms or recommendations. They set up a sub-committee to study the report but the only comment that is available was that 'the very generalised conclusions that were drawn from the survey' could not be sustained because the sample was too small. They refused to accept that the student nurse's time in wards was dominated by needless repetitive tasks.[11]

The RCN received the report in February 1953, arranged a conference to discuss it for May (when H A Goddard took the chair) and subsequently set up a working party to deal with matters relating to the report.

Goddard told the RCN annual conference in July that the job analysis did not claim to provide a solution to the many problems of the nursing profession; it was 'an essential foundation of long-term policy'. It was the end of a fact-finding stage, but the beginning of the policy-forming stage.

He believed that the nursing profession should have the prerogative to determine what its functions should be and he had therefore 'stoutly resisted the pressure which was put on me from certain quarters to provide a blue-print'. He emphasised that there should be no segregation of nursing activities into basic and technical 'since the prime reason for nursing care lies in the satisfaction of the total needs of the patient'. It followed therefore that the nursing of the patient should be in the hands of the trained nurse and that the group assignment system, which he had recommended in his report, would most contribute to that end.

Goddard spent some time in discussing the training of student nurses: '. . . it would appear that the end result of nurse training is not nursing but administration'. He told the meeting that at the May conference the question of the purpose of nurse training had produced many lively discussions.

The organisation of wards was a critical factor in the pattern of care and the matron should take an active part in reviewing this, if necessary by changing the routine of other departments and hospital staff. Too much of the ward organisation revolved around doctors; was it desirable that nurses should take on medical procedures?

What is now needed is action research by nurses themselves . . . reinforced by experimental work designed to test and evaluate the effectiveness of the research. Then with the whole weight of the profession behind them the results can be published and steps taken to apply them. Unless this is done, all that has gone before will be but a waste of time, energy and money.[12]

When the RCN comments came out in October, they immediately demonstrated that the central theme of Goddard's message, the preservation of the unity of nursing, had been misunderstood. The College accepted the distinction reported by Goddard between basic and technical tasks but could not accept that this distinction could be maintained at all stages of a patient's disease career. What might be basic for one patient could become technical for another patient. This was a tragic misunderstanding of Goddard's thesis, as a result of which patient care continued to be more and more fragmented and nursing became more and more divided by a hierarchy of tasks.

The College then continued, as it had invariably done since 1947, by shredding the remaining parts of the Goddard report and commenting on its separate recommendations. They did not agree that administration could be separated from the nursing duties of the ward sister; they remembered that Nightingale nurses had been trained for supervisory duties rather than bedside nursing; they considered that Goddard's prescription for a nursing unit of about 50 beds was far too large to handle. They went into a paroxysm of propaganda aimed at furthering the Horder proposals, making nursing more competitive and reducing student nurse wastage. There was a need, they said, to be realistic and to accept the fact of economic constraints; a need to reconcile the patient's needs with the available resources. It was not practicable to have trained nurses do bedside nursing nor was it economically possible: she should be the team leader. Non-nursing tasks should be reallocated to domestic, laboratory and clerical staffs.

They agreed that there was a preoccupation with medical needs and customs and that more equipment and work rationalisation was needed. They disputed that ward sisters did not give much teaching time to students but thought that sisters might give more if they were not so overworked.[13]

The College completely missed the point of Goddard's model and went for the peripheral points. It was significant that the nurses had permitted and encouraged the study and that they were open to discussions on the different mixes of skills in the nursing organisation, but they could not separate their thinking from the traditional ward organisation and, clearly, failed to grasp the different concept of a nursing unit worked by small nursing teams.

The College had latched onto the Horder model: they were too preoccupied with the 'pivotal' nature of the SEAN and the 'officer' type of SRN propounded by Horder to look coolly at a slightly different format. They were too concerned to be 'responsible' and 'realistic' in the face of manpower and economic constraints and with the need to reduce student wastage, to be able to understand the long-term implications of Goddard's proposals. They saw the SRN as the administrative leader of a ward team rather than as the clinical leader of a smaller team caring for a group of patients. They were too concerned with quantitative aspects and forgot about Horder's qualitative emphasis. They wanted a managerial status for the SRN rather than a clinical status.

If the College had agreed with the Goddard precept that the place of the nurse was at the patient's bedside, it would have enhanced the professional power and status of the SRN and it could have been woven into the Horder model. Goddard's ideas were not fundamentally irreconcilable with those of Horder. Acceptance of group assignment and all that went with it would have offered greater development of clinical skills and, possibly, have led more quickly to better professional training at universities. There is little doubt that it would have progressed to clinical specialisation and an improved clinical career structure. It might also have provided greater professional autonomy more quickly.

Implementation of the Horder model hinged on a reversal of the proportionate numbers of SRNs and SEANs. In spite of a great deal of rhetoric this had not been achieved and recruitment of pupil nurses was not successful.

The College, as well as the other nursing institutions, were trying to strengthen the position of enrolled nurses who had not been accepted by the profession. They were therefore inclined to defend enrolled nurses against suggestions that they were a second grade or that they gave second class care. By doing this they further confused the continuing problem of the respective roles of the SRN and SEAN, usually to the detriment of the former. The confusion of roles and the authorities' defence of SEANs tended to encourage SRNs to assume more administrative functions and to leave patient care to what SEANs were available. They did this partly to distance themselves from the SEANs and to bolster their own self-image. If the RCN considered that the skills of the trained nurse were more appropriate to an 'officer' role, how better to demonstrate her officer status than by allowing the SEAN to do the repetitive, routine nursing care?

Table 2   Nursing staff employed in hospitals 1949, 1957[14]

	1949	1957
Trained nurses:		
Whole-time	41,318	50,525
Part-time	6,283	12,407
Student nurses:		
Whole-time	46,182	52,831
Enrolled assistant nurses:		
Whole-time	12,177	9,614
Part-time	4,383	5,983
Pupil assistant nurses:		
Whole-time	1,658	4,443
Part-time		23

When the Sister Tutor Section held their conference on the NPHT report, their guest speaker was Miss M G Lawson, deputy chief nursing officer at the Ministry of Health. In her address she emphatically insisted that the SEAN

... is not a person who is trained to perform nursing duties to a lower level of skill than her colleague for registration. She is a person whose skill is essentially practical and who is trained in the duties proper to her grade, to no less high a standard than is demanded of the registered nurse. Naturally, the scope of her duties is more limited.[15]

Miss Lawson went on to ask why the NPHT report had discovered that 40 per cent of those interviewed by the Goddard team wished to leave to take further training? Why did trained nurses spend so much time in administrative duties and technical procedures?

Does this not point to the fact that the tasks now considered proper to the trained nurse (that is technical nursing and ward management) no longer have the same appeal to the nurse – that she misses the actual contact with patients with whom she no longer has the time to spend?[15]

Thus spoke the traditionalist, but she did not offer the whole Goddard package: she did not propose that there should be patient assignment and nursing teams which might help to keep the trained nurse at the bedside.

A letter from a ward sister put a different perspective on administrative chores. She complained that from five to eight forms were now needed when a patient died, whereas previously only two had been necessary. She did not ask for the Goddard package either; instead she wanted only clerical help and a domestic supervisor.[16]

In December 1953 the RCN held a further conference to discuss the College's comments on the NPHT report. This arrangement meant that the College's misunderstanding of the report was the main thrust of the discussion and it is possible that this reinforced the general misinterpretation of Goddard's model.

Miss M Houghton, education officer at the GNC (who had also been a member of the RCN working party which formulated the comments) complained that a 50-bed ward would be too large for one ward sister to handle; it would take her away from the patients. The increasingly elaborate procedures in patient care devolved mainly on the ward sister. She needed to be relieved of some of the burden. Staff nurses were 'shrinking' from the responsibility of ward sister posts and so left to take further training; there was the need to develop a clinical career for the ward sister and so to effect an improved status for her.[17]

Miss C Bentley (a ward sister at the time) agreed with the need for case assignment. She considered that ward sisters were acquiescent in taking on extra responsibilities and were hostile to parting with their present ones, but it was within their power to make any organisational changes in their wards.[17]

Miss M Powell discussed plans for case assignment at her hospital (St George's Hospital, London) but the Nightingale ward was not conducive to this system was, she agreed, the need for extra equipment as well as ient nurses or auxiliaries in order to turn over to case here had been no need for extra trained nurses a the scheme had been in operation for five years and by the nurses.[17]

The arg d on; the College persisted in arguing that there w trained nurses to nurse patients by assignment ould not be economical anyway.[18] The GNC continued to complain that ward sisters did not sufficiently accept their responsibility for teaching students.[19]

The Ministry of Health had referred the NPHT report to the Standing Nursing Advisory Committee (SNAC) and encouraged a few experiments in case assignment to test the system. In 1954 the SNAC issued a report on *The Position of the Enrolled Assistant Nurse within the NHS.*[20] In this they reported that the SEAN had a role in most fields of nursing so long as she worked under the supervision of a registered nurse. They considered that their duties should be restricted to basic nursing duties as described in the NPHT report, including

> ... care required in the interests of comfort and the well-being of the patient, for the maintenance of health and the prevention of infection, irrespective of the disease from which he is suffering.

The SEAN, they thought, had a place in the nursing team for patient assignment.

Their report on the NPHT report emphasised the need for trials of patient assignment. They proposed that these should be in four non-teaching hospitals which were 'not too favourably placed for staff'. The trial was to be assessed by a team of experienced nurses and a review of patients' comments. The report of this trial became very complex and was subjected to considerable amendments. First expected in 1954, it was not available until 1958. Even then it was inconclusive and called for further studies in the composition of the teams, flexibility between teams and the use of lay help in the wards. The sub-committee studying the scheme appeared to think that the system was sound. They could not yet say if it would need more nurses to work it but recommended that it should be introduced into hospitals as soon as possible.[21]

No details of the SNAC comments have been found and the only evidence available from the Central Health Services Council are sketchy. It can be inferred from these that there were considerable organisational problems in the introduction of case assignment, some of which must have been caused by difficulties of maintaining nursing cover by the team during off-duty periods (flexibility between teams). It can also be inferred that some form of assistance was given to the ward sister (use of lay assistance in wards) although the quality of this is not described.

In 1958 the King's Fund published a paper, *Noise Control In Hospitals*, which drew attention to 'the unnecessary noise' in hospitals.[22] The CHSC had previously published a paper, *The Reception and Welfare of In-Patients in Hospitals.*[23] It was thought by the

CHSC that both these reports linked with the NPHT report, and the sub-committee investigating case assignment was asked to include them in their work (CHSC, 1958). These tasks, specifically the in-patient's day, snowballed and when the SNAC was asked to consider a third report, published by the RCN[24] on the nursing services, work on the case assignment trials was overtaken. The investigation of the in-patient's day became very complex, involving hospital routines, hours of work, hospital services and medical routines. No final comments on the NPHT report appear to have been completed. It is possible that reorganisation of the in-patient's day may have been seen as a structural problem which should be resolved before ward organisation could appropriately be tackled.

No further comments were made by the Ministry about the NPHT report but they continued to discuss the need to make better use of trained nurses and to use SEANs more efficiently, and exhorted hospital authorities to transfer non-nursing duties to other grades of staff.[25] As medical technology gathered greater momentum, there was more discussion of the technical aspects of nursing and the need to look critically at the duties of nurses.[26] As the Ministry grew more and more keen on efficiency and method study, work study officers were appointed to hospitals, often to study the organisation of nurses in wards and staffing standards.[27] The emphasis was quantitative rather than qualitative and the turnover of patients increased dramatically.[28] But the organisation of the care of the patient remained the same: nurses still worked by task assignment and the division of work into basic or technical ranking continued. The difference was that as more technical tasks accumulated, the division between them shifted: basic nursing included more complicated procedures so that untrained nursing staff did more for their patients than previously.

In a leader article, *Nursing Times* discussed the situation that ward sisters had to contend with.[29] The ward sisters were faced with changing demands not only from the doctors but also from the patients. How was the sister to ensure that nursing did not disintegrate into a series of technical tasks? The medical profession was handing over tasks in order to lighten their increasing burden but medical science was also creating new demands for nursing. In one 30–bed ward there were 20 patients on quarter-hourly blood pressure recordings at one time. What was the proper task of the nurse? Was it to comfort, succour and support the patient? Or was it to assist, relieve and inform the doctor? If it had to be both, some services must be delegated to others and it must be the nurses who make that decision:

208

One of the essential characteristics of any profession is that it examines constantly its own standards and accepts responsibility for the service its members give.

A few months later the journal returned to the same theme.[30] It discussed the 'exacting task' of the ward sister to whom everybody turned. She had, it claimed, 40 or more patients in her care and their relatives to deal with. She might have 12 or more physicians or surgeons visiting the ward daily, a minimum of staff which was constantly changing. She might not have any other trained nurse on duty with her. There was a constant stream of people calling at the ward: administrative staff, ministers, family doctors, HMC members. Between 8 am and 11 am she would have spoken to 50 people, either personally or over the telephone. It was hard to measure the mental, emotional and physical drain on her, and this was a possible cause of the loss of trained nurses from the service.

It was impossible for one person to be the administrator, nurse, teacher, leader, adviser, friend, employee and manager, the pig in the middle of patients, students and doctors. One thing that would be helpful would be to start group assignment of patient care.

The College evidently accepted that something needed to be done and published a new statement on nursing policy, *Observations and Objectives*.[31] This paper, they said, built on the Horder report and updated it; the objectives were said to be realistic, not idealistic, and proposed a horizontal and a vertical expansion for nursing.

Horizontal expansion involved the growth of nursing teams composed of SEANs, student nurses (with priority given to their learning needs) and nursing auxiliaries. The team leader was to be a SRN.

Vertical expansion involved the development of advanced courses for specialist nurses in leadership positions. These included clinical nurse specialists.

The paper discussed the need for an improved standard of nursing for patients and better training for nurses. Training should emphasise total patient care, rather than nursing procedures. The paper illustrated the difference in the two approaches by contrasting the giving of a bed bath with bathing a patient. The College blamed service pressures for the deterioration in the standards of nursing.

If the paper had not clearly stated that this was the Horder model, it might have been talking about the Goddard model. There were many similar features in the two. Both recommended teams of nurses led by the SRN, both recommended further training for the ward sister or SRN; Horder had described a hierarchy of nursing tasks and Goddard had recognised these although he preferred to retain the unity of nursing. The main difference between the reports was that Horder had not looked at ward organisation and patient care in making up his model whereas Goddard had. Goddard worked through the local implications of his recommendations and described a system by which they could be implemented.

If the RCN had really analysed both models they could have grafted Goddard's on to Horder's to the great benefit of both nurses and patients. Horder's model left the ward sister with all the problems that have already been described. Goddard's relieved her of most of them.

Nursing teams were already developing: if there are three grades of nursing staff and two of them are subordinate to the first, there has to be some sort of a hierarchy or team. It was just a question of whether the entire ward staff comprised the team (Horder) or whether there were several mini-teams working under the ward sister (Goddard). The former method did not require reorganisation of ward routine and could perpetuate task allocation. The latter method did need the ward to be reorganised but also promoted patient assignment. The Horder model won over the Goddard model in the end.

It is probable that the serious shortage of trained nurses might have made the implementation of patient assignment impracticable at the time. The speedier turnover of patients meant that they were being discharged earlier than was the case ten years previously. The whole cycle of patient care had changed in the wards. In 1948 patients could roughly be divided into three groups. The first comprised those almost ready to be discharged, who were ambulant and able to help the nurses with many simple tasks such as giving out cups of tea in the early morning, fetching and carrying washing bowls and doing small services for other patients. The middle group of patients were those half way in their treatment who were sitting up in bed, possibly going out to the lavatories (with an escort) but who were able to feed themselves, wash in bed and get up for an hour or so during the day. These patients needed only a little care and some treatment. The third group were the very ill, highly dependent patients who needed much more nursing time.

By 1958 the first group had disappeared, the second group had been considerably reduced and the third group predominated. Patients in hospital were much more acutely ill and needed more nursing.

Although there had not been a decline in the numbers of trained nurses, the small increase hardly made up for these added demands which were exacerbated by the reduction in working hours from 96 to 88 per fortnight.

The shortage of trained and student nurses had been partly made up by an increase in untrained staff.[14]

	1949	1957
Other nursing staff:		
whole-time	16,060	21,264
part-time	11,465	18,370

Whereas whole-time trained nurses had increased by 22.3 per cent, whole-time auxiliaries had increased by 32.4 per cent.

The team nursing system had been introduced to some wards at St George's Hospital, London, in 1953. After five years, the experiment was written up by Vivien M Jenkinson.[32] Her account claimed more satisfaction for the staff nurse team leaders who liked having their own patients. They could plan and set their own patterns of nursing care, they had to explain and defend their decisions, they had more time for basic nursing and for supervising and teaching their juniors. Their work was at a higher and deeper level and there was friendly rivalry between team leaders who could compare their patterns of nursing with their peers.

The student nurses in the teams also preferred the system. They had fewer patients to get to know (9–13) and were able to establish better relationships. They were required to use a wider range of nursing procedures than under the task assignment method and they had better opportunities to observe the effects of their care and treatments. All learning was patient centred and included more understanding of social and domestic implications of the patient's illness. They were allowed to follow up the patient at home with a district nurse, and were able to present case histories to their peers. The patients' duration of stay appeared to be shorter (although Jenkinson acknowledged that other factors may have been involved) and the relatives were able to get to know the nurses more easily.

Team nursing was constrained by the design of wards: where a defined area was used for the patient group, the team was more able to confine their attentions to their own patients. This was not so easy in a Nightingale ward where the other patients made demands of the team.

Jenkinson concluded that team nursing did not save time but it did help to improve the quality of nursing and student training. The

211

students involved in teams were more likely to stay on as staff nurses but, in the early days, they needed help to adjust to the different style of nursing used in the other wards.

Team nursing helped with experiments in nursing and different methods of problem solving. It exposed the inadequate nurse and spotlighted deficiencies. Nursing administrators had to learn not to move members of the teams for relief duties on other wards. If the team was depleted it had to fall back on task assignment.

It was not so easy to meet crises on wards with teams as the extra load fell more heavily on the smaller number of nurses in the team. However, it did give the ward sister more time to spend with the students.

The crux of the system was to have small teams led by trained nurses. If there was a shortage of trained nurses the teams became larger. Evidently they had not tried the team system without trained nurses, and Jenkinson did not describe any other changes in ward organisation such as the Goddard package had proposed. The idea of teams was not wholly liked by the profession. One criticism was that it introduced more untrained nurses into the wards and that it further diluted the mix of skills. This argument was not a good one. It has already been shown that more auxiliaries were being employed irrespective of what system of nursing was used.

Some nurses wanted to get away from bedside nursing and preferred technical tasks. It therefore suited them to perpetuate the task assignment model. They were probably used to that way of nursing and had not had an opportunity of experiencing a more holistic approach – a bed bath was therefore a bed bath, not bathing the patient. Some preferred the stimulus of the new technical tasks. They liked working alongside doctors and enjoyed the new or extra knowledge and skills. For some it was simply a matter of status:

> If nurses persist in finding their only satisfaction in blanket baths, tepid sponges, poultices and the performing of techniques then they will be ousted in prestige by an army of social workers.[33]

There was also a school of thought that there was not a real shortage of trained nurses. These people believed that there was either a mal-distribution or a shortage of money to pay for trained nurses. There is little doubt that the teaching hospitals could recruit all the nurses they wanted. Non-teaching and non-training hospitals were less fortunate. The London hospitals had waiting lists for student nurses who often remained after registration to work as staff nurses. The provincial hospitals were more inclined to have difficulties in recruiting.

In *Nursing Times*, 'Wrangler', an iconoclastic writer, asked whether there was a shortage of nurses or a problem of establishments. She cited hospitals where there were staff available for recruitment but where the budgets did not permit their employment.[34] This point had strength. Nursing establishments had not, on the whole, been reviewed or changed since 1948. Regional hospital boards exerted considerable control over hospital budgets and were slow to respond to changing needs or new patterns of treatment.

Whilst the ratio of doctors to nurses and nurses to patients treated remained roughly the same between 1948 and 1958, the amount of treatment given to each patient had increased as medical science had developed. Patients were more acutely ill and the nursing establishments had not been increased to compensate for the reduction in working hours.[35] Furthermore, hospitals had been exhorted to restrict recruitment of domestic staffs as an economy measure and more work fell on the nurses as a consequence of this.[36] The shortage of trained nurses was therefore to some extent artificial or imposed.

Reaction to the Goddard report was confused and influenced by current preoccupations. Depreciation in the status of nursing, since the advent of the National Health Service, had caused the RCN to try to bolster the profession by turning to a managerial model propounded by Horder. The tenor of the Horder report had been one of acceptance of economic realities and the need to use fewer SRNs and more other grades. The RCN took on this argument and tended to let it overwhelm other perspectives. They sought to preserve the ward sister's role as the ward manager without allowing for any form of delegation.

At first, they failed to respond to Goddard's thesis of the unity of nursing because they, like many nurses, considered that basic care of patients was at the root of the loss of nursing's prestige. This was seen as having been de-skilled by modern medical science. In an age of specialisation, general nursing was falling in value. This could be partially redressed by giving greater emphasis to the skills required by technical tasks. In the choice between the traditional form of Nightingale nursing and the modern form of technical nursing, there was more visible prestige to be derived from the latter. Trained nurses should therefore be managers and technicians.

There were, too, considerable architectural problems attached to reorganising ward care into patient assignment. The open, Nightingale ward helped patients to see the nurses and to call for any one of them as she passed by. It was very hard for a nurse to say 'You are not my patient' and to restrict her responses to her own patient group. Furthermore, without the cooperation of the doctors, patient assignment was almost impossible. Used as they were to being escorted around the ward by the ward sister, they would not accept the need to discuss patient care with each of the team leaders; it was not good enough to be relegated to conversations with staff nurses.

It was also exceedingly difficult to reorganise staffing patterns and ward organisation to allow the formation of teams. Off-duty periods and student nurses' absence from the wards for lectures depleted the teams, often during hours of peak demands. The peaks and troughs of business were caused by routines outside the control of the ward: in the department, the operating theatres, meal hours, visiting hours and the doctors' routines. Jenkinson described the problems of responding to moments of crisis, when the team organisation tended to break down and nurses reverted to the task pattern.

The Ministry of Health probably kept an open mind on the subject and would have allowed team organisation if the profession had wanted it. They were, however, most concerned about the economical use of staff and would have jibbed if it had ever been proved that teams demanded more nurses. They did respond to the findings by Wood and Goddard that there was a need for more studies in patient dependency. In future years the principal direction of their manpower studies was towards seeking for a formula by which staff time could be assessed by patient dependency. These have so far not been successful because a central formula has little bearing on the local measurement of need; the studies have usually been sited in acute wards and there are too many variations between regions and units. Furthermore, they have usually been based on the division of nursing into basic, technical and administrative tasks.

By the time that the RCN published its *Observations and Objectives*[31] there was a shift of opinion. The position of the ward sister had become over-burdened, and early promotion of trained nurses had meant that the grade of staff nurse was rapidly becoming extinct. Young, inexperienced ward sisters, promoted too quickly to positions of considerable stress, were demonstrating their inadequacies. The loss of more experienced nurses made people realize that an improved clinical career had to be developed. There were more older patients who needed more nursing apart from technical care. Patients were more demanding and required a higher level of care in terms of their basic needs. The RCN paper accepted the need for clinical nurse specialists as well as policy makers and managers. The structure of nursing was beginning to lengthen and generate greater distance between the ward sister and the matron:

the position of the clinical nurse had therefore to be strengthened. Furthermore, there was a fairly clear feeling (if there was no proof) that standards of nursing were falling. *Observations and Objectives* therefore set out the need for 'total patient care' and set in train a new direction for nursing which reflected Goddard's unity of nursing and the current recognition of patients' rights.[37]

This new direction was not a return to the Nightingale tradition and went beyond the idea of the nurse as a technician. It became a third concept of nursing which took time to develop, since it lacked theoretical understanding until Henderson was able to describe it in more detail (see chapter 11).[38]

Whilst Goddard discussed the unity of nursing, he was unable to give it greater substance than by reminding nurses of the links between physical, mental and emotional nursing and of the need to nurse the whole patient. Henderson was able to take this further and to describe the unique function of the nurse which she initiates and controls:

> ... to assist the individual, sick or well, in the performance of those activities contributing to health or its recovery (or to a peaceful death) that he would perform unaided if he had the necessary strength, will or knowledge. It is likewise her function to help the individual gain independence as rapidly as possible.

Thus Goddard's unity of nursing became the caring role of the nurse. The nursing process later offered a theoretical framework for the caring role.

Chapter 11/University education
and nursing research

The first Horder report[1a] discussed the relative levels of the assistant and state registered nurses. It recommended that the level of functioning of the registered nurse (SRN) should be raised in order to make room below her for the assistant nurse grade who should be given a recognised qualification under the control of the GNC. There should be a new roll for assistant nurses.[2]

Section II of the report[1b] discussed the training of SRNs and considered it in the light of the general education for girls obtaining at that time. Girls' schools rarely offered science subjects and the syllabus was restricted to the arts, humanities and household sciences. Horder considered that nurse training could help to extend the nature of education of girls and, with improvements, it 'could be developed into one of the great national educational movements for women'. It would offer a system of further education, lacking for most women at the time.

He considered that there should be an honours level in basic nurse training to which the brighter candidates could aspire.

The Horder report also anticipated the need for nurse leaders and expected that the honours system would help to attract the more intelligent girls. It recommended that:

> ... every effort should be made to recruit girls whose education had continued to age 18 years and that the value of the Higher School Certificate and other academic qualifications be stressed.[1c]

By 1949 the last report of the series[1d] had been influenced by the 1944 Education Act which set up a system for secondary education for all children.

Section IV anticipated that the 'highly trained SRN and her specialist colleagues in other professions would be comparable' so long as the profession could develop an elite or officer grade. In Horder's terms, these were to be a relatively few selected candidates who took student nurse training. All other candidates would take pupil nurse training for enrolment:

> ... if all engaged in nursing service are to be considered as one group, then the relationship between nursing and its sister professions cannot be maintained.

This section also considered that ward management, as well as teaching and administration, should be regarded as specialist areas, 'equally important branches of the same tree, each with its own prospects of promotion and financial reward'.

Nurses should be prepared by further education for these specialist branches and should be able to contribute to public affairs and policy making. These qualifications should be of a higher and broader academic type, and the training should be paid from public moneys. In addition to these advanced qualifications, the report highlighted certain other post-basic trainings, such as that of the tutor or health visitor, which should be taken from a university.

Thus there was a gradual climb in the aspirations proposed for the profession and by 1949, for the first time in the series of reports, this section actually came out and stated the need for a degree in nursing. It described the opportunities for a degree at both post-basic and at undergraduate level.

The former would be directed towards achieving a higher standard of nursing whilst the latter, which should be either a science or an arts degree, would be combined with general nurse training. In addition, there should be diploma level courses, possibly at the then technical colleges.

In 1947, before publication of section IV of the Horder report, the Wood report had been published.[3] This recommended a shortened course of training for first level nurses and provoked a storm of disapproval from the profession. However, tucked away in appendix VIII was an extension to that recommendation which clarified the overall model set up by the working party but which was not explicitly described. Appendix VIII explained that the basic training set out in the main body of the report was not intended to prepare nurses for functions over and above those normally carried out by a staff nurse in a hospital:

> ... consequently we do not consider it unreasonable to assume that before a nurse proceeds to a post carrying new functions ... she should receive some training beyond that provided in the basic course.

The working party thought these courses should be met by an increasing number of university courses.

No nurse should claim to be a specialist (they also explicitly included ward sisters) until she had undergone further experience and 'post-graduate training'. Such training should be a pre-condition of promotion in any field.

The Wood report did not go so far as to recommend a degree in nursing nor even post-registration degrees, but it did consider that the student nurse should be a full student, working and studying through academic terms, with long vacations for self-study and gaining more experience of life outside a hospital.

By 1949, therefore, the seeds of the idea had been sown; that nurses should have opportunities for some university education and, more important, that there should be a degree course in nursing or a combined course leading to a degree and state registration. Both of these remarkable reports had identified that there was a need for the development of leaders in nursing, both had identified a specialist component in the ward sister's job, and both had included clinical nurses within their term 'leaders'. What was just as important in an age of specialisation, both reports offered a route for the general nurse to become a specialist.

There is no evidence that any nursing institution other than the Royal College of Nursing was at all interested in pursuing the matter of degree courses for nurses. With regard to post-registration training, there were already several universities and technical colleges which ran courses for health visitors. The first course for a diploma in nursing was started in 1921 at the University of Leeds; the universities of London, Birmingham, Manchester and Hull also had diploma courses. The precedent of holding second level or specialist courses for nurses in higher education centres was, therefore, established.

There were a few graduates in nursing: those who had first taken degrees and then their nurse training, and nurses who had graduated after their training. In 1953, G B Carter, a nurse and the Boots research fellow at Edinburgh University, wrote to *Nursing Times* to ask graduate nurses to contact her. She was setting up a list of nurses with degrees and had so far located 73 names.[4]

In 1956, Carter reported that her survey had produced 65 names including 39 with honours degrees in 15 different subjects ranging from mathematics to theology, 11 ordinary degrees and 15 higher degrees. There were other nurses who were currently studying for degrees. Many of the graduates felt that they had to hide their academic qualifications in nursing; they complained that they had no opportunities to use their critical faculties and that their additional qualifications offered no opportunities for quicker promotion nor extra salary.[5]

Since nurses insisted that their training and work should be practical, there was already an anti-education bias.[6] This bias was possibly inherited from Florence Nightingale's aversion to state registration and examinations, but was also probably confirmed by the open entry to nursing which was brought about in 1939 when the minimum education test was dropped. After that date, the number of candidates with secondary education declined and the majority of nurses soon became those with little formal education.

In 1947, after the publication of the first three sections of the Horder report, the general secretary of the RCN had unofficial conversations with two members of London University (Mr Clow Ford and Mr Knowles) about the possibilities of setting up a degree course for nurses. At first the RCN considered the possibility that its education department could be admitted as a college of the university. For this to happen, the staff of the department would have to be graduates and the level of the course would have to be acceptable to the university. Nothing came of this idea.

There seemed to be some agreement that an undergraduate school of nursing should be set up before a post-graduate school. The university representatives appeared to think that the timing of this innovation was appropriate and were encouraging in their responses.

In reporting these conversations to Council, the general secretary (Miss Frances Goodall) reminded them that if no nursing degree course were available, competition from other women's occupations would probably rob nursing of the better educated candidates. Council had adopted the Horder report as policy and they were therefore committed to setting up such a degree course.

Another reason given for the institution of undergraduate courses was that other countries had already achieved this breakthrough and Britain was slipping behind. If British nurses wanted to take their places in international nursing affairs, they would have to compete on equal terms. Already several influential posts with the International Council of Nurses had been lost to American and Canadian nurses because they had academic qualifications. Frances Goodall admitted that the idea of degrees for nurses was not popular with nurse leaders in the United Kingdom but believed that attitudes were beginning to soften.

Council set up a sub-committee from the Advisory Board in Nursing Education to investigate the ways and means, and Mr Clow Ford was appointed to it.[7] The sub-committee set about drafting a syllabus which should cover $5\frac{1}{2}$ to 6 years and agreed to approach the General Nursing Council and the university to discover their reactions to the proposal. They also set out their arguments for a degree course which they felt to be:

a To widen the education and outlook of the nurse.
b To give the nurse a better status.

219

   c To provide nursing leaders comparable to those from abroad.
   d To enable nurses to tap a wider source of recruits.
   e To provide suitable nurse leaders.

The course should provide three years in hospital, in order to cover registration requirements, and three further years for academic work.[7]

These discussions continued with little progress and not enough agreement to get the course started. In 1954 the Advisory Board in Nurse Education reported that there had been consultations about which faculty would be the most appropriate as a host for the degree course. Apparently their thinking was that a sociological base would be more suitable for nursing than medicine.[8]

In the meantime, the general secretary was investigating the possibilities of instituting some form of machinery for nurses to undertake nursing research on their own behalf, rather than to rely on other bodies. At the previous meeting of the Branches Standing Committee, Lincoln branch had put forward a resolution urging the RCN to take some action in this direction. Frances Goodall reminded Council that a small sum of money was available. An advisory committee was therefore set up.[9]

The idea for research into nursing had been put forward in 1947 by the Wood report which had found that few statistics were available for manpower planning and no evaluation of nurse education had been undertaken. The working party had set out to make their investigations on a scientific basis and used a series of field studies and surveys. The minority report written by Professor John Cohen had complained of

Committees composed of doctors, nurses, administrators and distinguished members of the public following the traditional procedure of compiling a report, namely, by an exchange of views supplemented perhaps by written oral evidence.[10]

One of the aspects that the working party had been asked to examine, but had failed to resolve, was the proper task of the nurse. They had therefore proposed a study of the work of the nurse. The Nuffield Provincial Hospitals Trust had undertaken to make job analyses of the work of hospital and public health nurses.[11] These studies were welcomed by most nurses who had deeply resented an earlier study undertaken by the Standing Nursing Advisory Committee in Nursing Techniques.[12]

Some of the profession, after 1948, were caught up by the exciting prospect of research into their activities but other nurses thought that outside bodies might lack understanding of nursing values and pressures. These, therefore, wanted nurses to be involved.

In June 1952, the RCN Scottish Board reported to Council that Boots the Chemists had funded a fellowship in nursing for seven years. The fund was to be administered by Edinburgh University and would be open to all graduates.[13] Later that year, the Florence Nightingale Memorial Committee announced the setting up of the Dan Mason Research Trust. This was to investigate basic nursing education, methods of training and nursing techniques. It was originally funded at £2,000 per annum for two years but this was subsequently extended.[14] Other moneys were received from the estate of the Dowager Countess of Peel and were earmarked for the College's research fund.[13]

In December, Council heard that Eileen Skellern's *Investigation into the Practical Application to Ward Administration of Modern Methods in the Instruction and Handling of Staff and Student Nurses* was to be published.[15] The report had been completed earlier that year and the costs of publication were to be paid by the Ward and Departmental Sisters' Section, of which Eileen Skellern was a member.

Early next year the appointment of the first Boots research fellow was announced. It was to be Miss G B Carter, BSc. She was a well-known sister tutor and was to examine the possibilities of converting the existing sister tutor certificate, at Edinburgh, to a degree course.[16]

The advisory group on research came to the decision that a research council should be set up and was asked to prepare a paper outlining its constitution, functions and methods of financing its activities. The group had approached the Medical Research Council for their expert advice. They had jointly concluded that the research council should consist of about twelve members of whom half should be nurses: the others should be scientists, doctors and university members.[17]

When the advisory group reported again in July, they presented their proposals for the functions of the research council. It should examine problems peculiar to nursing, sponsor such operational research as it thought appropriate, and test the application of research findings by experimental programmes. They considered that the research council could build up a body of scientific knowledge and help to formulate policy by the production of facts. They proposed that Mr (later Sir) John F Wolfenden, vice-chancellor of Reading University, should be chairman.

The objectives of the research council were given as follows:

1 To examine problems of the nursing profession.
2 To initiate research.
3 To examine findings of research activity.
4 To initiate controlled experiments to test findings.
5 To publish reports of research.
6 To become an information and resource centre.
7 To hold research conferences.

In November, Frances Goodall reported to Council that Mr Wolfenden had declined to accept the chair of the proposed research council. She was engaged in making informal approaches to other people and, for that reason, no further action was being taken on the constitution.

During these developments, the Scottish Board received a letter from Professor F A E Crew, Department of Public Health and Social Medicine, intimating the possibility of setting up a department of nursing within Edinburgh University. Discussions were current between the university and the Rockefeller Foundation regarding an initial five-year grant. The development of this possibility would depend on what kind of a degree could be agreed and how much control would be exercised by the Scottish Board.[18]

When the Scottish Board met Professor Crew in October, he urged the College to give immediate and active support to the proposals. This was given. Council thought that the College would be able to fund one lecturer post and proposed to write letters of appreciation to Professor Crew and the Rockefeller Foundation.[18]

The College was still not successful in finding a willing chairman for the research council but they went on with their search. The Advisory Board on Nurse Education continued to experience difficulties in establishing a degree course in London. But the Scottish Board was triumphantly able to announce that the Rockefeller Foundation had agreed £30,000 funding for a nurse teaching unit at the university.[19]

In 1956 the College published a new statement on nursing policy, *Observations and Objectives*, which was designed to up-date the Horder report. This document confirmed the need for graduate nurses to take leadership posts, and for research into nursing.[20] College policy was to seek for a nursing team of different grades, with a highly qualified nurse as leader.

A nursing degree was needed to produce these leaders for the ward team, as well as administrators, teachers and others who might represent British nurses at international organisations and in 'academic circles'. There was also a need for higher education at the post-registration level in order to develop specialists. The paper recapitulated the need for a research body and repeated the five functions previously identified for the research council.

In July of the same year (1956) the RCN was able to announce that Miss H M Simpson was to undertake part-time research into 'The Development of Nursing as a Profession' at the London School of Economics.

Negotiations obviously did not proceed very easily between the College and Edinburgh University in the planning of the nursing teaching unit. The College did not understand the strength of feeling in universities for their academic freedom and wanted too much control over the arrangements. The university resented this apparent officiousness. The Scottish Board of the RCN became the pig-in-the-middle: it was tied to RCN policy and dependent on Council's continuing goodwill but, on the other hand, it did not want to lose the opportunity of a department in the university.

Eventually the RCN went over the heads of the faculty representatives and wrote to the principal, Sir Edward Appleton, to ask about the policy of the unit and the content of the courses. Sir Edward replied asking the RCN to appoint two representatives to sit on the advisory committee. He also indicated that it would be wise to let the advisory committee get on with its task without too much detailed supervision. The chairman of the Scottish Board (Miss I G McInroy) and Miss Mary Carpenter (head of the RCN education department) were nominated as College representatives on the advisory committee.[21]

Later it was decided that the unit should be called the Nursing Studies Unit. The university nurse tutors' course was to be extended to two years and would start in October 1957. It would be a certificate course for non-graduates but a diploma course for graduates.[22]

At the same time, the appointment of the director of the new unit was announced. She was Miss Elsie Stephenson who had been the county nursing officer in Newcastle. Her appointment was warmly greeted but the selection procedure nearly brought about a serious breach in relationships which had anyway remained precarious.

The RCN did not understand the ways of universities and were affronted when they were not invited to be members of the selection committee. On the other hand, the university was obviously within its rights to want to appoint its own staff. A compromise was worked out: College representatives were invited to act as assessors and were therefore able to receive copies of the candidates' application details. The nurses took part in the interviews and were able to ask questions, but had to withdraw during the subsequent discussions when a decision was made.

Letters passed backwards and forwards between the College and the Principal who tried hard to keep the peace, but it was clear that the university members were doing their best to manoeuvre the College out of any part in the final selection.

At the same time, the second Boots research fellowship, following the completion of Miss Carter's term, was awarded to Miss Margaret Scott-Wright.[23]

Unfortunately, negotiations with London University did not progress as successfully. The university felt unwilling to set up either a new internal degree course or an external one. The College had to decide, therefore, whether they would try to negotiate an integrated scheme in sociology or some other subject already being taught.[24]

Such was the ingenuousness of Council that they sought, instead, to set up a degree course under their own administration. They also started discussions with University College Hospital, London, to explore the feasibility of establishing an integrated course for state registration with an external degree in sociology. They agreed to prepare a scheme for submission to the GNC and to investigate sources of financial support.[25]

Whilst these machinations were going on, the Edinburgh University scheme was progressing well. They drew up a plan for a five-year course offering registration and an MA degree. This was submitted to the Scottish GNC for approval.[26] They also prepared a scheme for a nursing degree but the University Grants Committee turned this down on the grounds that it was not appropriate for a grant.[27] The integrated scheme started in October 1960 with four students.

By this time, a small group of nurses in London, who were involved in research on their own account, had formed a self-help association in order to support each other in their work. Doreen Norton, a ward sister, had successfully applied to the National Corporation for the Care of Old People for a grant and was awarded £5,000 to make a study into nursing problems associated with the care of geriatric patients.[28]

Whilst the College continued trying to get a nursing degree course, it began to accumulate funds for a chair of nursing and, from time to time, they were able to report small amounts of money which had been donated.

The College continued in its sad efforts to set up a research council; permission had been received to style it The Countess Mountbatten of Burma Memorial Council for Nursing Research.[29]

A 'large number of eminent people had been approached [to take the chair] but none had accepted'.

In 1961 the Edinburgh Nursing Studies Unit was confirmed by the university and the advisory committee was disbanded. In its place a board of studies was set up and three nurses were invited to serve in their individual capacity.

The College in London never did manage to get their degree course, probably because they persisted in trying to control the nursing part of it and the university would not allow this. It was not until 1974 that a nursing degree course was set up at London university's Chelsea College. The moneys so carefully saved for a chair in nursing were finally put to use.

In 1960 Marjorie Simpson was appointed research officer, full time, at the College and in 1961 Mrs Winifred Raphael was appointed part-time research worker. It was not until 1981 that the RCN was able to set up its own research unit, but a nursing research council remains a dream.

There is little evidence that the profession at large was aware of these wheelings and dealings. Certainly, there was no discussion or comment about them in the nursing journals. The outcry against the main proposals in the Wood report had obscured the proposals for advanced training in appendix VIII and the total scheme implicit in the report was not, apparently, recognised. It is curious that discussion after publication of the report did not clarify the misunderstanding. The comments on the report that the RCN and the GNC published, never mentioned Wood's proposals for further specialist courses. The reactions of the profession were directed against the proposals for independent nurse training schools, repetitive duties, and the proposals for a curtailed basic nurse training.

Miss Cockayne, a member of the working party and, subsequently, the chief nursing officer at the Ministry, gave talks up and down the country but did not mention the implicit model, nor the scheme for advanced training.[30]

The main direction for change after the Wood report was to try to improve social relationships within hospitals, to make nurses more aware of their place in the community and the changes that were taking place in society around them. This thrust introduced nurses to elements of psychology and sociology and brought out manifestations of the anti-education feelings:

Britain's reputation for producing first class bedside nurses is being imperilled by the amount of theory crowded into the three year training.[31]

The American Committee on the Function of Nursing produced a similar reaction in this country.[32]

The health visitors were the group who were most in favour of university education for nurses but their aspirations were frequently debunked by the rest of the profession.

> By all means give the student health visitor the broader outlook but let her remember that she will need the detailed knowledge that only practical work and experience can give her.[33]

Greater exposure to international nursing affairs brought the realisation that British nurses were losing ground to graduate nurses. From 1953 onwards, larger contingents of nurses were sent overseas by the Ministry of Health, the GNC and the RCN. More nurses went to the United States to study or to observe nursing courses. Barbara Fawkes, the education officer at the GNC, spent a year at Teachers College, Columbia University, and was clearly influenced by the experience.[34]

If British nurses were to keep their end up at international meetings they had to appear to have adopted the same values. At the World Health Day celebrations in 1954, Miss Daisy Bridges, the executive secretary, ICN, spoke of 'The Nurse of Tomorrow' and declared the need for nurses to be trained in educational establishments.

Thoughtful academics and doctors could also see the need for an educated elite in nursing who might take their places alongside other professionals. Professor Crew, who had triggered the nursing department at Edinburgh University, was one of these. He could see that nurses were at a disadvantage when compared with the almoner or the psychiatric social worker: he wanted nurses to keep abreast of scientific knowledge.[35] Others observed the trend towards interdisciplinary teams and realised the need for graduate nurses to take a full place in them.[36]

These visionaries were usually limited to the community services, however. Hospital staff were still confined to the idea of the supportive role of the nurse, subject to the medical staff and regulated by discipline and spiritual ideals. 'The function of the training school is not only to teach the mind but to form the character': there was the need to send the student nurse out with a definite spiritual attitude of life.[37]

When the RCN's *Observations and Objectives* was published, there were several letters from upset doctors who disliked its proposals for university education for nurses:

... the poor patient will depend for his nursing on individuals whose claim to the title 'nurse' must be qualified by the words 'aide' or 'auxiliary' or 'assistant'. One might wonder whether it might not be more proper to retain the word 'nurse' for the person who really nurses and find some new title for this officer grade.[38]

Other doctors wrote in a similar vein, all concerned that the graduate nurse would remove herself from patient care, to the detriment of the patient. Many of them were influenced by developments in the USA where, it was said, graduate nurses spent most of their time at their desks, leaving the patients to the care of untrained aides.[39] Some doctors could not understand the relevance of degrees to nursing.

The views of the GNC were mainly coloured by their unwillingness to allow control of nurse training to pass out of their hands. This, they had discovered from the RCN's experience with London and Edinburgh universities, would be necessary if degree courses in nursing were set up. At any rate, the main objective and responsibility of the GNC was toward the minimum qualifying level of registered nurses.

Speaking at a conference of the Association of Hospital Matrons and the Sister Tutor Section, Miss M Houghton, education officer GNC, accepted the need to revise nurse education but warned that no hasty decisions should be made in setting up degree courses and that the profession must not hand over to a university its professional responsibility for preparing its own members.[40]

It may be significant that the president of the RCN, Miss G M Godden, preferred to allow nurses capable of leadership roles to emerge after the standard hospital training.[41]

One of the difficulties facing the profession was that there was no clear idea of how a university education might help nursing as a patient-centred occupation. It was not recognised as an academic discipline in its own right and the dominant ethos of universities, before the Robbins report,[42] was in academic education rather than in vocational preparation. The reasons given for nursing degrees were generally that leaders were needed, rather than that the nursing of patients might be improved by trained minds. Many people considered, therefore, that graduate nurses would quit the patient and move into administrative posts or, possibly, teaching.

Other reasons offered for nursing degrees were really no more convincing. It was of little interest to others if British nursing could not compete with foreign graduates in the international arena. Most people still considered that British nurses were the best in the world and the complacency of the profession reinforced this image. Nor was status for the sake of status of much interest to anyone but the College. Nurses did feel that they were not suitably appreciated by their fellow workers but they blamed their poor working conditions and salaries for this.

The difficulties in setting up a nursing research council were of the same order. It is significant that the main direction considered for nursing research was in operational studies. Few people could see anything in nursing procedures that merited study. Most of the research carried out after 1948 was on nurses and their organisation. The first suggestion that anyone was interested in nursing procedures was in 1956 in a leader article in *Nursing Times*, 'To Reason Why'.[43] This was, in turn, a response to a letter to *The Lancet* dated 21 January in which C Langdon Smith discussed the dangers of raising the foot of a bed, a routine nursing response to shock. *Nursing Times* leader considered the need for nursing to keep up to date with advances in medical knowledge and the need for other procedures to be examined. Doreen Norton's subsequent research was therefore of particular interest since it was a study which focused on the care of geriatric patients (of low medical and nursing status) and nursing problems attached to their care. It succeeded in exploding a time-honoured ritual, that of rubbing pressure areas, and demonstrated the merit of research into procedures. These entrenched positions were very hard to change as the many skills involved in nursing a patient had still not been identified. Although nursing was becoming more complex, it was difficult to explain why. Medical techniques were visibly more complex and, certainly, some of their routines were passed to nurses in order to relieve the doctors. But most nurses could sense that nursing was also becoming more demanding. Training focused on procedures rather than people, so it was the skills needed for procedures that were the point of attention, rather than the skills needed for the caring of people. It was not until the late 1960s that the skills needed for nursing were described.

The Goddard report[11a] found that nurses had themselves separated basic nursing from technical tasks. Nurses allocated basic tasks to the junior nurses and, later, to the nursing auxiliaries. The technical tasks were taken by the more senior nurses. It seemed common sense. If a nurse did half a dozen bed baths in a morning, it was bound to become a routine and rather boring; it did not require many skills. Until about 1958, the fundamental skill demanded of nurses was accurate observation and reporting.

In 1958, Virginia Henderson prepared a paper for the International Council of Nurses, *The Basic Principles of Nursing*.[44] She wrote: '... analysis of what any nurse does for any patient must rest upon a concept of the nurse's function'. She found that the nurse had a unique function:

> ... to assist the individual, sick or well, in the performance of those activities contributing to health or its recovery (or to a peaceful death) that he would perform unaided if he had the necessary strength, will or knowledge. It is likewise her function to help the individual gain independence as rapidly as possible.

This part of her work, of her function, Henderson wrote, the nurse initiates and controls; in this she is master. Additionally, she helps the patient to carry out the therapeutic plan as initiated by the physician. In cooperation with other members of the medical team, she helps to plan and carry out the total programme of care.

The more Henderson considered this concept of the nurse, the more complex did she find the nurse's function. Many of the activities, she argued, were simple until their adjustment to the particular demands of the patient made them complex. The primary responsibility of the nurse was that of helping the patient with his daily pattern of living, or with those activities that he ordinarily performs without assistance: breathing, eating, eliminating, resting, sleeping, moving, cleaning the body, keeping warm and properly clothed, social intercourse, learning, occupations that are recreational and those that are productive in some way.

But in fulfilling her primary responsibility, the nurse has to recognise and respect the patient's cultural pattern of living, his age and his values.

Where the Wood report had failed to find the answer to the question 'What is the proper task of the nurse?' Henderson had supplied it and had clarified the role of the nurse at the same time.

In Henderson's terms, the nurse needed extensive theoretical understanding of biological and social theories. If each patient was nursed according to his individual needs, principles had to be learned and applied at each occasion. Routine procedures were no longer appropriate. Here was the breakthrough.

Anyone could be taught procedures but only certain people could learn theoretical principles. At last there was the beginning of understanding of what had been intuitively known for so many years. There should be a level of nurse, Horder's 'officer', who would be the team leader and who would plan the care of the patient according to his needs. There would be a second level of nurse who would carry out the care plan with the team leader: the nursing team.

For this care planning, the conventional SRN was not enough. Her training lacked theoretical depth; this was where the graduate nurse was needed. But, although academic training taught people to think and to analyse, not all courses gave the mixture of biological and social sciences that a team leader needed. This was the unique *raison d'être* of a nursing degree: a blending of the two disciplines.

It was in 1974 that the first department of nursing was established in England. It was set up in Manchester University, with a post-graduate unit. After that date, degree courses for nurses proliferated.

In 1966 a working group of doctors, nurses, sociologists and civil servants were called together at the Department of Health. From this emerged a research project eventually called 'The Study of Nursing Care'. This was the first structured nursing research enter-prise but, with the support of the DHSS, nursing research became established quite quickly thereafter.

Chapter 12/Getting the nurses organised

At the start of the National Health Service, the nurses formed the largest body of workers; they were, however, not organised as an occupation and lacked national standards of salary, conditions of work, superannuation and consultative machinery.

The Rushcliffe committee[1] had made a start on setting a national salary but their reports were advisory rather than executive. This committee also made recommendations to establish a national form of superannuation and conditions of work which were not implemented before the start of the NHS.

At the onset of the NHS, the Whitley Council took over all negotiations for health service employees and the Rushcliffe committee was disbanded, handing over to the Nurses and Midwives Council.

Prior to the Rushcliffe committee, the Royal College of Nursing had picked up from the Athlone report[2] the need for local committees for consultation, but whereas the Athlone report had proposed a Burnham committee type of machinery which included hospital-based committees for consultation, the RCN had more ambitious plans. These included national, regional and local committees which would serve as a joint consultative structure as well as a salary negotiating machinery.[3] By 1941, the College appears to have changed its mind with regard to machinery for salary negotiations and advised the Ministry that they would prefer a Whitley Council form to that of the Burnham Committee.[4] In 1942, they acceded to the Ministry's proposals for a special nurses' salaries committee and appointed College representatives to it. This was their first experience of joint salary discussions with other oganisations and employers and it provided them with some preliminary experience before the Nurses and Midwives Whitley Council was set up.

Neither the Rushcliffe committee nor the Whitley Council provided for local consultation, however, and the College was determined to pursue the setting up of hospital committees, hopefully with a regional and national superstructure.

In 1945, the Ministry sent out a circular, *Staffing The Hospitals*,[5] setting out conditions of service, salaries and related conditions as the Rushcliffe committee had proposed. The circular also requested that nurses representative councils should be organised with a balanced representation of the different grades of staff. There should be free discussion of any matter affecting work and the efficiency of the nursing staff as well as their general welfare. The representative councils should reach a conclusion on an issue and be responsible for putting this to the matron and governing body in the form of a recommendation. The circular also requested that no obstacle should be placed in the way of nurses joining professional organisations or trade unions.

The RCN, in its new capacity as a negotiating body for nurses, was anxious that nurses should elect to join the College rather than a trade union. They set about trying to persuade matrons, medical superintendents and medical officers of health to encourage their nursing staffs to take out RCN membership.

The Labour Government had repealed the Trades Disputes Act 1927 in the previous year (1945) in order to strengthen the affiliation between the party and the unions. The Labour Party had had a landslide victory and many local governments were also controlled by its supporters. The College anticipated a growth of trade unionism amongst nurses on the inauguration of the NHS. Only a minority of trained nurses belonged to the RCN but it was already becoming clear that seats on the new Whitley Council would be allocated according to the numerical strength of nurse membership of the various representative organisations.[6]

There was a corresponding pressure by the unions for nurses to join them. They were often assisted in this by local authorities who were controlled by the labour faction. Willesden health authority required all their nurses to join a trade union and subsequently sent dismissal notices to those who had not done so. The RCN wrote to *The Times* (5 December 1946) reminding the public that the College had been recognised as a negotiating body and deprecating the actions of the Willesden authorities. They also appealed to the Ministers of Health and Labour. As a result of the outcry, Willesden council suspended its action and withdrew its notices of dismissal.[7] Similar occurrences, however, were repeated up and down the country during the next few years.

The RCN and other representative organisations were asked to con-sider the Minister's draft proposals for setting up the Whitley Councils. The College chose its representatives, including two Queen's Institute nurses. They rejected a request from the Institute to support its application for a seat as a negotiating body in its own right and concluded that too many sections would weaken the position of the nurses' side. Council wanted fewer, larger staff organisations with experience of negotiating, and had already arranged for the affiliation of several smaller organisations in order to strengthen its own position.

The Queen's Institute countered this rejection by the College by accusing it of discounting the views of the district nurses. The Institute subsequently made an application to the Management Side for a seat as an employer of district nurses but, once again, it was rejected as it did not qualify as a negotiating body.[8]

The College fought hard to gain a majority on the Staff Side and instructed their representatives to claim over 50 per cent of the seats, no matter at what cost, in order to ensure that the professional organisations were dominant. They also determined that their general secretary should be the honorary secretary of the Staff Side and agreed that Colin Roberts, the NALGO representative and former chairman of the nurses' panel on the Rushcliffe committee, should be asked to take the chair.

The employees' organisations set up a representative committee to determine the composition of the Staff Side. Seats on the representative committee were allocated on the same numerical basis as had obtained on the Rushcliffe and Guthrie committees. As there were no representatives of midwives and health visitors on the Scottish Guthrie committee, it was agreed that two additional members should be appointed to the representative committee to cover those specialties. Twelve Council members were selected to attend the meeting of the representative committee on 7 January 1948 and it was thought that the cost of each seat on the staff side in terms of servicing and representatives' expenses, might come to £250–300 a year.

The Staff Side set up a provisional advisory committee which met on 1 February 1948. Six unions and six professional associations were represented at the first meeting (one representative from each), and the member for the National Association of Local Government Officers (NALGO) was elected chairman. At this meeting it was agreed that applicants for seats on any of the Whitley Council's committees should be asked to submit evidence of nurse membership to support their claims.[9]

This was an important decision since many organisations were seeking to gain representation on the Whitley Council, on one or other of the sides, although not all could be justifiably recognised as being negotiating bodies. Some of the organisations did not restrict their membership to trained nurses, midwives and health visitors and represented other occupations besides nurses.

The Royal British Nurses Association had claimed to be a salary negotiating body and had asked for a seat on the council but had refused to submit evidence of its membership or activities. Its application was deferred until it agreed to furnish the required documents.

The provisional advisory committee (PAC) also agreed that no NHS worker would be required to belong to a trade union or a professional association, although it was hoped that they would. The PAC also set up an interim executive committee which subsequently set up four specialist committees for nurses, midwives, public health nurses and mental nurses. On the first two the professional organisations had a majority of seats and on the last two, the unions had the majority.[10] The executive committee was later kept as a permanent body which was responsible for administration and finance of the Staff Side.

One of the first items to be dealt with was to put in a claim for an increase of salary for student nurses, pupil midwives and pupil nurses. The executive committee also agreed that the matter was extremely urgent and that the learners' salaries should be dealt with, as distinct from other nurses and without regard to any possible repercussions on the other grades. The committee agreed to retain the principle of student status.[11]

During the remaining months of 1948, the executive committee discussed requests from many different organisations for seats on the Staff Side. Some were given a place on the specialist committees, including the Society of Registered Male Nurses (on the Nurses Standing Committee) and the National Association of State Enrolled Assistant Nurses (on any specialist sub-committee that might be set up for SEANs). Others were turned down on the grounds that they were not representative or had not supported their claims with sufficient evidence. These organisations included the Association of Nursery Training Colleges, the Queens League of Public Health Nurses, the Royal British Nurses Association, the National Federation of Hospital Officers, the Transport and General Workers Union, the National Association of Nursery Matrons, the British College of Nurses, the National Association for Prevention of Tuberculosis (sanatorium matrons section) and the London County Council Staff Association.[12]

In the meantime, there had been a full meeting of each of the sides of the Nurses and Midwives Whitley Council. On the Staff Side, they elected a NALGO representative to be their chairman, the Royal College of Midwives' representative to be vice-chairman and the general secretary of the RCN to be their secretary. All these, and a representative from the Association of Hospital Matrons, were elected to the Central (General) Council of the Whitley Council as staff representatives.[13]

In the understanding that the Whitley Council would pre-empt the RCN's attempts to set up a national and regional organisation of representative councils, Council agreed to abandon this project. Instead, they set up a labour relations committee which would be responsible for terms and conditions of service and for relationships between nurses and employers.[14]

There were some difficulties of procedure in nominating RCN representatives to the Whitley Council. The sections were asked to send forward names but not all the eventual nominations came from these. In the end, one each of the main sections was included: sister tutor, matron, ward sister, district nurse, local authority hospital matron, Society of Registered Male Nurses. Two Council members and the vice-chairman of Council were also nominated, together with the general secretary, secretary of the Scottish Board and secretary of the Public Health Section.[15]

In 1949, the General Council proposed that nursing auxiliaries, dental attendants and venereal disease orderlies should be allocated to the Nurses and Midwives Council. The College Council debated this and, influenced by the labour relations committee, decided that the proposal should be accepted.

The matter was not straightforward. As well as nursing assistants in the mental hospitals and nursing auxiliaries in some general hospitals, there were also orderlies. In some hospitals, these were styled 'ward orderlies' and their duties were more of a domestic nature; in other hospitals, they were called 'nursing orderlies' and their work was mainly simple nursing duties. If the nursing auxiliaries were to come under the aegis of the Nurses and Midwives Whitley Council, some of the orderlies would have to be re-styled as nursing staff and the others would remain with the Ancillaries Whitley Council as domestics.

On the Management Side, the chief nursing officer did not have any advice to offer on the question of the nursing auxiliaries but did advise against the inclusion of dental nurses because of their exclusion from the title 'nurse' under the Nurses Act 1943. The Management Side was, on the whole, in favour of accepting nursing auxiliaries, since they would then be in a position to control their salaries and ensure some comparability with those of the nurses.[16] The Staff Side also agreed to accept nursing auxiliaries.

During the early days of the Whitley Council, it became clear to both sides that the Management Side did not have the free hand which it might have hoped for. In 1949, the Government published a White Paper on the need to restrict personal incomes and put a pause on most nationally negotiated salary rises. Nurses were accepted as constituting 'a shortage field' but, in spite of this, the Minister asked the Management Side to delay a settlement for the public health nurses.[17] The Minister explained that the Management Side should act as a 'shock absorber' and protect him from coming into direct conflict with the workers. He also indicated that he did not like retrospective settlements. This demonstrated that the Minister would have the final say in all settlements irrespective of what might have been agreed by the two sides. There was, in fact, an over-representation of the Ministry on the Management Side and a remarkable lack of representation by hospital management committees.[18] In 1952, the number of seats was increased from 26 to 27 in order to include one member of the Association of Hospital Management Committees,[19] but the dead hand of the Minister continued to be felt. This could work in either direction: if the Minister received too many complaints from authorities, he could, and did, encourage the Management Side to take corrective action.

Apart from salary negotiations and the nursing auxiliaries, the Whitley Council at this time also discussed the formation of staff consultative councils and the position of regional nursing officers. It may be helpful if each of these topics is considered in turn.

Nursing auxiliaries

Once agreement had been reached in principle, the Staff Side set about trying to draw up some description of their duties as a preliminary to agreeing salary scales. Unfortunately, there was some difficulty in separating their duties from those of the ward orderlies and, by 1952, they had still not succeeded in producing a job definition.[20] There was evidently some change of heart about giving nursing auxiliaries 'official recognition' and the secretary of the Staff Side wrote to her counterpart, describing the problem and proposing that auxiliaries should be graded as ward orderlies and transferred to the Ancillary Staffs Council. She also asked that their designation should be changed in order to remove the word 'nurse' or 'nursing'.[21]

This change of heart had the hallmark of the RCN on it. Nurses did not like associating with untrained staff and disliked very much the decision that the auxiliaries should be included with them on the Nurses and Midwives Whitley Council. They were already smarting from the obvious lack of respect of the Ministry for their profession and some wished that the nurses had withdrawn from the Whitley machinery when the doctors and dentists had. On the other hand, absorption into the Nurses Council was not an unmitigated boon for the auxiliaries. Nurses did not receive overtime payments and expected to work many extra hours as a necessary part of their professional ethic. Ward orderlies, on the Ancillary Staffs Council, did receive overtime so that they were often much better off than their erstwhile colleagues.

The Management Side decided to resist the proposal to return nursing auxiliaries to the Ancillary Staffs Council and took exception to the idea of changing their title.

In the meantime, a standing committee had been set up for the auxiliaries on the Staff Side. This, in itself, provoked a considerable amount of aggravation between the unions and associations. The executive committee had recommended 13 seats, with the unions having eight of them. Some of the unions rejected this as they could not agree to the associations, who had no auxiliaries as members, being represented.[22] These inter-organisational rows appeared to take precedence over official business. It may be partly because of this that the matter of the nursing auxiliaries rumbled on for so long.

In 1953, the Staff Side agreed to keep the auxiliaries on the Nurses Council, offering the excuse that they thought that the auxiliaries should be free to become enrolled nurses if they so wished.[23]

The next hurdle was that of salary scales. The Staff Side put in a claim for the auxiliaries which was £20 pa less than the SEAN scale and higher than that of the pupil nurses. It was also, necessarily, less than the scale for ward orderlies.

Management Side were most upset by the level of the claim: '... it would kill the enrolled assistant nurse grade'. Other members thought that 'the pay of the nursing auxiliary grade should be a living wage and too much regard should not be paid to the rate of the students' allowances'. But if they did that, the students would quit and become nursing auxiliaries.[24] As was the technique at the time, the Management Side tried to resolve the conundrum by juggling with board and lodging charges in order to favour the auxiliaries without giving them a higher scale.

As the negotiations went on, it became more clear to the Management Side that the other side wanted the auxiliaries to be treated as SEANs. Management would not negotiate on this basis and wished to maintain a clear differential between the two grades. The Staff Side considered that, in this case, the difference should be marked by salaries rather than by juggling with charges.

There were problems, too, with nursing assistants in the mental hospitals. The Minister had issued RHB (53) 4[25] which set a policy 'intended to make improvements as economically as possible at the point where improvements are likely to do most good'. These 'improvements' raised the salaries of the nursing assistants whilst holding down those of the mental nurse students and the trained staff. The policy backfired because, with overtime, the attendants could earn more than the students, who started to refuse to do non-nursing duties. Some quit their training and took assistants' jobs.[26] Recruitment of student mental nurses, already poor, further declined. The Ministry received complaints from the regional hospital boards, and the Staff Side put in a claim for overtime payment for mental nurses at time and a quarter for the first two hours and time and a half for all additional hours.[27]

In 1955, complaints were sent to the Management Side by several regional authorities that salaries of nursing auxiliaries had fallen behind those of ward orderlies. It was, by then, difficult for the hospitals to recruit auxiliaries, even though their salaries were more than those of pupil nurses and overlapped those of the SEANs. Thus, it was equally hard to recruit or keep pupils or enrolled nurses.[28]

Complaints about salaries continued. By 1956, both auxiliaries and charge nurses were earning less than ward orderlies. If the salaries of the auxiliaries were equated with those of the ward orderlies, they would be earning more than the trained nurses.[29] Feeling in the profession was becoming noticeably warmer too. The RCN branches raised the issue of auxiliaries' salaries at their January 1950 meeting and Sheffield branch put a resolution to the effect that differentials should reflect the training, work and responsibilities of trained nurses.[30] To this the College replied that the maximum of one grade could not always be kept lower than the minimum of the next grade.[31]

The nurses were not mollified by this. Letters to the editors of the nursing journals complained that factory workers enjoyed better salaries and conditions of work.[32] Others continued to complain about the inclusion of nursing auxiliaries on the Nurses Council: 'the nursing profession was presented with a *fait accompli* in the recognition as part of the "nursing establishment" of the large number of untrained women and men ... to be called nursing auxiliaries'. There had been no preparation for this influx, no chance to define the duties of the various grades. The writer continued by observing that most of the auxiliaries belonged to unions and thus had upset the balance on the Staff Side. Auxiliaries were already sending representatives to joint staff consultative committees (and presumably upsetting the balance on those). She considered that the move had been a matter of expediency rather than of consideration for the care of the patient: '... it is strange that our College was not more informative'.[33]

Indeed, the correspondent had some justification in being anxious about the balance of representation, since admission of the auxiliaries (there were 21,264 whole-time and 18,370 part-time in 1957) had considerably strengthened the hands of the unions on the Staff Side.

In 1958, COHSE representatives proposed overtime payments for all nursing staff, but the association representatives were able to stave off this proposal for the time being.

The problem of the nursing auxiliaries subsided slowly: nurses had to accept the *fait accompli* and shortage of staff soon enabled them to be thankful for any help, trained or untrained. In the late 1950s, the shortage of senior staff became so acute that preference was given to them in salary considerations. By the end of the 1950s, all involved in the nursing service agreed that a complete restructuring of nurses was necessary. This was eventually achieved by the implementation of the Salmon structure.

The nursing auxiliaries were important, though. They had a very real effect by helping further to depress recruitment of pupil nurses and thus the growth of the 'pivotal' grade of SEAN. Their inclusion in the Nurses and Midwives Whitley Council also tipped the balance on the Staff Side. Although the associations retained their majority for some time, there was a change in the style of negotiation, the priorities for their claims and their attitudes. It became more difficult for the RCN to win their points on the Staff Side, and the College had to take on board union goals in order to maintain their position in other areas. The admission of the nursing auxiliaries to the Nurses and Midwives Whitley Council was agreed by the College, partly because of union pressure and partly in order to allow the matrons to retain control of them, but it was the first step towards the unionisation of the major professional association.

Staff consultative councils

The image of nursing had for years been one of severe (if not repressive) discipline, long hours, poor salary and dedicated submission. Box and Croft-White[34] portrayed this vividly and described the attitudes of the public as well as those of student nurses. This portrait of institutionalism was supported by the National Advisory Council on Nurses and Midwives[35] and, more explicitly, by the Wood report[36] which made recommendations to improve interpersonal relationships in hospitals, for the relaxation of discipline and the removal of nurse training from the institutionalism of hospitals. In 1939, the Athlone interim report[37] had recommended that nurses should take a more active part in hospital policy decisions via local consultative committees. The RCN *Memorandum to the*

Athlone Committee,[38] as well as evidence given by other organisations, had commented on recent hostile press reports of nursing conditions, and the College had subsequently warmly supported Athlone's proposals for joint consultation.

The Ministry was concerned to improve the image of nursing in order to aid recruitment. The Labour Government was also committed to giving workers more power in their work-places. Aneurin Bevan and the RCN both understood the need to make the profession more aware of the world and society outside hospitals. Friends of the profession thought that nurses had a contribution to make to the community if only they would come out from the sheltered life of their hospitals. Friends and relatives realised that patient care would be more sympathetic if the nursing staff left their cloisters and learned about normal people and their problems.

After publication of the Wood report, E E P MacManus wrote of the break-up of homes, the shortage of domestics, housing shortage, food shortages and other difficulties facing British society, and the need for nurses to take account of these in dealing with recruitment and training problems.[39] This was followed by a concerted campaign to make nurses more aware of societal attitudes and social policy.

Dr E Sherwood Jones wrote of the need for nurses to be more active in hospital politics.[40] The RCN held a third conference in the series 'The Nation's Nurses' and devoted it to human relations, the use of selection techniques, training within industry methods, negotiating machinery and personal problems. *Nursing Times* published a leading article on the need to review attitudes to patients' visitors.[41] The Queen's Institute for District Nursing set up a course on human relations and industrial sociology.[42] The RCN introduced 'a new technique' for its conferences called 'organised participation' and sought to develop more dialogue between speakers and audience.[43]

Stanley Mayne, assistant secretary at the Ministry of Health, spoke to an RCN conference of the need to inculcate in the nurse a realisation of the part she could play in running her hospital.[44] At the same time, the RCN arranged a series of meetings around the country to explain the Whitley Council system.[45] Miss Florence Horsbrugh, MP, talked about the nurse as a citizen,[46] and Aneurin Bevan spoke of the part nurses would have in how the NHS was run.[47] At the annual conference of the RCN, Mrs G Williams, author of section IV of the Horder report, gave a paper entitled 'The Nurse In The Social Order'.[48]

Later, the nursing journals started publishing articles with a social science approach,[49] and in 1952, the GNC introduced to the syllabus some simple aspects of sociology and psychology.

240

In 1948, Aneurin Bevan proposed the formation of joint consultative committees (JCC) as an important issue and set up discussions to provide a model constitution. He foresaw these committees as a route for consultation between the hospital authority and the staff.[50] By 1949, Hillary Marquand, the new Minister of Health, was able to claim that JCCs representing every grade of staff, as well as the management, were being set up.[51] This was certainly an optimistic view, since Stanley Mayne had earlier told an audience that only a few hospitals had followed this path since the Athlone report.[44]

The Whitley Council, in circulars GC13 and GC20, agreed the constitution for JCCs early in March 1950 and also stipulated that representatives need not yet be members of a staff organisation. They made this provision in spite of pressure from the unions on the Staff Side, which were anxious to enforce organisational representation.

According to the constitution, there was to be a central committee composed of representatives of all categories of staff and sub-committees for each category. Representatives from the sub-committees would form the membership of the main committee. Management would also be represented by nominees.

The RCN was anxious that its members should be active in these JCCs and that they should be elected as representatives. They therefore published information via their branch and section organisation in order to brief nurses about the function of the committees. Council was adamant that as the JCCs were for employees, student nurses should be excluded in order to safeguard their tenuous claim to student status.[52] This unilateral decision did not meet with general agreement. By July, Council heard that some HMCs were including student nurses in the election procedures. The RCN re-affirmed its policy and proposed, instead, that there should be student councils for all students undergoing training in hospitals.

Some hospitals accepted the RCN policy and excluded students; others ignored it. Some referred to the Minister for advice. Many committees were not sure of the machinery, the procedures or the purpose of JCCs, and the doctors opted to exclude themselves.

By November, there seemed to be general confusion and considerable dissatisfaction in the hospitals. Council began to think that it was a pity to be associated with a project which was showing itself to be unsatisfactory, but the general secretary bolstered their flagging enthusiasm by reminding them that it had been College policy for years to establish local consultative machinery. She thought that the present difficulties were due to the haste with which the scheme had been introduced and the paucity of preparation. Some members thought that there was already enough contact between nurses and their matron and did not think that JCCs would help an already satisfactory system. Some thought the scheme to be pointless if the doctors were not in it and others did not welcome the prospect of discussing nursing matters in front of domestic and artisan staff.[53] Clearly, many senior nurses were rather cool about the new system which would come between the matron and her nurses.

At a special meeting arranged in January 1951, Sir Frederick Leggett, chairman of the labour relations committee, advised Council not to withdraw from the scheme. The meeting agreed that participation should be voluntary and that the organisation should be flexible in order to suit different hospitals. The Whitley Council had stipulated that organisational representation should be mandatory after the two-year run-in, and Council was concerned that that might develop into a closed shop situation.[54]

The Management Side subsequently agreed that student nurses should be allowed to take part and supported the statement of the General Council to that effect.[55]

Council voted to complain about this to the Minister and, at the annual general meeting later in the year, they received unanimous support from the membership who re-affirmed the student status of student nurses and deplored the attitude of the General Council.[56] The College received little support from the Minister, who could not see how membership of JCCs would affect student nurses' status.[57]

Progress with the JCCs certainly did not go smoothly. There were complaints about excessive constitutionalism and rigidity and that neither management nor staff understood the principles of joint consultation. RCN members were anxious about the introduction in January 1952 of organisational representation, and the College seriously discussed the prospect of re-establishing the nurses representative councils as a channel of discussion for domestic professional affairs.

In 1953, the Society of Registered Male Nurses approached the Ministry to see if they could qualify for nomination as representatives on the staff consultative committees. The Ministry advised them that as an affiliated member association of the RCN, they could. This ruling upset some members of the Staff Side who were seeking a strict interpretation of the organisational representation rule.[58]

In fact, the College and its members did not need to be concerned.

Students at the King's Fund Hospital Administrative Staff College made a study of joint consultation in hospitals in 1953. They reported that many of the JCCs set up in 1950 and 1951 had already died and others 'cling tenuously to life on a meagre diet of complaints and grievances'.

The study found hospital staffs generally to be apathetic and unenthusiastic. The JCCs had considered only minor matters, had made little contribution to the better working of the hospital and feedback to complainants was poor.

The ready-made framework set out in RHB (50) 47 and HMC (50) 46 was criticised: divisions of status and work places within the hospital groups militated against collective consultative committees. The meetings had not been used as a means of communication by the management but, instead, the agendas were filled by complaints, administrative items and discussion of staff amenities. The JCCs had little effect on relationships or on involving the staff in running the hospitals. Many hospitals considered the JCCs as a safety valve for the ventilation of differences between staff and management. There was too little reciprocal consultation, and the restrictive clause in HM (50) 47 relating to membership had generated 'a good deal of feeling'.[59]

Some of these findings were supported by Sofer.[60] He also found that only a minority of staff either elected their representatives or took any other interest in the consultative committees. But, paradoxically, the new influence afforded to 'the rank and file' by this machinery had aroused unrealistic expectations. There was a clash of ideologies between staff and management who were made to feel that the committee was a way of by-passing them. These factors limited the degree of effective consultation that could be achieved. Meetings became a stage for acting out tensions generated by the hierarchical hospital system: responsibility for the problems generated by the system was cast on to management who had no solution and were as much prisoners of the system as were the staff.

Joint consultative committees slowly died, as had the nurses representative councils. When the College tried to set up nursing staff committees along the lines of the medical staff committees after the Bradbeer committee reported in 1954, the Minister rejected the idea. The nurses were left with no form of local professional consultation and when they eventually got professional advisory committees in 1975, they did not know what to do with them.

The drive to take nurses out into society contributed to the breakdown of the relationship between the matron and her nurses. The

JCCs put the matron on the management side of the table and the nurses on the staff side along with the 'domestic and artisan staffs'. The old reference groups of the nurses were broken down and they had to look elsewhere. They were pitched out of their secluded, enclosed hospital environment into the post-war world in which the labour movement was being given more power than it had ever had before. Unionised workers were winning greater wage settlements, shorter hours and better working conditions. The RCN was fighting for its place on the Staff Side and was compared rather unfavourably with the unions. College negotiators had to learn the aggressive tactics of the union negotiators. The unions were actively recruiting nurses to their ranks. There was a growth of bureaucracy and new paramedical groups over which nurses had no control and whose values were different. Nursing needs were subordinated to the needs of the service as a whole and the prestige of nursing subsided under the weight of the bureaucrats. There was a loss of vocationalism as the nurses perceived their growing deprivation. Open recruitment to nursing further emphasised their perception of themselves as hired labour only half a scale above that of the nursing auxiliaries. A process of proletarianisation was taking place: professionalism was visibly failing the nurses and they started to turn outwards, to the unions, for their new reference group.

The regional nursing officers

Nursing posts at the regional headquarters were really an afterthought. In 1945, when the general administrative structure was under discussion, there was no suggestion of a nursing presence at the regions (nor in the areas then under consideration), group or hospital level. In fact there was no suggestion either of a nursing advisory committee for the Central Health Services Council, or of a designated place for a nurse on the council itself, although one might have been included amongst the 'others'.[61]

A very lengthy letter in 1946 from Dr H Macauley, medical officer of health, Middlesex County Council, described in detail the administrative machinery of his medical and hospital services, the number of staff and their functions. He used the Middlesex County Council as a homologue for the proposed regional hospital boards and related the work of the MOH organisation to the future RHB. He described no nursing post at his headquarters and proposed none.[62] This is hardly surprising since, at that time, many local authority services had no senior nurse and the nursing staff were under the control of a medical officer.

Later, in 1947, headquarters staff were again discussed, and it was thought that senior staff should be appointed with some urgency. Three salary bands were agreed for regional medical officers and three subordinate medical posts were listed, but still no nursing post was described.[63]

The Ministry published HMC (48) 1 which discussed the appointment of hospital staff. The general scope of the work of hospital management committees and their relationship to regional hospital boards were set out. Hospital management committees (HMC) were seen as agencies of the RHB and would be responsible for the control and management of their hospitals. In this circular the Ministry advised HMCs to appoint professional advisory committees to act as an advisory body to the group.[64] No details of the composition of the advisory committee for nursing were set out and, ultimately, those HMCs that had one invariably packed it with lay people. It is clear therefore that nurses were perceived as functioning purely with patients and, exceptionally, teaching or organising the nursing service. There was, as yet, no acceptance of nursing advisers for the authorities, or of nursing administrators in the same sense as the chief medical officer of RHBs or MOsH of local authorities.

There were people who foresaw the need for a structured nursing administration however. Professor Mackintosh, dean of public health at the London School of Hygiene, looked forward to an 'active nursing division' in the hospital organisation and the development of a new nursing administration system.[65] After 1948, the local authorities did appoint more nursing and health visitor superintendents who still, often, reported to a medical officer, and the RCN set up a new training course for public health administrators. But nurses were more concerned with gaining seats on the RHBs and HMCs than with developing a nursing structure.[66]

Recruitment to the regional nursing officer posts, when they were established, was slow. Not all regions had succeeded in filling their posts by 1951, reportedly because the salary level was too low. There were already complaints about the salaries in July 1948. The Ministry had described the duties of these posts in RHB (48) 24: they were mainly to be those of recruiting nurses for the regional hospitals, liaison with voluntary nursing agencies (St. John's Ambulance Brigade, British Red Cross Society and Women's Voluntary Service), setting up nursing exhibitions and advising boards of governors and HMCs on nurse training. After the inception of the area nurse training committees, the RNOs represented their boards on those. Their salaries were based, in 1948, on those of the hospital matrons to whom they would act in an advisory capacity. Thus, compared with other regional headquarters' staff, the RNO had a very lowly status and this affected the value ascribed to her advice.

When the Staff Side asked for an increase in the RNOs' salaries in 1951, they were supported by the knowledge that at least one RHB had felt obliged to increase the salary in re-advertising the post after they had had no success in filling it with a suitable candidate. Nursing salaries had been raised since 1948 but not those of the RNOs, whose range was £650–800. A Ministry of Health nursing officer's range was £620–843, matrons of small hospitals (under 1,000 beds) received £825–1,005, those in charge of hospitals with between 1,000 and 1,500 beds received £930–1,110 and those in charge of hospitals with over 1,500 beds received £1,000–1,499.[67]

The Staff Side claim for RNOs was £1,200–1,500, but management proposed a scale £700–800. The Staff Side wrote to say that RNOs were 'of senior administrative status and are called upon to advise RHBs on all matters relating to nursing'. They considered that it was 'essential that the posts shall be regarded with the same respect that is shown towards other senior advisory posts under the jurisdiction of the Regional Boards' and that it was 'vital that the RNOs should enjoy conditions of service no less favourable than those of other senior administrative staff, including, for example, the expenses of first class travel and subsistence'.[68]

This last item was a real thorn in the nurses' flesh. Their status on the boards was measured by their salary rather than by their rank. Since medical and administrative salaries were much higher, the RNOs were equated with those of more junior officers. Other regional officers of equivalent rank travelled first class and received more generous allowances for both subsistence and leave. When the RNOs travelled with their regional colleagues, they had to pay the excess over their third class tickets or travel separately. Similarly, at overnight stays their subsistence allowances did not cover the cost of the hotels used by their colleagues.

During their discussion of RNO salaries, the Management Side was clearly flummoxed. 'What do these people do?' 'Do we need them at all?' They were not used in Scotland, why were they needed in England and Wales? The more knowledgeable members recalled that they did quite a lot with the area nurse training committees. A sub-committee was set up to discuss the matter, and the Ministry's chief nursing officer was invited to join them.[69]

The matter drifted on into 1953, when there was a joint meeting to discuss the problem. Management proposed three bands based on the relative size of the regions: they offered £680–860, £750–930 and £800–1,000. The Staff Side agreed the bands but would not accept the salary ranges. Management offered slightly higher scales and new job designations. The Staff Side said that the lowest scale would still not allow first class travel: this would be even more demeaning for the RNO as her nursing colleagues on the other two scales would have that advantage over her.[70]

Later, the Management Side wrote to the Staff Side to say that whilst they could not improve their offer, they would undertake to ask the Minister to relax the conditions entitling officers to first class travel so as to take in the only two RNOs in band C (Oxford and Cambridge RHBs).[71]

By the end of 1953, most of the negotiators had become confused over the issue. The Staff Side made a new proposal for one common grade with a salary range similar to their 1951 claim, £1,200–1,500. Failing any agreement on this, they proposed to take the matter to arbitration. Management did not welcome the idea of having only one grade as it departed from the arrangements made for other senior regional grades.[72] The Staff Side gave in. After further correspondence they agreed to the proposals for three bands, on condition that all should be entitled to first class travel and subsistence.[73]

The RNOs kept a very low profile and there was no further evidence to show how they developed their jobs. They were the regional authorities' representatives on the ANTCs and were responsible for preparing the budgets to be forwarded to the GNC. There were difficulties with the ANTCs because their priorities appeared to be oriented towards service needs. The GNC once or twice had to remind these committees that they were responsible for providing a training for student nurses rather than for recruiting labour for the hospitals.[74] On the other hand, the RNOs were responsible for recruitment and probably were chivvied by their own authorities when there was a shortage of candidates.

Another cause of complaint was that the ANTCs frequently prepared estimates for the schools of nursing without reference to the tutors. Alternatively, they altered estimates prepared by the tutors without prior consultation.

There is not much doubt that the RNOs adopted the values of their authorites and became the first nurse bureaucrats. Equally, they must have had quite a struggle in their early days to win acceptance for themselves. It took many years for the authorities to accept nurse administrators in the same way as they had the medical administrators.

In 1957, the National Advisory Council on Recruitment of Nurses and Midwives had been transferred from the Ministry of Labour to the Ministry of Health. In the change-over, the council was demoted and re-styled National Consultative Committee. The Minister anticipated that the assumption of responsibility by the Ministry for publicity and recruitment campaigns for nurses would entail extra responsibilities for the RNOs, and he therefore authorised additional posts for regional nurses. These new posts came under the authority of the RNO, thus establishing a regional nursing hierarchy. Since the status of the regional nurse was already equivocal, her assistants' positions were even more uncertain, both in respect of their regional colleagues and of the regional matrons.

Later in the year, Oxford RHB asked the Management Side to reassess the RNO's position. They asked that she should be taken out of the nursing structure altogether and be given a status equivalent to that of the regional assistant secretary with whose duties and responsibilities she could more reasonably be compared. After some discussion of the proposal, the Management Side decided to take no action in the matter.[76]

Recruitment of senior nurses from the assistant matron grade to RNO became more difficult owing to the flat nature of the nursing structure and the poor salary levels given to these nurses. Both sides had separately started to design a new hierarchy and all agreed that a new salary structure was urgently needed. Furthermore, the Ministry anticipated that the Hospital Plan (1961) would have a considerable effect on nursing grades, with many possible changes in hospitals.

There were further discussions about the RNO salaries and their work. The chief nursing officer thought that she was an administrator for 60 per cent of her time and a nurse for 40 per cent. Other management side members thought that she was an administrator, but in the nursing field. Her salary was pitched at that of the matron in a low to middle sized hospital: some members thought that it should, perhaps, be more nearly that of the higher reaches of the matrons' scales, or even more.[77] They thought that there was a need to bolster her position as the adviser to matrons of all hospitals, including the largest. They realised that the RNO's job was growing in responsibility and now included planning new hospital construction with other technical experts. On the Staff Side, the College representatives proposed that their salaries should be treated separately from those of other nursing staff. They wanted to widen the differential in order to attract the most senior and able nurses. The union representatives, who were more interested in the rates of the junior nurses, did not accept the College's proposal. In the end, the College was defeated and the RNO salaries remained with those of all other nurses.[78] They did, however, claim a salary for RNOs that was above the maximum for all matrons. This the Management Side rejected on the grounds that advisers should not be paid more than those they had to advise.[79]

The Staff Side salary claim became caught up with the Government's pay pause (1961) and the Ministry's concern with establishing a review of the nursing services at the higher levels. The Ministry therefore asked the Management Side to take its time over considering the claim.[80] The Minister, Enoch Powell, explained to the several functional Whitley Councils that he had to sustain the doctrine of responsibility by giving final approval, or otherwise, to their settlements and that he would not hesitate to withhold agreement for a pay settlement if necessary.[81] When the Staff Side pressed for a reply to their claim, Enoch Powell asked the Management Side to delay until the publication of Cmnd 1626, *Incomes policy: the next step.*[82]

The pay claim went to arbitration in 1962, and again in 1963. At the second occasion, the industrial court was advised by the Minister that an independent committee was to examine the senior nursing staff structure.[83]

The position of the RNOs was not successfully established until the Salmon structure was implemented after 1966. Under this arrangement they were given the highest grade 10, the equivalent of the chief nursing officers in the hospital groups.

As well as being the first purely administrative posts (in contrast to matrons who organised or administered a nursing service), the RNOs were probably the first nurses in the hospital service with a non-executive, advisory position. They had the task of demonstrating the need for a nurse to understand the complexities of the occupation, one who could give sound advice to the regional authorities. They had to fight for their status, both professional and bureaucratic, in order that their advice would be respected. The rather ludicrous reactions of the Management Side to their salary claims are evidence of the attitudes of the authorities to these first appointments. The development of a nursing authority structure (in contrast to a nursing presence at the RHBs) probably owes much to these first regional nursing officers.

At first sight, it seems strange that the authorities (including the civil servants and the Management Side) experienced so many difficulties in understanding the need for and functions of administrative nurses with no responsibility for the day to day management of a service. The posts of medical officers of health and regional medical officers produced no equivalent problems. Why then should a nursing adviser find the authorities so confused?

The problem probably lies in the attitudes of lay people and the authorities to nursing. Nurses had traditionally been seen as providing a service to patients. Nurses were seen as implementing the doctors' orders within an environment ordered by a lay administrator. Since all the tools and services required for nursing were provided, not much further organisation was required except that needed to provide the requisite number of staff at more or less the right moment. The flat structure of nursing tended to reinforce this view.

The bureaucratisation of the health service after 1948 and the growing division of labour, both in health care and in nursing, generated the need for a more vertical structure. The increasing complexities of health care brought about a need for more coordination between nursing and other health workers. After 1949, the structure of nurse education became more complex and needed to be tied into the provision of nursing services. In the meantime, the grouping of hospitals meant that further coordination between individual units and the many hospital groups had to be achieved satisfactorily at HMC and regional levels. It became noticed, slowly, that changes in one occupational group affected other occupational groups: this required some expert advice before changes were made in order to avoid dislocation. There began to be felt a need for expert nursing advice and it no longer served to consult doctors about nursing problems.

Hospital groups lacked a single nurse figure-head, and the weak nursing advisory committees could not provide the leadership that management committees might look for. Each hospital matron fought her own corner and looked after her own interests: how were management authorities to distinguish between their narrow interests? It needed a nursing adviser to weave a path through these and find what might be for the general interest.

One of the preoccupations of the 1960s was the question of staffing standards. There were none but historical establishments and no objective criteria: those who argued loudest often obtained the most nurses. When resources were spread thinly between groups, this often made for ill-feeling and inefficiency: the matron with the most nurses could claim greater status. Once again it was the nurse adviser at regional headquarters who might provide guidance and see to fair play.

Before 1948, there were fewer consultants and each had his whims more or less provided for. With the National Health Service came standardisation: this required a standardisation of nursing practice and procedures. Doctors might still try to assess quality of care, but it required a nursing adviser to speak with some assurance.

250

The division of labour and the increasing complexity of the health service, therefore, removed from non-nurses their former capacity to interpret and coordinate nursing needs, and generated the need for a nursing adviser who was removed from the local pressures and politics, who was a disinterested party and whose values and priorities were those of the policy makers rather than those of the practitioners. These were new posts, with new functions removed from patient care or the day to day provision of a service.

There may have been a further trigger in the growth of the RNO position. There was, and is, an informal channel of consultation and communication on a professional and scientific basis between Ministry officials and the medical Royal Colleges. There was no similar channel for the nurses since the Royal College of Nursing was not able to fulfil this function. In the first place, it was usually preoccupied with its negotiating functions and anxious to uphold or improve the status of the nurse. In the second place, it was a single body which tried to represent a host of different levels and, more significantly, a host of specialist interests, which were often irreconcilable. It was not a learned society and had no scientific expertise.

At one time there were hopes that the Standing Nursing Advisory Committee might have functioned as a central reference for nursing, but this hope was not fulfilled because, in political terms, the SNAC was a ministerial lapdog and, in professional terms, it spoke too much with the voice of the matrons and not enough with the voice of the practitioners.

In the end, it became the RNOs who were used as references for nurses since they could pick up opinions and discuss matters with them in their regions. That their values differed did not seem to matter, and it is true that many were fair in their presentation of opinion. They have continued in this informal function and the RNO Group, as it later became, is probably the most powerful section in the nursing profession today.

Chapter 13/Concluding discussion

Nationalisation and the nurses

Before the introduction of the NHS, nurses were employees of their separate hospital authorities. The local authority hospital nurses were the employees of the larger councils through the health committees, and the voluntary hospital nurses were employed by their boards of governors.

Nationalisation of the hospitals meant nationalisation of the nursing services and the nurses became the employees of the new group hospital management committees. Only the teaching hospitals were left out of this arrangement and their nurses remained under the boards of governors.

Although Sofer[1] looked at the staff relationships in the three hospitals (one voluntary, one local authority general and one local authority mental) he made no reference to the changed employment status of the staff, all of whom came under the authority of the new NHS. This had an unseen but dramatic effect on the nurses, in particular.

White[2] contrasted the social image of the voluntary hospital nurses with those of the poor law nurses. She argued that the nurses in the great teaching hospitals shared the charisma which attached to their establishments and that this charisma overflowed to the other voluntary hospital nurses. On the other hand, the poor law hospitals were tainted with the odium generally felt for the poor law authorities and the image of the nurses within those institutions was similarly coloured. Later, when the municipal hospitals grew up, their nurses were often regarded in a somewhat similar vein – as agents of social control.

After the regionalisation of the hospitals, the voluntary, municipal and mental hospitals were grouped together and the voluntary hospitals quickly lost their vicarious charisma. So did their nurses. The teaching hospitals which had stayed outside the regional structure, retained, for a while, both their character and their charisma, until 1974 when they too were regionalised.

The voluntary hospital nurses, then, lost their former prestige and became mere employees with none of their traditional charisma. This being so, their occupational status had to be re-established.

The doctors had a ready made status underpinned by their professional training and firmly legitimised by the agreements made between the Royal Colleges and the British Medical Association on the one hand and Aneurin Bevan on the other.

252

The administrators' status was ensured by the position of the group secretary, who had considerable power as the chief executive officer of the HMC, and by their access to information.

The nurses, coming between the doctors and the administrative staff, had to find a new image. The professional status of many of them was diluted by the loss of their charisma and they refused to acknowledge their 'hired hands' status, even though many of their colleagues were already used to it from their former employment by the local authorities. There was therefore a rift between the nurses who had been able to consider themselves as 'ladies' in the voluntary hospitals and those who were more used to being mere nurses employed by the local authorities.

We have seen in chapter 4 that the members of the new HMCs had mixed backgrounds. Some were used to the old voluntary hospital ways of administration and also regarded the nurses as 'ladies'; others were from the former municipal hospitals and regarded their nurses as employees, often as 'hands'.

The Ministry had little regard for nurses and never appeared to see them as anything other than labour. Their *Notes for the Guidance of HMCs*[3] clearly placed the nurses only one jump away from the domestic staff. The minutes exchanged between Whitehall departments during the preparation of the Nurses Bill in 1948 confirmed this attitude.[4] In the terms used by social scientists, when discussing the division of labour, the nurses were seen as generalists or semi-skilled workers.[5]

Whereas the entry requirements set by the General Nursing Council until 1939 had been a School Certificate or the equivalent, the majority of nurses had come from secondary education. The enrolment of assistant nurses in 1943 and the open entry policy since the war diluted the educational standards of nurses. The delay in re-introducing the minimum entry qualifications until 1962 and the imposition then of a low standard, two 'O' levels, further reduced the educational level of the majority. We saw in chapter 5 how these factors affected the training of nurses and in chapter 9 how they affected the numbers and quality of the nurse teachers themselves. The admission of the nursing auxiliaries to the Nurses and Midwives Whitley Council further proletarianised the nurses in the eyes of the Ministry and the employing authorities.

The better educated nurses and the more intellectually gifted ones found their training and their work lacking in stimulation. Many of them sought greater satisfaction by taking post-basic courses but were accused by the authorities and some of their colleagues of 'certificate hunting'. The rift between the 'ladies' and the 'nurses' changed over the years as one section of nurses sought for an improved social status through specialisation and the other section settled down under the imposed generalist ethic.

The race, after 1948, to recruit and train as many nurses as quickly as possible in order to staff the half million empty beds meant that the emphasis on numbers had to predominate over quality. Whilst Ministry officials and the employing authorities valued nurses only as 'pairs of hands', there was little reason for them to concern themselves with their social status. Material rewards, in so far as they could be reconciled with the need to run an economical health service, were thought to be the most important factor in recruiting more staff. But how could anyone determine a fair salary for the nurses?

The RCN claimed a salary commensurate with the professional responsibilities which they maintained the nurses carried. The Ministry, regarding nurses as semi-skilled workers, looked to other semi-skilled occupations for comparisons. The nurses, fed on the propaganda put out by the competing unions and College, began to feel more and more deprived.

The generalists amongst the nurses looked to material rewards to sustain themselves. They compared themselves to industrial workers who were receiving higher payments. The specialists, wanting greater professional status, looked to better educational standards to sustain their needs. They compared themselves to other specialists in the NHS and to the administrators who received better salaries but also had more power deriving from their managerial posts.

For many years, nurses taking further training had to revert to the salaries of third year students and, later, to those of first year staff nurses. They worked on the wards as learners but functioned as trained staff, which they were. This represented good value for the employing authorities, and post-basic training in midwifery, tuberculosis nursing, mental nursing and district nursing helped to keep the work moving on the cheap. These were courses with formal, structured training.

Other clinical areas, however, had no such structured courses. Fields such as operating theatres, medical or surgical wards, geriatric or casualty departments, were lumped together as 'general nursing' which required nothing more than the three years of basic preparation, particularly as these were not shortage areas.

The medical specialties, however, were quickly becoming more refined and narrower. Surgeons began to restrict their fields to a particular body system such as genito-urinary, respiratory, gastrointestinal. Their techniques developed and became more complex and they needed nurses to know more about the work. Nurses who worked with specialists often did learn a great deal more about their areas. They learned from the medical students whom they were teaching, from the resident medical staff and from the consultants themselves. Some nurses studied on their own and many accumulated a considerable theoretical understanding. These nurses were willing to accept heavy responsibilities of decision-making and professional judgment. Many of them became clinical specialists in all but name and official recognition. Other nurses were not so willing or able to improve their knowledge or understanding of the work. Whilst they might be ward sisters, because the shortage of trained staff was such that anyone could find a sister's post, they worked out the rest of their careers resting on their basic training and taking no more responsibility than they absolutely had to.

There were, therefore, many difficulties in rewarding the more professionally minded nurses or in distinguishing them from the semi-skilled generalists. Ward sisters were ward sisters and the common grading and salary structure failed to encourage the professionally minded and did not allow them any higher status. Often these nurses migrated to the teaching hospitals where they felt that their qualities and knowledge were more highly regarded. Others sought administrative posts in order to enhance their status and salaries.

During the 1950s, the hospitals became more bureaucratised. More administrators were appointed, more specialists were employed. After the Guillebaud committee reported in 1956[6] the Ministry of Health published HM(56)32 announcing a national training scheme for administrators. Administration in the health service became professionalised and graduates received speedy promotion. Managerialism entered the health service and bureaucratic values became more pronounced than ever.

The matrons, who had been slowly losing ground since the inception of the health service, observed the power of the administrators. They had few answers to the actuarial questions put to them by the budget-conscious hospital and group secretaries, and many found it more convenient to begin to take notice of the ways in which these people functioned. They began to absorb the bureaucratic values which seemed to give the administrators so much authority at committee meetings. They began to learn new forms of behaviour which rubbed off on to their subordinates.

If nursing was devalued and administration seen to be so prized, it is not surprising that the College rejected the Goddard proposals for a return to unitary forms of nursing (chapter 10). Since the Whitley Council had absorbed the auxiliaries into the nursing structure and since the authorities were trying to recruit more enrolled nurses, it seemed reasonable for a mini form of hierarchy to be exploited on the wards. The registered nurses were to be the administrators of those teams and the other nurses could do the bedside work. We may guess that this, substantially, was the attitude of the RCN in its response to the Goddard report.

The ward sisters, therefore, became more and more concerned with the administrative task on the wards. The bureaucracy of the NHS, with its increasing volume of forms, encouraged this transformation. But still the nurses found that the professional authority, for which many of them continued to search, evaded them.

Sociological criteria for professionalism in 1948 rested largely on organisation, service and altruism. Tawney[7] considered that professionals were a 'body of men who carry on their work in accordance with rules designed to enforce certain standards both for the protection of its members and for the better service of the public ... [its] essence is that though men enter it for the sake of a livelihood, the measure of their success is the service which they perform, not the gain which they amass'. Carr-Saunders and Wilson[8] wrote that 'the attitude of the professional man to his client or his employers is painstaking and is characterised by an admirable sense of responsibility; it is one of pride in service given rather than of interest in opportunity for personal profit.' Cole[9] offered three characteristics: technical efficiency and examination, a code of ethics which included service and a closed structure.

Later, sociologists began to concentrate more on the application of an intellectual technique, higher education and specialisation. Merton et al.[10] specified both theoretical knowledge and higher education, whilst retaining the characteristics of altruism and service. In the next decade, less emphasis was placed on altruism and this was often displaced by considerations of power, organisation and life-style derived from specialisation and monopoly (Jackson[11] and Johnson[12]).

In the 1950s, therefore, there was still the emphasis on altruism and service but the educational theme was gaining in strength.

Nurses had plenty of altruism and service but their training, taken outside the education system, lacked legitimacy and its educational or training standard could not be measured.[13] It was no use nurses thumping their chests and boasting of being registered: it meant nothing. Their training was tied to the minimum entry standard set by the Ministry of Health and GNC, and accepted by the RCN.

Although many hospitals required more than the two 'O' levels for their recruits, indeed some required university entrance qualifications, the final state examination had to be set to the entry minimum.

In the years after 1944, and certainly by 1962, the Education Act had enabled many more girls and boys to leave school with good General Certificate of Education levels, and the numbers of school leavers going into further and higher education were increasing rapidly. Whilst nurse training stood still, the standard of education generally was improving. Nursing was being de-skilled, at least in relative terms if not in real terms.

The Ministry of Health had no interest in improving the quality of nurse training. Indeed, it may be argued that they were more concerned to maintain the semi-skilled or generalist nature of nursing. Mr Wedderburn's prediction in 1956 (Chapter 7) that district nurses would become a 'semi-processed article' was becoming true of all nurses. The Ministry had reduced the training of enrolled nurses in 1949, abbreviated the training of nurse tutors in 1954, and shortened district nurse training in 1956. The Jameson report[14] confirmed the health visitor as a general family visitor. All the combined courses for multiple training effected a shortened period of preparation for those nurses and the Ministry delayed the return of the minimum education standard until 1962.

It was little wonder that so many nurses perceived a significant loss of status. Nursing lacked professional authority and, in compensation, many began to look elsewhere for an improved status.

The generalists, noting the growing affluence of industrial workers during the 1950s and 1960s, adopted more instrumental values and sought to improve their social standing in the hospitals by means of better material rewards and working conditions. Many preferred to belong to trade unions but those who were members of the RCN encouraged it to adopt a more union-like approach in its negotiations with the Whitley Council. Lacking much in the way of recognised educational qualifications, they assumed an anti-education ethic and insisted that nursing must be a practically based occupation, with their training emphasising practical skills rather than theoretical learning.

The specialists, recognising their lack of professional authority, sought to improve this by means of higher entry criteria, a more demanding training and post-basic courses in further and higher education centres. They insisted that there was a more intellectual meaning to nursing than was generally recognised. Whilst they welcomed higher salaries as a means of improving their lifestyle, their emphasis was on establishing professional authority through legitimate educational means.

The nurse administrators sought for greater authority in policy-making. Their search for status turned towards bureaucratic values in competition with the administrators and civil servants. If they were to win any arguments with bureaucrats, they had to be able to play the same game. Altruism, they noticed, meant little in the fight for resources, or power in policy-making.

Nursing, then, became a pluralist social system. Whereas before 1948 altruism had been the dominant ethic, the NHS drove it out and replaced it with the search for status. But status meant something different to each of the three main groups. For the generalists it meant a social or functional status within the hospital, based on instrumental and material values. For the specialists it meant professional authority supported by a legitimate education and a knowledge base. For the nurse administrators it meant power in decision-making and control of their own staff.

The pursuit of these three separate goals by means of separate strategies was severely hampered by the unitary policy structure imposed on the nurses.

There was only one system for training nurses. Whereas the 1949 Nurses Act had allowed the GNC to authorise experimental forms of training, it was slow to exploit this, particularly where nurse training could be taken outside the health service schools. The GNC was reluctant to let go of its control of nurse training or to allow outside examining bodies to hold their own examinations, even within a general policy framework set by the Council. This was one of the main reasons why the degree course negotiations with London University foundered in the early 1950s (chapter 11).

There was only one salary and grading structure for nurses. We saw in chapter 4 how, in the days before the Salmon report, this inhibited the growth of clinical specialties and made it virtually impossible for the nurses to respond to the growing needs of bureaucratic structure of the NHS. The Whitley Council, shackled by the Ministry of Health and heavily influenced by the employing authorities, could only react to immediate needs. There was no means of encouraging clinical expertise, no way of rewarding excellence. Salary levels were determined by the need to maintain differentials between the ancillary staff and the lowest grade on the nursing structure, the auxiliaries. Leads were given to nurses working in shortage areas rather than to nurses with additional training and qualifications or those accepting exceptional responsibilities. Indeed, further training was not encouraged except in those areas where there was a statutory requirement such as in the mental, midwifery and health visiting fields.

The salary structure reinforced the de-skilling process. The Whitley Council never accepted the need to allow separate structures for clinical specialists or the nurse teachers. The unitary structure always reinforced the use of student nurses as cheap labour on the wards. By regarding them as employees, the structure continued to maintain the matron's control over them.

Since the nurse administrators were compelled to bow to bureaucratic pressures and to adopt bureaucratic values, they became more conscious of the need for labour in their wards and the constraints of their nursing budgets. It was cheaper to employ student nurses and auxiliaries than to use trained staff. Since the generalists did not demand specialist courses, it was cheaper to use them than the more highly trained nurses. Except where there were statutory requirements, posts were not designated according to their requirements for specialised knowledge and the cheapest staff could be employed as the authorities wished. It was more convenient to employ generalists who subscribed to a class system and therefore to the authority of the nurse administrators, and did not challenge the *status quo*: the specialists were more inclined to subscribe to a status system and to question tradition and ritual.[15] The nurse administrators therefore slowly became more aligned with the Ministry and the employing authorities in their values and strategies and, without realising it, furthered the de-skilling process.

The unitary structure was able to support and satisfy the nurse administrators especially after the implementation of the Salmon structure. After this they became the nurse managers and adopted frankly bureaucratic values. As Froebe and Bain[16] pointed out, in a continuum between clinical values and management values, the further up the hierarchy a nurse gets, the further away from clinical values does she move. The unitary structure was also able to deal with the objectives of the generalists since it was designed for that kind of employee. It dealt with salaries and conditions of work rather than with professional values and needs.

The specialist nurses, therefore, were the group who were least satisfied by the system which had little to offer them. The system neither catered for their educational goals nor helped them with their search for authority. Indeed, the unitary system seemed almost designed to suppress this group.

During the period that we have examined, the specialists, or professionalists, were a relatively small group and, although articulate and vocal, they were not sufficiently well organised to compete either with the more numerous generalists or with the more powerful managers. Since 1961, however, they have increased in numbers. Whilst the level of general education has improved, the numbers of courses in further and higher education centres available to the professionalist nurses have also increased. Furthermore, the numbers of nurses who have graduated through university based training schemes, the Open University or the research fellowship scheme set up by the DHSS, have produced a steady trickle of nurses with graduate status. With the general nurse, training remained more or less static, the gap between the specialists and the generalists has grown and the difference between their objectives has become more marked; the lack of satisfaction felt by the specialists with the unitary policy system has become more pronounced.

The Royal College of Nursing and the decision-making process

In chapter 12 we saw that the College was determined, at any cost, to be recognised as the dominant partner with the Ministry of Health in policy making. Eckstein[17] described the determinants of pressure group politics, the most important of which he considered to be the structure of the government decision-making process itself. This was supported by Nettl[18], who also predicated that to be accepted as the official representative body, the interest group had to demonstrate certain characteristics. These included the adoption of government terminology and methods and the demonstration of concern for 'the common good' as defined by the civil service administrators.

Olson[19] agreed that interest groups existed 'to fulfil purposes which a group of men have in common' but also proposed that these groups are primarily organised for some other purpose, such as influencing policy decisions. He considered that these organisations could only have the strength and support to achieve power in a political direction if they managed to satisfy their members.

The official objectives of the College are set out in their charter and bye-laws and include the promotion of the science and art of nursing, the better education and training of nurses and their efficiency in the profession. It was only in 1978 that a new aim was included, 'to promote the professional standing and interests of *members* of the nursing profession' (my emphasis).

From the point of view of the College, the official goals must reflect the common interests of the membership but, as Olson pointed out, official goals are supplemented by 'by-product' goals, those of influencing policy. From 1948 onwards, the by-product goals almost displaced the official ones.

For some time it was possible to argue, and to believe, that the pursuit of legitimacy in the eyes of the Ministry was an acceptable means of gaining greater professionalisation. Similarly, it could be argued that negotiating for better salaries was commensurate with the College's official objectives. The latter was certainly popular with the membership, and that was very necessary.

Until the admission of the nursing auxiliaries to the Whitley Council, the professional organisations had the largest number of seats on the Staff Side and could sway both the nurses' demands and the negotiated settlements. After 1955, however, the trade unions gained the ascendency as the auxiliaries tipped the proportion of seats in their favour. Places on the Staff Side were allocated according to the size of membership of the several organisations and it became necessary for the College to recruit more nurses if its influence was not to be lost.

Since the foundation of the College in 1916, membership had been limited to women and only those whose names were on the general register. The Nurses Act 1957 did away with the general and supplementary registers and substituted one register with various parts. In 1960, the decision was taken at an extraordinary general meeting to permit all individuals whose names appeared on the register of a statutory body to join the College. In 1963, the College amalgamated with the National Council of Nurses and could fairly claim to have become the largest nursing organisation in the country. These moves also helped to strengthen the College's position on the Staff Side.

In opening its doors to all trained nurses, the College necessarily admitted to membership many who had not previously belonged to any organisation, as well as many who had been or remained members of trade unions. Dual membership was common, as these people thought that the unions were not only better negotiators at the Whitley Council and less restrained in their salary demands, but also gave stronger support to the staff at their places of work. Membership of the College enabled them to enjoy colleague support and exchange.

But this influx of new members diluted the strength of professional values which established College members (who had mostly come from the teaching and other voluntary hospitals) had, adding more instrumental and generalist sentiments. It also imported a more strongly anti-education element.

The College found itself in the position of having to legitimise itself with the Ministry and civil servants, strengthen its position on the Staff Side by less discriminating recruitment, satisfy a membership which was becoming increasingly activist in demanding better salaries, accommodate the matrons in their need for more labour and placate the professionalists who found their needs less and less well served.

In demanding more pay for the nurses the College risked upsetting the Ministry who could remind them of the need to be 'responsible'. It also upset the matrons, who were mindful of their own budgets and the need to maintain cover. On the other hand, a better salary level would please the generalists and, if it eased the supply position, would help the matrons' search for labour.

In demanding a return of the minimum education level, the College upset the generalists who did not think that it was necessary, as well as the civil servants who did not like the idea because they believed that it would hinder recruitment. In then compromising its own considered policy of three 'O' levels and meekly accepting two 'O' levels in 1962, the College upset the specialists but not the generalists or matrons. If the College negotiated aggressively, this too upset the nurse managers and the professionalists, even if it did please the generalists. Its concern to retain or revive the professional status of nurses by encouraging specialisation, ran counter to the de-skilling policy of the Ministry and appeared to be depressing the status of the generalists. Its concern with being 'responsible', to maintain the common good and be mindful of service needs ran counter to its search for professionalism. The paradoxical nature of the College's objectives was the cause of a considerable degree of conflict and stasis. The College was forced to attenuate its search for its official policy and put greater stress on its more popularist goals. It had to sacrifice its long term goals for short term gains.

Studying the minutes of most of the institutions suggests an apparent break in about 1956. This break is difficult to demonstrate but seemed to represent a change of tactics. There was a lull in major activity but the College had earlier set up a number of working parties and was obviously taking stock. It had appointed a new general secretary designate (who took office in 1957), published a major policy statement, *Observations and Objectives*[20] and was forcing through its paper on *The Duties and Position of the Nurse*[21] against the opposition of the BMA and with little help from the Ministry. The specialist sections of the College were becoming more numerous as well as more vocal.[22] The new generation of nurses, recruited after the war, brought up under wartime difficulties, many of them having served in the forces, was maturing in the profession and assuming leadership roles. Other nurses who had benefited from the Butler Education Act 1944 were coming forward. The climate in nursing took a turn.

The College grew in complexity as it had to handle more complex problems. It set up new departments and recruited more specialists to service the sections. In 1959 a firm of consultants was invited in and the organisation of the College was consequently changed. Ten years after the start of the NHS, the College too had become a bureaucratic organisation.

As the sections increased, the specialists tended to use them as their platform whilst the generalists met together at branch meetings. RCN Council increasingly forwarded papers to the sections for their interpretation, advice and reports. The sections became more authoritative and influential in policy decisions so that, from having been an elitist organisation, the College developed a more pluralistic system.

There was, however, still no recognisable framework for decision-making. Decisions rested largely on the majority interests of the current Council and were sometimes overturned as the composition of the Council changed or as the relative power of the sections shifted.

Council was largely held together by the general secretary but as Jones[25] said, 'the leader is as much the prisoner of the image of his party as the other candidates . . . the Prime Minister is only as strong as his colleagues let him be'. The affairs of the College have so increased and involve so many technical and complex factors that no one person is able to survey the whole field. Policy initiatives come from many sources, from the government and from administrative necessity. They come from pressure of events in the health service, from international affairs, from the demands of public opinion and from the membership. Nor is the general secretary's control over the agenda as absolute as may sometimes be supposed. She has to carry her colleagues and the members of Council with her. In doing this, she must woo and coax them to support her; there is necessarily a process of negotiation if not bargaining.

Without a clear reference framework, on what were decisions to be based? It is clear that during the years 1948–61, the central reference for decisions rested on the search for 'status'. The centre of the College managed to preserve its official objectives only because the periphery also wanted 'status'. The balance was maintained only because each gave 'status' a different meaning and this ambiguity could be exploited.

Observations and Objectives re-stated the College's official policies and gave great emphasis to specialisation and specialist education. It was a counter to the process of generalism and proletarianisation which had started with the health service. It encouraged even general hospital nurses to consider themselves as potential specialists and talked about the needs of the patient being best served by the establishment of a strong profession. Instead of subordinating nurses to the service ethic, for the first time a College document spelt out the needs of the profession as being equal to and supportive of the needs of the patient.

From that period on, the College voice became more confident and assertive.

Davies[23] has described the Florence Nightingale reforms of the 1860s as 'a very conscious selection of an occupational strategy'. Elsewhere,[24] she contrasts Nightingale's strategy with that of Mrs Bedford Fenwick. Ethel Bedford Fenwick was convinced that the trained nurse should be distinguished from the untrained nurse by a strictly controlled education process, similar to that of the doctors. Whereas Nightingale saw the nurse as a generalist, Mrs Bedford Fenwick saw her as a specialist. Florence Nightingale wanted nurses to be controlled by a nursing hierarchy; Mrs Bedford Fenwick wanted nurses within a professional monopoly.

It may not therefore be too far-fetched to describe the years after 1956 as the period when the College changed its strategy from that of Nightingale to that of Bedford Fenwick. It had been forced to go along with the Ministry's attempts to generalise nurses because of its prior needs to gain acceptance as the representative body in policy-making. By 1956, it became opportune to revert to the primacy of its official goal of furthering the profession of nursing and it was possible to take a stronger line in that direction using specialisation as a strategy.

It used the Salmon recommendations to gain greater policy-making powers in the health service and to develop manager specialists from the nursing ranks. Despite the common belief that the Salmon structure was managerial in orientation (which it was), we have shown in chapter 4 that by opening up grades and fitting these to posts (in contrast to the earlier need to fit posts to grades), it was possible to develop more clinical as well as non-clinical posts. The numbers and types of clinical posts proliferated after the implementation of the new structure. But the College, in this pluralist system, had to act as referee to the three interest groups now established in their membership. There is no evidence to show that either the College or the nurses themselves understood the division of goals nor the ambiguity in their collective search for 'status'. Whilst the centre called for harmony and consensus, it labelled the dissenters 'disloyal', 'rebels' or 'trouble makers' and sought to suppress their opinions and demands. The most influential group during the 1950s and 1960s, the public health section, declined in authority and the newly organised group, the nurse administrators section, became dominant.

After the implementation of the Salmon structure in the late 1960s, nursing became more managerialist and shaped the nursing ethic, driving the professionalists to the periphery.

The General Nursing Council for England and Wales

In so far as the thrust of this study has been towards examining the development of the nursing profession, and since the GNC was concerned only with training nurses to a minimum statutory qualification, it could be argued that its influence on nursing was minimal or, perhaps, negative. This statement needs to be examined more carefully.

The GNC first started agitating for the return of the entry test in 1944 and was very active in its search for new entry criteria. It was also concerned, at an early date, with the low standard of clinical experience available to many student nurses in the numerous small hospitals with training schools. Some of these could report no more than 20–54 occupied beds.[26] Its proposals to implement new criteria were repeatedly deflected by the Ministry.

On the other hand, the GNC did appear to take a very narrow view of its terms of reference. Since it repeatedly alleged that student nurses had to be taught clinical skills by ward sisters, why did it not consider that the qualifications and selection of ward sisters came within the GNC's purview?[27] Certainly, at the time of the Wood report, the GNC was very much on the side of the matrons and resisted an independent status for either the nurse training schools or the student nurses. It was also vehemently opposed to losing any vestige of control over nurse training and strongly resisted Wood's proposals to give the Government health departments responsibility for inspecting and approving schools. For the same reasons, it opposed the draft proposals for the new Nurses Bill in 1948, which would have taken the schools and the directors of nurse training right out of its control.

The GNC subscribed to the two tier system of registered and enrolled nurses but had nothing to say about Wood's proposals for mandatory advanced training for ward sisters.

Its reactions to the draft proposals and its subsequent skirmishing around the Nurses Bill showed that it had failed to gain a broader picture of nursing as it would or could be within a national service and, instead, continued to fight over details on a narrow basis, as if it were still negotiating with separate hospital authorities.

The concern of the GNC to keep the roll of nurses was more geared towards preventing the care of the chronic sick falling back into the hands of untrained staff rather than because it saw much intrinsic value in a second grade. It failed to recognise that the Nurses Act 1949 and the NHS would produce, for the first time, a nurse trained in both chronic and acute fields.[28] Half the Council thought that the SEAN training could be shortened in 1948 and the other half disagreed with this – mainly, it seemed, on the grounds of keeping up the numbers of pupil nurses in the long stay wards. In the end, Council agreed a compromise, to the pleasure of the Minister, including one year's training and a second year's supervised experience.

In 1948–49 the GNC did put up a very strong fight to gain control of post-basic training but failed, except for the roll of tutors, and lost control over the professionalisation of nurses. With the passage of time, especially in the light of the College's declared policy to professionalise nurses through post-basic training, the basic course could only be a preparation for generalists. When the GNC elected to make two 'O' levels the minimum entry level, it unwittingly subscribed to the Ministry's de-skilling policy and helped to institutionalise it. The differentials between the SEAN/SEN and the SRN became more and more difficult to defend and when the National Board for Prices and Incomes reported on nurses, they could find no difference between the two grades.[29]

In the case of the nurse tutors, the GNC agreed in 1950 that the length of training, taken with the London University course, should be two years. When then in 1954 did it go along with the Ministry in shortening the course? Two academic educationalists on the working party publicly disagreed with the decision and said that the proposals were educationally retrograde. The GNC made no comment on the shorter course nor did it explain its change of heart. The report, *Function, Status and Training of Nurse Tutors*,[30] used frankly economic and service arguments for this alteration and the GNC did not offer any evidence of resistance.

The membership of the GNC in 1944–50, which first set out the arguments for a return of the test and supported a two-year course for nurse tutors, was substantially different from the composition of the Council voted into office in 1950. Both the earlier council and the later one had a predominance of matrons but those on the earlier Council were still, largely, the pre-war ones who had qualified for training by taking the School Certificate, had been trained in the great teaching hospitals and who came, usually, from upper middle class families. Whilst education for girls, before the war, was poor and the curriculum thin, the women accepted for training in these hospitals generally came from educated families and were brought up in a cultured environment with strong ideals of service to the patients.

The nurses on the council of 1945–50 brought to their work the values and goals of their hospitals but, more important, the values and goals of hospitals before their nationalisation.

It is not surprising, therefore, that this Council started early negotiations with the Ministry for the return of the entry qualification in order to achieve, once again, a more stringent selection of recruits.

The later Council, that of 1950–55, inherited that policy and had to continue to pursue it. But this Council was of a different composition. Only five of the old Council were re-elected and nine were new faces. The most important change, however, was the change that had taken place in the hospitals themselves and the values and goals of their senior nurses. Whereas the dominant ethic of the pre-war and pre-nationalisation hospitals had been to do with the standards of nursing care, even by 1950, this had changed and the prior concern of senior nurses was recruitment and ward cover.

Therefore, whilst the earlier GNC called for a return of the entry test and based their arguments on the need for careful selection of students, the later Council continued this policy but based their arguments on the need to recruit more enrolled nurses and to make nursing more attractive for recruits. In fact, they searched for the minimum standard and, as their minutes said in 1956, some hospitals had no choice but to accept anyone who applied. Even those who failed the final examination had given three years of service.

The values of the 1950–55 Council were very different, therefore, from those of their predecessors: they were more interested in recruitment than in education. Certainly, there appeared to be a strong service orientation. On the other hand, the Ministry of Health treated the GNC with scant courtesy or respect and, until the middle 1960s, gave very little appearance of taking much notice of their advice. The Ministry spokesmen on the GNC were often able to sway the debate (as far as one can tell from the minutes and the curtailed accounts) and the medical appointees also appeared able to influence the voting. Furthermore, the nurses elected to the Council were put there by the nurses on the electoral role who had been able to study the manifestos printed in the nursing journals.

In the early days of this study, nurses still tended to regard their matrons as their natural representatives. There was little sign that the rank and file had discerned any plurality or conflict of values. It was not until the later part of the study period that the nurses began to show much consciousness of different views. By then, of course, the generalists were in a dominant position.

The GNC made a serious error in proposing that the area nurse training committees should be serviced by the regional health boards. It is not clear why they did not wish to have an independent organisation, and their stated fears of a proliferation of committees are not convincing, even if the RCN also shared these sentiments. The GNC quickly learned that they had made a mistake but by then it was too late. From then onward, the GNC had to spend an excessive amount of time struggling against the system, but they never succeeded in removing the service domination from these committees. The GNC also made a critical mistake in accepting the advice of the headmistresses regarding the new GCE examinations. Their confusion over the issue displayed their ignorance of the general education system which they considered, in so many ways, to be irrelevant to nurse training.

Over recruitment and wastage, the GNC took a convinced, commonsense line and closed its mind to any other possibilities. They had decided, for instance, that wastage in mental nursing was due only to the recruitment of unsuitable candidates. They *knew* that the return of the minimum education level would rectify the position.[31] They therefore refused to consider other factors and frequently rejected research based findings because these could not be reconciled with what they knew. The service orientation of the GNC members caused considerable dissatisfaction among the nurse tutors who should have been able to look for support and understanding from the Council. Instead, the GNC continued to support the position of the matron as head of the nurse training school and it was not until after the Aitken report[30] that the training staff were considered to have any part in selecting students. Even then, the GNC disliked the proposed title of 'director of nurse education' and preferred the watered down one of 'principal tutor'.

In the matter of nurse training, and in examining the activities of the GNC, we need to remember that there was a gulf between the ambitions of the RCN and the statutory responsibilities of the GNC. Whereas the College hoped to professionalise nursing, the GNC were concerned only with setting a *minimum* standard for the registration or enrolment of nurses. It is not clear that either of the institutions recognised this gap, although there was overlapping membership of the RCN and the GNC councils and much consultation between them. Furthermore, whilst no-one acknowledged the plurality of nursing objectives and the existence of several interest groups, everyone assumed a unity of interest and goals. This increased the confusion which enveloped their respective policies and strategies.

No-one had tried to describe what a minimum standard for registration should be. There was general acceptance that the nursing force should include a wide range of skills from the untrained auxiliaries through the SEAN/SEN grade to the registered nurses. Most patient care was given by untrained staff and the SRNs were commonly used only to supervise their work. What then were nurses being trained to do? If it was not to give nursing care, was it for administration? The GNC resolutely refused to answer this question and, as we have seen in chapter 11, there was no answer until Henderson's work became available.[32] Once again, therefore, we see that the GNC was making policy decisions (when it was allowed to) without any guiding frame of reference.

The role of nurses was always taken for granted: everyone knew what nurses did, didn't they? Although this matter became a topic for several pieces of research in the 1970s, no-one seemed to understand that a nurse's role could, and should, be whatever a statement of policy objectives made it. Since her role needed to be determined by policy, but never was, the confusion was bound to persist.

It was not until 1957 that the GNC appeared to take a firmer grip on matters and produced their policy document, *Conditions under which hospitals are approved as training schools*.[33] Even this, though, was rooted in the GNC's belief that a better entry standard would resolve most of their problems. There was still no recognition that nurse training lacked legitimacy and their proposals continued to be service orientated, hedged about, as the GNC was, by the ANTCs.

The GNC worked under considerable difficulties over the years and often gave the appearance of being the government's tool. It tried, repeatedly, to achieve the return of the entry test until, at last, in 1959 it succeeded. Even then, its preoccupation with screening-in candidates rather than screening them out persuaded it to set a level which seemed only to institutionalise the de-skilling process.

Its confused view of its functions and the need to work so closely with the Ministry of Health as well as the employing authorities, ensured that it worked as a recruitment bureaucracy rather than as an educational institution. Its statutory responsibilities were interpreted narrowly and its need to gain Ministry approval for all its major decisions ensured that government policy rather than the needs of nurse training were uppermost.

Concluding comments

The NHS introduced a number of new institutions to deal with the nurses in hospital and the community and also provoked the growth and development of several nursing institutions which already existed. These institutions had to reflect the health service bureaucracy and, therefore, became bureaucratised themselves.

The three former streams of nursing were absorbed into the NHS as a single force under the aegis of the Whitley Council. From having been a fragmented occupation, nursing was slowly brought under the control of the GNC, more by changes in morbidity patterns than by deliberate policy. But this unified control of nurses related only to basic training, and the GNC never did gain control of post-basic education. Under the influence of the bureaucratisation of the NHS and the growth of medical technology, nursing slowly separated into new groups, those of the generalists, the specialists and the managers.

The coming of the NHS removed the charisma enjoyed by the élite nurses employed in the voluntary hospitals and proletarianised nursing as an occupation. De-skilling of nurses was institutionalised in spite of the increasing demands of medical technology which assisted the growth of a small number of specialists or professionalists. The growth of the labour force as well as the bureaucratisation of the health service generated more nurse managers and made nursing into a pluralist structure.

The proletarianisation of nursing helped to drive out altruism and generated the greater unionistic tendencies which had been present in the former local authority hospitals but absent in the old voluntary ones. This unionism is only partly countered by the slow growth of the specialist/professionalist section.

Nursing was dominated by the Ministry of Health, and this required all other nursing institutions to suppress what professional goals they had to the over-riding needs of the common good. Common good values were short term ones with little regard to the long term and no-one questioned their rightness or the ways in which they should be achieved.

I have suggested, in the introduction, that an examination of macro nursing policy is strangely neglected. Indeed, to the best of my knowledge, this is the first study of that subject. The disdain felt by the civil servants for nursing was accepted by other disciplines in the health service, by other government departments, as well as, apparently, by most social scientists studying the health service. Nurses, themselves, failed to recognise the need for an evaluation of nursing policy or the constraints imposed by it upon their structure, training and function.

This study ends at about 1961 and it is possible that a later finishing date or a further study of the next period might alleviate the findings. Certainly, there has been much movement in nursing since 1961. The institution of the Salmon structure, the setting up of the DHSS research fellowships, the growth of nursing undergraduate and postgraduate courses and the establishment of a nursing research unit at the DHSS, all might indicate a change of heart at the centre. In chapter 4 I suggested that the Ministry of Health might have come to perceive the need for a balancing of power by the development of specialist nurse managers. It is possible that the escalation of the costs of medical care and the recognition of the demands made by an ageing population, as well as the long-term needs of the so far incurable behavioural diseases, will alter the priorities of the DHSS. As economic pressures grow, the policy of the Ministry of Health to de-skill nurses may be mitigated and the DHSS may find it necessary to encourage the growth of specialists who can take over responsibility for the care of certain groups such as the old and frail, the mentally handicapped and the long-term psychiatric patients.

The unitary policy making structure is no longer appropriate or helpful in a pluralistic nursing society and serves only to continue the de-skilling process. If the specialist group is to be encouraged, or even merely recognised, a new, separate policy structure will be needed. This is recognised in other occupations such as the civil service, the police, the armed services and the fire-brigade: why then have the nurses not been similarly treated? Why should the Salaries Review Board have to consider the salaries of the nursing auxiliaries together with those of the specialists and the managers?

One of the reasons, of course, is that senior nurses who are the managers (with, naturally, a vested interest) continue to be used as representatives of all nurses on the policy-making bodies. It is time that generalists, specialists and managers were allowed to speak for themselves and put forward their separate interests. If nursing were recognised as a pluralist system and if the respective representatives were encouraged to voice their needs, it is possible that the institutions would be able to perform their separate functions more fully and that nurses would be less 'apathetic' both in policy and political matters. Separate salary structures, designated posts for the specialists and a system for their training would not only prove more economical but would permit manpower planning more effectively.

In discussing the several nursing institutions, as well as the

Ministry of Health and the civil servants, I have not yet made clear that here, too, there were interest groups. The many reports and minutes which I studied failed to describe adequately the in-fighting and variety of opinion. I could not substantiate my understanding that there were many voices trying to halt or reverse the de-skilling process but I have every reason to believe this. The nursing officers at the Ministry were a small group and were advisory rather than executive: if the civil servant administrators felt a disdain for nurses, they probably tended to disregard the advice given by these nurses. If the RCN and the GNC majority felt the need to subscribe to the dictates of the Ministry, there were still other voices whose opinions were overwhelmed. Whilst many nurses absorbed the values of the bureaucrats, obviously there were also many who risked much and tried hard to reverse their decisions. Since there was no discernible point of reference, except the common good, by which to assess decisions, their opinions were not accepted and an unscripted definition of the common good prevailed.

The unitary system, as well as the insistence on harmony and consensus, served to repress dissenting voices and masked the growth of pluralism. In this way the different values emerging in the three groups were not distinguished, and provoked many people to regret that nurses did not know what they wanted. Where consensus was achieved it was at the cost of the minority group. Where consensus was not achieved, there was confusion and conflict. Both courses tended to inhibit constructive change.

If nurses do not appear to know what they want, how is anyone to judge what is good for them? It is only by accepting the pluralist nature of nursing and by understanding that nursing needs all these groups with their different goals, that we shall be able to develop a workable frame of reference.

We have accepted the need for a wide range of nursing skills and graded levels. We need the generalists, the specialists and the managers. So long as we accept this, we can come to terms with their separate goals. Satisfying the generalists should not be at the cost of the specialists. The encouragement of the specialists need not be at the expense of the managers or generalists. Both the generalists and the specialists want nurses to manage their service. By identifying these groups and their special goals, nurses can adopt a framework which will allow their separate needs to be fulfilled. It is only by insisting on a unitary form of policy-making that we perpetuate conflict of a destructive nature and inhibit the development of nursing.

An acknowledgement of the need for specialists, and a policy designed to develop and satisfy this minority group, would permit the identification of a suitable framework for decision-making. We should then be able satisfactorily to answer the question of the minimum entry standard: there should be one for the generalists and another for the specialists. We should be able to resolve the future of the SENs who are needed as the generalists. We should be able to resolve the thorny question of student status: the specialists need it and the generalists do not. We should be able to achieve educational legitimacy for the specialists even though this may not be necessary for the generalists. By designating posts for the specialists, we should be able to count them and open up a way to plan our manpower needs for this group.

Our present unitary framework not only is dysfunctional in that it prevents the development of specialists and continues the deskilling process. It is also uneconomical in that it prohibits adequate manpower planning and enforces excessive training, in a rather random way, for many of our nurses: training which is becoming more expensive and less effective.

The RCN's ambitions to professionalise nursing is manifestly unattainable so long as their goals include all nurses. Many do not wish to assume the demands and responsibilities of a professional role. Others are influenced more by instrumental values. Only some nurses are motivated by professional values. It is these, the minority, who will seek to achieve specialist status and should be encouraged. To try to professionalise all nurses is both too expensive and runs against their preferred goals. Nursing, as a generic occupation, cannot be professionalised. It is only the specialist who will form a profession of nursing. We must learn from history and use the lessons it teaches us to shape our future.

Chronology of relevant events

1939   Athlone interim report.
1941   Rushcliffe committee set up.
1942   Horder report on *Assistant Nurses*.
        Beveridge report.
1943   Nurses Act sets up GNC roll of nurses, two years' training.
        Horder report on the *Education and Training of the Nurse*.
1944   Butler Education Act stipulates that all school nurses should
        hold health visitor's certificate.
        White Paper, *A National Health Service*, Cmd 6502.
1945   National Advisory Council on Nurses and Midwives, *Recruit-
        ment of Nurses and Midwives to Training Institutes*.
        Horder report on *Recruitment of Nurses*.
        GNC appoints two full time inspectors.
        RCN and QIDN organise combined training for health
        visitors and district nurses.
1946   NHS Act passed, 14 RHBs in England and Wales, 377 HMCs
        (388 by 1957) set up.
        National recruitment drive for part-time nurses.
        Athlone sub-committee *Report on mental nursing*.
        Wood working party set up.
        National Insurance Act.
1947   Wood report.
        RN Association of British Columbia cancel reciprocal agree-
        ment with GNC.
        GNC get sanction to appoint education officer.
        QIDN offer to train male nurses.
1948   5 July, vesting day for NHS.
        CHSC and standing advisory committees set up, Statutory
        Instrument No 575.
        Qualifications for HVs and TB visitors mandatory in com-
        bined posts, SI No 1415.
        Cohen minority report.
        RCN memo on setting up training courses for HV tutors.
        Ministry of Health circular: notes for guidance of HMCs,
        Nursing and Domestic Staff in Hospitals.
        Whitley Council set up with functional councils.
        GNC conference on minimum educational standards for
        student nurses.
        Ministry of Health proposals for nursing legislation.

274

National Assistance Act.
1949 Nurses Act, reconstructs GNC, Mental Nurses Committee set up, ANTCs to be set up, experimental courses of training permitted.
Registration of nurse tutors by GNC, SI No 1104.
SEAN training reduced to one year plus one year supervised practice, SI No 1986.
Horder report on the *Social and Economic Conditions of the Nurse.*
1950 Admission of male nurses to general register, SI No 386.
New HV syllabus.
Whitley Council, *Hospital Staff Consultative Committees,* GC 13, GC 20.
RHB (50) 47, *Joint Consultation.*
GNC receives interim report re test for students.
Miss M E Davis appointed assistant secretary, Staff Side, Nurses and Midwives Whitley Council.
1951 The Nurses Order, Constitution of ANTCs. SI No 478.
The Nurses Rules and Consolidation of Nurses Rules, SI No 1372. Holders of RMPA transferred to mental register, Education and Examination Committee enlarged from 12 to 17; title of sister tutor changed to nurse tutor.
National Institute of Industrial Psychology report on experimental procedure for selection of student nurses.
Nurses representative councils disbanded, GC(S) 149.
Hospital Matrons with Extended Responsibilities, SAC(N) (52)9.
1953 CHSC, *Reception and Welfare of In-patients to hospitals.*
NPHT, *The Work of Nurses in Hospital Wards.*
First Boots research fellow, University of Edinburgh.
Royal Commission on Mental Laws set up.
Jameson working party set up.
Medical staffs committees set up, RHB (53)91.
Ministry of Health confidential report on *The Function and Status of Nurse Tutors.*
GNC receive final report from National Institute of Industrial Psychology on entrance test.
National Advisory Council on Recruitment of Nurses and Midwives report on *Wastage of Student Nurses.*
1954 CHSC report, *The Place of the SEAN in the NHS.*
Bradbeer report.
Ministry of Health et al, joint committee on the *Function, Status and Training of Nurse Tutors,* report.

HM (54)4, *Hospital Matrons with Extended Responsibilities.*
SNAC report, *The Position of the SEAN within the NHS.*

1955 Armer report on *Training of District Nurses.*
NPHT report on the *Work of the Public Health Nurse.*
University of Edinburgh set up nurse teaching unit.
Royal Sanitary Institute becomes Royal Society for the Promotion of Health.
Staff Side of Whitley Council decide to base future claims on responsibility rather than retail prices index. Salaries to be compared with other professions not necessarily in the NHS.
Staff Side first mention need to review salary structure to keep nurses in line with other grades in the NHS and outside.

1956 Guillebaud report, Cmd 9663.
Jameson report.
Oxford ANTC report, *Survey of training of nurses at general hospitals.*
RCN, *Observations and Objectives.*
Younghusband working party set up.
University of Edinburgh, post-registration courses, studies unit set up.

1957 Nurses Act, does away with supplementary registers.
The Nurses Rules, SI No 1476, set minimum age of entry at 18, prescribes qualifications for entry to nurse tutor training.
Nursing Mirror, *Overtaxed Nurses.*
South Eastern Metropolitan ANTC report, *The Work of Student Nurses and Pupil Assistant Nurses.*
Manchester RHB report *Standards of Nursing Staff.*
South Eastern Metropolitan ANTC report, *The affects of the pattern of the hospital on the work and training of the student nurse.*
Oxford ANTC second report, *Training of nurses in general hospitals.*
Dan Mason report, *Work of Recently Qualified Nurses.*
GNC introduces experimental syllabus for training mental nurses.

1958 RCN set up working party on salary structure of nurses.
National Council on Recruitment of Nurses and Midwives changed to National Committee on Recruitment of Nurses and Midwives under control of Ministry of Health.

1959 Mental Health Act.

Younghusband report.

Ingall committee report, *The Training of district nurses.*

Henderson, Virginia: *The Basic Principles of Nursing Care.*

University of Manchester award diploma in community nursing (SRN, HV, DN).

Doreen Norton research into geriatric nursing.

RCN working party to investigate shortage of recruits to nursing administration posts.

RCN working party on nurse education set up.

GNC syllabus revised, including five days' community observation.

1960 The Nurses (Amendment) Rules, SI No 409, minimum education qualifications for general student nurses (two 'O' levels) with effect 1962.

Edinburgh University sets up degree course for nurses (MA or BSc plus RGN)

Menzies, I: *Anxiety in Nurses.*

Dan Mason report, *Work of the Staff Nurse.*

RCN opens membership to all nurses on the general register.

RCN, *The Nurse tutor: a new assessment.*

RCN, Nursing Administrators Group set up.

1961 Nurses (Amendment) Act, SEANs re-styled SENs.

Health Visitors and Social Workers Training Act.

CHSC, *The Pattern of the In-patients' Day.*

RCN/BMA *The Duties and Position of the Nurse.*

RCN reform working party on nurse education into Platt committee.

1962 Ministry of Health, *A Hospital Plan for England and Wales*, Cmd 1604.

Council for Training Health Visitors set up.

Fever register closed, SI No 2139.

GNC new syllabus and minimum education standard introduced.

RCN and National Council for Nurses amalgamate.

1963 Salmon committee set up.

QIDN experimental course of instruction for SENs in district nursing.

Robbins report on higher education.

References and notes

INTRODUCTION

1 White, Rosemary. Social change and the development of the nursing profession: a study of the Poor Law nursing service, 1848–1948. London, Henry Kimpton, 1978.

2 Garrison W A. Influence in use. In: Castles F G, Murray D J, Potter D C (eds). Decisions, organisations and society. London, Open University/Penguin, 1971. Ch 9.

3 Ministry of Health and Scottish Home and Health Department. Report of the Committee on Senior Nursing Staff Structure. (Chairman Brian Salmon). London, HMSO, 1966.

4 Bellaby, Paul and Oribabor, Patrick.
The growth of trade union consciousness among general hospital nurses. Sociological Review, 1977, vol 25, no 4, new series, November, 801–22.
Determinants of occupational strategies of British hospital nurses. International Journal of Health Services, 1980, vol 10, no 2, 291–309.

5 Davies, Celia.
Experience of dependency and control in work: the case of nurses. Journal of Advanced Nursing, 1976, vol 1, 273–282.
Professionalising strategies as time and culture bound: American and British nursing circa 1893. In: Lagemann, Ellen Condliffe (ed). Nursing history: new perspectives, new possibilities. New York, Teachers College Press, 1983.

6 Ministry of Health and others. Report of the Working Party on Recruitment and Training of Nurses. (Chairman Sir Robert Wood). London, HMSO, 1947.

7 Reports of the Royal College of Nursing Reconstruction Committee. (Chairman Lord Horder). London, RCN, 1942–49.

8 Ministry of Health, Central Health Services Council. Report of the Committee on the Internal Administration of Hospitals. (Chairman Alderman A F Bradbeer). London, HMSO, 1954.

9 Acton Society Trust. Hospitals and the State. (Director of research, T E Chester). London, Acton Society Trust.
1955 Background and blueprint
1956 The impact of change
1957 Groups, regions and committees
1957 The regional hospital boards
1958 The central control of the service
1959 Creative leadership in a state service

10 Sofer, Cyril. Reactions to administrative change: a study of staff relationships in three British hospitals. Human Relations, 1955, vol 8, 291–316.

11 Menzies, Isabel. A case study in the functioning of social systems as a defence against anxiety. Human Relations, 1960, vol 13, no 2.
The criticism offered of her study, that it was too Freudian in orientation, cannot be upheld since Menzies based her work on that of Melanie Klein who, of course, was a notable critic of the Freudian school.

12 MacKenzie W J M. Power and responsibility in health care. Oxford, Oxford University Press for Nuffield Provincial Hospital Trust, 1979.

278

13 Abel-Smith B. A history of the nursing profession. London, Heinemann, 1960.
14 Report of the Committee on Nursing. (Chairman Professor (later Lord) Asa Briggs). Cmnd 5115. London, HMSO, 1972.
15 Barraclough, Geoffrey. An introduction to contemporary history. London, Penguin, 1969 (reprinted 1976).
16 Castles F G, Murray D J, Potter D C (eds). Decisions, organisations and society. London, Open University/Penguin, 1971.
   Simon H A. 1959, Ch 4
   Audley R J. 1967, Ch 5
   Lindblom C E. 1963, Ch 2
17 Shils Edward. Center and periphery. Chicago, University of Chicago Press, 1975.
18 Eckstein H. Pressure group politics: the case of the British Medical Association. In: Castles F G, Murray D J, Potter D C (eds). Decisions, organisations and society. London, Open University/Penguin, 1971.
19 Hall, Phoebe, and others. Change, choice and conflict in social policy. London, Heinemann, 1975.

CHAPTER 1

1 The Nurses Salaries Committee (Chairman Lord Rushcliffe) was set up in 1943 to look at salaries and emoluments for nurses in hospitals and public health. Its terms of reference were later extended to include tuberculosis and enrolled assistant nurses. The committee was told not to examine salaries of mental nurses. Subsequently two panels were set up for the nurses' organisations and the employers' organisations.
   One of their first recommendations was that the GNC should review and regularise the qualifications given by a variety of bodies so that payments could be considered. In their recommendations, nurses in the voluntary hospitals and local authority hospitals received the same treatment: nurses in public assistance institutions were treated differently.
   The Rushcliffe committee gave a differential to nurses with the Diploma of Nursing and other academic qualifications and instituted the principle of 'leads' for nurses in specialties with particular shortages of staff. Their first lead was given to nurses with the British Tuberculosis Association Certificate.
   The committee also provided definitions for a set of grades. Most grades thereafter were based on the ward sister with allowances.
   After the Committee's first report, a sub-committee was set up to deal with mental nurses.
2 The certificate awarded by this voluntary agency later came to be known as the Orthopaedic Nursing Certificate (ONC). The certificate given by the British Tuberculosis Association was known as the BTA Certificate.
3 Or, to be precise, one register with five separate parts.
4 Recruitment of Nurses and Midwives to Training Institutions. National Advisory Council on Nurses and Midwives, Ministry of Labour and National Service, Ministry of Health, Department of Health for Scotland 1945. The National Advisory Council was taken over by the Ministry of Health in 1958 and demoted to a National Consultative Committee on Nurses and Midwives.
5 Ministry of Health and others. Report of the Working Party on the Recruitment and Training of Nurses. (Chairman Sir Robert Wood). London, HMSO, 1947.
6 Nursing Times, 1948, 1 May, 310.

7 Royal College of Nursing. Nursing Reconstruction Committee. (Chairman Lord Horder). London, Royal College of Nursing.
  1942 The assistant nurse, Section I
  1943 Education and training, Section II
  1943 Recruitment, Section III
  1945 Supplement to section II, Post-registration nursing education
  1949 The social and economic conditions of the nurse, Section IV
8 See especially the correspondence columns of Nursing Mirror 1948.
9 Ministry of Health and Board of Education. Interdepartmental Committee on Nursing Services: interim report. (Chairman the Earl of Athlone). London, HMSO, 1939 recommended a 96 hour fortnight but reported that up to 120 hours per fortnight were being worked.
  These findings were confirmed by later reports and even in 1957, Nursing Mirror published a report, Overtaxed Nurses, which claimed that the average working week in general hospitals was 58-60 hours and 65 hours in mental hospitals.

CHAPTER 2

1 Ministry of Health and Board of Education. Interdepartmental Committee on Nursing Services: interim report. (Chairman the Earl of Athlone). London, HMSO, 1939.
2 Royal College of Nursing. Nursing Reconstruction Committee. (Chairman Lord Horder). London, Royal College of Nursing.
  1942 The assistant nurse, Section I
  1943 Education and training, Section II
  1943 Recruitment, Section III
  1944 The social and economic conditions of the nurse, Section IV
3 Ministry of Health and others. Report of the Working Party on the Recruitment and Training of Nurses. (Chairman Sir Robert Wood). London, HMSO, 1947.
4 The Association of Hospital Matrons. Memorandum of evidence to the Athlone committee. Rcn archives, 1938.
5 Superannuation arrangements for voluntary hospitals were not always transferable from one hospital to another. Arrangements for municipal hospital nurses were made under local authority superannuation provisions and could be transferred between local authorities but not to voluntary hospital schemes.
6 Not all voluntary hospital matrons had direct access to their governing boards. Municipal hospital matrons reported to their medical superintendents.
7 The Joint Consultative Committee of Institutions Responsible for the Training of Health Visitors. Memorandum of evidence given to the Athlone committee. Rcn archives, 1938.
8 The Voluntary Hospitals Committee. Memorandum of evidence given to the Athlone committee. Rcn archives, 1938.
9 White, Rosemary. Social change and the development of the nursing profession: the history of the Poor Law nursing service, 1848–1948. London, Henry Kimpton, 1978.
10 The East Suffolk and Ipswich Hospital. Memorandum of reactions to the Athlone report. Rcn archives, 1939.
11 The Society of Male Nurses. Memorandum of evidence to the Athlone committee. Rcn archives, 1938.
12 GNC. Memorandum of evidence to Athlone committee. Rcn archives, 1938.
13 The Lancet Commission on Nursing. London, The Lancet Ltd, 1932.

14 This referred to the Preliminary State Examination usually taken after the first year of training and the Final State Examination taken after completion of the full training period.
15 Since education for girls was not then as broad as that available for boys, Athlone thought that this innovation would have a profound effect on general education by introducing science subjects to the curricula in girls' schools.
16 The problem lay particularly with the nursing cooperatives or agencies. They were sometimes apt to provide private patients or nursing homes with assistant nurses either masquerading as registered nurses or allowing the clients to believe that they were trained nurses. Student nurses, Athlone found, were prone to leave their training after a short period and work for the agencies, sometimes returning to their own training schools, at much higher rates of pay than their erstwhile colleagues.
17 The Nurses Act, 1943, 6 & 7 Geo 6, Ch 1, provided for the establishment of a roll of nurses by the GNC and for the control of agencies. It also gave the GNC power to prescribe qualifications of teachers of nurses.
18 The College of Nursing. Memorandum of evidence to the Athlone committee. Rcn archives, 1938.
19 Nursing Times, 4 February 1939.
20 RCN Council minutes, April 1939.
21 King Edward's Hospital Fund for London. Comments on the report of the working party. London, King Edward's Hospital Fund for London, 1947.
22 RCN Council minutes, 1947, September, 225.
23 RCN. Memorandum on the report of the working party on the recruitment and training of nurses. London, RCN, 1948.
24 GNC. Memorandum to the Ministry of Health on the report of the working party on the recruitment and training of nurses. London, GNC, 1948.
25 The Ten Group proposals to the Minister of Health in commenting on the Wood report. Croydon, H R Grubb Ltd, 1948. Reprinted by Nursing Mirror, 10 April, 1948, 25. Comments on the paper, p 17.
26 GNC Annual Reports, 1951, 1979.
27 O'Connell P. Health Visitors Education at University. London, RCN, 1978.
28 a) National Board for Prices and Incomes. Report No 60. Pay of nurses and midwives in the NHS. Cmnd 3585. London, HMSO, 1968.
b) DHSS. Job evaluation: NHS nurses and midwives. London, DHSS, 1977.
29 GNC minutes, 1951.
30 Report of the Committee on Nursing. (Chairman Professor (later Lord) Asa Briggs). Cmnd 5115. London, HMSO, 1972.
31 Nuffield Provincial Hospitals Trust. The work of nurses in hospital wards. (Director of research, H A Goddard). London, Nuffield Provincial Hospitals Trust, 1953.

CHAPTER 3

1 The Nurses Act, 1949. 12 & 13 Geo 6. Ch 73.
2 Ministry of Health and others. Report of the Working Party on the Recruitment and Training of Nurses. (Chairman Sir Robert Wood). London, HMSO, 1947.
3 The National Health Service Act, 1946. 9 & 10 Geo 6, Ch 81.
4 Royal College of Nursing. Nursing Reconstruction Committee. (Chairman Lord Horder). London, Royal College of Nursing.
1942 The assistant nurse, Section I

1943 Education and training, Section II
1943 Recruitment, Section III
1949 The social and economic conditions of the nurse, Section IV

5 GNC minutes, 1948, September. 108.
6 RCN Council minutes, 1948, September. 252.
7 The NHS Act provided for hospitals to be grouped into more or less functional units under a single HMC. The GNC also had a policy to combine training schools into a single, larger unit in order to increase the numbers of students, economise on sister tutors and to provide wider clinical experience for the students.
8 Appeal against the refusal of the GNC to approve any institution for the purposes of training. After 1948, the Minister of Health was considered to be an interested party.
9 List of nurses not registered or enrolled who held certificates issued by institutions which appeared to the GNC to be satisfactory, stating that they had completed a course of training before the beginning of July 1925.
10 Until the 1949 Act, the GNC had powers to establish reciprocal certification with the Dominions but not with other countries.
11 GNC minutes, 1948, September. 108.
12 RCN Council minutes, 1948, September. 268.
13 RCN Council minutes, 1948, November. 314.
14 The GNC did not have powers to approve other than its own syllabuses and examinations.
15 GNC minutes, 1948, 22 December. RCN Council minutes, 1948, December. 363, 377.
16 Government papers. MH 80/44. Public Records Office.

CHAPTER 4

1 Ministry of Health, Central Health Services Council. Report of the Committee on the Internal Administration of Hospitals. (Chairman Alderman A F Bradbeer). London, HMSO, 1954.
2 Ministry of Health. Annual Report 1948–49.
3 King Edward's Hospital Fund for London. Evidence submitted to the Committee on Internal Administration of Hospitals. London, King Edward's Hospital Fund for London, 1951.
4 Government Papers MH 92/4 PRO London. Other files relating to the attendance of matrons at HMC meetings and general correspondence are still closed.
5 RCN Council minutes 1952.
6 Nuffield Provincial Hospitals Trust. The work of nurses in hospital wards: report of a job analysis. (Director H A Goddard). London, Nuffield Provincial Hospitals Trust, 1953.
7 Dan Mason Research Committee. The work of recently qualified nurses. (G A Ramsden). London, National Florence Nightingale Memorial Committee, 1956.
The work, responsibilities and status of the staff nurse. (G A Ramsden). London, National Florence Nightingale Memorial Committee, 1960.
8 These changes have been well documented. See, for example, G E Godber. Health services, past, present and future, The Lancet, 1958, 5 July. 1–6.
9 Maggs, Christopher. Nurse recruitment to four provincial hospitals, 1881–1921. In: Re-writing nursing history. Celia Davies (ed). London, Croom Helm, 1980.

10 See, for example, a running discussion in the Nursing Times about the power of the administrators:
'I think we Matrons are much to blame for allowing this to happen. We have not fought to defend our status, we have allowed ourselves to be pushed aside and to be placated with soft words and blandishments. Too many of us feel it is infra dig. to fight back and, in truth, we are sometimes afraid, because we feel we are fighting against the policy of a service which seeks any excuse to be rid of us. We want, and we should have, full membership of our management committees; we must demand this, not cap in hand and with a by your leave, but as an indispensable right which cannot be questioned.' (A matron)
Nursing Times 1958, 27 June. 751.

11 Nursing Times, 1957, 8 February. A survey of Scottish hospital matrons was reported:
of 224 returned questionnaires (280 sent out)
28 matrons attended management meetings
138 matrons attended management or house committee meetings
38 attended meetings only when invited
28 had no contact at all
96 received HMC papers
2 out of 5 Regions had no nurses on the RHBs.

12 Sofer, Cyril. Reactions to administrative change: a study of staff relationships in three British hospitals. Human Relations, 1955, vol 8. 291–316.

13 Menzies, Isabel E P. A case study in the functioning of social systems as a defence against anxiety. Human Relations, 1960, vol 13, no 2.

14 South East Metropolitan Area Nurse Training Committee. The work of student nurses and pupil assistant nurses. London, South East Metropolitan RHB, 1957.

15 Of all the senior hospital officers the matrons were alone in being required to be resident. This condition of employment persisted until the late 1950s and provoked The Practitioner 1959, May, to comment:
'If a hospital is adequately staffed, it is difficult to think of any good reason why a matron should be compelled to live in her hospital. . . . The time has obviously come for hospital authorities to revise their time-honoured regulations and allow their matrons to live in or out, as they like, and to ensure that they are supplied with deputies and sufficient staff to take over when they are off duty.'

16 Nursing Times 1953, 26 September. Leader article, The matron's position.

17 An example of the confusion that existed in this respect was the request of the Queen's Institute of District Nursing to the Management Side of the Whitley Council, in 1948, to be allowed a seat as employers. When this request was declined, the Institute applied to the Staff Side for a seat on the grounds that they were representatives of the district nurses.

18 White, Rosemary. Accountability: a necessity for survival? Nursing Mirror 1977, 17 and 24 November. 25–27, 30–31.

19 RCN Council minutes 1949, April. 181.

20 Nursing Times 1948, 12 June. 426. Report of a speech made by Aneurin Bevan. 'I rescinded the direction of nurses a long time ago and there is no intention to re-instate it', but he hoped for cooperation to secure the proper distribution of nurses where they were required.

21 SAC (N) (51) 4, CHSC, Ministry of Health.

22 RCN Council minutes 1951, May. 171, 282.

23 SAC (N) (52) 9, CHSC (52) 7, Ministry of Health.

24 Acton Society Trust. Hospitals and the State. (Director T E Chester). London, Acton Society.
1955 Background and Blueprint
1956 The Impact of Change
1957 Groups, Regions and Committees
1957 Regional Hospital Boards
1958 The Central Control of the Service
1959 Creative Leadership in a State Service
25 Also distributed as HM (53) 85 and BG (53) 87.
26 RCN Council minutes 1954, February. 34, 47.
27 Ibid. 233.
28 Ibid, December. 456.
29 RCN Council minutes 1955, February. 64, 73.
30 RCN Council minutes 1956, December. 401.
31 RHB (49) 25, RHB (49) 143, HM (54) 4, HM (54) 21.
32 Nursing Times, 1960, 4 November, 1361. Leader article, As spiritual descendents.
33 Nursing Times, 1958, 24 May.
34 Nursing Times, 1954, 14 August. 871.
35 Royal College of Nursing. The function, status and training of nurse tutors. London, RCN, 1954.
36 Nursing Times, 1955, 28 January. 121.
37 Ministry of Health and Scottish Home and Health Department. Report of the Committee on Senior Nursing Staff Structure. (Chairman Brian Salmon). London, HMSO, 1966.
38 The Cabinet had taken the decision in 1948 to allow a salary rise for trained nurses but to hold down the salaries for 'the higher ranges'. This was for two reasons: to keep these nursing posts less attractive than teaching posts since the priority then was to recruit teachers and both professions were recruited from the same pool; it was also because of problems related to equal pay for men and women. In nursing, the implementation of this would have cost about £450,000 but if this were done for the nurses, it would have had to be done for the teachers at a cost of £14–18 million. CP (49) 75 in CB 129–34 and CM 26 (49) 2 in CAB 128–15, PRO, London.

The salaries of matrons, especially those of the largest hospitals, were continuously held down throughout the period. A survey made by the RCN labour relations committee showed the following:

| | percentage increases | | | |
| | 1954–1959 | | 1949–1959 | |
	Min	Max	Min	Max
Staff nurses	21	20	54	47
Ward sisters	26	28	62	60
Deputy matron	20	20	40	40
Matron, non-training ‹50 beds	25	26	55	54
Matron, training ›50 beds	16	23	42	48

The salaries for the hospital matrons with extended responsibilities were not discussed by the Whitley Council until 1955 (NC (M) 596) and not finalised until 1957 (NC (M) 862) when it was agreed that the Minister should authorise ad hoc payments pending an agreed formula.
39 Whitley Council Minutes.
Night superintendents NC (M) 782, 913, 986, 991

Mental nurses NC (M) 450, 520, 567, 687
Nursing auxiliaries NC (M) 475, 544, 671
Departmental sisters NMC (S) 66, 70
40 Whitley Council minutes. NMC (S) 66. 1959.
41 RCN Council minutes 1959, May. 224.
42 The first course for a diploma in nursing was started in 1921 at the University of Leeds.
43 Subsequently published under the title A reform of nursing education, 1964. The working party was promoted and enlarged to a committee of enquiry under the chairmanship of Sir Harry Platt Bt LLD MD MS FRCS.
44 Whitley Council minutes.
1957 NMC (S) 57
1958 NMC (S) 63
1959 NC (M) 997, 1002, 1006
1960 NMC (S) 71, 72, 74, 474
45 Ministry of Health and Department of Health for Scotland. Report on the grading and structure of administrative and clerical staff in the hospital service. (Chairman Sir Noel Hall). London, HMSO, 1957.
46 Whitley Council minutes 1959. NC (M) 1002.
47 The RCN did not accept men as members until 1960.
48 Nursing Times 1950, 18 March. 273. Leader article.
This discussed the problems of matrons in the new groups and asked if the matron of the parent hospital retained the title 'matron', 'What was the position of the other matrons? Should they be down-graded?'
49 Farnworth, Mary. The social prestige of nursing. Nursing Times, 1952, 21, 28 June, 12 July, 684–5, 628–31, 688–90. This was a study undertaken for the Medical Research Council. Mary Farnworth was a nurse with a diploma in nursing and a social science degree.
50 Nursing Times, 1955, 4 February. 121. Report of the RCN winter conference of the Sister Tutor Section, discussing the report Function, status and training of nurse tutors. This report offered an interesting example of the growing amibitions of tutors and their challenge to the place of the matron as an active head of the nurse training school.
See also Nursing Times, 1955, 21 October. 1182. The changing functions of hospital matrons, Sir Zachary Cope.
51 Whitley Council minutes 1959. NC (M) 1006.
52 Although each RHB had, eventually, a regional nursing officer, the history of the salary negotiations for these nurses, demonstrated in the Nurses and Midwives Whitley Council minutes, shows that they were considered as advisers to the matrons rather than to the boards. The regional nursing officers were not seen to have any relevance to policy making in the RHBs until after the Salmon Report.
53 Nursing Times, 1958, 1 August. 884. There is a picture of eight matrons in the South West Metropolitan RHB who were retiring. Their total contribution of 289 years of service was reported.

CHAPTER 5

1 Before the 1939 War, and indeed until sometime after the Butler Education Act 1944, there were very few grammar schools that included the natural sciences in their curricula for girls. Many middle-class girls were educated privately and

were prepared for marriage rather than a working career. As late as 1953, a headmistress was able to declare, 'It is a woman's task to create an environment for other people and the schools try to give reality to this idea. . . . In educating a girl, we are educating a family.' Nursing Times, 1953, 19 September. 940.

It was because of the narrow and meagre education available to girls that the Horder report, Section II 1943, offered the progressive training, incorporated in its recommendations, as a means of improving the curriculum: '. . . the training of nurses in this country could be developed into one of the great national educational movements for women.'

2 The School Certificate required a pass level in five subjects taken at the same time. Matriculation level required passes at credit or distinction levels according to the requirements of the respective university boards. Matriculation level offered exemption from the university entrance examinations.

3 See Chapter 3.

4 Royal College of Nursing. Reports of the Nursing Reconstruction Committee. (Chairman Lord Horder). London, RCN, 1942–49.

5 See Chapter 4.

6 GNC minutes 1946, April, October.

7 GNC minutes 1947, November.

8 Ministry of Health and others. Report of the Working Party on the Recruitment and Training of Nurses. (Chairman Sir Robert Wood). London, HMSO, 1947.

9 Compare these figures with those of Box and Croft-White, 1943. Recruitment to Nursing, Ministry of Health. Their research demonstrated that 68 per cent of all student nurses in their sample had received some form of secondary education; 41 per cent of training hospitals demanded secondary education, 16 per cent preferred it and 43 per cent required 7th standard elementary education or had no definite requirements. Sixty-one per cent of voluntary hospitals and six per cent of municipal hospitals required secondary education. All their sample of student nurses had come from non-manual worker classes who could afford to keep their daughters at home until the minimum starting age, 18 years, of nurse training. In the voluntary hospitals there were more daughters of professional classes than in the municipal hospitals; 65 per cent of all the student nurses had fathers in social classes 1, 2 or 3.

10 Nuffield Provincial Hospitals Trust. The work of nurses in hospital wards. (Director of research H A Goddard). London, Nuffield Provincial Hospitals Trust, 1953. See Chapter 9.

11 As late as 1931 less than 20 per cent of the population aged between 11 and 14 obtained secondary education. Until the Education Act 1944 the vast majority of children was restricted to public elementary education. In 1947 the school leaving age was raised to 15 years and in 1951, it has been estimated, 17 per cent of the population between 15–18 years were receiving full-time education. Prior to the establishment of a public secondary education system in 1944, the chances of a boy (much less a girl) proceeding from a state elementary school to a grammar school were extremely small. Secondary education therefore was predominantly restricted to people whose families could afford to pay for it. See, Marsh, David C, The Changing Social Structure of England and Wales, 1871–1961. London, Routledge & Kegan Paul, 1977.

12 Nursing Times, 1948, 6 November. 824. Correspondence.

13 Nursing Times, 1952, 21 June. 604–5, 28 June, 628–31, 12 July, 688–90.

14 Nursing Mirror, 1948, 17 January. 271: 'wastage must be reduced by restoring into nursing training the simple, compassionate bedside nursing skills: the real

basic nursing training, which expresses the soul of nursing, not merely its brain, and which is something quite different from a comprehensive training.'

15 Nursing Times, 1947, 29 November. E E P MacManus, A critical survey of the Wood Report.

16 Nursing Times, 1953, 5 September. 899. BMA essay competition prizewinner, M Simson. Is nursing a vocation?

17 Crow, Jean. Effects of preparation on problem solving. London, RCN, 1980.

18 GNC minutes 1948. January, April.

19 GNC minutes 1949. Education and Examination Committee.

20 GNC minutes 1950. May, June, September.

21 GNC minutes 1952. June.

22 GNC minutes 1953. October, December.

23 Enquiry into Wastage of Student Nurses, 1948–1953. NAC 262. 1953. Ministry of Labour and Ministry of Health, Department of Health for Scotland.

24 Ministry of Health. Annual Report 1953, 6, 36.

25 RCN Council minutes 1950, September, 301; November, 349, 369.

26 RCN Council minutes 1952, May, 195.

27 RCN Council minutes 1953, October, 317.

28 Ibid, July, 194.

29 GNC minutes 1954, May.

30 RCN Council minutes 1954, February. 54.

31 Ministry of Health and others. Report of the committee set up to consider the function, status and training of nurse tutors. (Chairman Dr Janet Aitken). London, HMSO, 1955.

32 GNC minutes 1954, February.
   RCN Council Minutes 1954, February, September.

33 Nuffield Provincial Hospitals Trust. The work of nurses in hospital wards. (Director of research H A Goddard). London, Nuffield Provincial Hospitals Trust, 1953.

34 South-East Metropolitan Area Nurse-Training Committee. The work of student nurses and pupil assistant nurses. London, South-East Metropolitan RHB, 1957.

35 GNC minutes 1957, November, December.

36 a) Nursing Times, 1955, 19 August, 918. The education of the nurse, Joyce M Akester, HV Cert DipN (London).
   b) Ibid, 23 September, 1056. Lilian M Darnell SRN SCM RFN.
   c) Ibid, 23 September, 1075 and 14 October.
   d) Ibid, 16 December, 1184. A Altschul, BA SRN RMN STD.

37 Nursing Times, 1956, 4 May, 11 May, 18 May, 25 May.

38 Observations and objectives. London, RCN, 1956.

39 Nursing Times, 1956, 7 December, 1253, 14 December.

40 British Medical Journal 1956, 24 November, 1228. Degrees in nursing.

41 The Lancet 1956, 15 December. Correspondence.

42 The Lancet 1957, 5 January. Correspondence.

43 Ibid, 12 January. Correspondence.

44 Nursing Times 1957, 11 January. Leader.

45 Ministry of Health and Scottish Home and Health Department. Report of the Committee on Senior Nursing Staff Structure. (Chairman Brian Salmon). London, HMSO, 1966.
   This report established a managerial structure for nurses only. It tried to open out a limited structure for clinical nurses but the way in which it was implemented defeated that objective.

46 a) National Board for Prices and Incomes. Pay of nurses and midwives in the NHS. Report no 60. Cmnd 3585. London, HMSO, 1968.
  b) Department of Health and Social Security. Job evaluation: NHS nurses and midwives. Job Evaluation Unit, DHSS, 1977.
47 GNC minutes 1958, July.
48 Ibid, December.
49 The National Advisory Council on Recruitment had been taken over by the Ministry of Health in 1958 and had been demoted to be called the National Consultative Committee on Recruitment.
50 GNC minutes 1959, June, July, September, November.
51 GNC minutes 1960, July.
52 GNC minutes 1961, December.
53 Bendall E R D and Raybould, Elizabeth. A history of the General Nursing Council for England and Wales, 1919–1969. London, H K Lewis, 1969.
54 The Nurses (Amendment) Act 1961 changed the title of state enrolled assistant nurses to state enrolled nurse (SEN).
55 RCN Council minutes 1959, January, 5, 12; April, 162, 175.
56

1944–1950	Aneurin Bevan	Labour
1950	H A Marquand	Labour
1951–1954	Iain MacLeod	Conservative
1955	Robert H Turton	Conservative
1956–1959	Derek Walker-Smith	Conservative
1960–	J Enoch Powell	Conservative

57 For a description of this anti-education ethos see a) Reinkemeyer M H, A nursing paradox. Nursing Research, 1968, January/February. b) House, Vivienne. A degree of care. GNC Research Unit, 1977.
58 See Chapter 3 for full details.
59 See Chapter 4 for full details of the Ministry's unwillingness to allow nurses on the HMCs.
60 Government papers. MH 90/45. RHBs: Headquarters staff. MH 90/48. RHBs: Staffing policy. Public Records Office, London.
61 Government papers. T227/47. Minute ref SS 5/46/01.
62 Report of the Committee on Nursing. (Chairman Professor (later Lord) Asa Briggs). Cmnd. 5115. London, HMSO, 1972.
63 a) Scottish Home and Health Department. Experimental nurse training at Glasgow Royal Infirmary. (Director of research Margaret Scott Wright; Chairman Professor J H F Brotherston). Edinburgh, HMSO, 1963.
  b) Wright, Margaret Scott. Student nurses in Scotland: characteristics of success and failure. Edinburgh, Scottish Home and Health Department, 1968.
64 Pomeranz, Ruth. The lady apprentices. Occasional Papers on Social Administration No 51. London, G Bell & Sons, 1973.
65 These statements are taken from the GNC annual reports. Statistics of student nurses are available but as they relate to different courses, parts of the register and so on they are not helpful in this context.

CHAPTER 6

1 Walk, Alexander. The history of mental nursing. Journal of Mental Science, 1961, January, vol 107 no 446, 9.
2 The Medico-Psychological Association, founded in 1841, received a Royal Charter in 1925 and became known as the RMPA.

3 Walk, Alexander. 1961. op. cit. 13.
4 The Select Committee on the Registration of Nurses, 1904–05, Cmd 281, London, HMSO.
5 Bendall E R D and Raybould, Elizabeth. A history of the General Nursing Council for England and Wales, 1919–1969. London, H K Lewis, 1969.
6 GNC minutes 1945.
7 Royal College of Nursing. Reports of the Nursing Reconstruction Committee. (Chairman Lord Horder). London, Royal College of Nursing, 1942–1949.
8 RCN Council minutes 1946, January, 8, 31, 28.
9 Only mental nurses with general nurse registration were promoted to posts at ward sister level or above until 1955.
10 GNC minutes 1949.
11 Ministry of Health 1953, Annual Report.
12 Standing Mental Health Advisory Committee. Training of Mental Nurses. Central Health Services Council, Ministry of Health, 1953.
13 Central Health Services Council 1953. Annual Report, Ministry of Health.
14 In 1955 a survey conducted by the Liverpool RHB found that six per cent of general nurses and 66 per cent of mental nurses, particularly the males, belonged to trade unions rather than to the RCN. The College did not admit to membership male nurses or those who were not general trained, until 1960.
15 RCN Council minutes 1953. January, 9, 35.
16 Nurses and Midwives Whitley Council, Management Side minutes, 1953 NC (M) 412, 421, 450, 451, 520.
It is not clear whether the term 'untrained nurses' included nursing assistants as well as student nurses. Nursing auxiliaries were not included in the Nurses and Midwives Councils until after 1953. In the mental field, nursing assistants were the equivalent of nursing auxiliaries in the general field: all gave nursing care. If the nursing assistants were included, the ratio of trained to untrained nurses (said by the Ministry to be higher than in the general field) is surprising. If the nursing assistants were not included, the high ratio could easily be explained by the critical paucity of student nurses. The satisfaction expressed by the Ministry at the nursing ratios may be contrasted with findings published in 1954 by the King Edward's Hospital Fund for London in its Annual Report:

Student nurses: patients	General= 1: 3.1
	Mental = 1: 42.5
Registered nurses: patients	General= 1: 5.4
	Mental = 1: 12.5

17 GNC minutes 1953, June, July.
18 GNC minutes 1953, July.
19 Bendall E R D and Raybould, Elizabeth. A history of the General Nursing Council for England and Wales, 1919–1969. London, H K Lewis, 1969, 208.
20 Nursing Times 1953, 28 November, 1215.
21 Ibid, 1225.
22 Nursing Times 1954, 23 January, 86, 30 January, 3 February.
23 The Liverpool RHB had published a report of its survey in The work and status of mental nurses. This report commented that, since the war, there had been a move to introduce the standards and practices of general nursing to mental nursing, including the secondment of students to general hospitals. There had been a serious decline in the numbers of students: compared with 1938 (100 per cent) there were in 1953 only 12 per cent of male recruits and 16 per cent of

females. Since 1948, only 24 male students and one female had completed training. There was very little therapeutic work for the nurses as this was done by more highly trained staff. The dominant element in the work of the nurses was, therefore, custodial. The modern training given to mental nurses made them unfit for the work that had to be done: as the training became more like that of the general nurse, mental nurses were restricting their activities to those that resembled general nurses'. The poor status of mental nurses, their inferior educational standards and training gave rise to fewer nurses. This, in turn, gave rise to more custodial care, less therapeutic care and a further loss of status. The report complained that the attempt to model the mental nurses' training on that of the general nurse had led to a dysfunctional education which gave mental nurses unrealistic expectations of their role. Reported in Nursing Times 1955, 15 July, 776.

24 Nurses and Midwives Whitley Council, Management Side minutes, 1954. NC (M) 557, 567, 639.
Overtime had been paid at normal rates since 1941. Only mental and mental deficiency nurses received overtime payments.

25 Nurses and Midwives Whitley Council, Management Side minutes, 1955. NC (M) 655, 667.

26 Ibid, NC (M) 689.

27 The GNC had no powers to designate parts in the Roll of Nurses: enrolled nurses could not therefore be designated by their special training.

28 CHSC 1954, Annual Report.

29 GNC minutes, 1955.

30 RCN, Council minutes 1956, September, 282.

31 Ministry of Health 1958. On the State of the Public Health.

32 St Crispin Hospital Management Committee. Review of the hospital during the first 10 years of the NHS. Oxford RHB, 1958.

33 Biera, Joshua. The day hospital. London, H K Lewis, 1951.

34 Royal Commission on the Law Relating to Mental Illness and Mental Deficiency. (Chairman Baron Percy of Newcastle). Cmnd 169. HMSO, 1957.

35 Ministry of Health 1959, Annual Report, 6.

36 *Mental Nurses (Hospitals)*

	1949	1951	1954	1959	1960
Trained whole time	11056	11418	11255	11415	11453
part time	1147	1424	1581	1446	1436
Student nurses	5201	4248	3451	6178	5824
Other nursing staff W T	2610	3629	4783	7038	7130
P T	4398	4681	4993	5288	5001

Mental Deficiency Nurses

Trained whole time	2613	2766	3120	3343	3481
part time	250	336	413	406	383
Student nurses	1135		761	1289	1330
Other nursing staff W T	1706	2061	2625	3614	3847
P T	1496	1569	1772	2088	2060

Ministry of Health Nursing Statistics

The rise in the number of student nurses was said by the Staff Side to be due to the rise in the number of immigrants: 14 per cent of students came from Ireland and up to 38 per cent from other countries.

37 Nurses and Midwives Whitley Council 1955. Staff Side minutes, NMC/43 24 May.

38 Ministry of Health. Report of the Committee of Enquiry into the Cost of the National Health Service. (Chairman C W Guillebaud). Cmnd 9663. London, HMSO, 1956.
39 Ministry of Health and Scottish Home and Health Department. Report of the Committee on Senior Nursing Staff Structure. (Chairman Brian Salmon). London, HMSO, 1966.
40 Ministry of Health, Central Health Services Council. Report of the Committee on the Internal Administration of Hospitals. (Chairman Alderman A F Bradbeer). London, HMSO, 1954.
41 Sofer C. Reactions to administrative change: a study of staff relationships in three British hospitals. Human Relations, 1955, vol 8, 291–316.
42 A comprehensive mental nursing service. Report of a working party. London, RCN, 1960.
43 Bellaby and Oribabor. The growth of trade union consciousness among general hospital nurses. Sociological Review, 1977, vol 25, no 4, new series, November, 801–22.

CHAPTER 7

1 Ministry of Health. A National Health Service. Cmnd 6502. London, HMSO, 1944.
2 Stocks, Mary. 1960. A hundred years of district nursing. London, George Allen and Unwin, 1960.
3 Ministry of Health. Report of the Working Party on the Training of District Nurses. (Chairman Sir Frederick Armer). London, HMSO, 1955.
4 Government papers. MH 77/160. Nurses and nurses' associations. Representations, 1943–45. PRO.
5 Government papers. MH 77/161. Nurses and nurses' associations. Representations, 1946. PRO.
6 RCN Council minutes 1946, October, 264, 302; November, 335.
7 Ministry of Health and others. Report of the Working Party on the Recruitment and Training of Nurses. (Chairman Sir Robert Wood). London, HMSO, 1947.
8 Nurses and Midwives Whitley Council minutes 1949, NC (M) 45, 50.
9 Nurses and Midwives Whitley Council minutes, Staff Side, 1948. Interim Executive Committee IEC/4 November.
10 RCN Council minutes 1948, 252.
11 Nurses and Midwives Whitley Council minutes, 1950, NC (M) 95.
12 Ministry of Health Annual Report 1953, 124.
13 Nursing Times 1954, 7 August, 846.
14 Nursing Times 1955, 28 January, 95.
15 Queen's Institute of District Nursing, minutes of Council and committees, 1954, ad hoc committee, 1 February.
16 Ibid, General Executive Committee 1954, 8 February.
17 Ibid, 1955, 8 March.
18 Ibid, 1955, 19 April.
19 Ibid, 1955, 14 June.
20 Ibid, 1956, 10 April.
21 Ibid, 1956, June.
22 Ibid, 1956, November.
23 National survey concerning patients with cancer nursed at home. (Chairman Ronald Rowen). London, Marie Curie Memorial and Queen's Institute of District Nursing, 1952.

This survey of domiciliary cancer sufferers had shown the following:

% population	No. living rooms	% population	No. bedrooms
28	1	1	0
52	2	9	1
16	3	34	2
		45	3

Over-crowding was rare.

Public services and amenities available to the patients (per cent):

Main water	85
Running hot water	52
Main drainage	80
Gas	69
Electricity	78
Neither gas nor electricity	8
Bathroom	55
Indoors lavatory	52
Outdoors lavatory	53
Lavatory accessible	62
Adequate cooking facilities	95
Adequate washing facilities	95

Some town houses had a water tap outside the house.
Some town flat dwellers shared a sink and lavatory with up to six other households.
Survey population = 7,050 patients already being visited by the district nurse.
Survey done by district nurses, 1951.

24 The Wood report 1947 had proposed a 2 year training for general nurses and had calculated that this would be enough if the routine and repetitive duties which filled the student nurses' days were eliminated or delegated.
The Work of Nurses in Hospital Wards 1953, a report of a job analysis done by H A Goddard for the Nuffield Provincial Hospitals Trust, had confirmed that there were unnecessary tasks and poorly organised procedures which took up excessive time.
The GNC was in the course of organising shortened courses for nurses on one register to train for another register or supplementary parts. They had previously agreed to shortened SRN training for ex-service orderlies.
All these schemes were prompted by staff shortages rather than by educational criteria.
By 1956, the GNC had approved a total of 100 experimental courses, all for training in two parts of the register, with a reduced period of training. Also in 1956, the experimental combined training at the Battersea Polytechnic College was announced. This course was organised in conjunction with the Hammersmith Hospital and the Queen's Institute. Training over four years would offer the students full qualifications in general nursing, part I midwifery, district nursing and health visiting. Equivalent qualifications, taken separately, would have needed up to five years.
25 RCN Council minutes 1956, September, 256, 295.
26 Nursing Times 1955, 16 September, 1031. 'The training of a district nurse', Augusta Black, SRN SCM RSCN QN Cert. HV Tutor Cert. Education Officer, QIDN.
27 Ibid, 23 September, 1075.
28 Ibid, 30 September, 1169.

29 Ministry of Health. Report of the Committee of Enquiry into the Cost of the National Health Service. (Chairman C W Guillebaud). Cmd 9663. London, HMSO, 1956.
See also Abel-Smith B and Titmuss R. The cost of the NHS in England and Wales. London, Cambridge University Press, 1956.
30 Ministry of Health. Annual Report 1958.
31 Statistics for district nurses taken from the Annual Reports of the Ministry of Health:

	1951	1952	1954	1955	1960
Total	8700	8884	9642	9884	10322
Multiple duty	4979	5021	5233	5200	5137
Voluntary organisations: W T	1384	1400			
			2444	2316	1688
P T	1202	1032			
Males				315	336
Students				285	244
SEANs				1375	1144

W T = Whole Time   P T = Part time

32 Ministry of Health. Report of the Advisory Committee on the Training of District Nurses. (Chairman D H Ingall). London, HMSO, 1959.
33 RCN Council minutes 1960, November, 439.
34 Department of Health and Social Security and others. Report of the Working Party on Management Structure in the Local Authority Nursing Services. (Chairman E L Mayston). London, DHSS, 1969.
35 Nurses & Midwives Whitley Council
1952–3 NC (M) 395 Special payments
1953–4 NC (M) 486 LHA refusal to implement
1957   NC (M) 824 Comparison of salaries
            NC (M) 842 Special treatment for health visitors
1960   NC (M) 1113 Comparison of salaries
36 Ibid, 1959 NC (M) 997 Appointment of superintendents
37 There was an overwhelming majority of lay people on the Council, General Executive Committee and Education Sub-Committee of the Queen's Institute.
38 The Queen's Institute continued to organise refresher courses and developmental courses after that date.

CHAPTER 8

1 Owen, Grace (ed.) Health visiting. London, Ballière Tindall, 1977.
2 McEwan, Margaret. Health visiting. London, Faber 1962 (4th edition).
3 SI, 1948, no 1415.
4 The National Health Service Act 1946, 9 & 10 Geo 6. Ch 81.
5 Ministry of Health and Department of Health for Scotland. Report of the Working Party on Social Workers in Local Authority Health and Welfare Services. (Chairman Miss (later Lady) Eileen Younghusband). London, HMSO, 1959.
6 Ministry of Health Annual Report 1953.
7 Nursing Times 1948, 31 January 83. Recent developments and new approaches to the work of the health visitor, E K Trillwood.
8 Nursing Times 1954. Leader article.

9 RCN Council minutes, 1955, May, 222, 252, 277, 293.
10 Nursing Times, 1954, 814. The health visitor, Professor F A E Crew, Professor of Public Health and Social Medicine, University of Edinburgh.
11 Ministry of Health Annual Report 1949–50, 47.
12 Report on a study of the work of public health nurses, 1954. London, Nuffield Provincial Hospitals Trust, (unpublished).
13 Ibid, Table 13 gave details of visits:

Type of visit	% all visits
Children 0–5 years	73.9
No answer	10.5
School follow-up	5.9
Infectious diseases	1.4
After care, over 15 years	0.3
Aged, 60+, women	0.7
65+, men	0.2

No travel time was recorded.
14 Nursing Times 1948, 24 April, 301. Miss B M Langton, SRN SCM DN.

Work	% of all time
Clinic work	37.0
Clerical work	8.0
Travel	3.75
Visiting	12.25

15 Williams M. The integrated nurse/health visitor course: a report of the first five years of the experimental course. Southampton University, 1962.
16 RCN Council minutes 1950, November, 374. The proposal to make the GNC responsible for HV training was pre-empted by the Nurses Act 1949 which gave the GNC responsibility only for basic training and nurse tutors.
17 Ministry of Health and others. An Inquiry Into Health Visiting. Report of the Working Party. (Chairman Sir Wilson Jameson). London, HMSO, 1956.
18 Ministry of Health. Report of the Committee of Enquiry into the Cost of the National Health Service. (Chairman C W Guillebaud). Cmd 9663. London, HMSO, 1956.
19 Nursing Times 1955, 9 September, 996. Reorganisation within health visiting, Mary E Davies.
20 Ibid, 14 October. Report of the public health section at York. The education of the nurse. J M Akester, HV Cert DN (London).
21 Ibid, 1956, 1 June, 490. The health visitor in a changing field of social work. Ilse Windmuller, specialist HV for neglected children in Salford.
22 The definition in this chapter of the term 'health education' appears to be very much broader than the definition given in Chapter 10, para 293. In the second instance, it is given as being practical advice on personal health to members of families in their homes. We believe that this ambiguity was subsequently exploited in different ways by authorities and individual workers.
23 Ministry of Health and others. Report of the Working Party on the Recruitment and Training of Nurses. (Chairman Sir Robert Wood). London, HMSO, 1947.
24 The Council for the Training of Health Visitors was set up under the Health Visiting and Social Work (Training) Act 1962, 10 & 11 Eliz 2 Ch 33, which also set up the Council for the Training of Social Workers. In 1971, the CTHV became the Council for the Education and Training of Health Visitors (CETHV) which was disbanded in 1983 when it was absorbed by the UKCC.
25 RCN Council minutes 1956, November, 359, Education Committee.

26 Ibid, December, 401, Public Health Section.
27 Nursing Times 1956, 15 June. Leader: Report on health visiting.
28 Ibid, 22 June, 561.
29 Ibid, 28 September, 966.
30 Ibid, 1957, 24 May, 586.
31 These included the provision of health centres, care of mothers and young children, prevention, care and after care, tuberculosis, venereal diseases and the mental health service.
32 Wilkie, Elaine. A history of the CETHV, 1962–1975. London, George Allen and Unwin, 1979.
33 Ministry of Health, Annual Report 1960, 126f.
34 RCN Council minutes 1960, September, 316.
35 Ibid, 1961, January, 12 March, 130.
36 Ibid, 1961, May, 204.
37 Ibid, 1962, November, 506.
38 The Royal Sanitary Institute became the Royal Society for the Promotion of Health in 1955. The society later became known as the Royal Society for Health.
39 Ministry of Health, Annual Report 1957, 190f.
40 Ibid, 1958, 163.
41 Ibid, 1959, Chapter I.
42 Ministry of Health. Report of the Maternity Services Committee. (Chairman the Earl of Cranbrook). London, HMSO, 1959.

Annex:

Statistics for Health Visitors, taken from Annual Reports,
Ministry of Health

	1951	1953*	1955	1958	1960
HVs general duties: W T	1626	1181	1112	WTE	WTE
P T	4314	4883	5125	4217	4391
Voluntary organisations: W T	11	WTE	WTE		
P T	204	3796	3989		
Numbers practising without statutory qualifications				517	413

*Change in method of counting after 1952

W T	Whole time
P T	Part time
WTE	Whole time equivalent

CHAPTER 9

1 Ministry of Health and Board of Education. Interim report of the Interdepartmental Committee on Nursing Services. (Chairman the Earl of Athlone). London, HMSO, 1939.
2 Ministry of Health and others. Report of the Working Party on the Recruitment and Training of Nurses. (Chairman Sir Robert Wood). London, HMSO, 1947.
3 Royal College of Nursing. Reports of the Nursing Reconstruction Committee. (Chairman Lord Horder). London, RCN, 1942–49.
4 The preceding paragraphs have been based substantially on Bendall E R D and

Raybould, Elizabeth. A history of the General Nursing Council for England and Wales, 1919–1969. London, H K Lewis, 1969.

5 GNC minutes 1948, October.
6 Ibid, 1950.
7 Nurses and Midwives Whitley Council, Management Side minutes, 1950, NC(M) 163.
8 Ministry of Health and others. Report of the Committee set up to consider the Function, Status and Training of Nurse Tutors. (Chairman Dr Janet Aitken). London, HMSO, 1954.
9 GNC minutes 1954, February.
10 Nursing Times 1955, 4 February, 121. See also Chapter 5.
11 Ibid, 9 December.
12 Ibid, 16 December.
13 GNC Annual Report 1956–57.
14 Nursing Times 1958, 29 August, Letters, 1019.
15 Ibid, 1959, 20 February, Letters, 237.
16 Ibid, 1960, 15 January, 66. Shortage of tutors, a symposium.
17 Nurses and Midwives Whitley Council, Management Side, 1961, NC(M) 1130.
18 Royal College of Nursing. The nurse tutor: a new assessment. London, RCN, 1961.
19 Nurses and Midwives Whitley Council, Management Side, 1961, NC(M) 1172.
20 GNC Annual Report 1960–61.
21 GNC. Teachers of Nursing. London, GNC, 1975–76.
22 Bendall, Eve. So you passed nurse. London, Rcn, 1975.
23 Ministry of Health. Report of the Working Party on the Training of District Nurses. (Chairman Sir Frederick Armer). London, HMSO, 1955.
24 Ministry of Health. Report of the Advisory Committee on the Training of District Nurses. (Chairman D H Ingall). London, HMSO, 1959.

CHAPTER 10

1 Nuffield Provincial Hospitals Trust. The work of nurses in hospital wards. (Director of research H A Goddard). London, Nuffield Provincial Hospitals Trust, 1953. (This report is referred to variously as 'the Nuffield report', 'the Goddard report' and 'the NPHT report'.
2 Ministry of Health and others. Report of the Working Party on the Recruitment and Training of Nurses. (Chairman Sir Robert Wood). London, HMSO, 1947.
3 Ibid, Minority Report. Professor John Cohen. London, HMSO, 1948.
4 Ministry of Health, Annual Report 1949–50. Chapter V.
5 Nursing Times 1948, 10 January, 35.
6 Nursing Times 1948, 31 January, 83.
7 RCN Council minutes 1948, February, 28.
8 Royal Commission on the National Health Service. (Chairman Sir Alec Merrison). Cmnd 7615. London, HMSO, 1979. See McFarlane, Jean. Essays in nursing. King's Fund Project Paper no RC2, 1980.
9 Shryock R H. The history of nursing: an interpretation of social and medical factors. Philadelphia, Saunders, 1959.
10 Royal College of Nursing. Reports of the Nursing Reconstruction Committee. (Chairman Lord Horder). London, RCN, 1942–49.
11 GNC Annual Report 1954.
12 Nursing Times 1953, 25 July, 750.

13 Royal College of Nursing. Comment on the NPHT job analysis of the work of nurses in hospital wards. RCN, 1953.
14 Ministry of Health Annual Report, 1958, Table 33, 60.
15 Nursing Times 1953, 15 August, 817.
16 Nursing Times 1953, 15 August, 830.
17 Ibid, 5 December, 1238, 12 December, 1273.
18 Nursing Times 1954, 21 August.
19 Nursing Times 1955, 11 February, 145.
20 Ministry of Health, Central Health Services Council. Standing Nursing Advisory Committee. The position of the enrolled assistant nurse within the National Health Service. London, HMSO, 1954.
21 Central Health Services Council, Annual Reports, 1953, 1954, 1955, 1956, 1957, 1958. Ministry of Health.
22 King Edward's Hospital Fund for London. Noise control in hospitals. London, KEHF, 1958.
23 Ministry of Health, Central Health Services Council. The reception and welfare of in-patients in hospitals. London, HMSO, 1953.
24 Royal College of Nursing. The problems of providing a continuous nursing service, especially in relation to night duty. London, RCN, 1958.
25 Ministry of Health. On The State of the Public Health, 1957. Report of the Chief Medical Officer.
26 Ibid, 1960.
27 Ibid, 1958, 1961.
28 Ministry of Health, Annual Report, 1960, 20.
Since 1948:
Number of available beds had declined by 2,000.
Number of occupied beds had declined by 3,000.
Number of patients treated per available bed had increased by 10 per cent.
Deaths and discharges had increased by 141,000.
29 Nursing Times 1957, 27 December, leader article.
30 Nursing Times 1958, 7 February, leader article.
31 Royal College of Nursing. Observations and objectives. London, RCN, 1956.
32 Jenkinson, Vivien M. Group or team nursing. Nursing Times, 1958, 17 January, 63. 24 January.
33 Nursing Times 1958, 18 July, 844. Letters to the Editor. College Member 54162.
34 Ibid, 1958, 8 August, 927. Talking Point.
35 1948 = 96 hour fortnight.
1958 = 88 hour fortnight.
36 Ministry of Health. Economy in manpower. 5 December 1952. HMC (52) 121. This circular put a standstill on all hospital staff and called for reductions wherever possible. A reduction of five per cent in professional and technical, domestic and maintenance staff was required.
37 The concern for the welfare of the patient was demonstrated by a series of reports: Ministry of Health, Central Health Services Council. The reception and welfare of in-patients in hospitals. London, HMSO, 1953.
Royal College of Nursing. Memorandum on out-patients departments. London, RCN, 1955.
King Edward's Hospital Fund for London. Noise control in hospitals. London, KEHF, 1958.
Ministry of Health, Central Health Services Council. The welfare of children in hospital. London, HMSO, 1959.

Ministry of Health, Central Health Services Council. Services available to the aged and chronic sick. London, HMSO, 1961.
Ministry of Health. Communications between doctors, nurses and patients. London, HMSO, 1963.

38 Henderson, Virginia. Basic principles of nursing. Reprinted by Nursing Mirror 1958. See Chapter 11.

CHAPTER 11

1 Royal College of Nursing. Nursing Reconstruction Committee. (Chairman Lord Horder). London, RCN.
   a) Section I, The assistant nurse, 1942.
   b) Section II, Education and training, 1943.
   c) Section III, Recruitment, 1943.
   d) Section IV, The social and economic conditions of the nurse, 1949.

2 The Nurses Act 1943, 6 & 7 Geo 6. Ch 17 set up a Roll of Assistant Nurses. These were known as state enrolled assistant nurses (SEAN) until 1961 when they became state enrolled nurses (SEN).

3 Ministry of Health and others. Report of the Working Party on the Recruitment and Training of Nurses. (Chairman Sir Robert Wood). London, HMSO, 1947.

4 Nursing Times 1953, 5 December, 1249.

5 Nursing Times 1956, 7 December.

6 This has been described by:
   a) Reinkemeyer, M H. A nursing paradox. Nursing Research, 1968, vol 17, January, February.
   b) House, Vivienne. A degree of care. GNC Research Unit, GNC, 1977.

7 RCN Council minutes 1947, January, 30, 52; April, 97; July, 204–5.

8 RNC Council minutes 1954, September, 310.

9 RCN Council minutes 1952, March, 80.

10 Ministry of Health and others. Working Party on the Recruitment and Training of Nurses. Minority Report. London, HMSO, 1948.

11 Nuffield Provincial Hospitals Trust. (Director of research H A Goddard).
   a) The work of nurses in hospital wards. London, NPHT, 1953.
   b) A study of the work of public health nurses. 1954. NPHT (unpublished).

12 Standing Nursing Advisory Committee. Nursing techniques. SNAC, Central Health Services Council, Ministry of Health, 1950. The committee at that time had a majority of non-nurses and the profession complained of being told how to perform nursing techniques by those people.

13 RCN Council minutes 1952, June/July, 277, 234.

14 Ibid, October, 345. Also 1953, July, 194.

15 Ibid, December, 548, 575.

16 Miss G B Carter had been co-author with Miss Evelyn C Pearce of a pamphlet Reconsideration of nursing: its fundamentals, purpose and place in the community. This was subsequently published by Nursing Mirror 1946, January, February and March.

17 RCN Council minutes 1954, March, 71, 106; July, 229; November, 396.

18 Ibid, June/July, 274; October, 323.

19 RCN Council minutes 1955, July, 245, 253, 284.

20 Royal College of Nursing. Observations and objectives: a statement of nursing policy. London, RCN, 1956.

21 RCN Council minutes 1956, May, 143, 175; June/July 240.
22 Ibid, December, 409.
23 RCN Council minutes 1956, December, 409. Margaret Scott Wright was a ward sister at St George's Hospital, London, at the time of her appointment. She later became the first professor of the Nursing Studies Unit. This was the first award of a Chair to a nurse in the UK.
24 RCN Council minutes 1957, October, 322, 341.
25 RCN Council minutes 1958, January, 34; April, 149.
26 RCN Council minutes 1959, June/July, 320.
27 RCN Council minutes 1960, March, 99.
28 This self-help group later became the first Nursing Research Discussion Group and was the germ of what was later to become a widespread movement. Discussion groups were set up by nurses throughout the UK. The London group flourished and subsequently affiliated itself to the RCN to form the Research Society in 1976.
   Doreen Norton's work was later published. Norton, Doreen, McLaren, Rhoda, Exton-Smith A N. An investigation of geriatric nursing problems in hospital. London, National Corporation for the Care of Old People, 1962. Reprinted Edinburgh, Churchill Livingstone, 1975.
29 RCN Council minutes 1960, January, 8; February, 32; April, 133.
30 For example, see Nursing Times 1947, 27 December, 90, A talk by Miss E Cockayne; or, 1948, 31 January 88, reporting an open conference on the working party report.
31 Nursing Times, 1950, 15 July, 733. E H Hodsoll (sister tutor), The assistant nurse.
32 A programme for the nursing profession. Report of the committee on the function of nursing. (Chairman Professor Eli Ginzberg). New York, The Macmillan Co, 1950.
33 Nursing Times 1950, 28 January, 81. Editorial article reporting the Public Health Section meeting to discuss the future training of health visitors.
34 Nursing Times 1954, 14 August, 871; 25 September, 1 October.
35 Ibid, 1954, 31 July, 814; also 1955, 6 May, 483.
36 Ibid, 1954, 820. Phyllis M Stott, Teamwork in social service.
37 Ibid, 1954, 14 August, 871. Annual conference of the RCN Sister Tutor Section. Miss M E Gould, Principal Tutor, Nightingale School of Nursing.
38 The Lancet 1957, 5 January. Correspondence, Dr Thomas Anderson, Glasgow.
39 Ibid, 1957, 12 January. Correspondence, Dr Ronald Macbeth, Oxford.
40 Nursing Times 1956, 4 May, 11 May.
41 Nursing Times 1957, 8 February, 153.
42 Committee on higher education. (Chairman Lord Robbins). Cmnd 2154. London, HMSO, 1963.
43 Nursing Times 1956, 31 August, leader article; and article by C Langdon Smith, 841.
44 Henderson, Virginia. The basic principles of nursing care. Paper prepared for consultation by member countries of the International Council of Nurses and reprinted by Nursing Mirror 1958. Geneva, International Council of Nurses, 1969. Revised edition.

CHAPTER 12

1 Nurses Salaries Committee. (Chairman Lord Rushcliffe). 1943–48.
2 Ministry of Health and Board of Education. Interim Report of the Inter-departmental Committee on Nursing Services. (Chairman the Earl of Athlone). London, HMSO, 1939.

3 RCN Council minutes, 1939, May.
4 RCN Council minutes, 1941, December, 123.
5 Staffing the Hospitals. Ministry of Health, Ministry of Labour and National Service. 1945.
6 The RCN did not accept as members any male nurses or nurses who were not on the general register. In 1960, membership was extended to all nurses (including males) who were on the register of a statutory nursing body in the United Kingdom.
7 RCN Council minutes, 1946, December, 368.
8 Nurses and Midwives Whitley Council (Management Side) minutes, 1949. NC (M) 45, NC (M) 50.
9 Provisional Advisory Committee minutes, 1948. PAC/1, 17 February.
The organisations represented at this meeting included:
Association of Hospital Matrons
Association of Supervisors of Midwives
Confederation of Health Service Employees
National Association of Administrators of Local Government Establishments
National Association of Local Government Officers
National Union of General and Municipal Workers
National Union of Public Employees
Royal College of Midwives
Royal College of Nurses
Scottish Matrons Association
Scottish Health Visitors Association
Women Public Health Officers Association
10 Interim Executive Committee, 1948, 1EC/2, 18 August.
11 For an account of the student nurses' situation during the first days of the NHS see: Abel-Smith, Brian. A history of the nursing profession. London, Heinemann, 1960.
12 IEC/4, 1948, 9 November.
13 NMFC/1, 22 June. The representation was:

Association of Hospital Matrons	3
Association of Hospital and Welfare Administrators (formerly National Association of Administrators of Local Government Establishments)	1
Association of Supervisors of Midwives	1
Confederation of Health Service Employees	4
National Association of Local Government Officers	3
National Union of General and Municipal Workers	2
National Union of Public Employees	4
Royal College of Midwives	6
Royal College of Nursing	12
Scottish Health Visitors Association	1
Scottish Matrons Association	1
Women Public Health Officers Association	2

Thus, the professional organisations had a majority of places.
14 RCN Council minutes, 1948, February, 50.
15 Ibid, April, 121; May, 167.
16 Nurses and Midwives Whitley Council (Management Side), 1949. NC (M) 44, NC (M) 50.
17 Ibid, 1950. NC (M) 95, NC (M) 120.
18 Ministry of Health. Report of the Committee of Enquiry into the Cost of the

National Health Service. (Chairman C W Guillebaud). Cmd 9663. London, HMSO, 1956.

In 1956, more hospital and regional representatives were appointed and the number of Ministry representatives was further reduced.

19 Nurses and Midwives Whitley Council, 1952, Management Side, NC (M) 391, 395.

20 Nurses and Midwives Whitley Council, 1951, NMC/22, Staff Side, 25 September.

21 Management Side, 1952, NC (M) 361.

22 Staff Side, 1951, EC10; NMC/19.

23 Management Side, 1953, NC (M) 452.

24 It is considered that the term 'students' in this quotation was loosely used for pupil nurses. However, the salary differentials were so small that it could equally well have applied to both categories in practice.

25 See Chapter 5.

26 Management Side, 1954, NC (M) 520.

27 Management Side, 1955, NC (M) 639. Overtime had been paid at plain time for mental nurses since 1941.

28 Management Side, 1955, NC (M) 671.

29 Management Side, 1956, NC (M) 770.

30 Nursing Times 1955, 11 February, 150.

31 Ibid, 22 April, 439.

32 Ibid, 20 May, 577.

33 Ibid, 22 July, 822.

34 Box, Kathleen and Croft-White, Enid. Recruitment to Nursing. London, Ministry of Health, 1943.

35 National Advisory Council on Nurses and Midwives, 1945. Recruitment of Nurses and Midwives to Training Institutions. Ministry of Labour and National Service, Ministry of Health, Department of Health for Scotland.

36 Ministry of Health and others. Report of the Working Party on the Recruitment and Training of Nurses. (Chairman Sir Robert Wood). London, HMSO, 1947.

37 Ministry of Health and Board of Education. Interim Report of the Inter-departmental Committee on Nursing Services. (Chairman the Earl of Athlone). London, HMSO, 1939.

38 RCN memorandum to Athlone committee. London, RCN, 1938.

39 Nursing Times 1947, 29 November.

40 Nursing Times 1948, 3 January, 3.

41 Nursing Times 1948, 17 January, leader article.

42 Ibid, 1948, 17 January, 38.

43 Ibid, 1948, 21 January, 59.

44 Ibid, 1948, 28 February, 157.

45 Ibid, 1948, 6 March, leader article, and 178.

46 Ibid, 1948, 3 April, 238.

47 Ibid, 1948, 12 June, 426.

48 Ibid, 1948, 10 July, 496. Section IV of the Horder report was not published until 1949.

49 Nursing Times 1953, 27 August, 839. Barnes M E. The psychological approach to the orthopaedic patient.

50 Ministry of Health, Annual Report, 1948–49.

51 Ibid, 1949–50.

52 RCN Council minutes 1950, March, 101.
53 Ibid, 1950, July, 229, 261; October, 315; November, 345.
54 Ibid, 1951, January, 30–45.
55 Management Side 1951, NC (M) 229, NC (M) 231.
56 RCN Council minutes 1951, July, 247, 259.
57 Ibid, September, 273.
58 Ibid, 1953, September, 260.
59 Hospital Administrative Staff College. Joint consultation in hospitals. Research undertaken by students on a two year training course. London, King Edward's Hospital Fund for London, 1958 (typescript).
60 Sofer, Cyril. Reactions to administrative change: a study of staff relationships in three British hospitals. Human Relations, 1955, vol 8, 291–316.
61 Government papers, MH77/30B, PRO, London.
62 Ibid, MH90/48.
63 Ibid, MH90/45.
64 Ibid, MH92/4.
65 Nursing Times 1948, 7 February, 98.
66 See Chapter 4.
67 With effect from 1 January 1951. Management Side, 1951, NC (M) 285.
68 Management Side, 1951, NC (M) 311.
69 Ibid, NC (M) 312, 1951.
70 Ibid, NC (M) 426, 1953.
71 Ibid, NC (M) 427, 1953.
72 Ibid, NC (M) 461, 1953.
73 Ibid, NC (M) 474, 1953.
74 GNC minutes, 1952.
75 Management Side, 1957, NC (M) 823.
76 Ibid, NC (M) 862, 1957.
77 Ibid, NC (M) 1139, 1142; 1961.
78 Staff Side, 1960, NMC/72, 24 May.
79 Management Side, 1961, NC (M) 1142.
80 Ibid, NC (M) 1162, 1169, 1961.
81 Ibid, NC (M) 1009; 1959.
82 Ibid, NC (M) 1182, 1185; 1962.
83 Ministry of Health and Scottish Home and Health Department. Report of the Committee on Senior Nursing Staff Structure. (Chairman Brian Salmon). London, HMSO, 1966.

CHAPTER 13

1 Sofer, Cyril. Reactions to administrative change: a study of staff relationships in three British hospitals. Human Relations, 1955, vol 8, 291–316.
2 White, Rosemary. Social change and the development of the nursing profession: A study of the Poor Law nursing service, 1848–1948. London, Henry Kimpton, 1978.
3 Nursing and domestic staffs in hospitals: notes for the guidance of HMCs. London, Ministry of Health, 1948.
4 Government papers T227–47, PRO.
5 The expression 'division of labour' was adopted from Adam Smith by Durkheim in his thesis Division of labour (1933). Durkheim equates it with social differentiation and points to the significance for social relationships in occupational

groups for the development and maintenance of moral ideas. Friedmann (1961) contrasts the generalist with the specialist who takes control over the process, of which the generalist is the task worker. I have used the term 'specialist' interchangeably with 'professionalist'.

6 Ministry of Health. Report of the Committee of Enquiry into the Cost of the National Health Service. (Chairman C W Guillebaud). Cmnd 9663. London, HMSO, 1956.

7 Tawney R H. The acquisitive society. London, Bell, 1921.

8 Carr-Saunders A N and Wilson P A. The Professions. Oxford, Clarendon Press, 1933.

9 Cole, G D H. Studies in class structure. London, Routledge & Kegan Paul, 1955.

10 Merton R K, Reader G G and Kendall P L. The student physician: introductory studies in the sociology of medical education. Harvard, 1957.

11 Jackson J. (ed). Professions and professionalisation. Cambridge, CUP, 1970.

12 Johnson T. Professions and power. London, Macmillan, 1972.

13 It is for this reason that the work of nurses and, therefore, their fair remuneration, cannot easily be compared against other occupations.

14 Ministry of Health and others. An inquiry into health visiting. (Chairman Sir Wilson Jameson). London, HMSO, 1956.

15 Prandy, Kenneth. Professional employees. London, Faber, 1965.

16 Froebe D J and Bain R J. Quality assurance programs and controls in nursing, 37. St Louis, Mosby, 1976.

17 Eckstein H. Pressure group politics: the case of the British Medical Association. London, Allen and Unwin, 1960.

18 Nettl J P. Consensus or elite domination: the case of business. In: Castles F G, Murray D J, Potter D C (eds). Decisions, organisations and society. London, Open University/Penguin, 1971. Ch 14.

19 Olson M. Groups and organisations and their basis of support. In: Castles et al. Decisions, organisations and society. London, Open University/Penguin, 1971.

20 Royal College of Nursing. Observations and objectives. London, RCN, 1956.

21 Royal College of Nursing. The duties and position of the nurse, London, RCN. 1961.

22 The Public Health and Sister Tutors Sections were set up in 1921. The Ward and Departmental Sisters Section was established in 1949, the Occupational Health Nurses Section in 1953 and the Administrators Section in 1960. Many other sections have been set up since.

23 Davies, Celia. Experience of dependency and control in work: the case of nurses. Journal of Advanced Nursing, 1976, vol 1, 273–282.

24 Davies, Celia. Professionalising strategies as time and culture bound: American and British nursing circa 1893. In: Lagemann, Ellen Condliffe (ed). Nursing history: new perspectives, new possibilities. New York, Teachers College Press, 1983.

25 Jones G W. The Prime Minister's power. In: Castles et al. Decisions, organisations and society. London, Open University/Penguin, 1971. Ch 12.

26 GNC minutes 1946, April, October.

27 GNC memorandum to the Minister of Health on the report of the working party on the recruitment and training of nurses. London GNC, 1948.

28 The voluntary hospital nurses had been trained only in acute nursing care; most of the local authority nurses had been trained only in chronic nursing care.

303

Before the Nurses Act 1949 there had not really been a general nurse who had received training in both these areas of care.

29 National Board for Prices and Incomes. Report No 60. Pay of nurses and midwives in the NHS. Cmnd 3585. London, HMSO, 1968.

30 Ministry of Health and others. Report of the committee set up to consider the function, status and training of nurse tutors. (Chairman Dr Janet Aitken). London, HMSO, 1955.

31 GNC minutes 1953, July.

32 Henderson, Virginia. Basic principles of nursing care. Reprinted by Nursing Mirror 1958. Geneva, International Council of Nurses, 1969. Revised edition.

33 GNC minutes 1957, December.

Bibliography

PRIMARY SOURCES

Able-Smith B and Titmus R. The cost of the NHS in England and Wales. The National Institute of Economic and Social Research, Occasional papers XVIII. Cambridge, Cambridge University Press, 1956. Paper prepared for the Guillebaud report, 1956.

The Association of Queens Superintendents. The place of the district nurse in the health services of the future. (Chairman Miss E J Merry). 1943.

Athlone Committee (1938). Evidence given by:
Association of Hospital Matrons
British Medical Association
East Suffolk and Ipswich Hospital
Federated Superannuation Scheme for Nurses
General Nursing Council for England and Wales
Headmistresses Association
Joint Consultative Committee of Institutions for Training of Health Visitors
Joint Tuberculosis Council
National Council for Women
NALGO
Queens Institute of District Nursing
Royal College of Nursing
Society of Registered Male Nurses
TUC
Voluntary Hospitals Committee
Women's Employment Federation

Box, Kathleen and Croft-White, Enid. Recruitment to nursing: an inquiry into the attitudes of student nurses to their profession, with special reference to the present recruiting campaign. London, Ministry of Health, 1943.

British Hospitals Association. Personal support for hospitals in the National Health Service. London, BHA, 1948.

Central Health Services Council, Annual Reports, 1949–1962.

Central Health Services Council, Ministry of Health:
1952 Standing Nursing Advisory Committee, SAC(N)(52)9, CHSC(52)7, The appointment and duties of principal matrons and group matrons, Report and Recommendations.
1953 The reception and welfare of in-patients in hospitals.
1954 Standing Nursing Advisory Committee. On the position of the enrolled assistant nurse within the National Health Service. (Chairman Miss K G Douglas.
1954 Report of the committee on the internal administration of hospitals. (Chairman Alderman A F Bradbeer).
1959 The welfare of children in hospital. (Chairman Sir Harry Platt).
1959 Report of the maternity services committee. (Chairman Earl of Cranbrook).
1961 Services available to the aged and chronic sick. Standing Medical Advisory Committee.
1961 The pattern of the in-patient's day. Standing Nursing Advisory Committee.

305

1961 Human relations in obstetrics. Standing Maternity and Midwifery Advisory Committee.

1961 Control of noise in hospitals. Standing Nursing Advisory Committee.

1963 Communication between doctors, nurses and patients. Standing Nursing Advisory Committee, Standing Medical Advisory Committee.

Council for the Training of Health Visitors, Annual Reports, 1962–64.

Dan Mason Nursing Research Committee:

1956 The work of recently qualified nurses.

1960 The work, responsibilities and status of the staff nurse.

1962 The work, responsibilities and status of the enrolled nurse.

1963 Some aspects of the work of the midwife. National Florence Nightingale Memorial Committee.

General Nursing Council for England and Wales:

1945–63 Minutes.

1951–63 Annual Reports.

1948　Memorandum to the Ministry of Health on the report of the working party on the recruitment and training of nurses.

1957　The work of student nurses and pupil assistant nurses: Reply to South East Metropolitan RHB/ANTC review.

Government Papers:

Cabinet Papers:

CP(49)75 – CAB 129–34

Remuneration of Trained Nurses

CM26(49)2 – CAB 128–15

Continuation of above

CM(50)18 – CAB 128–17

Cost of the NHS

Ministry of Health Papers:

MH 55/765, Setting up Roll of Nurses

MH 77/30B, re CHSC, 1944

MH 77/35, Conference with nursing organisations re future NHS, 1946

MH 77/121, NHS, nursing services, policy, 1944–45

MH 77/160, Nurses and nurses' associations, representations, 1943–45

MH 77/161, Nurses and nursing associations, representatives, 1946

MH 77/162, Nurses and nursing associations, representations, 1947

MH 80/44, Nurses Bill, December 1948–December 1949

MH 90/5, re NHS RHB areas correspondence with organisations

MH 90/6, RHBs, areas, correspondence

MH 90/45, RHBs, headquarters staff

MH 90/48, RHBs, staffing policy

MH 92/4, HMCs, appointment of hospital staff

Treasury Papers:

T227 47 ref Nurses Act 1949

Public Records Office, London.

Institute of Hospital Administrators. Making the most of present resources (Conference Papers). 1953.

King Edward's Hospital Fund for London:

1944 Memorandum on National Health Service: comments on the White Paper.

1947 Comments on the report of the Working Party on the recruitment and training of nurses. (Wood).

1950 Memorandum on supervision of nurses' health, second edition.

1951 Evidence submitted to the committee on internal administration of hospitals.

1953 Joint consultation in hospitals, research undertaken by students in Hospital Administrative Staff College. Typescript.

1955 Report of the sub-committee on mental and mental deficiency hospitals in the London area.

1958 Noise control in hospitals.

1961 Staff College for Matrons: prospectus.

Management Consultants Association. Report on survey of specified services in selected hospitals. 1959.

Manchester Regional Hospitals Board:

1957 Report of the working party on standards of nursing staff for hospitals.

1959 Report of the working party on standards of nursing staff for mental and Mental Deficiency Hospitals.

Menzies, Isabel E P. A Case Study on the Functioning of Social Systems as a Defence Against Anxiety. Human Relations, 1960, vol 13, no 2, 95–121.

Ministry of Health:

1939   Interim Report, Interdepartmental Committee on Nursing Services (Chairman The Rt Hon the Earl of Athlone). With Board of Education.

1943–48 Reports of the Nurses' Salaries Committee (Chairman Lord Rushcliffe). With Ministry of Labour and National Service, Department of Health for Scotland.

1944   A National Health Service, White Paper, Cmnd 6502.

1944–61 Annual Reports.

1945   Recruitment of nurses and midwives to training institutions. With Ministry of Labour and National Service, Department of Health for Scotland.

1945   Staffing the hospitals. With Ministry of Labour.

1947   Report of the Working Party on the Recruitment and Training of Nurses. (Chairman Sir Robert Wood). With Department of Health for Scotland, Ministry of Labour and National Service.

1948   Working Party on Recruitment and Training of Nurses, Minority Report. (Chairman Dr J Cohen).

1948   Nursing and domestic staff in hospitals: notes of guidance.

1949   Report of the Working Party on Midwives. (Chairman Mrs [later Lady] Mary Stocks).

1950   Joint Consultation RHB(50)47.

1951   Principal matrons and group matrons, memorandum by Ministry of Health, SAC(N)(51)4.

1951   Nursing and midwifery, reference note no 6.

1952   Economy in manpower, HMC(52)121.

1954   Hospital matrons with extended responsibilities. HM(54)4.

1954   Report of the committee set up to consider the Function, Status and Training of Nurse Tutors. With Department of Health for Scotland, GNC for England and Wales, Scotland.

1955   Report of the Working Party on Training of District Nurses. (Chairman Sir Frederick Armer).

1956   An inquiry into health visiting, report of the Working Party (Chairman Sir Wilson Jameson). With Department of Health for Scotland, Ministry of Education.

1956   Report of the Committee of Enquiry into the Cost of the National Health Service. (Chairman C W Guillebaud) Cmnd 9663.

1959   Report of the Working Party on Social Workers in Local Authority
        Health and Welfare Services. (Chairman Miss [later Lady] Eileen
        L Younghusband). With Department of Health for Scotland.

1959   Training of district nurses, report of the Advisory Committee (Chair-
        man D H Ingall). With Department of Health for Scotland.

1966   Report of the Committee on Senior Nursing Staff Structure. (Chairman
        Brian Salmon).

National Association of State Enrolled Assistant Nurses. The position of the state
enrolled assistant nurse in the National Health Service. Memorandum submitted
to the Ministry of Health. 1953.

Nuffield Provincial Hospitals Trust:

1946 Nurse staffing in hospitals. Medical Committee of Scottish Advisory
     Committee.

1948 Comments on the Wood report.

1953 The work of nurses in hospital wards, report of a job analysis (Director of
     research, H A Goddard).

1954 Report of a study of the work of public health nurses. Unpublished
     typescript.

Oxford Regional Hospitals Board:

1956 Training of nurses in general hospitals. A report on a survey of four training
     schools.

1962 The experimental ward. Report number 1. Oxford RHB, publication
     number 81.

Parliament:

1946   The National Health Service Act, 9 & 10 Geo 6, Ch 81.

1949   Nurses Act, 12 & 13 Geo 6, Ch 73.

1957   Nurses Act, 5 & 6 Eliz 2, Ch 15

1957   Nurses Agencies Act, 5 & 6 Eliz 2, Ch 16.

1961   Nurses (Amendment) Act, 9 & 10 Eliz 2, Ch 14.

1948–62 Statuory Instruments (various, selected)

1954–57 Report of the Royal Commission on the Law Relating to Mental Illness
        and Mental Deficiency. (Chairman Baron Percy of Newcastle). Cmnd
        169, London, HMSO.

1972   Report of the Committee on Nursing. (Chairman Professor [later Lord]
        Asa Briggs). Cmnd 5115.

1979   Report of the Royal Commission on the National Health Service.
        (Chairman Sir Alec Merrison). Cmnd 7615.

Queen's Institute of District Nursing:

1949 Houses for district nurses. With Royal Institute of British Architects.

1952 National survey concerning patients with cancer nursed at home. (Chair-
     man Ronald Raven). With Marie Curie Memorial Trust.

1957 The training and work of district nurses.

1964 Survey of district nurse training, 1962–63. (Researcher L Hockey).

Royal College of Nursing:

1928–78 Aims and objectives of the RCN

1936–63 Minutes of Council

1939   Reaction to Interim Report of the Interdepartmental Committee on
        Nursing Services

1942–61 Annual Reports
        Reports of the Nursing Reconstruction Committee (Chairman Lord
        Horder):

1942 I The assistant nurse
1943 II Education and training
      III Recruitment
1945 Supplements to the report on education and training, Parts A & B
1949 IV The social and economic conditions of the nurse
1948 Memorandum on the report of the Working Party on the Recruitment and Training of Nurses
1952 The Nation's Nurses, conference no 11. Mental health services. Report.
1953 Comment on the NPHT job analysis of the work of nurses in hospital wards.
1954 Nursing libraries in hospitals and libraries in schools of nursing.
1955 Memorandum on out-patients departments: Ward and Departmental Sisters' Section
1956 Observations and objectives: a statement on nursing policy
1957 Welfare of children in hospital: memorandum to the Central Health Services Council Committee.
1958 The problem of providing a continuous nursing service: especially in relation to night duty
1959 Memorandum on the establishment of education committees in schools of nursing
1960 A comprehensive mental nursing service: the part of the ward sister and charge nurse
1961 The nurse tutor: a new assessment. Report of a working party, Sister Tutor Section.
1961 The health visitor and the family doctor. With the Royal College of General Practitioners.
1962 The enrolled nurse. Report of the Nurse Administrators' Section.
1964 A reform of nursing education. Report of a special committee. (Chairman Sir Harry Platt).

Royal College of Physicians. Report on the care of children in hospital. 1957.

St Crispin Hospital HMC. Review of the hospital during the first 10 years of the NHS. St Crispin HMC, Oxford RHB, 1958.

Scottish Home and Health Department. Experimental nurse training at Glasgow Royal Infirmary. (Chairman J H F Brotherston, researcher M Scott Wright). Edinburgh, HMSO, 1963.

Socialist Medical Association. Memorandum of shortage of nurses. 1945. Typescript.

Sofer, Cyril. Reactions to administrative change: a study of staff relationships in three British hospitals. Human Relations, 1955, vol 8, 291–316.

South East Metropolitan RHB. The work of student nurses and pupil assistant nurses. (Director of research H A Goddard). 1957.

The Ten Group. Proposals to the Minister of Health, in commenting on the Wood report. Croydon, H R Grubb Ltd, 1948.

Voluntary Hospitals Committee for London. Memorandum on the (Wood) working party report.

Nurses and Midwives Whitley Council:
1948–63 Management Side Minutes
1948–60 Staff Side Minutes

Williams, Heather. The integrated nurse/health visitor course: a report of the first five years of the experimental course. Southampton University, 1962.

SECONDARY SOURCES

Alford R R. Health Care Politics. Chicago, University of Chicago Press, 1975.
Acton Society Trust. Hospitals and the state. (Director of research T E Chester). London, Acton Society Trust.
  1955 1 Background and blueprint
  1956 2 The impact of change
  1957 3 Groups, regions and committees
       4 The regional hospital boards
  1958 5 The central control of the service
  1959 6 Creative leadership in a state service
Allen, David.
  A short history of the health service in England and Wales. Working paper no 26, Manchester Business School, 1976.
  A case study of decision making: the development of the 1962 hospital plan for England and Wales. Working paper no 22, Manchester Business School, 1976.
  Hospital planning. London, Pitman Medical, 1978.
Barnes, Elizabeth. People in hospital. London, Macmillan, 1961.
Barraclough, Geoffrey. An introduction to contemporary history. London, Penguin Books, 1969.
Bellaby, Paul and Oribabor, Patrick. The growth of trade union consciousness among general hospital nurses. Sociological Review, 1977, vol 25, no 4, new series, November, 801–22.
  Determinants of the occupational strategies adopted by British hospital nurses. International Journal of Health Services, 1980, vol 10, no 2, 291–309.
Bendall E R D and Raybould E. A History of the General Nursing Council for England and Wales, 1919–1969. London, H K Lewis, 1969.
Bierer, Joshua. The day hospital. London, H K Lewis, 1951.
Bligh, Donald, 1979, Educational principles in inter-professional learning. In: Education for cooperation in health and social work: papers from the symposium on interprofessional learning, University of Nottingham, July 1979. London, Journal of the Royal College of General Practitioners, 1980. Occasional paper 14.
Bowman, Gerald. The Lamp and the book: the story of the Royal College of Nursing, 1916–1966. London, Queen Anne Press, 1967.
Burrage, Michael. Nationalisation and the professional ideal. Sociology, 1973, vol 7, pt 2, May, 253–72.
Brown, Muriel. Introduction to social administration in Britain. London, Hutchinson University Press, 1971.
Briggs, Lord Asa. The growth of the social services. New Society, 1978, 16, 23 November.
Carter G B and Pearce, Evelyn R. Reconsideration of nursing – its fundamentals, purpose and place in the community. Nursing Mirror, 1946, January, February, March.
Castles F G, Murray D J, Potter D C (eds). Decisions, organisations and society. London, Penguin Books, 1971.
Chester T E. The Guillebaud report. Public Administration, 1956, vol XXXIV, 119–210.
Cohen, Percy. Modern social theory. London, Heinemann Educational, 1968.
Coltham J B and Fines J. Educational objectives for the study of history. London, Historical Association, 1971.

Davies, Celia. Experience of dependency and control in work: the case of nurses. Journal of Advanced Nursing, 1976, vol 1, 273–282.

Past and present in nursing education. Nursing Times, 1980, September, 1703–7.

(ed.) Rewriting nursing history. London, Croom Helm, 1980. Christopher Maggs, ch 2.

Professionalising strategies as time and culture bound: American and British nursing circa 1893. In: Lagemann, Ellen Condliffe (ed). Nursing history: new perspectives, new possibilities. New York, Teachers College Press, 1983.

Davies E A B Report of a special study on the future scope of the District Nursing Service and the personnel needed. London, Queen's Institute of District Nursing, 1955.

Dingwall, Robert and McIntosh, Jean. Readings in the sociology of nursing. Edinburgh, Churchill Livingstone, 1978.

Elton G R. The practice of history. London, Fontana, 1975.

Etzioni, Amitai (ed). A sociological reader in complex organisations. Holt International, 1971 (second ed).

Social Problems. Prentice Hall, 1976.

Farndale, James (ed). Trends in the National Health Service. Oxford, Pergamon Press, 1964.

Ferguson, Sheila and Fitzgerald, Hilde. Studies in the social services. (History of the Second World War, UK Civil Series. Sir Keith Hancock, ed) London, HMSO and Longmans, Green, 1954.

Ferrer H P (ed). The health services: administration, research and management. London, Butterworth, 1972.

Fitzpatrick, M Louise (ed). Historical studies in nursing. New York, Teachers College Press, 1977.

Forsyth G and Logan R F L. The demand for medical care. Oxford, OUP for Nuffield Provincial Hospitals Trust, 1960.

Forsyth, Gordon. Doctors and state medicine. London, Pitman, 1973 (2nd ed).

Fraser, Derek. The evolution of the British welfare state. London, Macmillan, 1975.

Friedson E. Professional dominance: The social structure of medical care. New York, Atherton Press, 1970.

Gamarnakow, Eva. Sexual division of labour: the case of nursing. London, Routledge & Kegan Paul, 1978.

Godber G E. Health Services, past, present and future. The Lancet, 1958, 5 July, 1–6.

Guthrie, Douglas. Nursing through the ages. Nursing Mirror, 1954 (reprint).

Hall, Phoebe and others. Change, choice and conflict in social policy. London, Heinemann, 1975.

Halmos P. The personal social services. London, Constable, 1970.

Hardy G M. Nursing as a career and livelihood. London, E O Beck, 1954 (2nd ed 1955).

Hayward J. A growing partnership: inaugural lecture, Chelsea College. Nursing Times, 1978, 7 December, 2028–2033.

Haywood, Stuart and Alaszewski, Andy. Crisis in the Health Service. London, Croom Helm, 1980.

Henderson, Virginia. The basic principles of nursing care. Nursing Mirror 1958, reprint.

Hill C P. British economic and social history, 1750–1975. London, Edward Arnold, 1977.

Illsley, Raymond. Professional or public health? London, Nuffield Provincial Hospitals Trust, 1980.

Jackson J A (ed). Professions and professionalization. Cambridge, Cambridge University Press, 1971.

Jefferys, Margot. The uncertain health visitor. New Society, 1965, 28 October, 16–18.

Johnson R. Socialist humanist history. History Workshop Journal, 1978, Autumn, 79–101.

Johnson T J. Professions and power. London, Macmillan, 1972.

Jones, Kathleen, Brown, John and Bradshaw J. Issues in social policy. London, Routledge & Kegan Paul, 1978.

Joseph, Sir Keith. The health services: the second decade. London, Conservative Political Centre, 1958.

Kenner, Charmian. The politics of married working class women's health care, 1918–39. Seminar, 18 November 1980, Department of History of Science, UMIST.

Lamb, Anne. Primary health nursing. London, Ballière Tindall, 1977.

Lindsay A. Socialised medicine in England and Wales, 1948–61. The University of North Carolina Press, Chapel Hill, 1962.

Long, Frank. King Edward's Hospital Fund for London. London, KEHF, 1942.

McEwan, Margaret. Health visiting. London, Faber, 1962.

McFarlane, Jean. Essays in nursing. Kings Fund Project Paper, RC2. London, Kings Fund, 1980.

McGhee, Anne. The patient's attitude to nursing care. Edinburgh, Livingstone, 1961.

MacGuire, Jillian. The expanded role of the nurse. Kings Fund Project Paper, RC3. London, Kings Fund, 1980.

MacKenzie N. The nurse and the modern community. Nursing Times, 1950, October, November.

MacKenzie W J M. Power and responsibility in health care. Oxford University Press for Nuffield Provincial Hospitals Trust, 1979.

McLachlan G, Stocking B and Shegog R F A (eds). Patterns for uncertainty. London, Oxford University Press for Nuffield Provincial Hospitals Trust, 1979.

MacQueen I A G. From carbolic powder to social counsel. Health Visiting Centenary Lecture at Battersea College of Technology. Nursing Times, 1962, vol 58, 866–868.

Marsh, David C. The changing social structure of England and Wales, 1871–1961. London, Routledge & Kegan Paul, 1977.

Marwick, Arthur. The nature of history. London, Macmillan, 1976.

Matthews, Olive. Hospital improvements: how to improve the daily life of the patient in the ward. Published, privately 1950.

Merton, Robert. 1968, Social theory and social structure. New York, Free Press, 1968.

Mitchell, Juliet. Woman's estate. London, Penguin, 1971.

Mishra, Ramesh. Society and social policy. London, Macmillan, 1977.

Nisbet, Robert. Social change and history. Oxford, Oxford University Press, 1969.

O'Connell P. Health visitor education at university. London, Rcn, 1978.

Owen, Grace (ed). Health visiting. London, Ballière Tindall, 1977.

Parry, Noel and Jose:

The rise of the medical profession. London, Croom Helm, 1976.

Professionalism and unionism: aspects of class conflict in the National Health Service, Sociological Review, 1977, vol 25, no 4, new series, November, 823–841.

The teachers and professionalism: the failure of an occupational strategy. In: Flude M and Ahier J (eds). Educability, schools and ideology. London, Croom Helm, 1978.

Parsons T. The structure of social action. New York, Free Press, 1937 (reprinted 1967).

Pater, John. The making of the National Health Service. London, King's Fund, 1981.

Pinker, Robert. Social theory and social policy. London, Heinemann, 1973.

Popper K R. The poverty of historicism. London, Routledge & Kegan Paul, 1961.

Revans R W. The measurement of supervisory attitudes. Manchester Statistical Society, 1961.

Ross J S. The National Health Service in Great Britain. London, Oxford University Press, 1952.

Rostow W W. The stages of economic growth. Cambridge, Cambridge University Press, 1971.

Seebohm Rowntree B and Lavers G R. English life and leisure. London, Longmans Green, 1951.

Wright, Margaret Scott. Nursing and the universities. Nursing Times, 1973, vol 69, no 7, 222–227.

Shils, Edward. Center and periphery. Chicago, University of Chicago Press, 1975.

Shortell, Steven M. Occupational prestige differences within medical and allied health professions. Social Science and Medicine, 1974, vol 8, 1–9.

Shryock R H. The history of nursing: an interpretation of social and medical factors. Philadelphia, Saunders, 1959.

Simpson, Marjorie. The Rcn 1916–76: role and action in a changing health service. The Nursing Lecture, 24 November, Rcn, 1976.

Stern, Fritz (ed). The varieties of history. New York, Meridian Books, World Publishing, 1956.

Stocks, Mary. A hundred years of district nursing. London, Allen and Unwin, 1960.

Teggart F J. Theory of history. Cambridge, Cambridge University Press, 1960. Reprint of Theory (1925) and Processes of history (1918) in one volume.

Timms, Noel (ed). Social welfare: why and how? London, Routledge & Kegan Paul, 1980.

Titmuss, Richard M. Social policy: an introduction. London, Allen and Unwin, 1974.

Walk, Alexander. The history of mental nursing. The Journal of Mental Science, 1961, vol 107, no 446 (new series no 410), 1–17.

Wilkie, Elaine. A history of the Council for Education and Training of Health Visitors. London, Allen and Unwin, 1979.

Willcocks A J. The creation of the National Health Service. London, Routledge & Kegan Paul, 1963 (reprinted 1973).

Wilson A T M. Hospital nursing auxiliaries. Human Relations, 1950, vol 3, 1–32.

NEWSPAPERS, JOURNALS

The Lancet 1943–61
Nursing Mirror 1939–61
Nursing Times 1937, 25 September. College and TUC policy: a comparison.
Nursing Times 1939–61
The Times 1948–61

Index

Note: Government committees are entered under their function. Reports are found under their chairman. Acts of Parliament are entered directly under name.

factions, major xix
see also interest groups
Farnworth, Mary 82, 94
Fawkes, B N 77
Fenwick, Ethel Bedford 264
Ford, Clow 219
Froebe, D J 259
Function, Status and Training of
Nurse Tutors, ad hoc
committee *see* Aitken report
funding of hospitals 2, 30

Garrison, W A xi
GCE examination 17, 97–8, 257,
268
general nurses 33, 51, 108, 254,
257, 259, 260
General Nursing Council for
England and Wales (GNC) 2,
265–70
aptitude tests 95–6, 98–101,
102–3
and Athlone committee 9–10
and entry qualifications 89,
90–1, 265, 266–7, 268, 269
and the general nurse 34–5, 266
and the Goddard report 202
Horder's view of 16
influence xix, 267
membership 266–7
Mental Nurses Committee 43, 47,
124, 128–9, 134–5, 268
and Nurses Act (1949) 35, 38–9,
41–2, 43, 44, 45, 265–6
reconstitution of 25, 26, 27, 36, 40,
42–3, 46–7, 48
and training 26, 36, 38–9, 40, 42–3,
46–7, 50, 62–3, 96, 181, 258, 265
and tutors 186–7, 190, 266
and university training 227
and Wood report 26–7, 265
general practitioners (GPs) 163
and health visitors 164, 168, 171,
183–4, 185
Goddard, H A 104, 132, 196, 202
Goddard report (1953) 33, 93, 103,
196–215, 228
reaction to 202–8, 213–14
Goddard report (1957) 104
Godden, G M 227

Goodall, Frances 14, 25, 188, 219,
220, 222
grades of nurse 12, 13–14, 15–16, 20,
29–33, 49
see also hierarchy
Grading and structure of administrative
and clerical staff in the health
service, report (1957) *see* Hall
report
group hospitals *see* hospital groups
Guillebaud report (1956) 139, 156–7,
158, 170, 255
Guthrie committee 233

Hall report (1957) 81
Hall, Phoebe xviii
Health, Ministry of, attitude to nurses
4, 6, 115–17, 141, 256
Health Visiting, committee of inquiry
see Jameson committee
Health Visiting and Social Work
(Training) Act (1962) 182
health visitors 159, 161
case loads 168, 169, 174, 184
consultant 166–7, 171, 174
duties 161, 162, 163–4, 166–7, 168,
169, 171, 173, 174, 176, 183
entry qualifications 162, 169, 173
funding 161–2
nursing background 172–3
recruitment 167, 169
shortage 170, 183
specialist 167, 168, 183
training 35, 161–2, 164–5, 167,
169–70, 172, 180–1, 184
tutors 162
university courses 167, 169–70, 171
Henderson, Virginia 215, 229
hierarchy, nursing 15, 24, 28, 32–3,
78–9
Himsworth, E W 175
Holland, D L 77, 191
home care *see* community nursing
services
Horder reports (1942–49) xiv, 5,
14–20
and assistant nurses 15–16
and Goddard report 204, 209–10
and hierarchy 15, 20, 24, 28, 49,
110, 200, 204, 209–10
reaction to xiv, 5, 18, 29, 34, 106

Registration of Nurses Act (1919)   121
repetitive tasks   21, 24, 26, 103–4, 196
research   220–3, 224, 227–8, 230
residential homes   3
RHB(53)4, ministry circular on mental
   nursing   127–8, 130, 131, 133, 237
Robbins report (1965)   19, 227
Rockefeller Foundation research
   grant   222
role of nurse   108, 220, 229, 269
Royal British Nurses Association   233
Royal College of Nursing (RCN)   xi,
   35
  and Athlone Committee   13, 14,
    231, 239–41
  and Bradbeer report   72, 74
  decision-making   xix, 5, 260–5
  and district nurses   145, 159
  and entry qualifications   90, 262
  expansion   263
  and Goddard report   202–6, 209–10,
    213, 255–6
  and group hospitals   57
  and health visitors   162, 170, 171,
    175–6, 180–1
  and Horder report   14, 29, 35, 204,
    209–10, 213
  labour relations committee   60
  matrons   65, 75, 87
  membership   261
  and mental nursing   126–7
  mental nursing, nurse's conference
    (1954)   130–1
  and negotiating machinery   231,
    232–3, 234–5
  and Nurses Act (1949)   35, 38, 39,
    40, 44
  and nursing administration   79, 80–1
  objectives   260–1
  and principal matrons   66, 67–8, 83,
    84
  and research   220–3, 224–5
  and salaries   80, 81, 254, 262
  tactics   262, 264
  and tutors   77, 186, 193–4
  university training   218, 219–20,
    223–5
  and Whitley Council   235
  Wood report   24–6, 35
Royal College of Nursing
   Reconstruction Committee *see*
   Horder reports

Royal Commission on the National
   Health Service (1979)   197
Royal Medico-Psychological
   Association (RMPA)   9, 120–1
Royal Society for the Promotion of
   Health (earlier Royal Sanitary
   Institute)   161, 166, 167, 173, 174,
   181
Rushcliffe Committee (1943)   2, 4,
   145, 231
Russell, Ritchie   107
Russell-Smith, A   187
Russell-Smith, Dame Enid   73

St Crispin Hospital   135–7
salaries:
  mental nursing   79, 81, 125, 127–8,
    131–3, 139–40, 142
  negotiation   13, 94, 254
  structure   78, 79, 83, 258–9
Salford Ladies' Sanitary Reform
   Association   161
Salmon Report (1966)   xi, xvi, 78, 81,
   83, 84, 110, 133, 195, 239, 258,
   259, 264
Scott, Phyllis M   176
Scott-Wright, Margaret *see* Wright,
   Margaret Scott-
SEAN *see* state-enrolled assistant
   nurses
self-image, nurses'   4–5, 253
SEN *see* state-enrolled nurse
Senior Nursing Staff Structure,
   Committee on (1966) *see* Salmon
   report
senior posts   81, 83
Shils, E   xvii
shortage of nurses   4, 7, 15, 34, 61, 66,
   90, 210, 212–13
  mental hospitals   124–5, 126, 127,
    139, 141
Shryock, R H   200
Shuttleworth, Dr   121
Simon, H A   xvi
Simpson, H Marjorie   223, 225
Skellern, Eileen   221
Smith, C Langdon   228
social workers   177–9, 180
  and health visitors   171–2, 174,
   179–80